A TOTEM POLE HISTORY

STUDIES IN THE
ANTHROPOLOGY OF NORTH
AMERICAN INDIANS SERIES

Editors
Raymond J. DeMallie
Douglas R. Parks

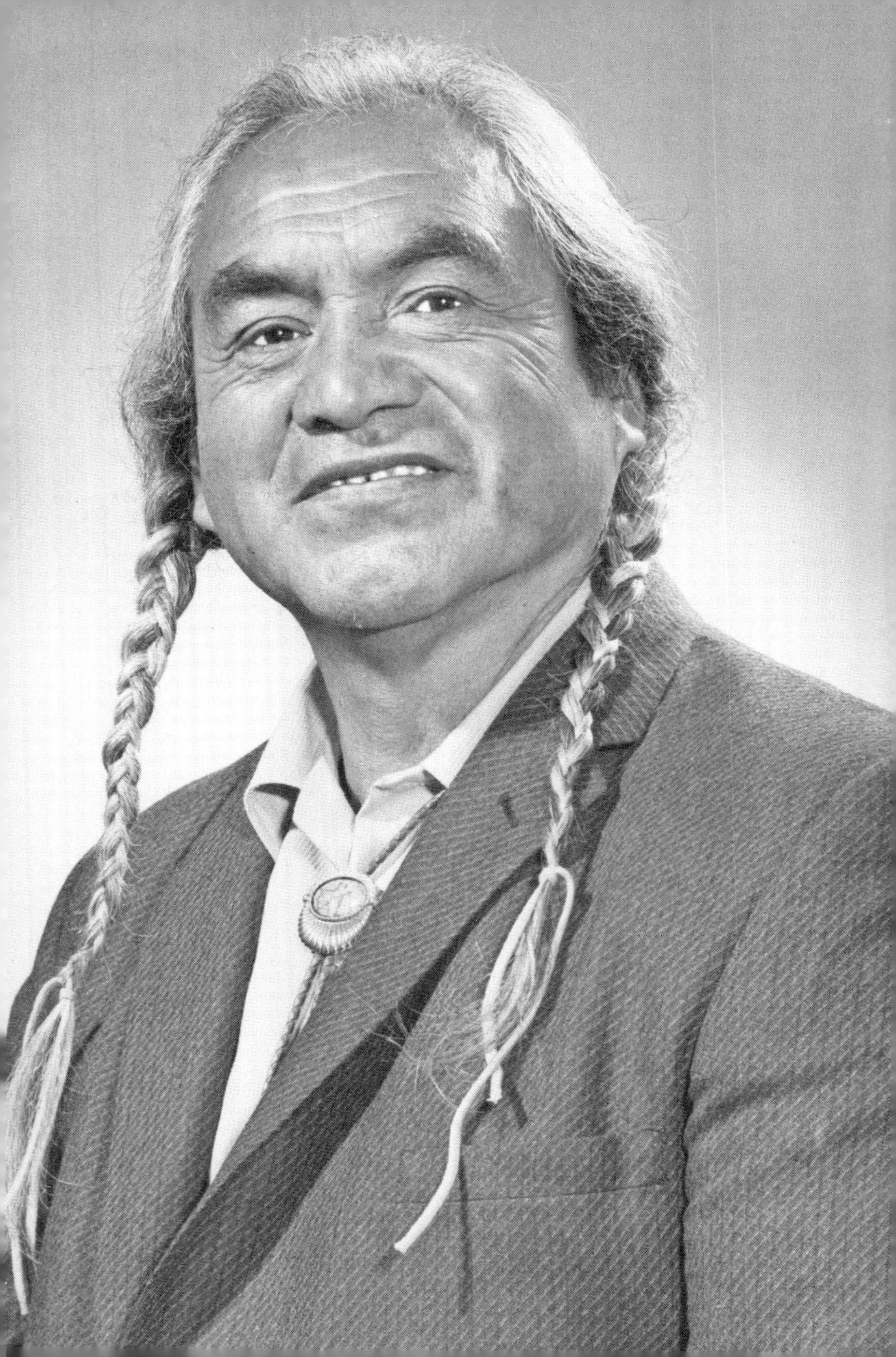

A Totem Pole History

THE WORK OF LUMMI CARVER JOE HILLAIRE

Pauline Hillaire | EDITED BY Gregory P. Fields

Published by the University of Nebraska Press / Lincoln and London
In cooperation with the American Indian Studies Research Institute, Indiana University, Bloomington

Frontispiece: Joseph R. Hillaire (1894–1967), Kwul-kwul'tʷ, Lummi. Courtesy of the Seattle Municipal Archives, ca. 1961.

Manufactured in the United States of America

Library of Congress Cataloging-in-Publication Data
Hillaire, Pauline, 1929–
A totem pole history: the work of Lummi carver Joe Hillaire / Pauline Hillaire, edited by Gregory P. Fields.
pages cm. — (Studies in the anthropology of North American Indians)
Includes bibliographical references and index.
ISBN 978-0-8032-4097-1 (hardback: alk. paper)
1. Hillaire, Joe, 1894–1967. 2. Lummi Indians—Biography. 3. Indian artists—Washington (State)—Biography. 4. Indian wood-carving—Washington (State) 5. Totem poles—Washington (State) I. Fields, Gregory P., 1961– II. Title.
E99.L65.H55 2013
704.03'97—dc23
[B] 2013021876

Set in Garamond Premier by Laura Wellington.
Designed by Nathan Putens.

For assisting Pauline Hillaire with preparation of the manuscript, thanks to the Lummi Tribe Archives & Records Office

For assistance with photographs and historical information, thanks to Barbara Brotherton, Seattle Art Museum

Contents

PART TWO: *Coast Salish Art and Carving*

PART THREE: *Totem Poles of Joe Hillaire*

Illustrations

MAPS

A Note on Lummi Terms

For their expertise and generous assistance with Lummi terms, we are thankful to Lummi hereditary chief Tsi'li'x^{w} Bill James and Dr. Timothy Montler, Department of Linguistics, University of North Texas. Bill James provided assistance with the Lummi terms used by the author, and Timothy Montler provided spellings of the terms with diacritical marks for pronunciation using the Americanist Phonetic Alphabet. In general, we have used the terms as spelled by users of Lummi, and after the first appearance of each term in a chapter, it is followed by the spelling with diacritical marks.

Nomination of Pauline Hillaire for the National Heritage Fellowship

TAQ^{W}ŠƏBLU VI HILBERT

Transcribed by Barbara Brotherton

I WOULD LIKE TO SUPPORT THE NOMINATION OF Scälla, Pauline Hillaire for the NEH National Fellowship Award. I was privileged to receive the award many years ago, and I know that its intention is to highlight our living treasures. Scälla most surely belongs with those who have spent their lives practicing and perpetuating the best of our American traditions. As a Native American artist and teacher and storyteller she has filled the important role of many before her, including her father and mother, Joseph and Edna Hillaire.

I have known Scälla since she was young, as her father and my father worked together in the logging camps on the Skagit River. I am ninety years old, so that was quite some time ago. Joe was a beautiful speaker and carver. Joe and Edna raised their children to be culturally alert, even at a time when it was frowned upon.

Scälla learned the spirit of sharing. Her grandfather was a cultural historian, and she prepared in the same manner to honor the ancestors through our oral traditions. I have participated side by side with Scälla at many community gatherings and public events and have seen the beautiful way she shares her culture with all those who have an open heart to listen.

A Call to Carvers

SCÄLLA, PAULINE HILLAIRE

MY NAME IS PAULINE HILLAIRE. I COME FROM THE Lummi Nation. My Indian name is Scälla, which means "Of the Killer Whale." I'm making an all-out call for young people with dreams and visions for the future of their children and the survival of their children. To carve, some of you think it's a mystery, but no.

You've got to have heart, and I know you do. To carve as the Coast Salish people did, you've got to have heart. It has also been said, "Once a carver, always a carver." The love of cedar or whatever medium is used, the love of the stories, the adventure of the entire event, from picking up the carving tool and picking the right tree or other medium, featuring in your mind, at first, the final carved product—every work of this art becomes a work of love, not just a challenge.

To say, "Once a carver, always a carver," becomes a challenge to the workings of your mind as a young carver. Carving, no matter how long, brings more to the surface of the art than you expect. You've already become a storyteller or a historian once you carve, once you study the totem pole and finally cover and add your personal touch to it. Your world has expanded without your knowing it. You are already a very important person to your family and your community without knowing it. It may be better if you don't know it.

Please hear this story. My father learned from his father, who was born in about 1846. He also learned from his grandfather Salaphalano, a priest of the Longhouse tradition who must have been born close to 1800. Without a formal education, my father built a two-story home for us. And this is how I know a carver can switch from art to building, and building may be an art. And so he built this two-story house for us. Sadly, it was burned down. It was on the corner of Slater Road and Lake Terrell Road. Now that spot is empty. It was a beautiful sight to see. It had a stairway that started with a turning spiral of three steps and then fourteen to the upper level. My brother, who was one year old at that time, and I watched as he completed the entire house, and he turned to us and said, "This house belongs to you." How happy a memory is that, because it was a beautiful home. But without an education to build, without any assistance whatsoever, carving gives you the tools. Carving gives you the tools, the physical and mental and spiritual tools, and the adaptability to switch from carving to building. They're both art forms requiring similar tools.

As Lummi stands now, it has very little history evident to the visitor. A visitor can come and look at the place and see nothing but the birds and the trees and the road and maybe an Indian or two walking. They have no evident history, and that's what we need. So we need you to present your stories to the community: your interpretation, your knowledge. Carvings are few, and those that are evident are not as obvious to the community or visitor or as close to the history books of recent years as they should be. Totem poles of various shapes and media around the world hold valuable history of their localities. They carry more than what your school's history books can say. The heartfelt feelings that caused them to be created remain for centuries beyond their initial creation. History books need help. Families need help. For their history, tribes had best not deny the history you have for your first totem pole.

Today's carvers are standing ready to help you pass along your knowledge with this art. All they need is for you to share. I was never so pleased as when I was seated at a recent funeral and a young man unknown to me came up to me and introduced himself as David Wilson's son. David Wilson is a very good carver and has a history of carving. And so this young man came up to me and introduced himself to me and was pleased that I was a storyteller and that he received some knowledge from me. And so I was so happy for that opportunity. Please make yourself known wherever you go as a carver. Release that knowledge. Your family needs you, and so does your tribe.

Now this history of carving goes a long, long way, mentally and physically, physically and spiritually. Carving is the result of a dream, of a vision, of a spiritual message. It is possible for anyone, any age, and for young people in particular to remember their dreams.

And so, my beloved people, when you hear my voice, remember that my voice is carrying a message to you. To you who are listening to me from anywhere, our Indian history is lacking in your knowledge. It is lacking in your spirit of survival. Wounded Knee was only about a hundred years ago. It was not much more than a hundred years ago that Washington State became a state and the tribes were forced to sign peace treaties. But when things are removed, they are always replaced by the Great Spirit. Anything that's removed by the Great Spirit, like carving, art, history, and love, is replaced, is rebuilt, is revitalized and brought to your children and grandchildren. I thank you for being wherever you are, but we need you.

Thank you.

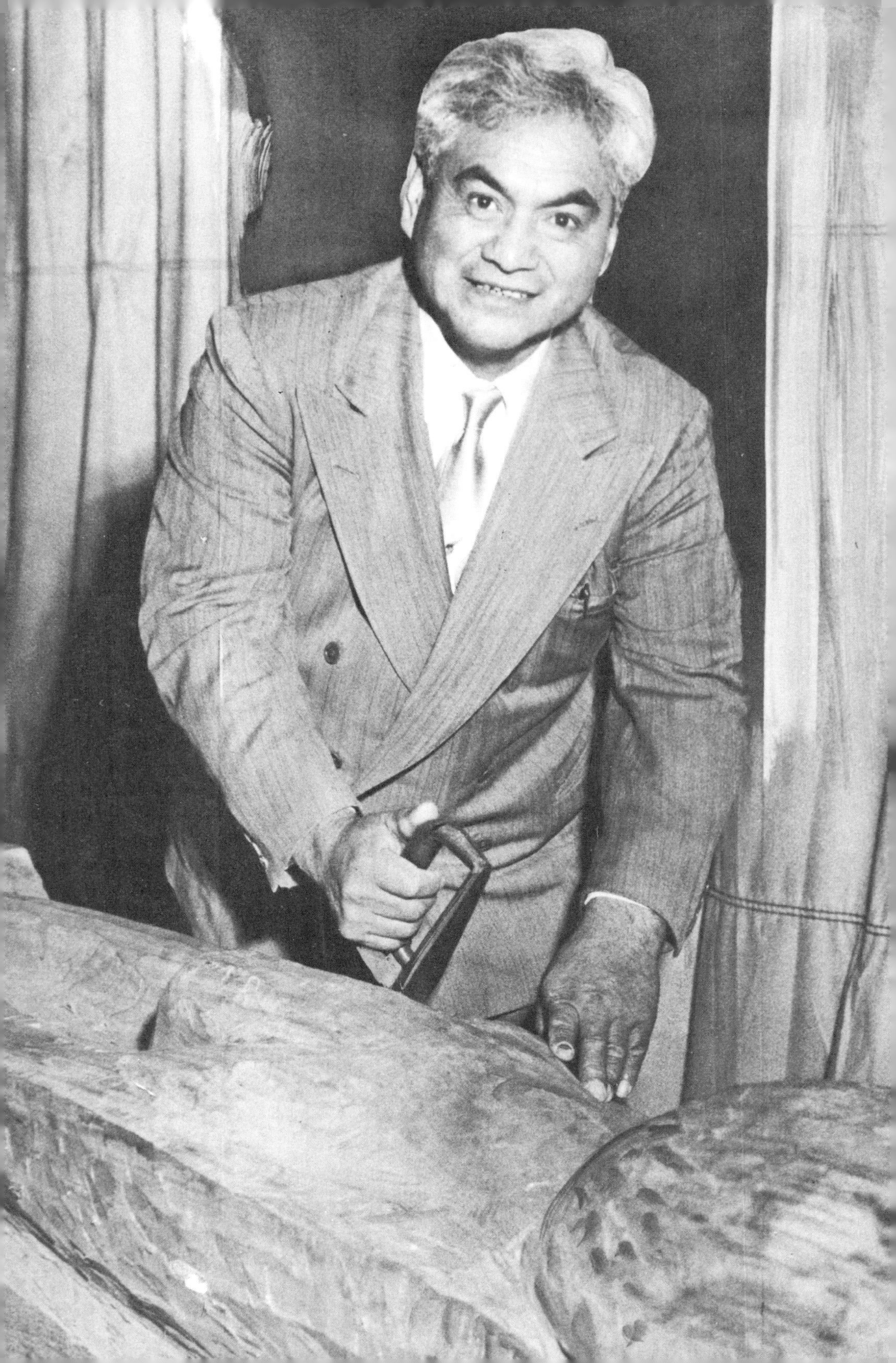

Introduction

GREGORY P. FIELDS

THE BEST-KNOWN TOTEM POLES ARE THOSE OF THE northern Pacific Coast, that is, the totem poles of Alaska and northern British Columbia from tribes such as the Tlingit, Haida, and Kwakwa̱ka̱'wakw (see map 1). However, south of these tribes, a number of Coast Salish tribes in Canada and Washington State also carve totem poles. Among American Coast Salish tribes, the tradition of totem pole carving is particularly strong at Lummi both historically and currently. The United States and Canada established a national border at the forty-ninth parallel with the Oregon Treaty of 1846. Before the arrival of Anglo-Europeans, the Lummi Tribe was a large tribe whose ancestral territory covered an expansive area of coastal northern Washington extending into southwestern British Columbia (see map 3). The Lummi Tribe is the northernmost American Coast Salish tribe, so it is not surprising that this Washington tribe, just twenty miles south of the border of British Columbia, is among the totem pole tribes of the Pacific Northwest (see map 2).

1. Joseph Hillaire carving the Kobe-Seattle Sister Cities friendship pole, 1961. Reprinted by permission from the Seattle Post-Intelligencer Collection, Museum of History and Industry, Seattle.

The Lummi are also known as Lhaq'temish ("LAHK-temish"), People of the Sea. The Lummi tribe is the third largest tribe in Washington State, with over 4,500 members as of 2011. In the past century and a half, the population of the Lummi Tribe has recovered significantly from the few hundred persons who survived after Anglo-Europeans began to arrive in the late eighteenth century. In the nineteenth century, new diseases, loss of homelands, loss of food-gathering places, and impaired livelihoods caused the decimation of Native populations on the northern Pacific Coast.[1] In 1854, the year before the Lummi and other western Washington tribes signed the Treaty of Point Elliott, Isaac I. Stevens, governor of Washington Territory and superintendent of Indian Affairs, estimated the number of Lummi people at 450.[2] Fifty-five years after the treaty was signed, the 1910 Census listed 395 residents of the Lummi Reservation (including the non-Native Indian agent and his family). Among the residents of the Lummi Reservation in 1910 was Joseph Hillaire, age fifteen.

Lummi elder Pauline Hillaire, Scälla, Of the Killer Whale, was born, as she understood it, in 1929 (U.S. records identify her birth year as 1931). She has written this book about the totem poles carved by her father, master carver Joseph R. Hillaire, Kwul-kwul'tʷ, Spirit of the War Club (Lummi, 1894–1967), in order to document her father's major works and to share some of the ancestral stories and teachings, as well as the contemporary history, carried by these totem poles. Scälla learned by experience and instruction from her mother and father, and other elders, about Lummi cultural teachings. Throughout her life she watched her father carve, so she can convey with great depth of understanding the history, stories, and interpretation of these totem poles. She presents this history of Joe's totem poles with a number of aims, primary among them, to help prevent loss of the ancestral art of totem pole carving and its associated cultural teachings and to encourage and inform artists of this and future generations. Like her father and his father before him, Haeteluk Frank Hillaire (born in approximately 1846), Scälla has educated wider audiences about Coast Salish Lummi culture, and this book is also a contribution to humanity and the humanities globally. Scälla has created this book, with its companion media (two audio CDs and a DVD), for the sake of cultural preservation and continuation: to inspire carvers and artists and to encourage young people to take up cultivation of the ancestral arts. For all humanity, her contribution can inspire — aesthetically, intellectually, and spiritually — and help to generate commitment to the perpetuation of ancestral spiritual arts.

The term *totem pole* is an Anglo-European term for monumental wood pillars carved by people of the northern Pacific Coast. Although the Pacific Northwest, with its massive cedar trees, is the homeland of the totem pole, the word *totem* is not a Northwest Coast Indian term. The word comes from the Anishinaabe word *ototeman*, which pertains to kinship. The terms *totem* and *totemism* are anthropological terms that refer to a variety of beliefs and practices concerning relationships between human groups and natural phenomena, usually animals but also plants, celestial bodies, and other living beings, places, and powers of nature. Two important kinds of relationships exist in totemism: a relationship with other people who have the same totem (e.g., the bear) and a relationship with the spirit of the bear. Marjorie Halpin, who was curator of ethnology at the University of British Columbia Museum of Anthropology, explains these relationships: "Just as bears differ from wolves and eagles, so do the people of Group A (whose totem is the bear) differ from those of Group B (whose totem is the wolf) and Group C (whose totem is the eagle). This does not mean that the people of Group A consider themselves to be like bears, or to have bear characteristics. When a Northwest Indian says 'I am a Killerwhale,' he means he belongs to a kinship group which has a legendary relationship with the killerwhale."[3] The figures on totem poles of the northern Pacific Northwest cultures (i.e., north of the Coast Salish) generally represent supernatural beings with whom the ancestors of a family had encounters and formed relationships. The family therefore acquired a right to display those particular figures as crests: symbols of their family identity and records of their history. Many Coast Salish poles have the characteristic feature of being "story poles" or "history poles," which convey myths, legends, or episodes of history. Story poles and history poles also have family crests and tribal symbols and motifs. Joe Hillaire's works are primarily story poles and history poles. We could have titled this book *A Story Pole History* but chose *A Totem Pole History*, since story poles and history poles are types of totem poles and because of the familiarity of the term *totem pole*.

The book has four parts: "Joe Hillaire," "Coast Salish Art and Carving," "Totem Poles of Joe Hillaire," and "Lummi Oral History and Tradition." The main part of the book, part 3, presents images of nine of Joe's major totem poles along with Scälla's interpretations and some stories associated with each of these poles.

The essays in this book offer a range of perspectives on Coast Salish totem poles and oral tradition and on Joe Hillaire's contributions to this art form and cultural practice. Pauline's longtime collaborator, Rebecca Chamberlain, member of the faculty at the Evergreen State College, provides a short biography of Pauline Hillaire. Bill Holm, professor emeritus of art history and curator emeritus of Northwest Coast Indian art at the Burke Museum at the University of Washington, has written an introduction to the history and nature of Straits Salish carving entitled "Straits Salish Sculpture." Barbara Brotherton, curator of Native American art at the Seattle Art Museum, has provided the essay "Joseph Raymond Hillaire: Lummi Artist-Diplomat." The essay provides insight into Joe Hillaire's carving in his work for Native rights and better intercultural relations in the mid-twentieth century. Carver Felix Solomon, Lummi/Haida, who operates the carving studio Chulh tse X'epy (Tradition of Cedar), is especially known for his efforts to bring back ancestral knowledge and procedures of canoe carving. He speaks about the challenges and power of carving in his essay, "Coast Salish Carving: Our Work Is Our Identity." In the essay "I Look to the Old People," carver Scott Kadach' āak'u Jensen, who operates the studio Speaking Cedar and whose works are exhibited at the Stonington Gallery in Seattle, shares reflections about Joe Hillaire's legacy, carving, and the creative process. Melonie Ancheta is an artist and authority on pigment and paint technology of Northwest Coast art. She has taught at Northwest Indian College and consulted for the Canadian Conservation Institute, and her works are exhibited at the Stonington Gallery. Her essay, "A Thin Red Line: Pigments and Paint Technology of the Northwest Coast," offers findings about pigments and paints used for Coast Salish poles along with observations about the painting of several of Joe Hillaire's works. Art conservator Andrew Todd worked with Canada's two major conservation facilities, the Conservation Division of Parks Canada and the Canadian Conservation Institute, before establishing a private practice based in Vancouver. His essay, "Maintaining Integrity: Totem Pole Conservation and the Restoration of the *Centennial* History Pole," addresses both methods and imperatives for preservation of Coast Salish totem poles. An essay by the book's editor, philosopher Gregory Fields, entitled "Archetypes from Cedar: Myth and Coast Salish Story Poles," talks about how Coast Salish totem poles convey myths: stories that express profound and healing truths. In the final essay, "Artists Were the First Historians: Spiritual Significance of Coast Salish Carving," CHiXapkaid (Michael Pavel), an artist, carver, and culture bearer of the Skokomish Tribe and professor at the University of Oregon, speaks to the cultural and spiritual significance of Coast Salish carving.

Available with this book is a media companion: a DVD and two audio CDs. This utilization of multimedia (integrated text and audio and video recordings) provides a more comprehensive account and, importantly, a presentation style that is more culturally appropriate to an oral tradition than a text would be by itself. Audio CD volume 1 includes songs and commentary from Joe Hillaire. Eighteen of the songs were recorded in 1953 by Leon Metcalf as part of the Metcalf audio collection held by the Burke Museum at the University of Washington. Commentary by Joe Hillaire and some additional songs were recorded at Suquamish in 1965 by Thomas R. Speer. Audio CD volume 2 contains Pauline Hillaire's "A Call to Carvers" and her telling of stories of several of the totem poles. The CD concludes with commentary from Pauline Hillaire and from master carvers Felix Solomon and Scott Jensen. The audio version of Scälla's telling of the "Land in the Sky" story was recorded by Jill Linzee of Northwest Heritage Resources (recorded at Jack Straw Productions in 2008). The same recording appears also on Scälla's audio CD, *Lummi Legends: Tales Told by My Father, Kwul-kwul'tʷ* (Northwest Heritage Resources, 2008).

The DVD has three chapters. The first chapter is a presentation in which Scälla speaks on how totem poles are "read" or interpreted. The presentation was video-recorded at Southern Illinois University Edwardsville in June 2008 when Scälla was seventy-nine years old. In the second chapter of the DVD, Scälla's voice narrates a version of the myth that goes with the *Land in the Sky* totem pole, along with photographic images of the pole. The third chapter is a short film originally produced in 1965 by Prof. Erna Gunther of the Burke Museum, with Joe's voice telling the story "Grandmother Rock and the Little Crabs." Postproduction of the DVD was done by Aaron Bourget of Seattle, Nicholas Cline of Indiana University, and editor Gregory Fields. Audio material for the project was recorded and mastered at Jack Straw Productions in Seattle in May 2010 (audio engineer, Tom Stiles) and in July 2011 at Sound Wise Studio in Bellingham, Washington (audio engineer, Travis Jordan). Additional audio mastering was done at the Center for Documentation of Endangered Languages Sound Laboratory, American Indian Studies Research Institute, Indiana University Bloomington (audio engineer, Jon Bowman). The media companion was produced by the book's editor, Gregory Fields.

Scälla wrote this book in 2009 and 2010 and was assisted by the Lummi Office of Archives and Records. In 2010 and 2011 I (the editor) carried out additional research and writing, integrated transcriptions of recorded materials into the book, edited the text with Scälla, located additional images, obtained the essays, and produced the companion media.

Marjorie Halpin wrote the following about the meaning of totem poles:

> When a totem pole was commissioned, the artist was told which crests it was to show, but there was considerable evidence that he was given freedom in how he chose to portray them. It appears also that the artists put into their designs hidden meanings and visual puns of their own. The meaning of a totem pole was therefore very personalized: to know exactly what a totem pole signified it would be necessary to ask both its owner and the carver what they had intended it to mean. Recorded information of this kind is surprisingly meager, so that we know only the meanings of totem poles in the most general and, thus, superficial ways. Most of their meanings have died with the people for whom and by whom they were carved.[4]

Scälla's book, with its companion media, makes a valuable contribution by conveying, in the voice of a knowledgeable culture bearer, teachings and meanings represented by the major works of a particular carver, her father, Joe Hillaire. There are many topics related to totem poles that this book does not aim to address but that are addressed in several outstanding works on the subject. Hilary Stewart's book *Cedar: Tree of Life to the Northwest Coast Indians* contains drawings and descriptions of tools and methods used to fell and work cedar for the making of totem poles and many other objects of utility and art. Stewart's *Looking at Totem Poles* provides a guide to a number of poles in British Columbia, with information on how to locate them and insights concerning the meanings they convey. Halpin's book *Totem Poles: An Illustrated Guide* discusses the role of totem poles in Northwest Coast culture, offers guidance on understanding totem poles culturally and aesthetically, and provides images and descriptions of totem poles within the collections and grounds of the University of British Columbia's Museum of Anthropology. Edward Malin's *Totem Poles of the Northwest Coast* provides a detailed account of the history and styles of carving by northern tribes of the Pacific Coast (the Haida, Tsimshian, Tlingit, Kwakwa̲ka̲'wakw, and Nuu-chah-nulth) and contains many contemporary and archival photos. *The Totem Pole: An Intercultural History* by Aldona Jonaitis and Aaron Glass is a magnificent, profusely illustrated work of art history and anthropology that examines the intercultural history of totem pole art in the Northwest, particularly the influence of colonialism on the proliferation of totem poles in the nineteenth century.

This book, *A Totem Pole History: The Work of Lummi Carver Joe Hillaire*, does, however, make some significant contributions that have not been made by the several excellent publications already available on the topic. First of all, as noted, Scälla's book provides a knowledgeable Native voice that recounts the history and the cultural and spiritual significance of the totem poles of a particular Native carver. It is an opportunity of inestimable value to read and hear the voice of this elder culture bearer, who lived through most of the past century and is well acquainted with Indian life as it was lived in the early postcontact period that was experienced by her grandparents and parents. Scälla presents the stories and teachings of various totem poles from the standpoint of her personal, familial, and tribal knowledge and as a lifelong student of the carver, her father. At the time of the publication of this book, the early twenty-first century, there are few Native American elders still living who are descendants of the immediate postcontact generations. In many areas of the United States, the first arrival of European Americans occurred two to five centuries ago. However, the Pacific Northwest was one of the last regions of the United States to be affected by the influx of traders, settlers, and missionaries, the creation of Indian policy, and the establishment of treaties and reservations.

Scälla was born of parents born in 1894 in the region where the Treaty of Point Elliott (1855) had been signed during the lifetimes of her grandparents and great-grandparents, among whom were signatories of the treaty. Chowitsut (Chow-its-hoot), her great-grandfather on her mother's side, and his brother Tsi'li'xw (Tseleq) signed the treaty, along with Chief Seattle and the chiefs and subchiefs of over twenty western Washington tribes. On her father's side, Salaphalano, the father of Joe Hillaire's father, Haeteluk Frank Hillaire, also signed the Point Elliott Treaty. The knowledge and traditions shared by Joseph Hillaire and Pauline Hillaire in the present work, therefore, come to us from persons strongly connected with Indian life as it was lived in precontact and early postcontact times.

The second major contribution made by the present work concerns the fact that scholarship and museums have given a greater share of attention to the culture and arts of the more northern tribes of the Pacific Northwest, while in many respects, less attention has been given to the Coast Salish tribes of southern British Columbia and Washington State. Although the art, architecture, and ceremonies of the more northern regions of the northern Pacific Coast may be considered more large-scale and dramatic, Coast Salish philosophy, arts, and cultural practices are no less profound.

In this book and media collection, Scälla has shared a range of cultural teachings that provide insight into the depth of Coast Salish thought and culture. The carving of totem poles was not originally a Coast Salish practice. Although the Coast Salish people carved large planks that were attached both inside and outside their ceremonial houses, the carving of free-standing poles was not evident in the Coast Salish area until the late nineteenth or early twentieth century, when the practice developed as a result of diffusion from the more northern regions of the Pacific Coast. Jonaitis and Glass provide this historical summary:

> Totem poles were not evenly distributed on the coast. They likely originated in one particular region, around Haida Gwaii (the Queen Charlotte Islands) or possibly in the neighboring Tsimshian Territory, spreading over time to both northern and southern groups. Nor were they a unitary phenomenon, as the widespread application of the term "totem poles" implies. There were and are a variant of carved columns of the coast (most with distinguishing terms in the local, indigenous languages in which specific types are found): "House posts" are interior structural features that hold up the roof beams of large cedar plank houses; "house frontal poles," "portal poles" or "entry poles" are attached to the exterior façade of the house and occasionally include a carved out passage that can act as a door; "memorial poles" are freestanding posts, often erected in front of houses in burial grounds, which memorialize individuals; and "mortuary poles" containing the remains of the memorialized individual, often interred in a box attached to the pole itself. Furthermore, there were types of carvings in narrower distribution, such as "speaker figures" used to depict host chiefs or their orators, "welcome posts" placed at the entry points of villages, and "shame poles" or "ridicule poles" erected to humiliate or challenge rival chiefs. All of the carved posts have been subsumed under the generic term "totem pole," the idea-typical version of which is a freestanding, painted, multifigured pole, often with outstretched wings.[5]

It is not known exactly when totem poles were first carved in the Pacific Northwest, particularly since the cedar wood of which the poles are carved, although very enduring, eventually deteriorates in the humid coastal climate. In the late eighteenth century, European explorers of the Northwest Coast documented totem poles in regions including Haida Gwaii.

In interviews conducted for the preparation of this book, Scälla has said that her father, Joseph Hillaire, whose father and paternal grandfather were

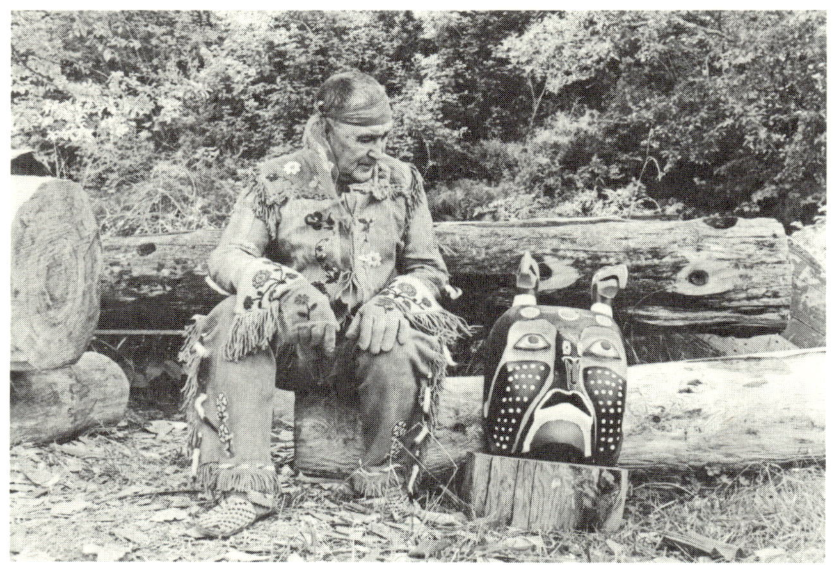

2. Lummi carver Al Charles. Photo by Mary Randlett. Reprinted by permission from University of Washington Special Collections, UW29786z, 1970.

carvers and mask makers, started carving when he was twelve to sixteen years old, as early as 1906. He carved many works, large and small, and continued to carve until a few years before his death in 1967. Owing to the work of Joe Hillaire and a small number of Lummi master carvers, the art of totem pole carving became a well-established part of Lummi culture and art in the twentieth century, and it remains significant in cultural recovery and continuation.

In 1970 a Ford Foundation grant was received by the Whatcom Museum of History and Art (Bellingham, Washington) for apprenticeships in totem pole carving for four young men of Lummi. They were instructed by Lummi master carvers Al Charles (1896–1984) and Morrie Alexander (1915–73). The apprentices were Dale A. James, Israel L. James, Floyd D. Noland, and Al N. Noland.[6] The staff of the Whatcom Museum created a book titled *A Report: Master Carvers of the Lummi and Their Apprentices*, with photographs by Mary Randlett; the book includes a list of carvers. The report's text and images illustrate elements of the technology and art of carving. Nearly half a century later, Lummi totem poles are well known to Americans on the East Coast and across the United States. Ten Lummi carvers, under the direction of master carver Jewell Praying Wolf James, House of Tears Carvers, carved a thirteen-foot healing pole, installed in 2002 in New York City in honor of persons who lost family members in the attacks of September 11, 2001. The next year an honoring pole was installed in Shanksville, Pennsylvania, in memory of the passengers of the airliner lost there, their families, and all past and present members of the armed services. Finally, Lummi carvers under the leadership of Mr. James carved the *Liberty* and *Freedom* totem poles with the *Sovereignty* crossbar, presented in honor of those who lost their lives in those attacks. In 2004 the poles were raised for a welcoming ceremony at the Pentagon and then were placed at the Congressional Cemetery in Washington DC.

In academic studies of indigenous cultures conducted during the nineteenth and early twentieth centuries, scholars made efforts to collect arts, artifacts, and photographs that were free of European American influence. This trend is evident in early twentieth-century photographs by Edward Curtis, who composed photographs first by removing trade items, such as metal cookware and clocks, and then by arranging Indian people in

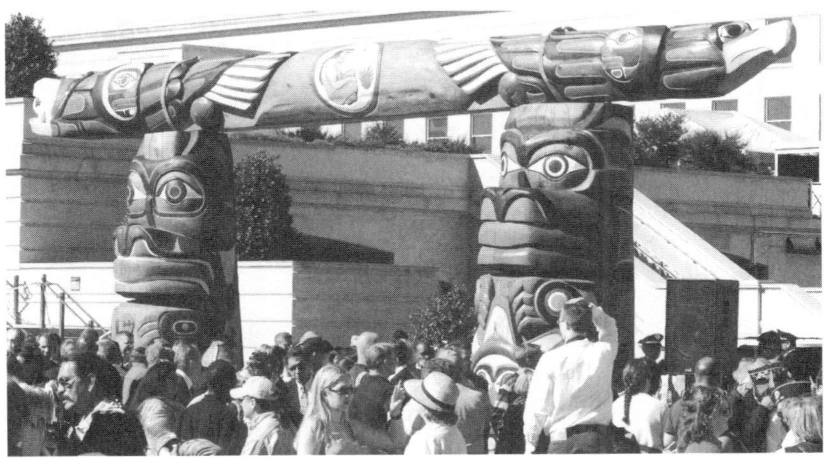

3. *Liberty* and *Freedom* totem poles with the *Sovereignty* crossbar by Lummi carvers led by Jewell Praying Wolf James. Photo by Rudi Williams, U.S. Department of Defense.

scenes to capture the appearance of a time considered bygone and pure. In a similar vein, anthropologist Franz Boas, who organized the Jesup North Pacific Expedition in 1897–1901 to investigate and collect artifacts from cultures on both sides of the Bering Strait, instructed field collectors to seek "traditional" (i.e., unacculturated) items and to avoid items made with trade goods, such as button blankets made with commercial buttons rather than with shells, the old way. A better understanding has evolved since then: innovations adopted by indigenous people that utilize new materials and methods, including those introduced by European Americans, are not, for that reason alone, inauthentic. The assumption that only precontact methods and materials were "traditional" rested in part on a presumption that Indians were a "vanishing race" and that indigenous people and their lifeways would soon pass out of existence. This presumption has been replaced with more informed understandings of how cultures utilize adaptations and innovations. Importantly, there are deeper understandings of the term "traditional," whose meanings are not limited to "precontact style" or "the way it was always done." "Traditional" connotes, among other things, faithfulness to general and coherent forms of practice and meaning within a particular cultural tradition, along with informed reverence for that which is signified by those forms. Totem pole carving, although not practiced at Lummi until fairly recently, is a natural development of the diffusion of practices from neighboring tribes, a practice consonant with the ancestral Lummi art of carving cedar and an art form that expresses ancient teachings and meanings unique to Lummi culture, in some cases, in response to interactions with non-Indian culture.

As regards influence and cultural diffusion among groups, factors such as travel, trade, warfare, and intermarriage have resulted in countless instances of adoption and adaptation of cultural materials and practices among Indian cultures. A major example of this is the carving of freestanding totem poles, which was eventually taken up by Coast Salish carvers. It was a natural development for Lummi carvers, who for centuries had been making cedar canoes, longhouses, boxes, utensils, masks, and other items, to transfer their skills to the carving of totem poles. Cedar was the primary material for making the majority of items required not only for shelter and transportation but also for clothing, housewares, implements, and ceremonial purposes. Oral and lived traditions were transmitted by oral history, song, dance, legend, ceremony, and art, and carving was the fundamental form of nonperformance art. The totem pole lent itself naturally to serve as a sensorially and spiritually impactful medium, to record and to memorialize important cultural and family history and teachings.

The third way that this book and media make a significant contribution is that none of the available works on totem poles addresses in detail the totem poles of any non-Alaskan Indian cultures of the United States; existing works focus instead on the totem poles of Alaskan and Canadian Indian cultures. One book that focuses on U.S. totem poles was published in 1948 by the University of Washington Press: *The Wolf and the Raven* by Viola Garfield and Linn A. Forrest. It documents a U.S. Forest Service project to collect and restore totem poles of southeastern Alaska, a project that was begun in 1938 and employed Native carvers through the Civilian Conservation Corps.

The fourth contribution of this book and media collection, as a history of the work of a particular carver, is its illumination of some themes in the relations between Natives and non-Natives in the twentieth-century Pacific Northwest. Notable in this connection are Joe's carving of the *Land in the Sky* totem pole for the 1962 World's Fair in Seattle, the *Schelangen* story pole carved for the General Petroleum Refinery in Ferndale, Washington, and the *Bellingham Centennial* history pole. This book and its companion media offer glimpses into the historical period in which Joe lived and the continuation of Lummi culture and philosophy through the present, made possible in part by the unbroken legacy of knowledge and practice carried forward by culture bearers such as Joe Hillaire.

When European Americans arrived in larger numbers in the Northwest, their presence changed the practice of totem pole art in a number of ways. Techniques of production changed as carvers adopted the use of metal drills, axes, and other tools that were more efficient than the tools of stone, bone, shell, and copper that carvers had used formerly. In some instances poles were carved to cater to a market of Anglo-Europeans, whose cultural backgrounds did not permit them to grasp the significance that the symbology of totem poles held for Native persons and communities. The trade of furs and other goods from Indian to white hands produced a greater amount of wealth that Indian carvers could invest in the creation of new works, resulting in a large number of poles being carved in the late nineteenth century. Although totem poles were carved in this period for purposes including commissions by new white residents who wanted to possess totem poles, this very active time of production of commissioned poles in the Northwest existed alongside the fundamental practice of totem carving as a significant Native cultural expression and record that white residents and visitors in the Northwest lacked the context to understand. Given the history of misappropriation of both tangible and intangible forms of cultural property and the sacred elements of cultural art forms, books like the present one should go only a limited distance in helping outsiders to a culture gain insight into Native cultural life and meanings. Yet there is much insight that non-Native people can appropriately receive from a work such as this one about Native art and culture and about universal human experience in the domains of the earth and waters, the human community, and the spirit. For Lummi and other First Nations people, we hope that this book will add to resources for the strong continuation of aboriginal practices and philosophy.

Finally, this work helps to document the legacy of the honorable Kwulkwul't^{w}, Joseph Hillaire, a remarkable gentleman who possessed many talents, who cultivated those talents, and who worked tirelessly in behalf of Lummi and Coast Salish people for the continuing vitality of cultural arts and practices that he knew would help sustain Native people in a new era of coexistence with Anglo-Europeans.

Thanks to the University of Nebraska Press and to our editors and reviewers for making possible the publication of this book and its companion media. We are indebted to Raymond DeMallie and Douglas Parks and the American Indian Studies Research Institute at Indiana University for assistance and resources provided for this project. Special thanks to Jon Bowman, audio engineer for the AISRI's Center for Documentation of Endangered Languages Sound Lab. For funding, we thank Artist Trust; Jack Straw Productions; Loran Olsen, Professor Emeritus, Washington

State University; the Potlatch Fund; Southern Illinois University Edwardsville; and the Center for Spirituality and Sustainability at SIUE. Thanks to SIUE research assistants Lauren Gibson, Jenna Tucker, and Wendy Wyrostek. Special thanks to the Philadelphia Friends (Quakers) and community members of Bellingham, Washington, for supporting this project. Many thanks to the individuals and institutions that contributed images and to Melonie Ancheta for expert assistance with the images. To the essayists who contributed to this work, we are thankful for the years of expertise they have cultivated in support of the ancestral arts and for their generous gifts of time and effort to help create this book. Thanks to Scälla's chosen biographer, Rebecca Chamberlain, for many contributions, including traveling with Scälla to Illinois and assisting her during some of the recording done for this project. Finally, great thanks to Scälla, Pauline Hillaire of Lummi, for the opportunity to work with her on this project and for her lifetime of dedication to the continuing vitality of Lummi arts and cultural philosophy.

NOTES

1. Boyd, *The Coming of the Spirit of Pestilence.*
2. *Report of the Commissioner of Indian Affairs*, 454.
3. Halpin, *Totem Poles*, 16.
4. Halpin, *Totem Poles*, 18.
5. Jonaitis and Glass, *The Totem Pole*, 4.
6. Whatcom Museum staff, *A Report*, 6–8.

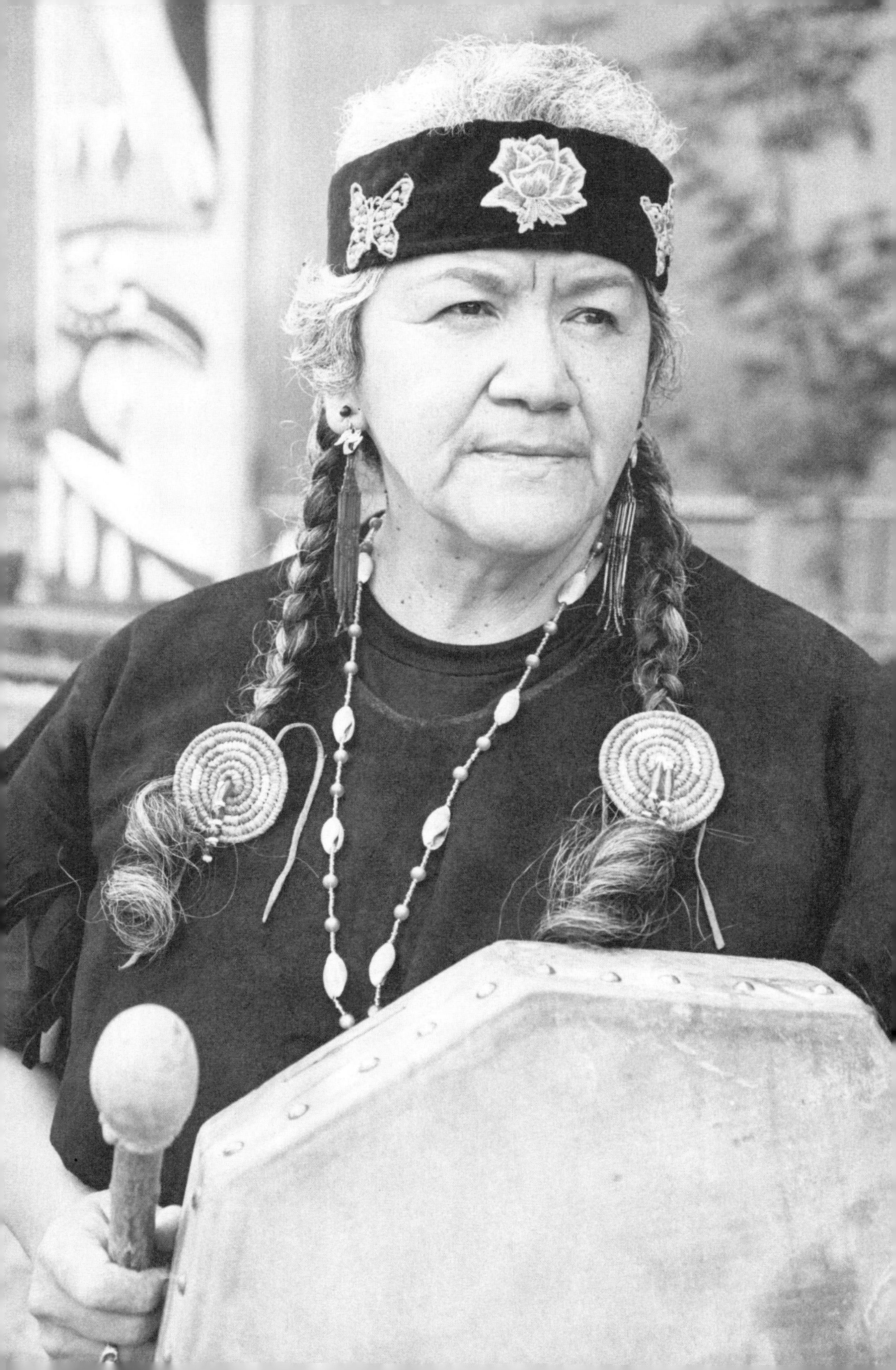

Scälla, Of the Killer Whale

A Brief Biography

REBECCA CHAMBERLAIN

> Long ago, when the world was new, everything and everybody had a spirit. With that spirit they could communicate with each other. Rocks could talk, animals could talk, fish and little crabs could talk. Many Native American songs express this communication between people and nature.
>
> As Native people, our value system is based on our relationship to the land. Our environment is part of every aspect of our lives. The land will sing to you, if you listen. It is the source of songs. Many have stopped listening, but the spirits are still there.
>
> — PAULINE HILLAIRE, *Sharing the Circle*

PAULINE HILLAIRE AND I SIT ON THE BEACH AT Gooseberry Point witnessing a breathtaking sunset as the autumn sun hangs in the sky.[1] Two young men paddle out to pull in their purse seine as we look across Hale Passage toward Lummi Island. A seal noses its head out of the water in front of them, and then, bobbing up and down, it swims toward us. Songbirds, ignited by the brilliant afternoon light, sing in a trilling chorus. Flecks of gold and silver dance on the water and

4. Pauline R. Hillaire (b. 1929), Scälla (Lummi), 1992. Photo by Jill Sabella.

illuminate the leaves of a nearby ocean-spray bush. A lone seagull strolls toward us on the beach, while others execute aerobatic flights overhead. As the sun colors the world in vibrant hues, families make their way home for dinner, and fishermen around the bay check gill nets, strung from narrow poles, and bring in their evening catch of silver salmon. The seal that has been eyeing us swims off to join its companions. Pauline says, "Smell the freshness of the air. This is the most magnificent view anyone could imagine."

On this September afternoon I understand how this western shore has inspired four generations of Setting Sun Dancers, who have been active for the past 150 years, beginning with Pauline's paternal grandfather, Frank Hillaire (Haeteluk), who was born on ancestral homelands across the strait on Orcas Island in approximately 1846 and who started the group when he was in his twenties.[2] This beach, stretching for miles around the Lummi Reservation on the Salish Sea in Washington State, is a hub of life, as it has been for generations. Past and present converge as people go about their lives. A realm rich in resources and resonant with the mystery of life and myth, it is a doorway between worlds, framing the transitions between earth, sky, and water. Isolated for years, the Lummi Peninsula is now seen as prime real estate. In places the beachfront has been sold off through allotments and is crowded with the houses of newcomers. To our left is the fishing operation run by the descendants of the first Indian agent. Pauline says with a laugh, "They tried to turn us into farmers, but we turned them into fishermen. Now they are the biggest fishing fleet in the region."

Gooseberry Point is one of Pauline's spiritual centers. As we talk, I wonder if it is possible to know anyone apart from the forces of family and nature that shape her. This is where Pauline went to meditate as a young woman, listening to the wind and water and drinking in the scenery. It is her place of healing, where she gathered birch bark and other medicinal plants when she recovered from two bouts of pneumonia. Rich in resources, it is where one of the main villages was located. It is the original site of the Stommish grounds, a summer canoe and water festival. Pauline's family gathered seafood here — crabs, flounder, sole, cod, salmon, skate, shellfish, and other delicacies that they cooked over bonfires. Each spring the blackfish — little minke or pilot whales — migrate past this point on sunny days in March or April, when Mount Baker — Cuomo Kulshan, the white shining mountain — stands radiant in the east, and skies are clear enough to see all the way down to Mount Rainier.

Joe Hillaire, Pauline's father, carved canoes and totems on this beach. It was here that he cultivated her political awareness, spiritual gifts, and poetic imagination. One afternoon, as they walked along the beach, he stooped to pick up a handful of sand. As the grains ran through his powerful fingers, falling to the beach in a sparkling cascade, he said, "There is someone greater than I, for this is where He has been. There is someone greater than I, for this is what He has given me." As sand crystals, symbolic of the wealth of the universe, flowed freely through his hands, Pauline understood that he was passing on an ancient teaching. That moment contained an eternal message, rich with meaning, for those who could interpret his gesture, tone of voice, and intention.[3] Brought up in a family that values poetic expression and spiritual insight, she was deeply moved. She told him, "Your words are going to be in a poem someday." She now tells me, "Sure enough, I wrote them in a poem."

A quarter of a mile behind us was Pauline's main childhood home. Unlike newcomers who build up to the water's edge today, it was typical of the homes of its time; it overlooked the bay but was nestled in the shelter of protective trees. Built on 160 acres, the two-story home is no longer there, and new houses have crowded in, but the orchard behind it still bears fruit, and a fir tree that was split in half stands like two sentinels marking where the property began.

An old grove of fir trees still protects the site of the original spring. It was one of the largest natural springs on this side of the reservation, and Pauline's family cleared brush to maintain the site on their property where water flowed up in two gentle cascades, pooling into a small wetland below. Every day she walked down the forest trail to the spring, hauling five-gallon milk cans. She says, "We had fresh spring water from the glacier. It was so clean and freezing cold. Many people across the reservation came to get their water here. It never dried up until a Gooseberry Point resident obtained the water rights and drilled, diverting the water to his cistern. Drilling dried up the spring."[4]

Gooseberry Point is all the more dear to Pauline because of the tragic and blessed circumstances that brought her here. As we talk, she bears witness to the challenges and heartbreak that people endured as well as the joys that they cultivated during times of what she calls "severe survival." How does anyone face cultural decimation, loss of life, and loss of land? As a tribal genealogist, historian, and storyteller, Pauline feels an obligation to pass on what she received from her elders, recounting stories of hope as people found the strength to endure unthinkable hardships. Smallpox, tuberculosis, flu, and other illnesses raged through the generations, altering the futures of tribes and individuals. Political, cultural, and economic struggles were unending, and each generation faced a different challenge. Pauline discerns the truth of compelling stories that were barely whispered. Life was beautiful, but it took every part of one's being to survive and thrive.

When her father, Joe, was a young man, her grandfather Frank Hillaire (Haeteluk) was forced to burn eighteen homes of the Silahilano tribe at Skathlan on the west side of Orcas Island — across the strait from where we are sitting. The families were relocated to Tealish, Sandy Point, at the north end of the Lummi Reservation. This western coast had a vast, sandy beach flanked by abundant forests and wetlands and was steeped in ancient history. However, like many families, they had to agree to remain on their allotment and were prevented from gathering in their accustomed areas. One of the ways that the authorities justified the injunction to burn down homes and village longhouses was by saying that it was to protect people from smallpox and other diseases, though everyone knew it was a way of forcing people from their homelands. Pauline says, "That would be tragic for me. It's a sad story to be an Indian anytime, anywhere. We cope — that's our ability."

Tealish, Sandy Point, was her mother's homeland. It was here that Pauline's parents, Joe Hillaire (Kwul-kwul't^{w}) and Edna Petoie Price, were married.[5] Both parents were born in 1894, her father a descendant of spiritual leaders and her mother of the chiefs' clan. Joe had already been married, but his first wife, Edith Price, died of tuberculosis, leaving him with three children. As was the custom, he married her sister, Edna. Pauline was born in 1929, the thirteenth of fourteen children.[6]

Her family fished and gathered seafood along the beaches, and they set nets to catch ducks and waterfowl in wetlands. Forests and meadows were thick with deer, which feasted on a variety of berries and edible plants that her family also gathered. Wildlife was so abundant that black bear and wolves were occasionally seen. Her mother maintained a garden and grew specialty items such as strawberries. They made clothes from whatever secondhand items they could find. However, as talented and resourceful as her parents were, it was not easy to raise children during the wars and the Great Depression. They lived off the land, but it was hard to feed a large family, especially since they were limited from gathering in accustomed areas. Government annuities did not come through, and health care was virtually unheard-of. Suffering from flu or tuberculosis, seven of their fourteen children died.

Pauline's earliest memory is of living in a tent on the corner of what is now the corner of Terrell Road and Slater Road.[7] She was in a crib and looked out, through a flap, to watch her family work. Her father, an artist in every detail, was building a two-story home with a spiral staircase. She was too small to participate, but she was curious. Always aware and alert, she said, "My strong eyes and ears saw and heard everything."

Pauline recounts many childhood adventures that instilled in her the wonder and mystery of life. During these years, her parents continued her education in earnest both by their example and by what they expected of their children. With a single look they could communicate a silent conversation, indicating what needed to be done, their approval, or their disapproval. Masters of the art of the one-liner, both parents prized a highly developed intellect, memory, and sense of humor. They were athletes, strong people who knew how to survive against the odds. They were artists, valuing the intuitive and spiritual insights that give life meaning. They were strong-willed, but they loved their family and the natural world around them. When they separated when Pauline was seven, she was grief-stricken. However, she could see that they still respected each other as they demonstrated how loving people could cooperate despite challenging circumstances. Throughout her childhood, they continued to foster love and devotion, along with an independent spirit and inquiring mind. Pauline says, "My father taught me to have a well-rounded intelligence, to never forget beautiful logic or common sense. My mother taught me to maintain self-control. If you have self-control, you can go anywhere." She continues, "What I share comes from the source of hours of thinking, reflecting their talent coming through me out of love."

One afternoon the family gathered in the orchard behind the house. Pauline's brother Bert had returned from World War II, and Joe was visiting. Her father put his hand against one of the fruit trees to brace his arm, and Bert, now a full-grown man, stood on Joe's arm, bouncing and talking, just to show how strong their dad was. Another day, as they visited in the orchard, her father sliced an apple in half and said, "Here is the Creator's art," showing her a star inside. Later, the family stood in the orchard watching dozens of shooting stars falling above the bay. Originating from a single point in the center of the sky, this visual portal opened Pauline's imagination to the mystery of the sky world.[8] She recalled her father's teaching about the star inside the apple, along with other stories about wetland flowers that originated from the reflection of stars in water. These connections opened her to the wonder of the cosmos and the relationship between large and small, earth and sky, and humans with nature.

Pauline loved school and attended high school in Bellingham and Ferndale. Academic work came easily, and this was not lost on her parents. They trained her remarkable memory and mind. One day her mother stopped her in church when she was running with another girl. She sat Pauline down and made her read a chapter of the Bible silently in the foyer. When Pauline finished, Edna turned her around so that Pauline's back was to her mother and took the Bible from her. Edna followed along as Pauline repeated the passage word for word, reciting twelve to fourteen verses. Her mother recognized that Pauline had a nearly photographic memory and was proud of her ability.

After Pauline's parents' divorce, Joe came regularly to Gooseberry Point to train her and the other children, and he continued to prepare Pauline to complete her life's work as a tribal genealogist and historian. Talking for hours at the dinner table or as he carved at the beach, they recounted tribal history and worked on nuances of language, stories, songs, and dances, the symbolic meaning of the visual art, how to make Native paint, and other details. They discussed complex questions about political issues. A well-read man, he asked hard questions about culture and identity while maintaining a spirit of integrity and goodwill. He wanted Native history and perspective to be included in the canons of history. How could it be that Native people helped and supported newcomers to their land but that this fact had been overlooked? There were many stories of heroism and generosity, but they were not in the public record. In return, his own people had been treated criminally, yet he still believed that most people want to act in good faith. He didn't preach or demand but worked silently and effortlessly, making learning seem natural and opening her mind to new questions.

Joe Hillaire had incredible vision and influence: he was a leader in tribal politics and restoration; he danced for Theodore Roosevelt; he recorded songs and stories for the Library of Congress with Willard Rhodes; he was an international ambassador to Kobe, Japan, after World War II, carving a pole to represent healing between indigenous people of the United States and nations of the Pacific; and he served as an ambassador for the 1962 World's Fair in Seattle, carving two story poles, *Man in Transition* and *Land in the Sky*, with symbolic messages that embraced ancient tradition and the modern space age, earth and sky, past and future, and the potentials and quest of the human spirit. He was a talented artist and visionary thinker, intent on making the world a better place and making sure that Native people were understood and acknowledged for their gifts and contributions. Like other celebrated artists of his time along the Northwest Coast, he experienced tribal differences and constraints, but individual artists had unique signatures, and he successfully blended tradition with innovation. Joe was also a charismatic orator, speaking with wisdom and a big heart. Many admired him. Some may have misunderstood him, and a few tried to exploit his goodness. However, as his daughter, Pauline understood the depth of his sincerity and genius. She saw him up close.

With all the demands on his time and energy, he made his children feel special. All of his success as an accomplished artist, historian, and cultural leader meant nothing unless he could pass on his insights, and he let her know that he saw in her a person who could master highly spiritual and intellectual work. His belief drew out her potential. He knew that the seeds of his conversations would grow with her in the future.

After high school, Pauline left home to attend the Haskell Indian College in Kansas (known today as Haskell Indian Nations University), earning straight As and a business degree. She got a job right out of college, working for the Colville Confederated Tribes in northeastern Washington, east of the Cascade Mountains. One day Pauline was visiting her mother and there was a knock on the door. Her father, Joe, and Frank George of Colville walked in and offered her a job as secretary to the tribal operations manager. She took it. This was her chance to see Native culture from a different perspective. For the next eight years, she managed payroll accounts, supervised staff during fire season, was a whiz at typing and shorthand, managed meetings, wrote correspondence and reports for the business council, traveled to negotiations, and worked day and night to make herself indispensable. She married Edward Covington, a traditional leader who still lived off the land, which she admired. She had four children. Her mother came to live with her in Nespelem.[9]

In 1954 Congress passed the Klamath Termination Act, and the Colville Tribe got involved. Pauline accompanied council members to meetings in Oregon. Her job included visiting members of the Klamath Tribe and interviewing them about how they felt. Pauline typed up the interview notes and wrote summaries. This experience opened her eyes and made her intimately aware of the effects of legislation on Native communities. It allowed her to see firsthand how indigenous people react personally to "black and white laws" that have been legislated to disenfranchise them. This lit another fire in her, and she was motivated to do deeper work. It wasn't just that people wanted more land. Pauline understood that, from the president on down, people must have a change of heart. She understood what her father had taught her: people needed to be educated and to develop a deeper understanding and respect for each other. She says,

"We were born with the conditions to get along, and we must enhance, educate, and train our minds. Let's survive openly and together. Our future, and the earth, is dependent on this."

Pauline needed a change. She divorced her first husband and in the 1960s moved to Seattle to work as a secretary for Boeing in an electrical engineering department. Then she got a position at the University of Washington as a level-three secretary in the Personnel Department. It was here that she met Erna Gunther, who was professor and chair of anthropology and director of the Burke Museum at the University of Washington. Professor Gunther encouraged her to write a book. Pauline wrote a short monograph entitled "Indian Policy: Crime or Reason?"[10] Professor Gunther saw its value and wanted Pauline to expand it into a book, but Professor Gunther also criticized it, saying that each section should be a chapter. Instead of feeling encouraged, Pauline initially gave up. She tried to write political analysis, but her message was expressed in a condensed form, more like poetry. She needed time to gestate these ideas. She carried the information around for forty-four years, clipping every article and report she came across and taking notes on the Indian policy documents in the U.S. Senate and House reports, especially from the decades surrounding the 1855 Treaty of Point Elliott. She quietly carried her pain around too, trying to understand it. The research and writing was a way to transform that pain into something meaningful.

By the time Pauline was in her thirties, Joe's work had achieved international acclaim, and he continued to carve at sites around western Washington. In the 1960s he worked regularly at Blake Island, and he invited Pauline and her second husband, Tommy Noyes, to visit and carve with him. This allowed Pauline to express her creativity and to forge a new relationship with her aging father. He praised her perseverance and delighted in her work, letting her know how talented he thought she was and including her in his carving life in several ways. First, he put her carving of a female figure in one of his canoes and photographed it. Then, when she carved a totem of Tsats-mun-ton — the hunter who would not listen to his elders — Joe was intrigued. Pauline did not paint the pole; she varnished it, leaving the natural lines of the cedar visible. Joe acknowledged her by borrowing this idea and varnishing the celebrated *Land in the Sky* totem pole for the World's Fair.

Various Native artists lived and worked at Blake Island at different times. However, when Pauline stayed with Joe in the 1960s, he was teaching the Boy Scouts. The Scouts were living in trailers, learning to carve and to perform songs and dances, working to keep up the facilities, and feeding audiences. Training them was controversial, but Pauline indicated that Joe didn't have a choice. He couldn't find traditional dancers from among Lummi or Suquamish tribal members who could make the commitment to live there full time. A Native couple, Hyacinth and Winifred David of the Nuu-cha-nulth on the West Coast of Vancouver Island, along with several of their children, also helped found Blake Island with Bill Hewitt. Like Joe Hillaire, they saw that the arts and culture could help educate people, and they felt that this opportunity would help increase understanding and appreciation of Native traditions. They worked to carve, sing and dance, roast salmon, and feed the guests. When Joe lived there, he felt that the Scouts would do a responsible job. He was a devoted mentor, making sure they understood what was expected of them. He encouraged them to thrive as human beings, with the same kind of attention that he gave to his own children. This training had a strong impact on two of the Scouts who remained lifelong friends with Pauline.[11]

When Joe had a stroke, Pauline continued to visit him at his home in Suquamish, spending whatever time she could to support him as he recovered. One day she read a poem that she had written in tribute to the cedar tree. The next time she visited, he sang a song, "Tall Cedar Tree," in response to her poem. He then encouraged her further by giving her the song and saying, "Someday your poetry will set the world into harmony."[12]

> Our environment sings to us, like the Cedar Tree. Did you ever watch the wind in the branches? We love our land; we are one with our environment. All of our songs are from the elements. We don't often sing of a lost love or a new love. We sing of our land. Today, many have stopped listening, but the spirits are still there.

> For every song that the Coast Salish sing, there is a story. For every story, there is a dance, and for every dance there is a special movement. In the song "Tall Cedar Tree," the movement is the graceful dance that cedar trees make.
>
> Many years ago, when my father was very sick, I wrote a poem for him called "Tall Cedar Tree." By writing the poem, I was saying, "Thank you, Cedar Tree, for everything you have ever given to my father." He was able to carve canoes. He was able to carve totem poles. He was able to make storage boxes, paddles, and houses. In the old days our people were able to make many things: baskets, clothing, anything we needed. I was thanking the cedar tree for all the ways it helped us.
>
> After I read the poem, my father didn't say a thing. He was thoughtful as I left his bedside. The next week when I went to see him, he sang this song. When he said "tall," he smiled, because I am tall. I knew that "tall cedar tree" also referred to me. I felt honored when he sang this song.
>
> — PAULINE HILLAIRE, *Sharing the Circle*

When Joe Hillaire died in 1967, Pauline began her work in earnest. She became a member of the Human Rights Commission in Seattle. She served on the Washington State Board against Discrimination. She was a member of the Seattle Indian Center Women's League. She completed an applied sciences degree at Seattle Central College and then attended the Evergreen State College, where she focused on Indian education and continued her research. There Pauline joined her sister Mary Ellen Hillaire, who was a founding member of the faculty. Mary Ellen was a force. Not only was she the first female faculty member hired by the college, but she developed one of the first Native American studies program in the nation. Pauline, along with others, was asked to join a task force to support Mary Ellen. After Pauline completed her bachelor of arts degree in 1974 and returned to Lummi to deepen her cultural work, she continued to collaborate with Mary Ellen. When Mary Ellen died in 1983, Pauline was asked to join another task force to carry out Mary Ellen's vision, continuing the Native studies curriculum and building the first Native longhouse on a college campus. This project brought together a large and diverse group, solidifying Mary Ellen's twenty-year vision for an indigenous studies program.

Pauline continued to consult with the Evergreen Longhouse and academic programs and was honored by Evergreen, along with her sister Mary Ellen and other influential elders, as one of the pillars of the Longhouse. Likewise, she is honored among elders of Puget Sound tribes and is one of the grand cultural teachers of our age. She is a master artist and teacher, recognized by the Seattle Art Museum's Day of Honoring (1995), a Governor's Heritage Arts Award (1996), and a National Heritage Fellowship (2013). With her diverse abilities — intellectual, artistic, and cultural — she blends traditional arts and ancient knowledge in modern contexts, working with dignity and grace to pass on an unbroken lineage of Lummi and Halkomelem stories, songs, dances, material arts, genealogy, and cultural and ceremonial traditions. She humbly embodies artistic integrity and generosity, teaching how to learn from the past as we move into the future. At tribal gatherings, in Lummi schools, and at Northwest Indian College, she has passed on the traditional teachings to grandchildren, great-grandchildren, and members of the Lummi Nation. She also shares stories, songs, and teachings at schools, colleges, universities, and museums and at cultural, arts, historic, and environmental organizations throughout Puget Sound and western Washington.

Like her parents, sister, and other family members, Pauline Hillaire is a force. With quiet intensity and practical applications, Pauline embeds cultural teachings in the minds and imaginations of all who meet her. A dynamic orator, storyteller, singer, and choreographer, she uses traditional arts to explore issues of sustainability, cultural survival, tribal sovereignty, colonization, and other issues. The core of Pauline's artistic practice celebrates a deep relationship to the natural world. She asks people of all backgrounds four basic questions: What is your relationship to land? What is your relationship to work? What is your relationship to others? What is your relationship to exchange?

To answer these questions, she challenges people to express these dynamic relationships through a variety of media. How do you express creativity through the integrated arts — music, dance, language, myth, poetry, visual arts, and ceremony — in ways that embrace everyday life? How do you build community and live sustainably with others and the natural world? How do you enhance perception and experience through awareness of body, mind, emotion, and spirit? How do you acknowledge the past and embrace the future, not only surviving but thriving amid the challenges of transformation and change, personally, locally, and globally?

Pauline demonstrated this process during the Sharing the Circle project, an innovative multicultural music program with Northwest Folklife and the Shoreline School District that brought Native American musicians into the schools to work with second- and fifth-grade students.[13] Pauline told them, "I am passing on the songs that my father shared with the children of the universe. . . . As his daughter, all I am doing is fine-tuning the songs for this age. As I teach, I share the correct words, information, and stories behind them. Now is the time to make sure they are passed on correctly. We work hard to pass on our traditions with integrity."[14]

It is a marvel to watch Pauline bring out the depth of each student's creativity and understanding. When sharing Joe Hillaire's story and song "Grandmother Rock and the Baby Crabs," recorded by Willard Rhodes for the Library of Congress (1954), Pauline gives a full-spectrum experience that engages students with the natural world. As they learn the Lummi (xʷləmi'chosən [xʷləməčásən]) words and choreography, they gain confidence and coordination in singing and dancing. Everyone becomes an important character as the group brings to life an intertidal drama. As students observe how ancient rocks protect fragile rock crabs, they discern how elders protect the young from the storms of life. By the end everyone looks with new friendliness and appreciation toward the ordinary creatures they encounter on Puget Sound beaches.

During the spring of 2009, Pauline was invited to speak at the Evergreen State College program Ecology of Language and Place and was asked to address issues of language, art, culture, change, human creativity, and the natural world.[15] She began by teaching several Lummi songs, stories, and dances that her father had shared with the public along with other songs that were one-time-only "gifts" given in the celebration of the moment, to be recorded only in our memories. She complimented all the students on their abilities and one student in particular for his graceful movements as an eagle-dancer. Then she shared teachings from her father, asking:

> What challenges do you face? How do you solve problems? Be silent. Observe. Examine. Interact. Explore. Get acquainted with nature and the elements. Don't rush in recklessly or needlessly. Probe the core of your question. Use the vision of your imagination to see the inner dimension of your question. There are differences between people and cultures. We must respect those differences. When you can do as well with what is strange as with what is familiar, then you are a superior person. There are also times when what seems superior is inferior. That is when you must come to terms with your spiritual self. From this understanding you develop your artwork and your partnership with nature.

She asked participants to refine these aspects of their creativity by asking, "What do you see when you observe the natural world? What is the face of thunder? What is the face of the 'sound' that goes with thunder? Observe, examine, and interact. How do you see the face of clouds or trees? What does your spiritual self see and express when you do artwork? You can create your own stories if you have the mind, imagination, and wherewithal to work from." Then she told them:

> When my father was a young man, he went out and saw, in the face of the clouds, a gigantic thunderbird picking up a whale. From that vision, he became an artist and carved thirty- to forty-foot totem poles. He took a spiritual design from nature and the Creator. Later he had dancers make the sound of thunder and do an eagle dance with their arms on top of the thunder. That's how an eagle flies, turning to the right and to the left. How do they fly when they move between trees? Watch them. Eagles are nesting right now, coming back from their migration. They're beautiful, with their sparkling white heads. I love them.
>
> My father also observed the straightness of the tree, its bark, and its breadth. He left a frog-leaf, a favorite medicine, with a rock on top, to thank the tree. Expressing gratitude; this is one of the best things you

can do for the environment. The tree communicated with him, "Stand back and I shall know what I will be. Then I will see what I will be."

There was a partnership between him and the tree. In the old days they made everything from the cedar tree. It answered every need. They called it the tree of life. They treated it with honor and respect. "Stand back and I shall see what I will be." There was an immediate exchange.

There were special words for different aspects of life, and Pauline described her father's beautiful language through Indian song and prayer. Artistic and creative expression is often demonstrated more through the body, emotions, and subtle forms of communication rather than through words. Pauline indicated that words can detract from the beauty of the inner experience of the artist or spiritual person. Her father's artistic, or metaphysical, sensibility was alert and vibrant but was often unspoken. She asked the students how they experienced this in their own lives.

Even as she gave students a sense of the respect and maturity it takes to succeed in an artistic or spiritual vocation, she illustrated her father's humor. In one prayer he said, "I asked for strength, and you gave me challenges. I asked for love, and you gave me all manner of behavior. I asked for this, and you gave me that. Thank you. All of this made me as strong as I am today." Her father was strong enough to see all the events of life as a blessing. This ability to transform suffering into strength is primary to Pauline's worldview. With this perspective, one is powerful to make change.

Pauline told the students how her father showed tolerance toward people who didn't understand. As he was carving the *Land in the Sky* totem pole in downtown Seattle, he described various tools: sharp wedges from wood, stone, bone, antler, and black obsidian; steelhead bones for needles; plant fibers and ingenious applications of the material culture. However, he was using iron axes and steel carving tools at the time. A man came up and announced, "Indians didn't use those things." Catching the irony of the situation, her dad answered with a smile, "Yes, but a long time ago they used common sense."

Then Pauline taught students the "Song of Hope: Song of Tomorrow," which reveals how to develop confidence and courage to face life's challenges and overcome obstacles. It portrays a journey of hope that links past, present, and future, strength and weakness, illustrating how to thrive and survive as we work together in times of hardship and change. It demonstrates how the power of traditional myths can be applied to our lives today. The song describes warriors from the North who captured twins at Gooseberry Point. Each brother had a different gift. They worked together to overcome overwhelming circumstances, demonstrating strength and character. However, in the end, it was the crippled brother — not the strong one — who had the fortitude and vision to escape, saving both of them.

No matter how difficult or impossible a situation seems, Pauline advises, we have inner resources to face the challenge. These very circumstances are sometimes what bring out our best. Giving students hope based on traditional philosophy, she then brings them into their bodies to re-create the myth through song and dance and reinforce its message. Students pass beneath canoe paddles that are crossed in an arch, moving hopefully and joyfully into the future. Like the twins from Gooseberry Point who recovered their freedom, the students are strong and confident as they sing in English and Chinook Jargon, "Tomorrow, tomorrow, we will make it, you will see."

Pauline shares this song with groups of all ages; however, when speaking to teachers or college students, she goes into detail about the challenging circumstances of her people. Reciting her genealogy back seven generations, she describes how her family came to terms with the heavy history of colonialism and the suffering it caused. She says, "We had to live by laws that were made by the very people who were breaking them." Yet somehow each generation lovingly transformed their grief and pain, passing on their strength and insight. Life includes beauty along with suffering and loss. Both must be embraced.

She goes on to relate the history of smallpox and illness on the coast, saying, "In an account from government documents of 1854, just before the signing of the treaty, an old blind woman from the Spokane tribe claimed to know a cure for smallpox. She found a flower along the trail that looked like an iris and brought it home. The old blind woman simmered and strained it. It was the cure for smallpox." Humans are given tremendous insight when they learn to engage with their imaginative capacities. Pauline said, "The Indians found a cure, but it took awhile. The old blind woman used the same technique my father taught to me and that I am teaching you. Observe, examine, and interact. There's your data."

Pauline continued with a family story about the smallpox epidemic. "Many Indians accepted death as if they were expecting it, as if it was an everyday thing, which it is. When the disease came through, Petulie, a man from Nooksack, dug his own grave and waited in his coffin to die. I can imagine what that would be like myself, sitting in my own grave during that epidemic."

Then she told a story from Portage Island, just across from Gooseberry Point. A couple had a beautiful baby. They loved it dearly, but they were affected by smallpox and were waiting for their demise. To save their beloved child, they built a raft, wrapped the baby in buckskin and soft bark, and pushed it into the outgoing current along Hale Passage. That baby had love in its heart for the rocking waves. It was kicking softly, moved by

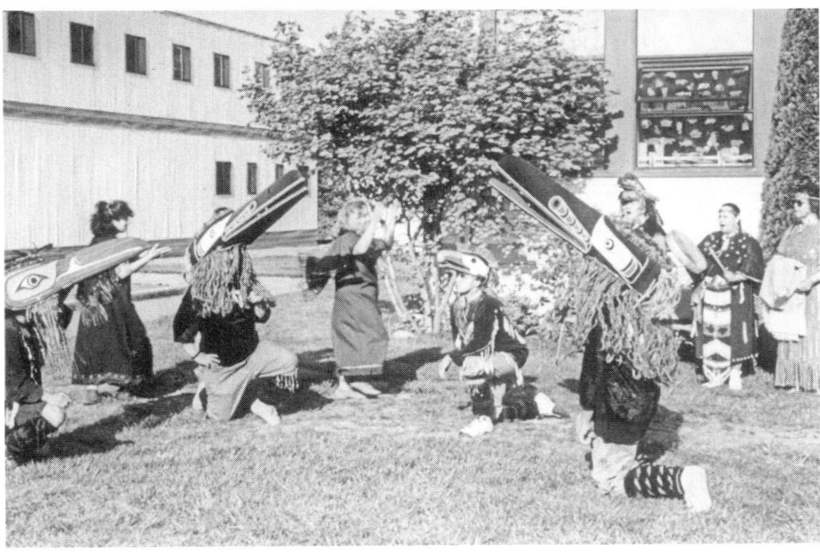

5. Pauline Hillaire (*third from right*) teaching song and dance to the Children of the Setting Sun Dancers, Northwest Indian College. Masks carved by Scott Jensen, 1970s. Courtesy of the Pauline Hillaire Archives.

the waves. As the baby floated along the beach it met a crane, fox, eagle, rabbit, and seagull. Each time the baby was so happy and thought, "Is this my mother?" It pushed it away, but it was still happy. Even when it was rejected, it didn't feel alienated. The baby drifted as far as the Stommish grounds today. There was a gorgeous, shining, white-headed eagle. He made a whistling sound, and the baby looked up at the beautiful eagle and said, "That's my father."

The eagle criticized the baby: "Don't you know where you come from?" The baby asked, "Don't I come from you?" "Look west," the eagle told the baby. The baby looked to the west, and the sun was setting, gold, orange, red, and purple colors in the sky and on the water. The eagle said, "That's where you come from." That's where the dance group got its name: Children of the Setting Sun.

As I listen to Pauline's stories, I move between joy and sorrow. I wonder, "How do we heal the past? How do we heal Mother Earth?" I am grieving too. As we sit on the beach at Gooseberry Point, the sun continues to set. It is a perfect evening, but my heart is heavy. I say, "I am sorry. We owe you a lot. It takes a big person to absorb such pain and trauma."

Pauline has been thinking about these issues for decades, and in 2007 she decided to do something about it. Recovering from two strokes, she began in earnest to complete her book *Rights Remembered: A Salish Grandmother Speaks on American Indian History and the Future*. The questions that she asked so many years ago still compelled her. How could she make sense of what her father had told her in light of the government documents? Her father encouraged people to educate themselves and to understand each other; this was essential to moving forward. However, Pauline felt a strong sense of frustration at the injustice. How could she channel her feelings into something useful? She says:

> I was so angry at the government that I had to stop. I had to think harder than that. I began to ask deeper questions. What is the measure of unfairness? My father told me that we helped the newcomers, but where was that in the record? I concentrated my research on the political

officials, because others had focused on the military. In the book, I put my research together with my father's teachings. Those years of talking with Mary Ellen also had a lot to do with how I understood these issues. My father taught me that we must work for change. We were born with the conditions to get along. How do we enhance, educate, and train our minds to do that?

The first law of the Smokehouse is acceptance, and this was hard for me. I had to get through that pain. But if you understand the first law of acceptance, it allows you to hold our relationship to the land in trust. Mother Earth is the common denominator. She will survive if we are kind to the land. We don't do anything to preserve Mother Earth. Yet it's common sense. We can't overrun her. Europeans are always running away. We didn't have to run away. We need to love where we are. Our hope is that the coming generations can do the same. They must protect the land.

My father knew that I would do this work and that it would not be easy. He said he couldn't get into the ring with me, but he would stand on the sidelines and cheer. That's where he is now. The dead are not powerless. They are powerful.

Pauline's book *Rights Remembered* offers a sensitive perspective on how we can acknowledge and begin to reverse generations of abuse and thoughtlessness against indigenous peoples and the ecological fabric of life on earth. What are the long-term consequences of historical inequity, appropriation, and abuse? Can social justice and psychological healing begin when we witness and begin to heal the wounds of the past? Pauline has asked us to join her and to begin a collective journey of understanding, renewal, and transformation.

As we look out over the sunset in silence, I am still grieving, but I realize what she has done. By sitting in the fire of past wrongs, she guides us toward recognition of new cultural and social possibilities. Grounded in the traditional education, sustainable practices, and spiritual insights of her ancestors, Pauline shares insight into how we can renew our present world by reestablishing bonds to the earth, developing sustainable economies, and cultivating healthy social relationships. Through her research into government documents, she challenges readers to look clearly at the systems of oppression that we have inherited, assess how they have gone wrong, and accept responsibility for witnessing the wounds of the past and transforming our lives in the present.

Pauline breaks the silence and repeats her father's prayer from so many years ago. "There is someone greater than I, for this is where He has been. There is someone greater than I, for this is what He has given me." She continues, "That is the strongest prayer that I have ever heard. It is the Spirit of the Earth, reaching into our hearts. Look at the beautiful sand, the crystal sandy beaches, the smell of the air, the sun as it hovers toward the west, sparkling on the water. You can see beauty in every quivering detail. The birds are singing their little hearts out in celebration; they can't keep it in, thrilling in the beauty of the afternoon. Knowing that prayer has made all the difference in the world."

Looking at the sun setting over the water, I see the road into the sky world. For a moment, I see it. There is a road into the sky, and I see the image of Joe's signature sun dog reflected on the water. In that moment I recognize more of the symbolism behind Joe's celebrated totem poles, *Land in the Sky* and *Man in Transition*. The sun dog is a doorway; it is a road into the sky world, and it is beautifully expressed at the top of both poles. Painted on the chest and wings, the double sun dog rises as an eagle, in victory. The sun dog is an ancient symbol passed through Pauline's father's family. She says, "Sun dogs were the vision of Chief Chowitsut, who lived two generations before my great-grandfather. He was born in the 1700s. He was the leader of the Silahilano."

Joe's vision of the past, recorded on these poles, is also his vision for the future. His *Land in the Sky* and *Man in Transition* totem poles are symbolic doorways. His symbolic message embraces both the struggle and beauty of life. His story poles weave together the relationships between earth, sky, and water, the life of flesh and spirit, past and future, human and natural worlds, ancient tradition and modern space age, and the potentials and quest of the human spirit.

Joe Hillaire and Pauline Hillaire were aware of the significance of this age of great transition, and they have done their part to help us make that journey together. Pauline maintains the same generosity, integrity, and protectiveness in passing on the culture that her father did. Combining practical knowledge of hands, heart, and head, they both became well-rounded human beings. Centered and content within themselves, they felt an awe and obligation to pass on the best of what they received from their elders to the coming generations and to the earth and all its creatures. Joe and Pauline too are symbolic doorways, reminding us of the past and guiding us into the future through the expression of their lives.

Pauline, because of you, we listen to the songs and stories of the world around us in a new way. Because of you, when we hear the sound of the cedar branches moving in the wind, we hear a song. Because of you, we know that these songs and stories have been sung since the beginning of time. *Haishka* (háy sxʷ q'ə), dear Grandmother, for weaving the circle of life.[16]

I give thanks for what Pauline, Joe, and the Hillaire family have so generously shared with so many through the years and for the beautiful way they have honored the ancestors and the spirit of the people of the Salish Sea.

NOTES

1. This biography of Pauline Hillaire is based on more than two decades of our collaboration and, in particular, conversations held at Lummi over several days in September 2011.

2. The U.S. Census of 1910 lists Frank Hillaire's age as sixty-three. In the 1927 case *Duwamish et al. Tribes of Indians v. the United States*, Frank Hillaire said that his age was eighty-two. Based on these two items of information, his year of birth was approximately 1846. Frank Hillaire's original Setting Sun Dance Group was composed of men, and Pauline indicates that they performed for a U.S. president. Later, Frank's son, Joe Hillaire, included his wife, children, and family in the group, and the Setting Sun Dancers performed for Theodore Roosevelt, with Pauline's mother dancing the "Star Song: Song of the Universe." This was during the first decade of the twentieth century, prior to World War I. The Setting Sun Dancers participated in tribal events and major events honoring Native American traditions in western Washington and beyond for well over a century. Joe Hillaire continued the dance group through the 1960s; Joe Washington of the Lummi Tribe also led the group. Pauline continued the group from the 1980s into

the twenty-first century. Lummi tribe members Clarissa Young Finkbonner, Sadie Jones, and others supported the group over the years. Pauline's daughter, Debra Paul, sang the "Star Song: Song of the Universe," and Debra's son, Benjamin Covington, received training to carry on the dance group.

3. Years later, in the 1960s and early 1970s, Joe Hillaire taught the Boy Scouts on Blake Island the tradition of letting sand fall through their fingers, an ancient teaching that came from his grandfather.

4. Pauline's mother, Edna, was forced to sell this valuable property for a mere fifty dollars per acre. Since it was condemned as having no water, she could not get a fair price. For years a water association owned the water rights on her land; however, the Lummi Tribe regained the water rights and turned the area around the spring into a reserve. Non-Native neighbors who seem sensitive to the history own the property adjacent to the spring. There is currently no access to the spring, which is tucked away in forest and wetlands.

5. An ancient family name, Petoie, became Anglicized as Price. Edna's parents were Harry Petoie Price and Emily George Price.

6. Pauline includes a half-sibling, bringing the number of children to fourteen.

7. When we pulled up to where this home was, a deer stood in the road. Pauline said, "This is the land of the deer. The deer stopped us and came to say hello."

8. This phenomenon was different from the normal Perseid, Orionid, or Geminid meteor showers of late summer through early winter, and the family could never explain this phenomenon. Pauline has shared a number of these star songs and stories in educational programs such as Spring Star Stories at the Evergreen State College, programs for the Jack Straw Foundation, and other events. Pauline recorded several star stories and songs in an interview that I did with her at the Jack Straw Foundation, Seattle, May 2010 (produced by Gregory Fields; audio engineer, Tom Stiles).

9. Four children were born to Pauline: Debra, the eldest, followed by Robert, David, and Audrey. Debbie (Debra Covington Paul) cared for Pauline until Debbie's passing in 2011. David passed away in childhood. Robert (Bobby) passed away in 2007.

10. Pauline Hillaire, "Indian Policy: Crime or Reason?," monograph published by the *Omak (WA) Chronicle*, 1982.

11. Joe Hillaire was the beloved teacher of two of the Scouts, Joe Tougas and Tom Speer, and their work with him was one of the important and cherished parts of their lives (see chapter 17).

12. The song "Tall Cedar Tree" has become popular throughout the Pacific Northwest. Pauline included her father's original version on *Sharing the Circle* and has taught it freely to audiences and school groups around the region. She also shared the song with her beloved nephew, Gary Hillaire (Native name, Sealthluk, Lummi), who was a noted Lummi artist, storyteller, and teacher. Gary appreciated the song, and he recorded it

on an album with Tickle Tune Typhoon, a popular Seattle music group, changing the melody slightly. The late Fred Jameson (Lummi) sang Gary Hillaire's version of the song at gatherings with Johnny Moses (Nuu-chah-nulth and Tulalip). This is the version of the song that most people know. Pauline appreciates the popularity of her father's song and the affection that people have for it, as well as the fact that it has inspired so many. She recognizes that both versions of the song are beautiful and vary only slightly, but she hopes that people will take the time to learn her father's original version.

13. Pauline Hillaire, Johnny Moses (Nuu-chah-nulth and Tulalip), and Kevin Paul (Swinomish) conducted teacher workshops, taught classes for second- and fifth-grade students, led assemblies, and worked with students to give a culminating performance at the Shoreline Center. Throughout the program, we consulted with elders, scholars, folklorists, and educators. As we implemented and documented the project, we made the distinction between public songs and private songs that belong to individuals or families. The songs Pauline shared include "Tall Cedar Tree," "Grandmother Rock and the Baby Crabs," and "Song of Hope: Song of Tomorrow." Pauline's grandson, Benjamin Covington (b. 1980), then a high school student, taught with her by demonstrating songs and dances in the same way she had been trained by her father. It was an extraordinary model of mentorship. The Sharing the Circle project sprang from the vision of Paul de Barros of Northwest Folklife, Vicki Hinchey, Ken Noreen, and music teachers from the Shoreline School District in Seattle. Support was provided by Dr. Willie Smyth, coordinator of folk arts for the Washington State Arts Commission, and by the King County Arts Commission. I served as the coordinator for Northwest Folklife to administer the project.

14. Hillaire, *Sharing the Circle*, 14.

15. Ecology of Language and Place was a program for fifty students taught by linguist Rick McKinnon and myself during the winter and spring of 2009. That May, five of the Thirteen Indigenous Grandmothers came to the Evergreen State College as part of the Willie Unsoeld Lecture Series, and Pauline's presentation was timed to coincide with the Grandmothers' visit.

16. Rebecca Chamberlain, tribute to Pauline Hillaire, Day of Honoring, Seattle Art Museum, May 5, 2005.

A TOTEM POLE HISTORY

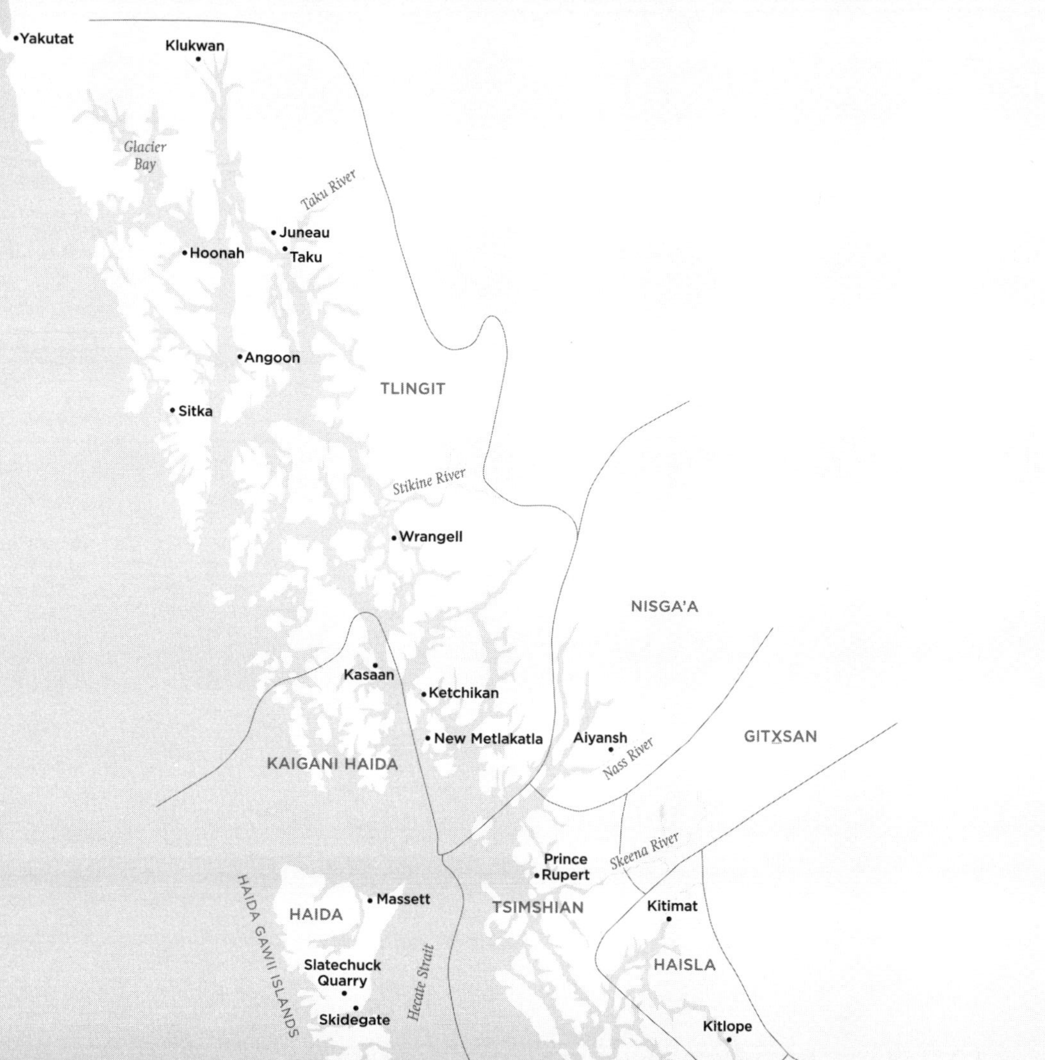

Yakutat
Klukwan
Glacier Bay
Taku River
Juneau
Hoonah
Taku
Angoon
TLINGIT
Sitka
Stikine River
Wrangell
NISGA'A
Kasaan
Ketchikan
New Metlakatla
Aiyansh
GITX̲SAN
Nass River
KAIGANI HAIDA
Prince Rupert
Skeena River
HAIDA GAWII ISLANDS
Massett
HAIDA
TSIMSHIAN
Kitimat
HAISLA
Slatechuck Quarry
Hecate Strait
Skidegate
Kitlope

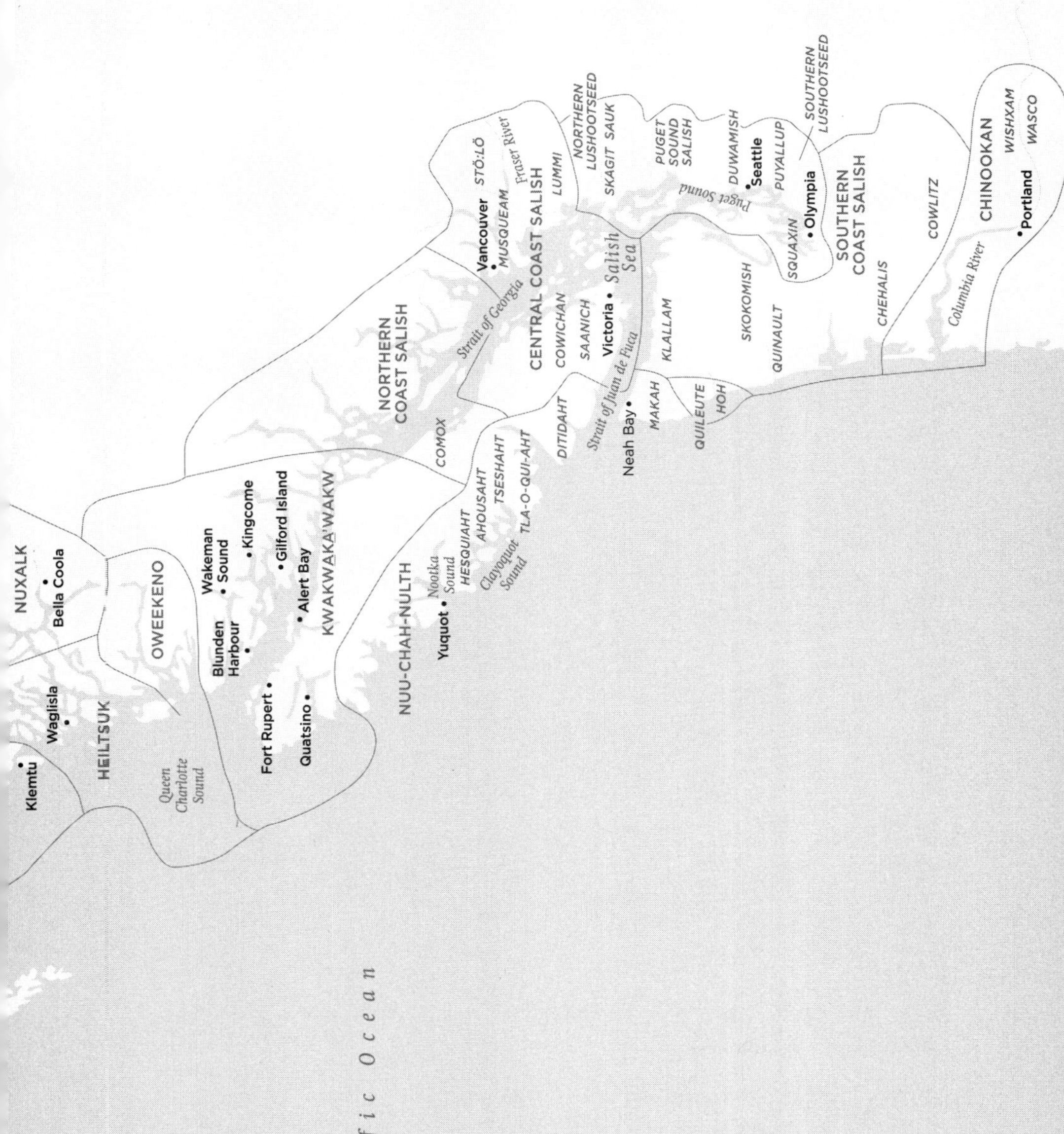

Map 1: Culture groups of the North Pacific Coast. Cartography by Jennifer Shontz. Courtesy of the Seattle Art Museum, 2011.

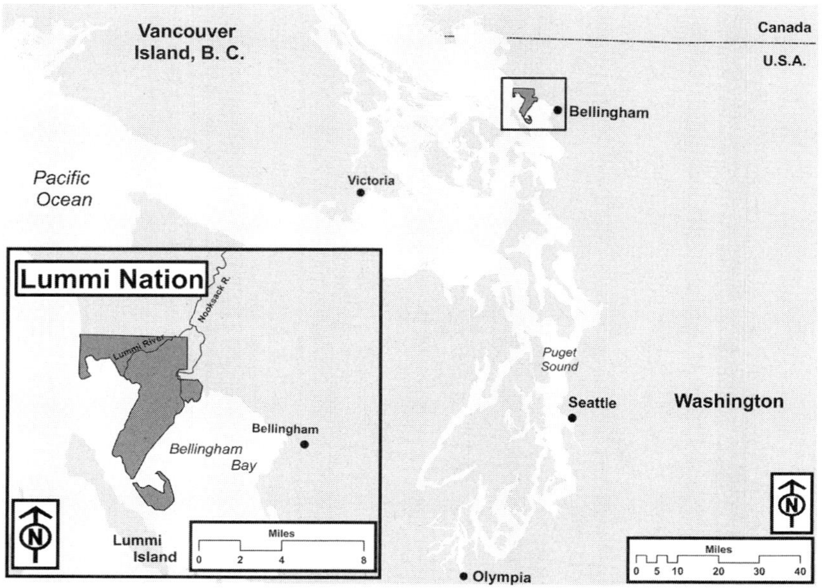

Map 2. (*above*) Location of the Lummi Indian Reservation. Map by Gregory P. Fields. Cartography by Charles Yeager, 2011.

Map 3. (*right*) Approximate boundaries of pretreaty Lummi lands. The boundary line shows the central ancestral lands of the Lummi before the 1855 Treaty of Point Elliott. Lummi territory extended beyond the boundary shown and across the current border between Canada and the United States. The Lummi and other Straits Salish–speaking tribes, the Semiahmoo north of the Lummi, and the Samish to the south, along with tribes based on southern Vancouver Island — Saanich, T'Sou-ke, and Songhees — traveled and gathered food in the straits and among the Gulf Islands (British Columbia) and the San Juan Islands (Washington State). Map by Gregory P. Fields. Cartography by Charles Yeager, 2011.

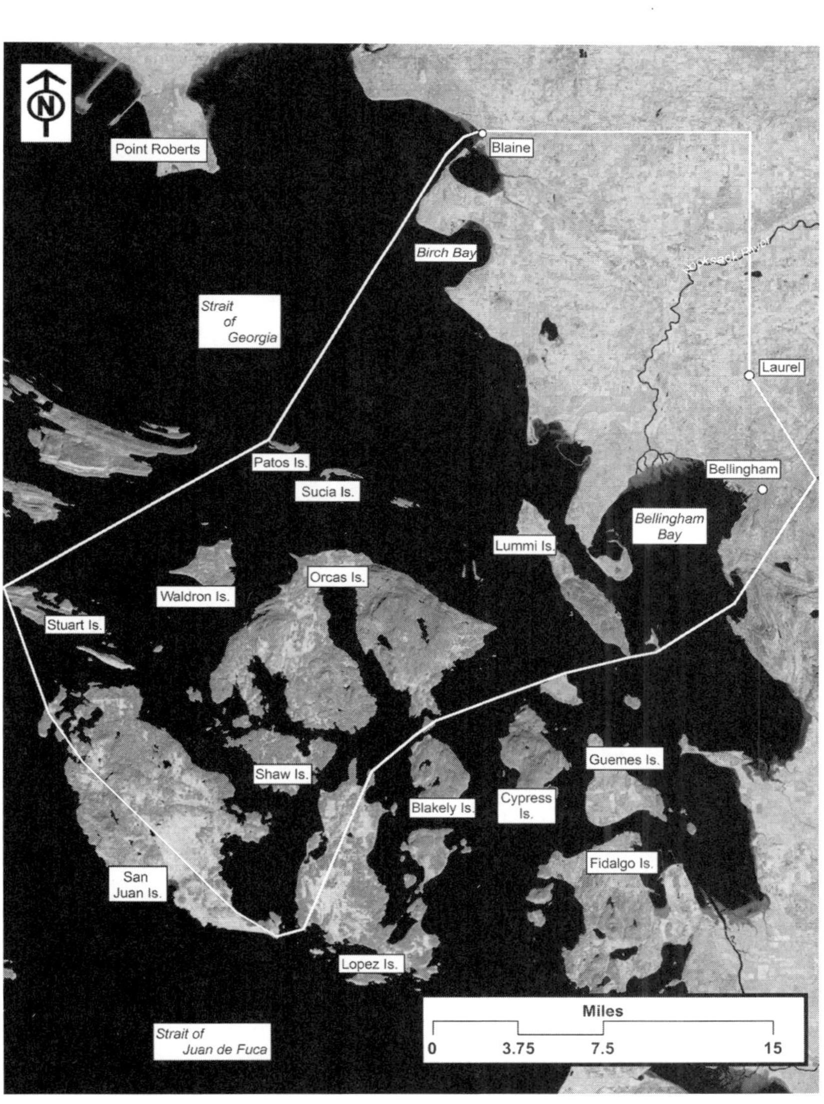

N
Point Roberts
Blaine
Birch Bay
Strait of Georgia
Laurel
Patos Is.
Sucia Is.
Bellingham
Bellingham Bay
Lummi Is.
Orcas Is.
Waldron Is.
Stuart Is.
Guemes Is.
Shaw Is.
Blakely Is.
Cypress Is.
Fidalgo Is.
San Juan Is.
Lopez Is.
Miles
0
3.75
7.5
15
Strait of Juan de Fuca

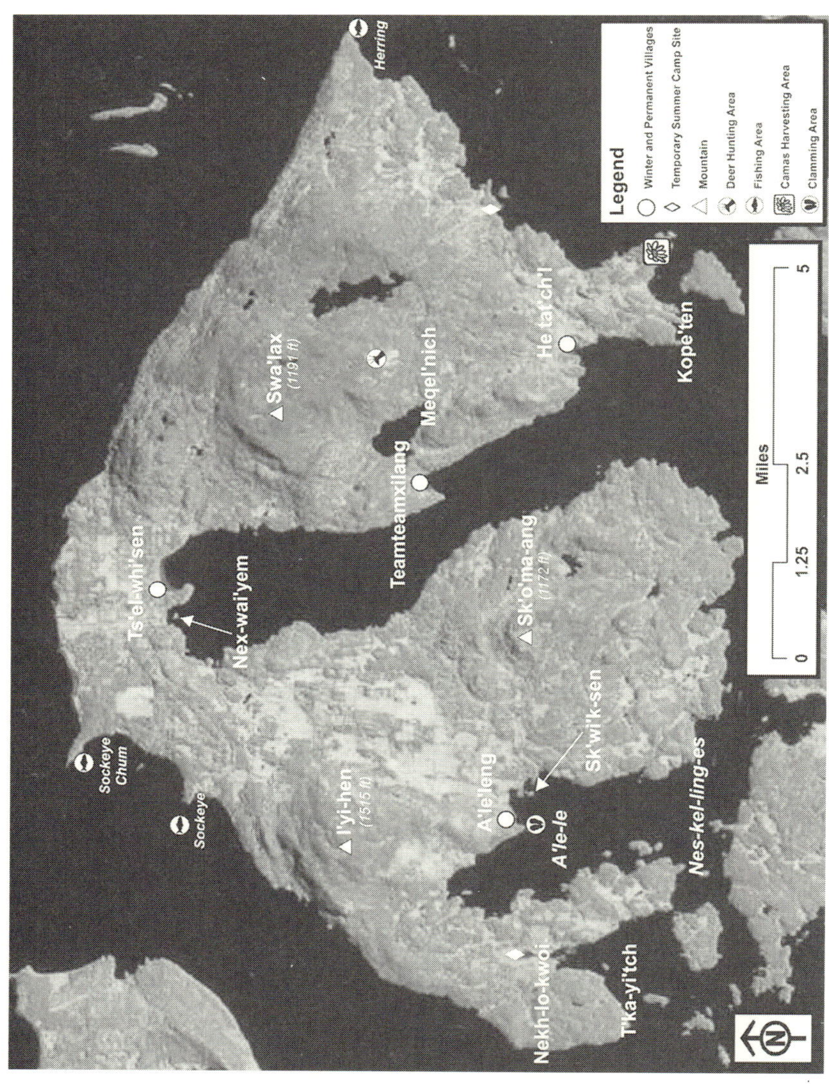

Map 4. *Tl-qol-qs*: Orcas Island, with Lummi place-names. Map by Tsi'li'x^w Bill James, hereditary chief, Lummi Tribe. Cartography by Charles Yeager, 2011.

PART ONE

Joe Hillaire

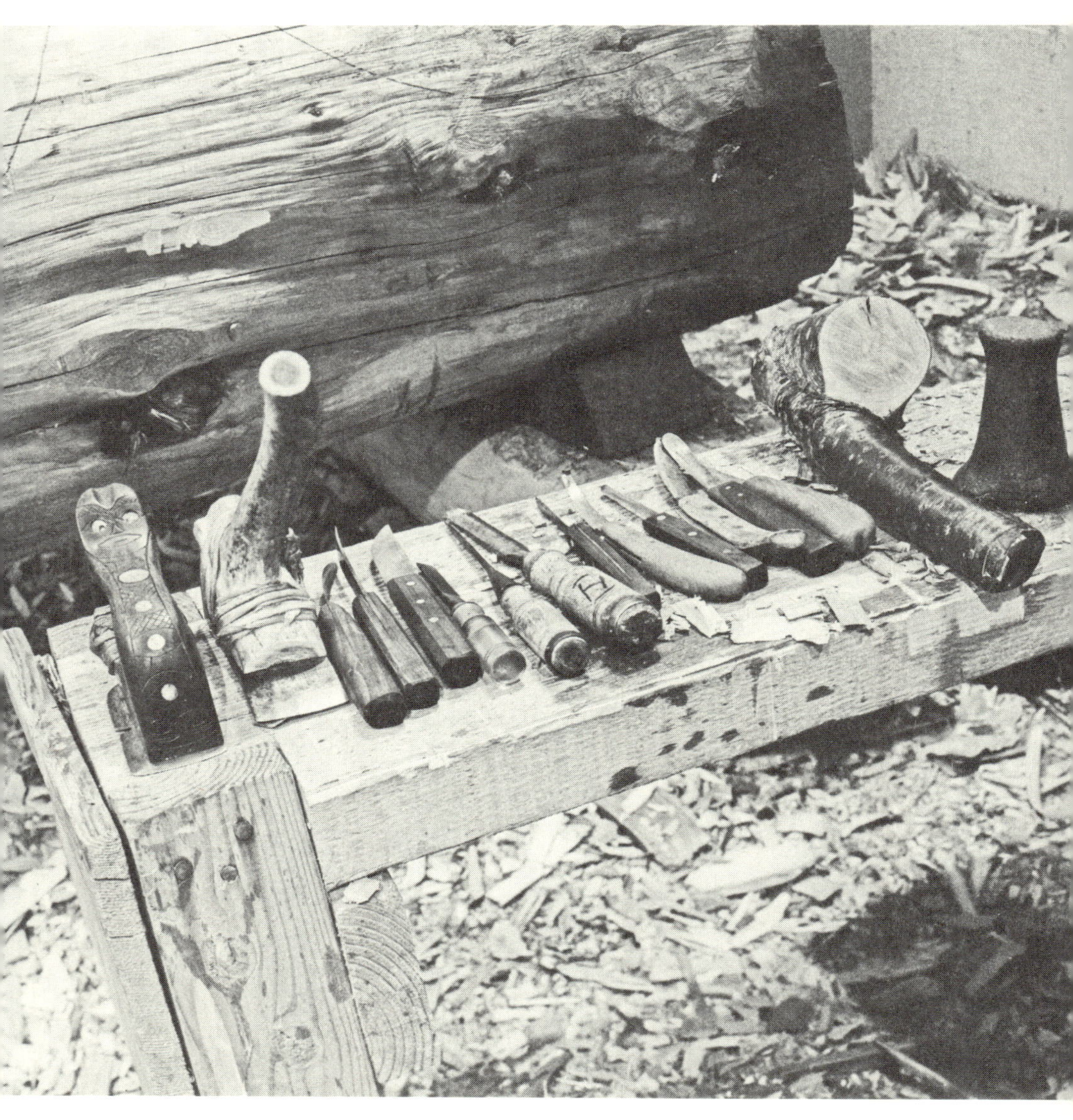

6. Carving tools belonging to Lummi carver Morrie Alexander, Bellingham, Washington, 1971. Photo by Mary Randlett. Reprinted with permission from University of Washington Libraries, Special Collections, MPH 329.

I Carving

PAULINE HILLAIRE

CARVING IS SUCH A FASCINATING SIGHT TO WATCH. The reason I say this is because I've watched several family members as they carved from beginning to end: totem poles, grave markers, boxes, utensils, masks, hats, canoes, paddles, and many other useful and artistic items.

I must admit that I watched my father carve more than anyone else did. He told stories of nature, legends of the old times, and Indian teachings as he carved without missing a stroke or losing his place in the carving. He also had a great voice, strong and gentle. As he talked, his intonations added color as well as definition to his stories and legends. My favorite times were when others in my beloved family and circle of friends would join us, listening. He fascinated everyone who listened to him. He shared his knowledge of the culture, of the past, of place-names of our local area, and of sacred prayers and Indian teachings. He lived the cedar tree, he loved the cedar tree, and many times he simply bragged happily about the cedar tree, which he called the "tree of life." He mentioned the many things that were made by him and others among our tribal artisans. When he'd go on and on about this tree of life, one could easily understand his love for the red cedar tree. He not only admired the beauty of the cedar tree but was grateful, giving thanks to the Great Spirit for the existence

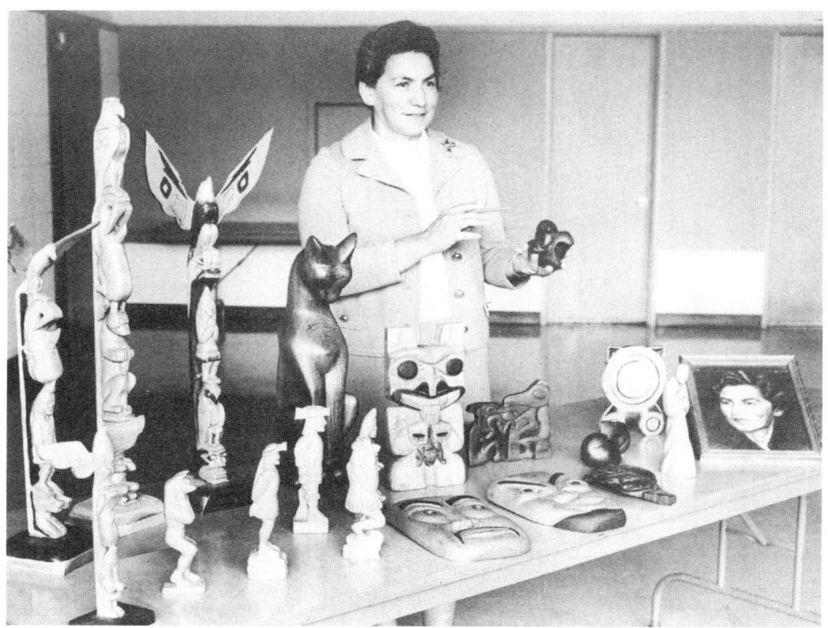

7. Mary Ellen Hillaire (daughter of Joe Hillaire), a carver, leader in Indian education, and faculty member at the Evergreen State College, 1969. Photo by Jack Carver. Reprinted by permission from Whatcom Museum of History and Art, Bellingham, Washington, image number 1995.1.001.

of this tree of life. Perhaps I'm actually spelling out the reasons why I love the red cedar tree so very much. My outlook upon this wonder of nature is perhaps more juvenile than my father's. However, I have learned how to peel cedar bark off the tree to make baskets and have made headbands and other small articles of the inner bark, but I am not an expert. If I had a stronger inclination toward weaving, I would stop whatever I am doing now and stick to the art of weaving. But, alas, my interests stretch beyond my patience.

My gift is the love of trees. I love trees. Why? Because they offer so much to us: shelter, shade, beauty, the stalwart personality, the strength of unity. And when the wind blows you see the movement, the dancing of the leaves or the branches. My mate once asked my father how he picked a tree. My mate had gone hunting with my father and knew from experience

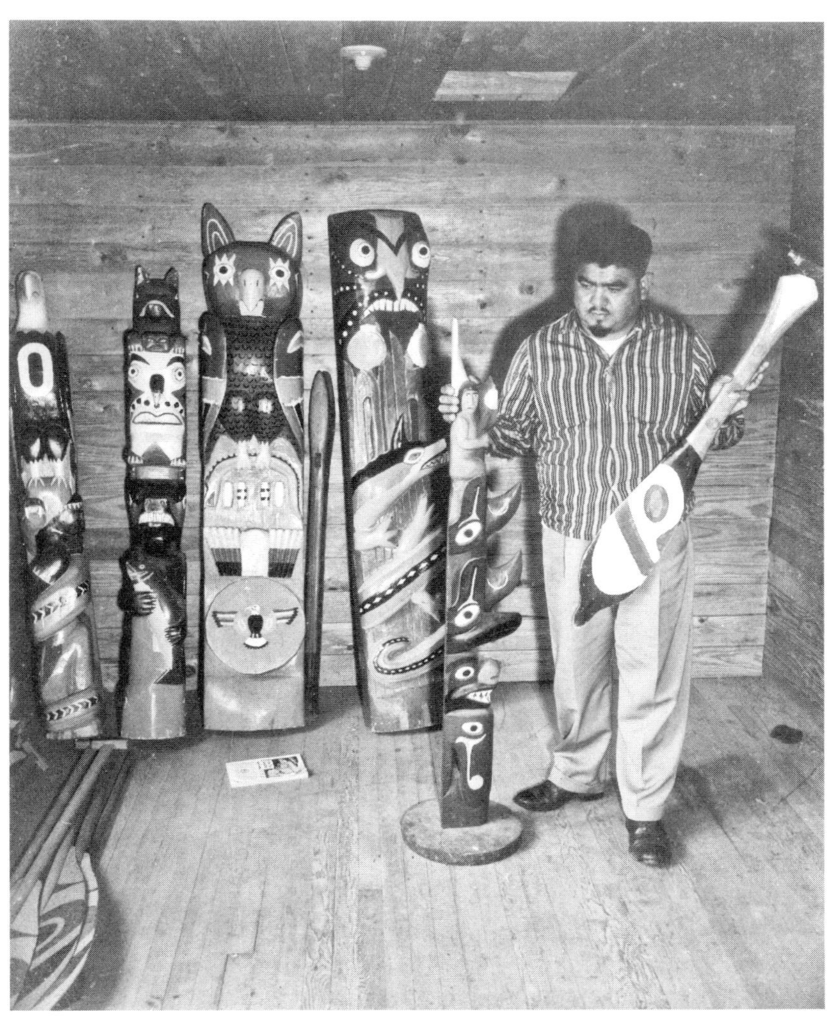

8. Lewis Hillaire (son of Joe Hillaire), Lummi Island, with some of his carvings, 1958. A totem pole carved by Joe and Lewis Hillaire is featured in chapter 19. Photo by Jack Carver. Reprinted by permission from Whatcom Museum of History and Art, Bellingham, Washington, image number 1995.1.021609.

how he could walk through the forests and mountains without getting lost or tired. My father kindly acknowledged my mate's question. At that moment my father was carving a canoe. He turned toward us as though with a strong sense of purpose. Looking toward the nearby forest, he said, "Sometimes it is easy, and other times it takes awhile to find the tree that is just right. And, finally, when you do spot a tree and think, 'That's the one,' you carefully look and, most importantly, listen. The tree will talk. It says to the artisan, 'Stand back, and I shall see what I will be.'" The artisan stands back, gazing at the tree. He talks to the tree respectfully. He moves about the tree and, finding the right space, plants another tree or some other plant that assures the spirits of the forest that he will not waste the tree in this taking. He then fells the tree and gratefully takes it home and carries out his plans for it. When it is taken care of in this way, it becomes a work of love, a remarkable work of art. And so my father always stood back and looked at the tree, whether it was going be a totem pole, a canoe, a log for a building, or just a box.

My father's focus as a carver was very strong; he could hold complete conversations as he studied his work. It is understandable when you know that he had been carving since he was perhaps twelve years old. He respected everyone's opinion; their point of view was important and their right to speak at all. In this way, in his older years as well, visiting with him as he carved was a great pleasure too. He added just how to read the totem pole: to begin where the carver started to carve or to create the first image on it. Then we read the story from the bottom to the top, and if the totem pole story should continue on the back of the pole, we read the rest of the story from the top down to the bottom, on the back. In this way, my mate and I learned more than what we had asked my father about. But that's the way he always talked; he never limited the conversation.

I know from the experience of visiting my father as he carved that each figure he carved on the totem pole had a correlation to the rest of the pole. Putting the story together as you read the totem pole, each figure represents a different "chapter," like in a book. As the story comes together in this way, it is easier to read it the second and third time. Or one can look at each figure as a different "paragraph" of the same story. My experience reading totem poles helped me learn to read fairy tale books in school. Your answer can be as true as the spirit, as true as the spirit of the legend or the fairy tale. But there's a difference between the fairy tale and the legend. The fairy tale gives a reward for being beautiful, but the legend gives an inner reward for listening and behaving.

I'd like for you to note that the art before you is very rare these days. There are not many carvers of totem poles. Totem poles are never to be worshiped. They are not something to worship; they're just a piece of art by a master carver, in this instance, my father, Joe Hillaire. When my father chose a tree to carve on, he'd go out to the woods, and he'd bring with him Indian medicine for the tree. And this Indian medicine, whether it was herbs, roots, or berries, it was a medicine, and he'd bring it in offering to the tree before he'd carve it. He'd go before the tree, and if it was tall and straight, he'd talk to that tree and tell the tree what he intended to do. He was going to entertain the centuries of people that could observe, and then he would lay the offering down at the foot of the tree. Nowadays we plant wildlife. We just plant wildflowers or something wild at the foot of the tree that we're going to cut down for a canoe.

There may be some carvers out there who know what I mean when I say, "Once a carver, always a carver," whether you want to be or not. There are ideas flying around out there, locked in a spiritual place. And every now and then someone, meaning no particular person, catches one. And it's this type of person who sometimes carries his ideas, and in some clever way he turns his idea over to a carver. A carver is a person who realizes the importance of a dream or vision caught in such a way, and eventually this carver helps the wondering dreamer realize that his dream could be a reality, and with a little encouragement, maybe even he, the new dreamer, can realize other dreams of his own. And suppose he learned the magic of creating a carving, a reality, out of his dreams. Eventually he will find someone to share his best dream. Partnerships are often created in this way.

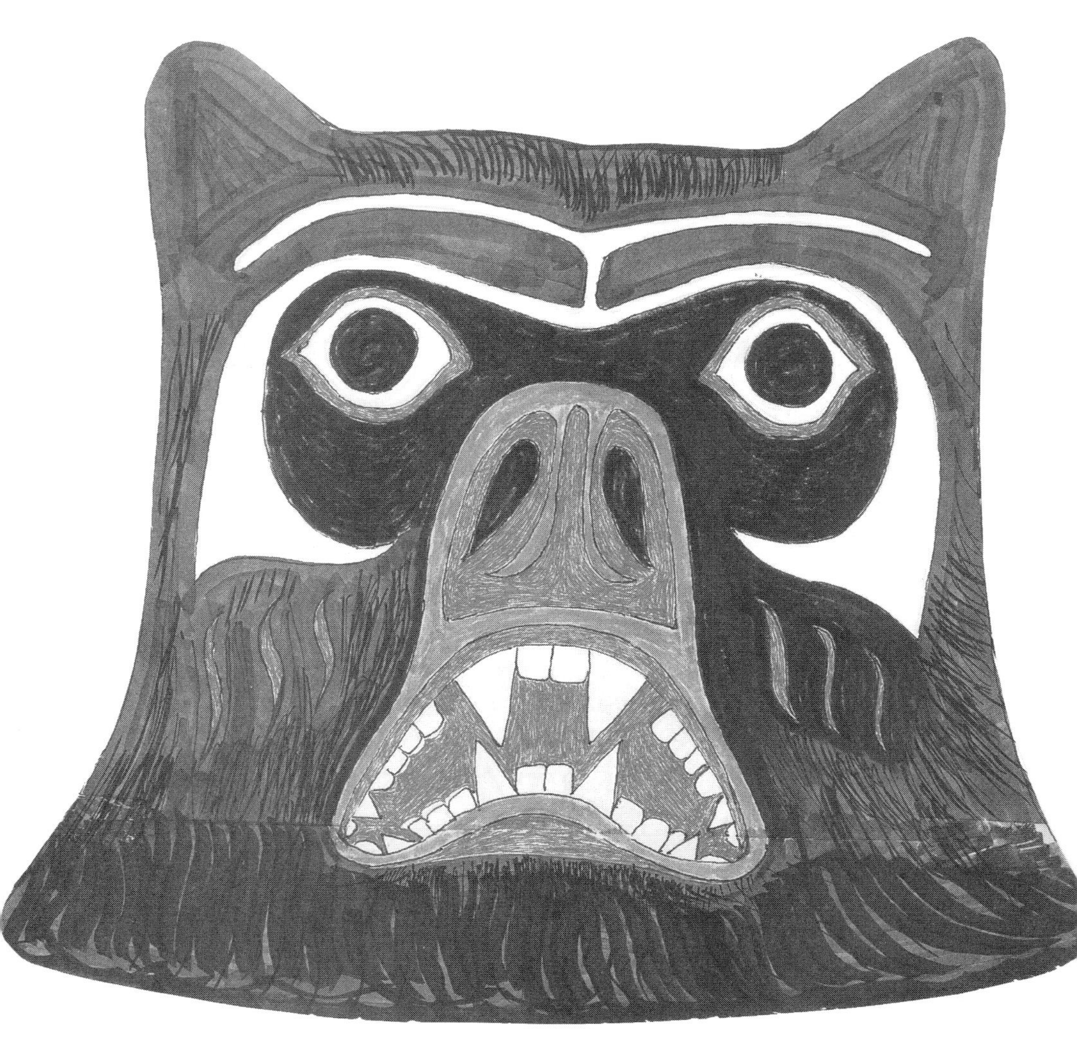

9. Drawing of a bear by Pauline Hillaire based on the design of a drum belonging to her grandfather Haeteluk Frank Hillaire. Courtesy of the Pauline Hillaire Archives.

2 Power of the Bear

Memories of My Father, Joe Hillaire

PAULINE HILLAIRE

JOE HILLAIRE, KWUL-KWUL'T[W], SPIRIT OF THE WAR Club, was born on December 25, 1894. First of all, he is my dad, and I am extremely proud of him. My effort in this book is to tell you about him as much as possible while knowing that telling about just one part of his life — his work as a carver — is extremely limited. He completed the sixth grade at the Tulalip Indian School. His father's name was Haeteluk Frank Hillaire. Haeteluk means "Formidable Man." Haeteluk's father was Salaphalano the Priest. They were both holy men, teaching our Indian way of life in the Winter Dance Longhouse. My father's full name is Joseph Raymond Hillaire. He began carving at twelve to sixteen years of age, being taught by his father and grandfather. His grandfather, Salaphalano, was one of the signers of the Treaty of 1855 at Point Elliott near Seattle. No one ever tracked my father down for his biography. Perhaps Don McQuade came the closest to writing a biography on him on their trip around the United States with the totem pole that my father carved for the Seattle World's Fair in 1962. I collected many newspaper articles about my father, saving them, admiring them.

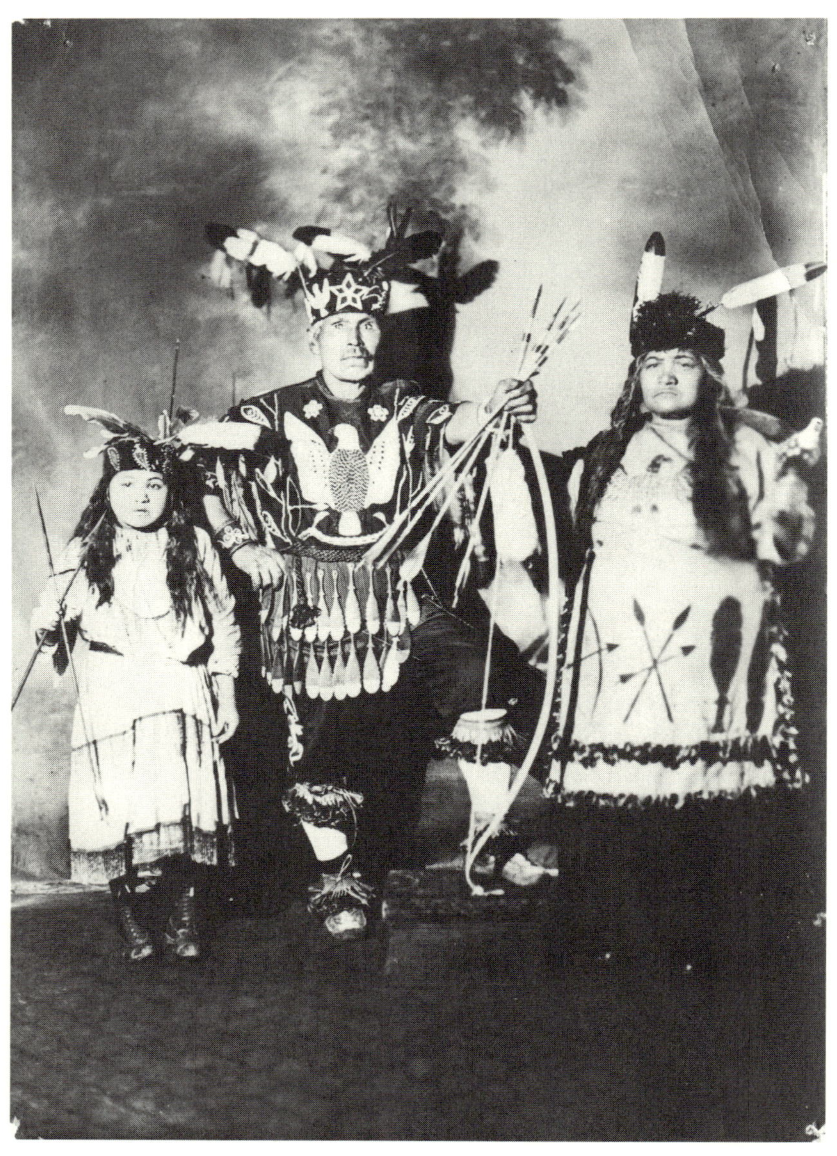

10. Haeteluk Frank and Agnes Hillaire with granddaughter Ethel, ca. 1920–30. Courtesy of the Burke Museum of Natural History and Culture, catalog number 06.

Joe Hillaire's mother, Agnes, was part Polynesian. Her father, Henry Haumea, was one-half Hawaiian. She was an extremely talented lady at weaving baskets and knitting. After the sheep were sheared she would collect the wool. It was kept in big bundles. She would wash it and hang it out in the sunshine, weather permitting. It was always strung out; I'd see it when I was a child. When it was dry she would spin it into strands for knitting. Granny Hillaire showed me how to card the wool and pick out little leaves and twigs. I'd also kill the bugs as I sat at her feet. She knew how to make baskets and mats of all sizes and cooked truly great meals. To me, she was one in a million. I am thankful that she was my father's mother and that I learned from her. My father was a lucky man to have such wonderful parents, and the biggest wonder of all was their cultural mastery in all things. They taught my father how to survive, and they

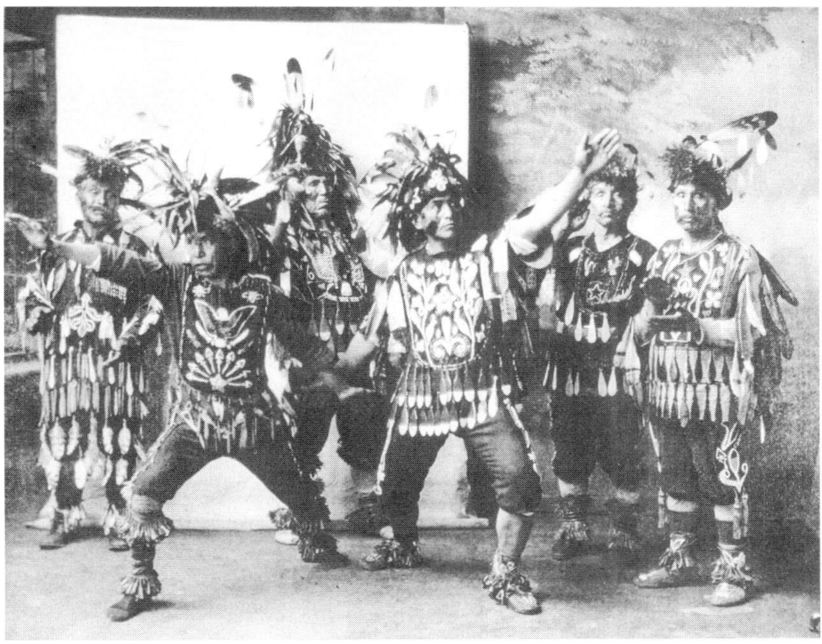

11. Adult dancers in Frank Hillaire's Setting Sun Dancers performing in Washington DC, 1922. Pictured from left to right: Joseph Bill, Thomas Tom, Frank Hillaire, Joseph Hillaire, Matt Paul, and Chief August Martin. Courtesy of the Pauline Hillaire Archives.

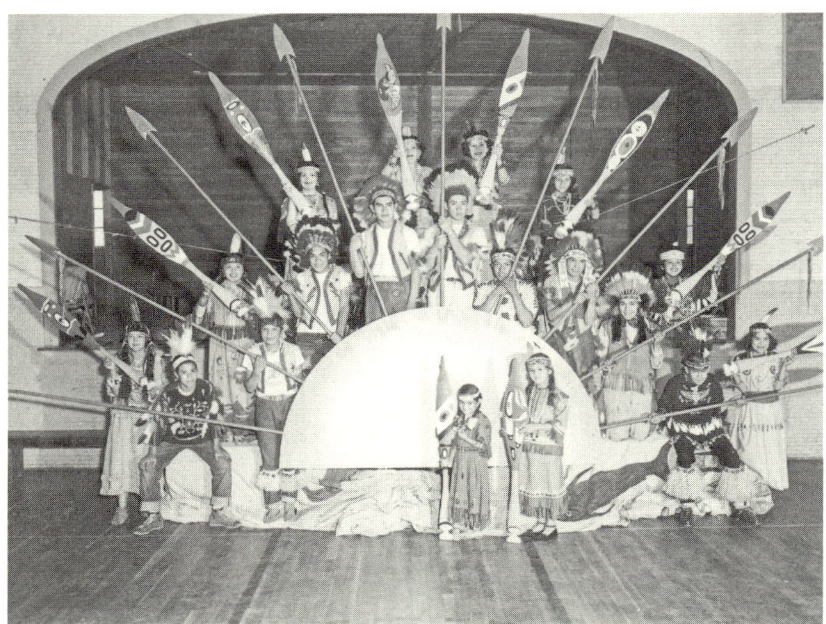

12. Youth dancers in Joe Hillaire's Setting Sun Dance Group. Courtesy of the Pauline Hillaire Archives.

were also teaching me. My elder brothers and sisters danced in Gran'pa Hillaire's Setting Sun Dance Group.

Dad was first married to my mother's sister, but when she died of tuberculosis, he married my mother. This was the law of the culture. Our mother had such a difficult time at first caring for her stepchildren because of the cold weather and — because of the treaty and the land allotments — the inability to gather foods in the usual and accustomed places. No one knew what money was or how to use it. But the women of the family gathered foods within the allotment acreage, which was very small compared to their usual and accustomed grounds. The treaty allowed Indians of the Northwest to fish in their usual and accustomed areas, but gathering wild food was not included in that freedom.

My grandfather was born in about 1846 [see "Scälla, Of the Killer Whale: A Brief Biography," note 2]. His regalia is much different from the regalia of the Plains Indians. On top of his head is what we call the

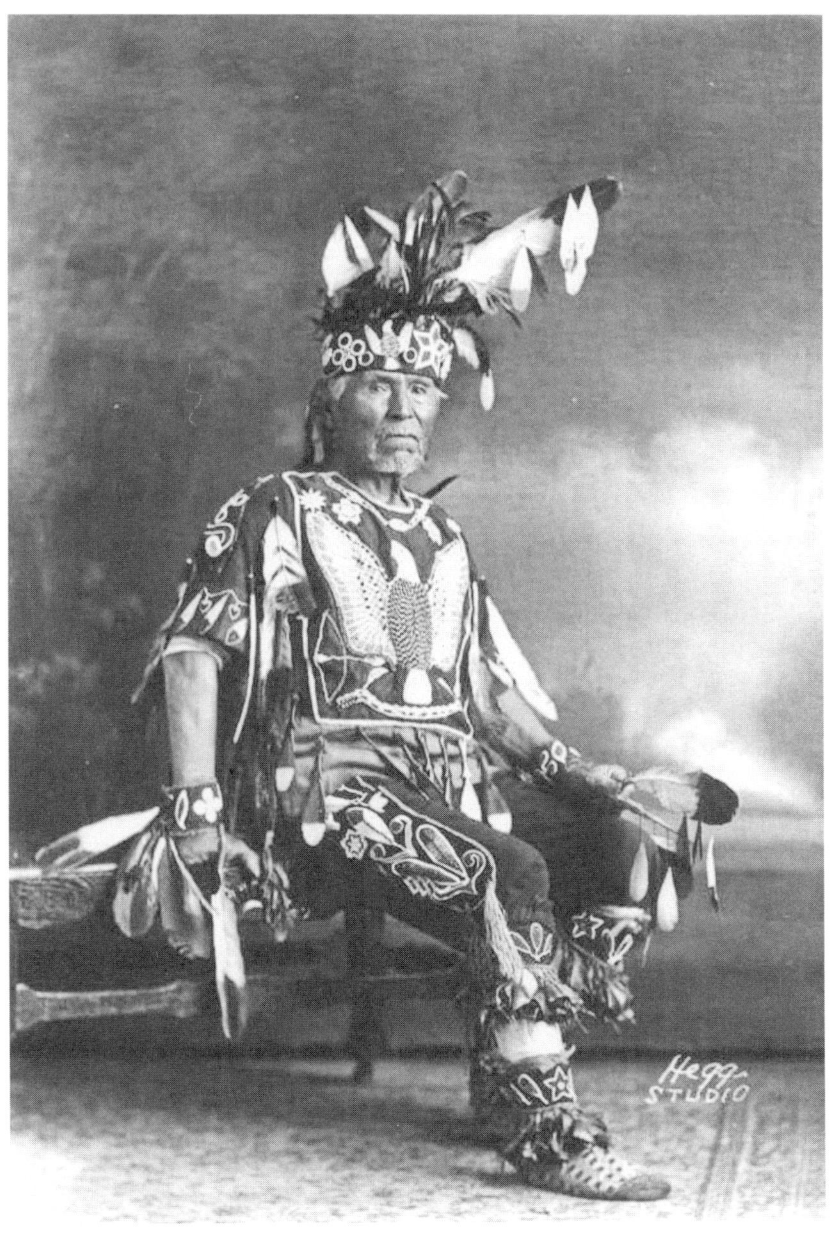

13. Haeteluk Frank Hillaire (ca. 1846–1937), portrait ca. 1920. Courtesy of the Pauline Hillaire Archives.

broken feather of the chief. The broken feather of the chief means that a chief has died, but the other feathers remain solid; those feathers represent the chiefs who are still alive. And so he's telling the world that he has one, two, three living chiefs and two or maybe three who have died.

His costume is his message to the world: "This is who I am. I need not say a single word; you just have to read my regalia," just like the totem pole. See the deer hooves at the bottom and the paddles in the middle? They are the music to his dance; they're like the drum to his dance, even the swishing of feathers as he turns. The swishing can be heard when they dance. The headgear is made out of cedar and velvet. We got velvet because we refused the rum. In trading, we refused the rum for so long that the president said, "Well, give them something else." And they gave us the velvet for the shirts, and they gave us cotton for our wing dresses, and they gave us silk for bandanas and belts. And that's how we got velvet on that shirt. That's a family crest; it's the house of Haeteluk. It identifies the house. They don't say "clan," they don't say "tribe," they don't say, "I come from Bellingham." They say, "I come from the house of Haeteluk."

My mother has a different format of feathers; you can see the chiefs that are alive, and the ones that have died, by the drooping of the feathers. She has buckskin on. Many people have said, "I want that picture, I'll draw her for you." And I have never let it go so that they could draw it; I'm afraid I might never get it back. She didn't braid her hair; she twisted it: just takes four pieces and twists each one, and ties it with her own hair. So there are different hairdos for those old folks.

Hers is the "Star Song." She did the "Star Song" for President Roosevelt. She was a beautiful lady, and when she went to school, she was punished for speaking her Lummi language. She told us they put her in a cave on the beach that had bars and a closed door. There was no place for her to sit, no place for her to lie down. The tide came in, about to her waist, she said, about to her waist. It was dark, and she couldn't tell what the things were, creeping along her toes. And that was what she got for talking her language. It was removed from us, in trying to make us become white, but we can't become white, can we? I can't right now, and she was born in 1894, and I was born in 1929, according to Lummi census. But that's

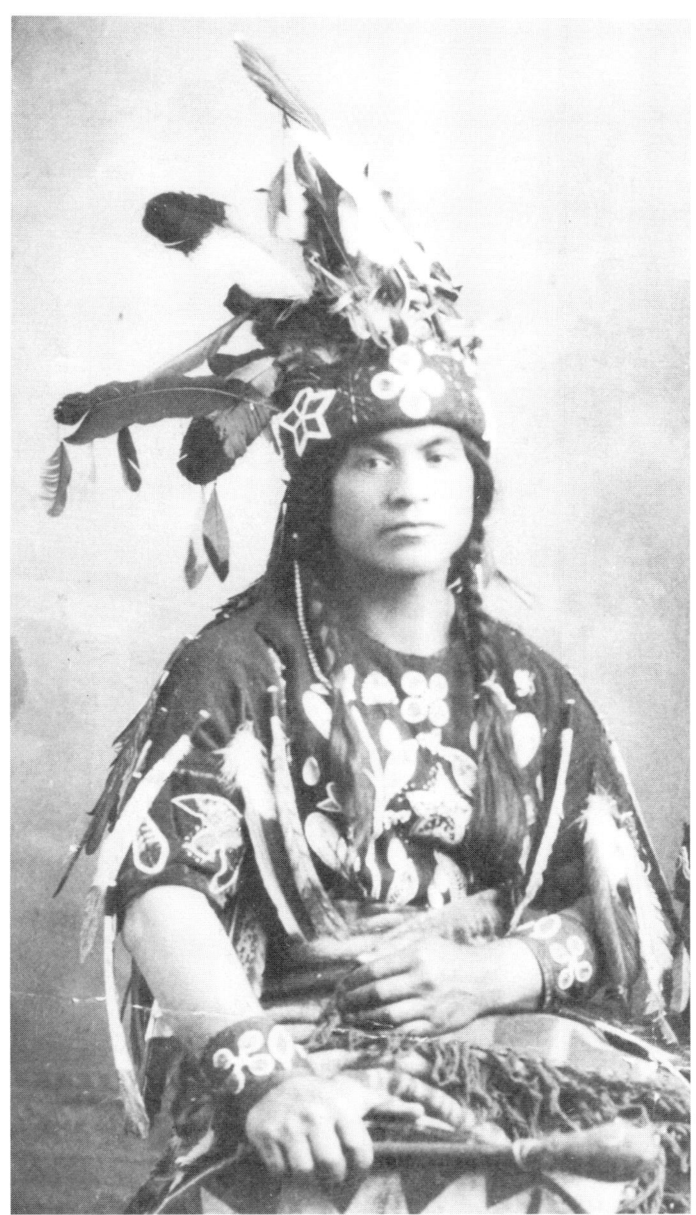

14. Joseph Hillaire (1894–1967), portrait ca. 1919. Reprinted with permission from the Center for Pacific Northwest Studies, Western Washington University, Bellingham WA 98225-9123. Howard E. Buswell photograph 178.

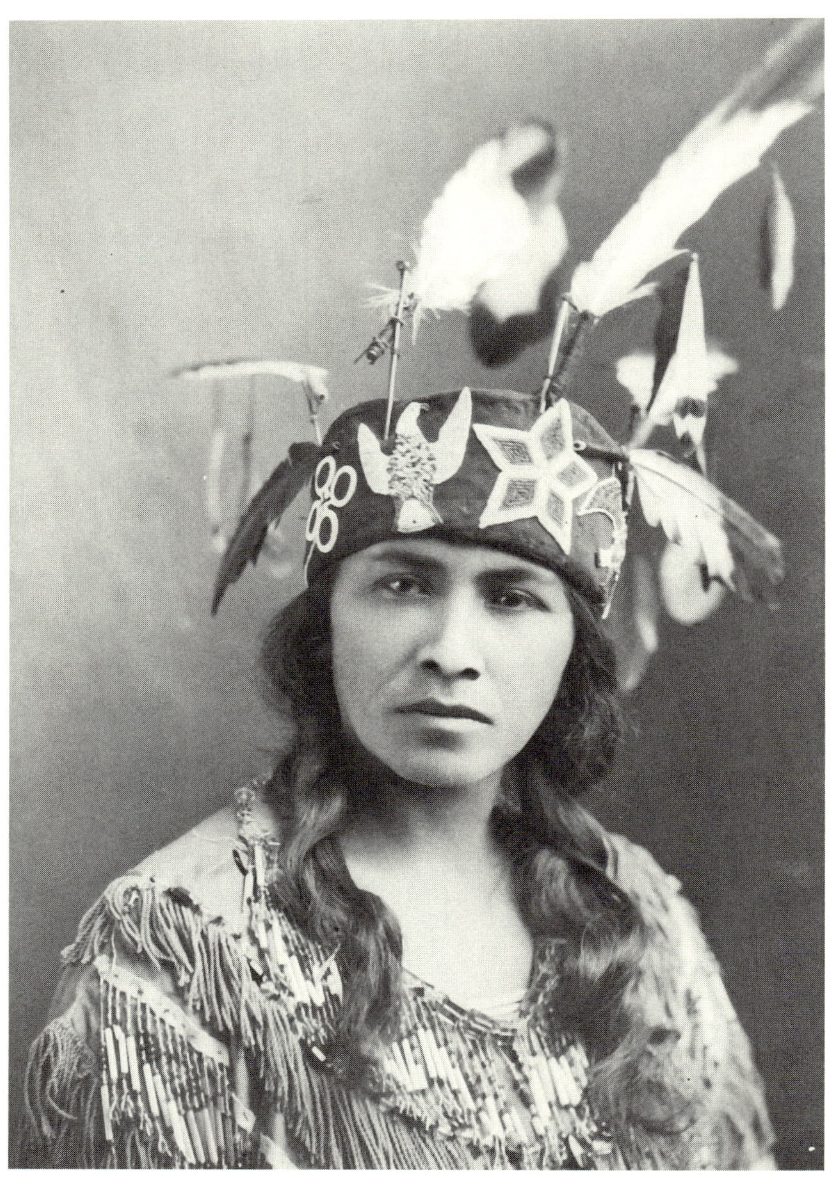

15. Edna Price Hillaire Scott (1884–1958), portrait ca. 1919. Courtesy of the Pauline Hillaire Archives.

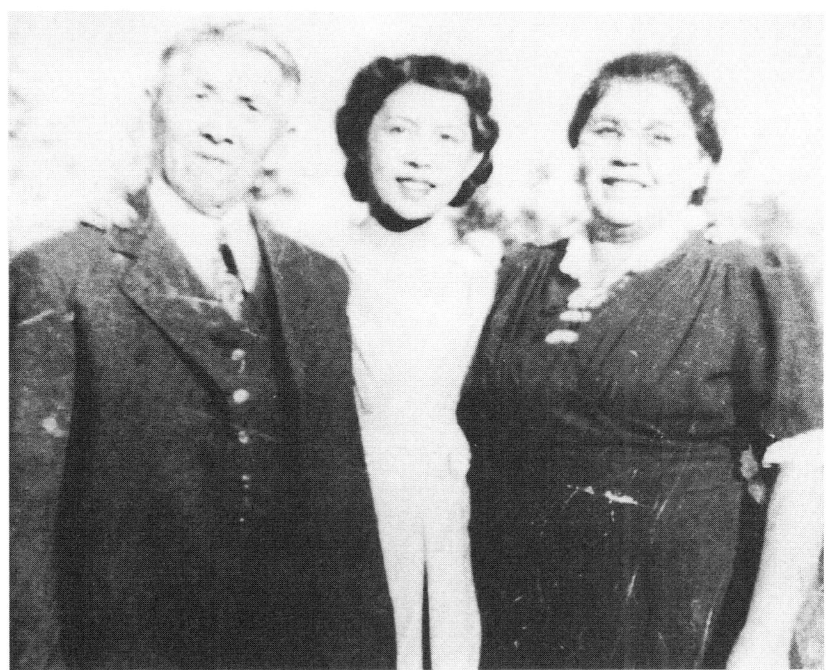

16. Charles and Louise Anderson and daughter taqʷšəblu Vi Anderson Hilbert (Upper Skagit, 1918–2008), ca. 1940. "My parents, Charley and Louise Anderson, told stories and historical information to each other all the time just to remind and refresh themselves. They also sang our ancestral songs to remember them, often when we were driving or alone in the mountains. . . . My father was laconic, soft-spoken, and detailed. My mother was dramatic, making much of the personalities and situations." (Vi Hilbert, *Haboo: Native American Stories from Puget Sound* [Seattle: University of Washington Press, 1985], xii). Courtesy of the family of Vi Hilbert.

what they did to her; they made her stop using the Lummi language, and she would even whisper at home. "Go get me some of this," and she'd just whisper it in Indian: "Go get me some of that *xexmein* (q'əx̣mín). Go get me some of that birch bark." So we'd just go out and gather it for her.

Mom and Dad were very happy together traveling around the country where my father was invited to teach and preach. Mother helped him with Bible reading. They were a very good team. People from every reservation knew my parents. There was a couple by the names of Charlie and

Louise Anderson, parents of Vi Hilbert, who were close relatives. The Andersons housed my mom and dad when they were close to their area, but that was before I was born. These four people got along perfectly in all they ever did.

My mother and father had thirteen children. They had very good farmland, deeded to my father by his father. They handled the newness of farming like old pros. We had wheat, strawberries, a greenery garden, gooseberries, crab apple trees, and a very nice root house built into the natural hillside of the property within yards of the house. My father built and completed this around 1930. It was a two-story home. He didn't go to carpentry school, but he was able to build our home. The staircase had one turn in it, and it turned out perfectly for a carpenter who never went to school; he was a natural-born carpenter.

My father was, by the time we were all born and growing like weeds, deeply involved in the Lummi Tribe's politics. He traveled near and far for tribal council (government) business: back and forth to Olympia, then back and forth to Washington DC. Then he met a woman by the name of Lena Capoeman. He and Mom divorced. As it ended up, they both remarried, my father to Lena Capoeman and my mother to a man from Swinomish named Bill Scott. Mom and Dad went through an Indian divorce and a white divorce. The Indian divorce required four well-known witnesses who knew them both really well. They had a spokesperson. Dad had to leave everything to Mom. That included the children and all the land (the land needed to be transferred in court). My dad was left with nothing but the clothes on his back. They experienced this when I was about seven years old. It broke my heart. I fell asleep in school (second grade) and stayed asleep for about two weeks. My mother had to retrieve my father and bring him home. As soon as he sat on my bed I woke up and gave him a big hug. He had such a strong and sturdy back, I hung my arms around his neck, and then I was okay. He saved my life. He didn't stay; he just made sure I understood, because when he left again, I was okay.

The white marriage and divorce and their Indian marriage and divorce were required by the tribe and by the state. They had to do twice as much as other couples getting married and divorced. White courts did not recognize the Indian culture, so the double ceremonies were done to accommodate both societies. Pictures taken of them are beautiful, showing not only their good-looking qualities but the seriousness of their eyes. What a treat to see those pictures. Joe Hillaire carried on his work with Lena Capoeman. He carved and built homes and churches. He talked extensively to the various tribes, preached at various tribal gatherings, and made a name for himself on the Quinault Reservation. Bill Scott helped my mother raise us, and we are ever grateful to our stepfather. He was a very humble man. He became a policeman with the Swinomish Tribe after he quit drinking. He attended church with us and enjoyed the family time. He and my mother were very hardworking people.

As I learned how to log and cut wood, I enjoyed the smell of the wood. Whenever they would brag about my work, it would make me work harder. We each had our own jobs that we did every day. My brother Ruben drove the horses for each task. My brother Bert handled the axe when he returned home from World War II. My job was using the blue-steel crosscut saw for cutting the logs. Bert measured the logs. Mary Ellen helped us load the trucks or pile the cut wood into ricks and cords, which would later be sold.

Joe continued to gain recognition by carving about twelve major totem poles as well as canoes and other artifacts in Suquamish, where he lived from his forties for the rest of his life. He visited us between those times. When he carved the *Bellingham Centennial* pole, he moved to Lummi and stayed in Marietta with his sister Amelia. She was the care provider for my father's mother. Grandma Agnes lived to be over one hundred years of age (we are uncertain of her exact age).

Please understand that Joe Hillaire had multiple talents such as carving, organizing, singing, and oratory and as a significant Indian cultural master and historian and in doing political work for tribes that needed his help. With his organizing ability, he began to revive the Lummi Stommish Water Festival and Chief Seattle Days in Suquamish, and he taught the Boy Scouts Order of the Arrow in Seattle when he could not get Indian men to join him in keeping the Indian songs and dances alive. Some of the songs were kept alive thanks to the Boy Scouts. A few of those Boy Scouts visit me from time to time. I've heard them singing the songs, and they do very well.

At Lummi, my father helped Earl Thomas Sr. develop into the Lummi Stommish master of ceremonies for the canoe races, the Indian games, and other activities. Mr. Thomas acknowledged my father's teachings in public; this made me so proud. Joe Hillaire was a good teacher. He was very proud of his accomplishments in participating with the dignitaries who constructed the Bellingham Vocational and Technical School: proud because it brought home a similar curriculum from Chemawa Indian School in Oregon but without the dormitories. In later years, my daughter attended school there for cosmetology and haircutting. This had special meaning to me and other Lummi who had attended school there. There was a school and a small park named after Joe Hillaire in Seattle. While he was working for Bill Hewitt, he was asked by a garden company to name a new dahlia. He suggested both Chief Kitsap Dahlia and Setting Sun Dahlia.

Looking back in time, I remember when he went to the Grand Coulee Dam and helped in the dedication ceremonies alongside of President Franklin D. Roosevelt. The lake was named after the president: Lake Roosevelt. The president took the opportunity to talk to my father for two and a half hours, so it is said. He explained to the Colville Tribe dignitaries that he thought Joe Hillaire was a very scholarly gentleman. He was self-taught after leaving the Indian School in Tulalip, Washington, as a young boy.

After my father's death, someone broke into his carving shed in Suquamish, Washington, and stole his remaining carvings. I would recognize the carvings if I ever saw them again. This, after all the years of work and dedication it took to do all that carving, plus a lot more that is not mentioned here.

Once he was talking about art in a church sermon that I attended as a young person, and I saw him cut an apple in half and show the audience the artful perfection of God's work. There was a perfect star design in the middle of the apple. He went on and on about the beauty of God's

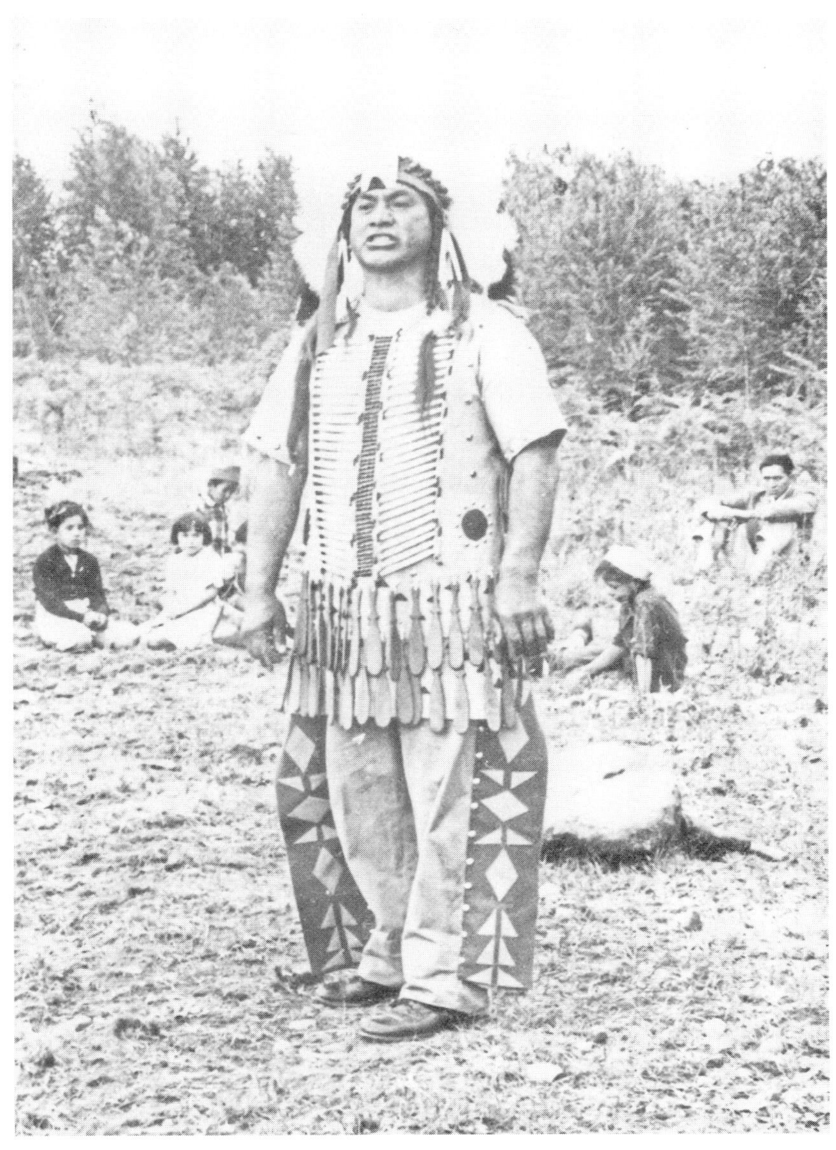

17. An oration delivered by Joseph Hillaire at the Muckleshoot field dedication. Photo by David W. Hopkins. Reprinted with permission from the Center for Pacific Northwest Studies, Western Washington University, Bellingham WA 98225-9123. Howard E. Buswell photograph 75.

creations. My mother exclaimed, "How can you get bored when Mother Nature is doing her best to entertain you with the artful creation of Our Father in Heaven?"

Bill Hewitt hired my father to help design and build the Tillicum Village Resort and Restaurant on Blake Island near Seattle. My father participated in full regalia onstage there, demonstrating how the dances are done locally. It was at Tillicum Village, in conversation with my father, that I told him his words would be poetry someday. He told me that my poetry would set the world in harmony with the Creator one day. This made me feel great.

When my dad began carving the *Land in the Sky* totem pole in Seattle's Pioneer Square, a well-dressed man from King's Garden walked up to him and had the following conversation with him. "Didn't they use stone tools a long time ago? I see you're using a metal axe." My father paused and then answered, "Oh, yes, but they also used common sense a long time ago." The well-dressed man slowly walked away. The people with him asked my father to sign chips for them. Whenever he carved he left behind big, slightly curved chips. He signed the chips for the people and thought it was a great idea.

One time, my mate and I had bought a trailer near Neah Bay, Washington. On the way home, the hook-up broke, leaving us stranded not too far from my dad's home. Instead of asking Dad to fix it, we asked nearby friends. No one could fix it, so finally we told Dad. He accompanied us to the broken-down trailer alongside of the road. Lying on his back beneath the broken hook-up, he asked my mate to hand him the tools that would be needed. Not long after that it was fixed, and we drove the rest of the way home. We were able to live in the trailer while visiting my father's second family. Their home was very crowded, but everyone was happy and content. At the evening meal, my father told my mate, "Necessity is the mother of invention," and that ended our plight. Soon after that, Dad asked my mate to go hunting with him (elk were then plentiful in the Quinault Peninsula mountains). My mate said that my father walked fast and had turned and told him, "Take long steps; you'll save shoe leather." My dad was very near out-walking my mate; we chuckled about that when they got home from their elk hunt. This proved my dad was in great physical shape in his early seventies. Dad had many profound one-liners that he used in his teachings. He would say, "You're born learning, you learn to eat, to talk, to walk, to carry on conversations short or long. You learn all your life, back and forth, and then you learn to die, or you die learning." Back and forth: learn to die or die learning. And so it becomes the endless circle of life.

This bear totem pole represents or identifies a person's power, and the bear is Joe Hillaire's. Joe was deeply involved with the Lummi Indian Business Council. He also held fast to the importance of teaching Indians how to read. He did this on his own and wherever they lived, using the Bible as a teaching tool. He knew so much about the Bible and Christian songs. He had the voice for it, too, as his voice was deep and clear, loud and easy to understand. Starting in the 1940s, he helped the Lummi veterans and Lummi tribal government to carry on the annual Stommish Water Festival. Native cultural activities had been banned for years by the U.S. government. He did the same for the Chief Seattle Days in Suquamish, Washington. Many people got involved as a result.

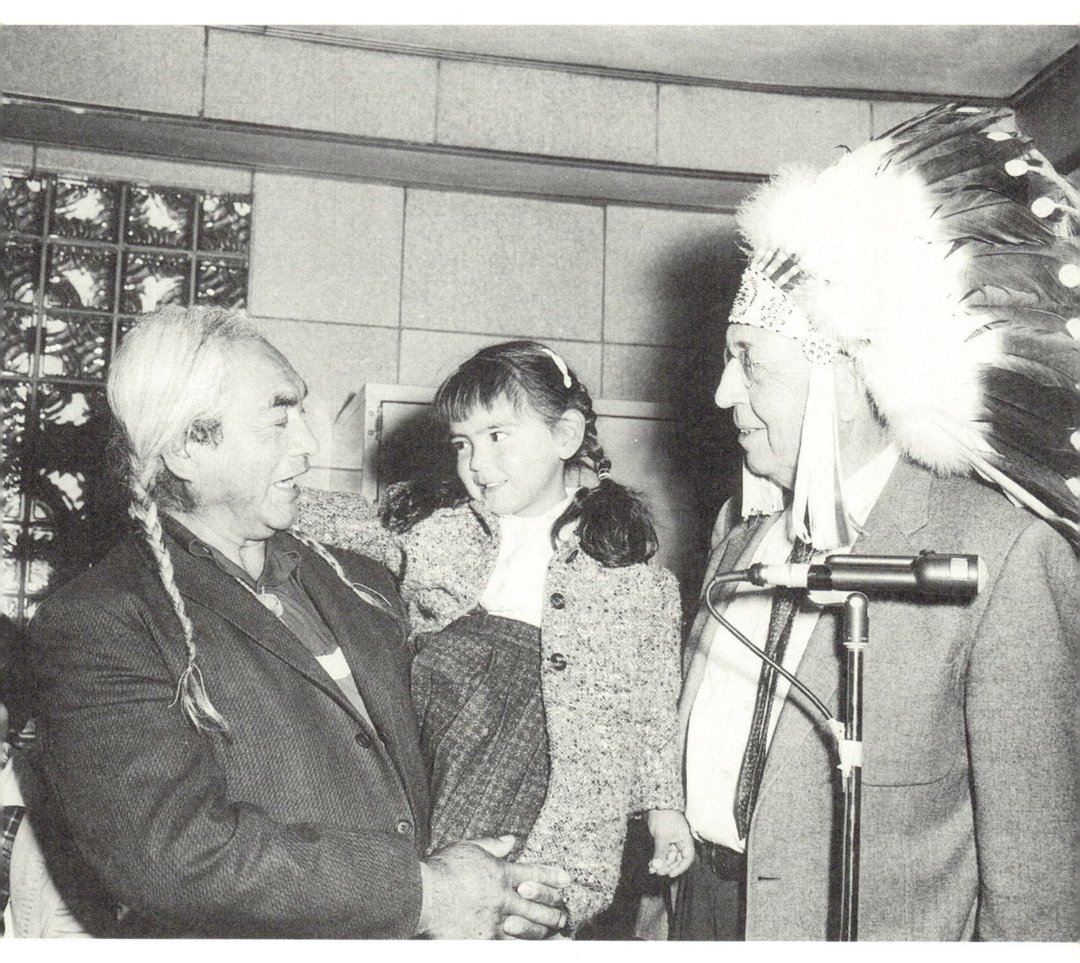

18. Joe Hillaire, granddaughters Debra and Audrey, and Martin Sampson (Skagit/Swinomish). Courtesy of Washington State Historical Society and the Pauline Hillaire Archives.

3 Kwul-kwul't^w, Spirit of the War Club

Religious Man, Renaissance Man

GREGORY P. FIELDS

SUQUAMISH TRIBAL MEMBER PEG KWI-ALQ DEAM remembers being away from home at a government boarding school, the Institute of American Indian Arts in Santa Fe, New Mexico, in the 1960s. Sometimes, when she was homesick, she would go to the school library and listen to the Library of Congress recording of Joe Hillaire's story and song, "Grandmother Rock and the Little Crabs." She loved to hear Joe's voice, and it helped her through her time away from home. An elementary school in Bellevue (across Lake Washington, a few minutes from Seattle) was named Hillaire Elementary School in 1962 in honor of Joe Hillaire. It was open from 1962 to 1979, and Hillaire Park is still operated by the city of Bellevue. Joe Hillaire's fame as a carver was at a high point in the early 1960s when he carved the totem poles that received national and international exposure. But seeds of his contributions took root and continue to manifest themselves in forms such as the resurgence of Coast Salish carving and his work for cultural preservation, Indian rights, and intercultural cooperation.

Kwul-kwul't^w, Spirit of the War Club, was born on December 25, 1894, only thirty-nine years after his tribe, the Lummi, along with more than twenty other western Washington tribes and bands, entered into the Treaty of Point Elliott with the United States in 1855. He was born into an Indian community radically changed by the arrival of the Anglo-Europeans and the resulting decimation of peoples, loss of lands and waters, loss of livelihoods, and a host of difficulties related to U.S. Indian policy. Yet this early postcontact time of Joe's birth was a time when a large share of ancestral knowledge and practices were still strongly in place. By the end of his life in 1967, Joe, and all Americans, had seen tremendous changes in culture and technology. The U.S. moon landing in 1969 was emblematic of the amazing developments of the twentieth century. Joe's *Land in the Sky* totem pole, carved for Century 21, the 1962 Seattle World's Fair, was itself emblematic of the imminent U.S. moon landing but also of humankind's archetypal yearning to travel to — or be connected with — the sky world. In particular, the pole was emblematic of an ancient Lummi myth of such a journey.

When we refer to someone as a renaissance man or woman, we are acknowledging that individual as a master of several diverse areas of knowledge and practice. Joe Hillaire was a renaissance man because of his expertise as an artist-carver, a carpenter and technician, an oral historian and culture bearer in possession of ancestral songs and dances, an orator, a civic leader and diplomat, a poet and playwright, a teacher, and a lay minister. His abilities in diplomacy and public speaking allowed him to work for Indian rights and — at the same time — to work for Indian participation in American civic life and for greater cultural cooperation between Indian and Anglo-European Americans. He was a Renaissance man in a second sense as well: seeds sown in his work — both artistic and political — continued to grow after his lifetime in support of the rebirth and continuation of Lummi and indigenous cultural art, identity, and vitality.

Joe ministered independently as a Christian evangelist, and in his earlier years, he preached and established congregations for Indian people. His daughter Pauline Hillaire (Scälla, Of the Killer Whale) tells of Joe's combining his commitment to Indian literacy with his teaching about the Bible, which served as a text when he taught other Indian people to read.

His gift as an orator, cultivated as an important part of the Longhouse way of life, the spiritual tradition of his forefathers, remained central in his spiritual work in his Native communities; it was also significant in his preaching the gospel. Joe was a member of the Church of Jesus Christ of Latter-day Saints (Mormon Church) in Poulsbo, Washington, in the Suquamish area.[1] He also embraced the Bahá'í faith, a religious tradition that holds that the various prophets of the world's different religions and eras of history were legitimate prophets who brought needed teachings from God.[2] The moral teachings of Joe's ancestral Longhouse spiritual tradition, his Christianity, and the Bahá'í perspective of respect for the world's many faiths all informed Joe's way of being. Pauline speaks of her father as a powerful man, as a father who led by example and "who used only loving words." He encouraged us, she said, "to go to church instead of to drink." In recordings that Pauline made in June 2008, she spoke more than once about the qualities that a leader must have. She was speaking at those points not of her father but rather of tribal chiefs, chairs, and U.S. presidents. A leader, she said, must have honor, integrity, courage, and generosity. Joe's Longhouse training, grounded in these values, guided his conduct and the respect he extended to others, Indian and non-Indian.

For the first half of his life, Joseph R. Hillaire (1894–1967) lived on the Lummi Reservation near Bellingham, ninety miles north of Seattle, where he began his family with Edith Price, who passed away, leaving him with three children. Following custom, he married her sister, Edna Price. After Joe's remarriage to Suquamish tribal member Lena Capoeman, he lived at the Port Madison/Suquamish Reservation on Bainbridge Island, just west of Seattle. Edna Price Hillaire also remarried, to Bill Scott of Swinomish. Although Joe was and is well known as a carver, he was involved in efforts to seek justice from the U.S. government concerning Indian rights and ancestral lands. He was a consultant to major scholars who conducted research on Lummi history, language, and culture, and he generously educated non-Indian people about elements of Coast Salish culture that can be shared outside the culture. Joe was featured in approximately thirty articles and announcements in the *Seattle Times* newspaper in the three decades between 1938 and his death in 1967 at age seventy-three. Many of the articles concern his work as a carver, notably, activities related to the Seattle World's Fair totem pole and its national tour and the Kobe-Seattle Sister Cities friendship pole. The histories of several of his totem poles show that he envisioned and labored for the hope of intercultural fellowship. His diplomatic activities, many with totem pole artwork as the medium, extended to regional, national, and international domains. Joe's friend and colleague Don McQuade (Anishinaabe) wrote press releases for the U.S. tour of 8,470 miles on which he accompanied Joe while Joe carved the *Land in the Ṡky* totem pole for the 1962 World's Fair. McQuade wrote: "Joe lived on the reservation as a logger and commercial fisherman until World War II, when he worked in the U.S. Naval shipyard at Bremerton, Washington. Since then he has returned to Indian lands to function as a liaison between his people and the industrialized society that has grown up around them."[3]

Joe's dedication and skill as a communicator took him to various Indian communities of the Northwest, to the nation's capital, and to Kobe, Japan, on a mission of international goodwill, where he presented the Kobe-Seattle Sister Cities pole after World War II. Joe's Setting Sun Dance Group — started by his father, Frank Hillaire, in the nineteenth century and continued by his daughter Pauline Hillaire until the twenty-first — danced at Native as well as public venues in western Washington and as far away as Washington DC, for audiences including President Franklin D. Roosevelt, who conversed with Joe at some length when Joe participated in the dedication of the Grand Coulee Dam.

As a carver of approximately twelve major totem poles and other works, Hillaire was both a traditionalist and an innovator. His work was influenced by his father, Haeteluk Frank Hillaire (b. approx. 1946) and Frank's father, Salaphalano the Priest (i.e., a priest of the Longhouse tradition), both of whom were carvers and mask makers. Joe also credited as his teachers of carving Arthur Howeattle (Quileute), "Young Doctor" (Makah), and Chief William Shelton (Snohomish/Tulalip).[4] The earliest of the *Seattle Times* articles, in 1938, lists Joe Hillaire among those who submitted a bid to restore the totem pole in Seattle's Pioneer Place, which had been damaged by fire.[5]

As an innovator, Joe developed his own carving style, which maintains design features and symbolism of historical Lummi carving and also shows his unique aesthetic style, expressing insight into psychology and events of historical significance. McQuade gave these details in press releases about the Century 21 totem pole's national tour:

> Hillaire's masterpiece, carried in a special van, will be on public display in major cities that include New York, Washington DC, Cincinnati, Chicago, St. Louis, Kansas City, Las Vegas, Los Angeles, San Francisco and Portland, Oregon. The idea is to acquaint people across the nation with the World's Fair and the Pacific Northwest's unique heritage in tribal art and lore. The pole will be returned to Seattle in time for the opening of the Century 21 Exposition on April 21.
>
> He is being accompanied on the trip by Don McQuade, an Ojibwe and specialist in Indian customs. McQuade serves as narrator and tour manager. The totem log, three and a half feet in diameter, is cradled in one of the world's largest trailers, provided for the occasion by Dean Van Lines. Sides of the van open fully, so that onlookers may easily view Hillaire as he works. The floodlighted interior is outfitted with a picturesque profusion of North Coast Indian drawings and artifacts. McQuade and Hillaire will explain the totem legends and traditions as the carving progresses. They will also pass out photographs and literature and gifts for children. No beads, however. "Joe is a great storyteller and loves to visit with people," McQuade says, "but I have to keep him working so he will get the pole finished before the fair ends in October." Joe Hillaire has this to say about it: "The legend goes back to prehistoric times, but it remains appropriate to this day as an Indian way of expressing the man-in-space theme of the World's Fair. Men have always wanted to conquer the moon."[6]

Joe Hillaire's totem poles provide a literally monumental record of his life's work as a carver, but his work has had lasting influence in thought and policy as well. Joe served as chair of the Lummi Indian Business Council (tribal council), and he worked in many capacities for the rights and well-being of his tribe and other Native people of the Puget Sound region. Joe's activism for Indian rights took place in a period when U.S. Indian policy underwent two major shifts of direction.

> Between 1930 and 1960 national and economic and political trends reversed course twice. Each time they did, policies toward Indians changed as well. First, the Great Depression and Indians' especial poverty motivated lawmakers to listen to critics of the fifty-year-old assimilation policy, and Congress acquiesced in a new program aimed at protecting rather than eliminating Indian enclaves. Little more than a decade later, World War II and postwar prosperity provided a rationale for recanting the Depression-era deviation. By the 1950s the government once again planned to abolish the institutions and laws that set Indians apart.[7]

The Indian Reorganization Act (IRA), a reform initiative led by U.S. Commissioner of Indian Affairs John Collier, was signed into law by President Roosevelt in 1934. It reversed the policies of the General Allotment Act (Dawes Act, 1887), which had divided tribal lands into individual allotments, eroding tribal unity and leading to further loss of Native lands through sale of land to non-Natives and the government's taking over "unused" lands. Although the IRA supported greater independence of tribal governments, it was a controversial matter among tribes nationally and in Washington State. Joe Hillaire supported the Indian Reorganization Act, and he wrote a letter directly to Commissioner Collier with ideas for rewording sections of the bill.[8]

Joe Hillaire testified for Indian Claims Commission case *Lummi Tribe of Indians v. U.S.* (docket 110, 1951), in which the tribe submitted a claim of $30 million (plus interest) for 249,800 acres ceded in the Point Elliott Treaty, for which the tribe had received an estimated value of $13,636. The claim was denied by the commission. In his younger years, Joe also testified at the 1927 hearing of *Duwamish et al. Tribes of Indians v. the United States*, concerning land loss and treaty rights of the Point Elliott Treaty tribes. He and Norbert James, who also testified, were the only Lummi in their thirties to testify at the 1927 hearing; August Martin was fifty-four and Jack Pierre sixty-eight years old at the time. The five other Lummi tribal members who testified were all gentlemen over eighty years of age: John Andrew Wilson, Louis Mike, Frank Hillaire, Albert Descanum, and Patrick George. Joe Hillaire testified that it was he who drew the map of historical Lummi lands and village locations as identified by the elder men who also testified.[9]

U.S. Indian policy threatened the termination of the federal tribal status of the Puget Sound tribes. Joe Hillaire brought to the attention of Congress that the Bureau of Indian Affairs (BIA) land services were in "a most deplorable state of entanglements" and that it would take a long time to straighten out land titles before termination could even be considered. As Alexandra Harmon observes, it is not clear whether Indian leaders such as Hillaire intended to employ such remarks as a stalling tactic, but "they indicated why the BIA could not hurry away from Puget Sound."[10]

A number of articles in the *Seattle Times* concern Joe's political and civic leadership. A front-page article in 1944 tells of Joe's successful effort to form an organization called the Bow and Arrow Victory Club for American Indians in the war industry at the Puget Sound Naval Yard, where he began work as a rigger in 1942. Joe explained that he had three sons and a son-in-law serving in various branches of the armed services overseas and stateside and a daughter working with him at the navy yard: "I was proud [of them] and anxious to help." The preamble to the constitution of the organization states in part that the goal of the club was "to uphold the honor of the American Indian by being patient, reliable, industrious, courageous and efficient and to impress upon our members the intent of the Four Freedoms and to remember the brave men living and dead after this war, who shall have consecrated these freedoms far beyond our poor powers to add or detract."[11]

In 1953 a short article in the *Seattle Times* identified Joe Hillaire as spokesman for an initiative under consideration by the Lummi Tribe and the Indians of the San Juan Islands (a neighboring tribe that was not federally recognized) to form an alliance. The aim was to strengthen the resources and position of each tribe in suits against the United States concerning treaty rights.[12] A 1963 article in the *Bainbridge (WA) Review* reports on Joe's efforts to establish a National American Indian Day.

> A National American Indian Day "to pay tribute to an important part of our national heritage" is a major goal of planners of Chief Seattle Days, says Joe Hillaire of Suquamish. Hillaire, an Indian of Lummi descent, has long urged all Indians to assume an active position in civic affairs. He advocates an Indian day "to recognize the many contributions that have been made by the American Indian to this country." Indian Franchise day, June 2, is the day that Hillaire would like to set aside for the nationwide observance of American Indian day. It was on this date in 1924 that Congress granted citizenship and the right to vote to the American Indian.[13]

Joe Hillaire served as an historical and cultural consultant for the University of Washington and for several leading scholars. Wayne Suttles does not list Joe Hillaire among his main consultants for his 1974 work *Coast Salish and Western Washington Indians*.[14] However, in his article "The Plateau Prophet Dance among the Coast Salish," he speaks of consulting with Hillaire, whom he refers to as "a well-educated man in middle age."[15] A short film narrated by Joe and produced in 1965 by University of Washington professor and Burke Museum curator Erna Gunther appears in the media companion available with this book. Bernard Stern acknowledges Joseph Hillaire in his 1934 book, *The Lummi Indians of Northwest Washington*: "The author is especially indebted to Joseph Hillaire, a Lummi Indian whose sincere interest in preserving the tradition of his people made him an eager and intelligent informant."[16]

Joe's generation was the last generation of Lummi people to include speakers of their Native language, xʷləmi'chosən (xʷləməčásən), a dialect of Straits Salish, and he served as a court interpreter in tribal affairs. Currently the University of Washington Language Learning Center offers online audio files of the Lummi dialect.[17] These recordings, from the Metcalf Collection (tape #36, recorded by Leon Metcalf in 1953), feature Lummi elder Julius Charles (b. ca. 1865) and Joe Hillaire speaking entirely in the Lummi language. About thirty minutes long, the recording concerns the story "How Deer Got His Stiff Legs." These audio files are among the few existing recordings of the Straits Salish Lummi dialect, spoken currently by just a handful of speakers. There is additional Lummi material in the Metcalf Collection: tape #11 contains songs by Lummi elder Agnes Cagey and a story and some lessons in Lummi vocabulary by Joe Hillaire.[18]

Several of Joe's children and grandchildren became carvers (see chapter 1). But other significant lines of his legacy were also carried forward by his daughters Mary Ellen Hillaire (1927–55) and Pauline Hillaire (b. 1929). Mary Ellen Hillaire was the first female faculty member to be hired by the Evergreen State College in Olympia, Washington. She founded the Native American studies program there in 1972, and her vision and leadership led to the establishment of the Longhouse at Evergreen, the first Native studies and indigenous cultural center of its kind on a U.S. campus.[19] Pauline Hillaire shares this personal history in the first chapter of her book *Rights Remembered: A Salish Grandmother Speaks on American Indian History and the Future*.

> My father, Joseph Hillaire, on his deathbed, shared extremely valuable information with me about the clash of our two cultures that went on during his youth; he was born in 1894. He asked me to find certain laws, certain letters, remembering one thing: Too many years have gone by and the government has forgotten what was ceded by what the U.S. Constitution calls the supreme law of the land: the Treaty. I gathered that information, but reading it caused me such depression, sadness, and disappointment in our government. . . . His interest remained focused upon Indian causes throughout his life. . . . My father had told me to look up the Treaty of 1855, the Omaha Treaty, the Wheeler-Howard Act (the Indian Reorganization Act), and letters between Washington Territorial Governor Isaac I. Stevens and President James Buchanan. And my father told me his version of the explorers crossing the Atlantic to North America. It was of great interest to me. I wanted to make this investigation a reality.[20]

Pauline began writing *Rights Remembered* in the late 1960s, around the time of her father's death, and completed it in 2011. Her book examines Indian history, policy, and life in the Puget Sound area from the time of the Point Elliott Treaty through the twentieth century along with her commentary about life for Indian people currently and in the future.

Toward the end of his life, Joe was working on the Chief Kitsap totem pole on Blake Island, but shortly after his death, the pole was stolen, along with several other carvings and works in progress. Pauline has maintained hope that at least some of these works will be recovered. One of the final articles to appear about Joe Hillaire was "Joe Hillaire Defies Paralysis to Carve."

> Recently a little Indian girl approached carver Joe Hillaire, an internationally famous totem pole carver, who is bedridden with a stroke in a small frame house here. Joe's left arm has been paralyzed nearly a year. All Suquamish knows it. But the girl took a message of hope. She had just had a dream, she said, in which Joe Hillaire carved again, using only his good right hand. Taking the dream as a sign, Joe got up from his bed, steadied himself with a crutch and made it to the kitchen table. He called for a small piece of cedar and a sharp carving knife. Holding the wood with the weight of his dangling left arm, Joe carved with the right hand. It was slow, tedious, frustrating work. The wood kept slipping. At times, tears came. But Joe did not quit until the wood had been challenged and at least partly conquered.

Joe tells of how his father, who lost three fingers in his middle years, one day decided to overcome his sorrow for the loss by lashing a knife to his thumb so that he could carve again. The article tells of Joe spending most of his time in a plain bed in a simple room; there is nothing to occupy him, so he meditates. Joe tells the reporter that he hopes to attend the upcoming Chief Seattle Days. He spoke "in the rolling, sonorous tones of a natural orator."

> Joe wants to deliver a speech too, his mind is bubbling with it; his mouth is filled with it. If his health permits, he will begin by reciting the Declaration of Independence and will call upon Indians to adopt it as their own. He will decry federal "mismanagement" of Indian affairs, implore Indian people to fight for ancient fishing rights, to

organize and get loans to repossess Indian lands that have fallen into non-Indian hands.

Joe will say that it is far past time for Indians to set higher education as a goal for all, "so we can run our own affairs." And we will argue that now, today, is the time for Indians to "wage their own all-out fight against job discrimination that is every bit as real as that practiced against the Negro. . . ."

Speaking powerfully of "the evolution of culture," of "man's concept of himself," of "the image builders," Joe is every inch the college graduate, though he had only a few years of formal schooling. As we talked, wind hummed through fir and madrona trees outside. Little waves lapped at Suquamish's barnacled beach. Joe turned his face to the plain board wall and began:

"When in the course of human events, it becomes necessary for one people to dissolve the political bonds which have connected them with another . . ." He said it all the way through, fading almost to a whisper as he recited: "We hold these truths to be self-evident, that all men are created equal."[21]

Joe died on Thursday, December 28, 1967, at age seventy-three in a Bainbridge Island nursing home. The funeral notice indicates that services for Joseph Hillaire, chief of the Lummi Indian Tribe and a totem pole carver, would be the following Monday at the Owyen Funeral Home, Bainbridge Island, with burial at the Chief Seattle Cemetery, Suquamish. Surviving him were his wife (Lena, great-granddaughter of Chief Kitsap), four daughters (Mrs. Pauline Covington, Seattle; Mrs. Walter Fowler, Spartanburg, North Carolina; Mrs. E. Dorothy Vercoe, Anchorage; and Mary E. Hillaire, Bellingham), four sons (Benjamin W. Hillaire, Ferndale; Bert V. Hillaire, Lummi Reservation; Ruben G. Hillaire, Bellingham; and Lewis G. Hillaire, Makah Reservation), a brother (Benjamin Hillaire, Ferndale), a sister (Mrs. Delphine Tom, Seattle), forty-four grandchildren, and thirteen great-grandchildren.[22]

Peg kwi-alq Deam remembers Joe Hillaire in his later years, after she returned home from Indian boarding school to her native Suquamish

Reservation, where Joe lived in his later years. She remembers how Joe would carve the top portion of a totem pole by leaning it up against his house so that the top of the pole came through a second-story window, and he could carve from indoors. A man of ingenuity, a powerful man well into his later years who was not fazed by the enormity of a cedar log as his medium of art, Joe Hillaire was likewise unfazed by the enormity of Native justice issues and intercultural relations, which he also engaged with confidence and grace.

NOTES

1. A representative of the Public Relations Office of the Church of Jesus Christ of Latter-day Saints (Mormon Church) at the church's headquarters in Salt Lake City, Utah, regretted that further information about Joe Hillaire's membership status in that church could not be provided, because the Mormon Church is not able to respond to inquiries from the public regarding membership information about individuals.

2. Joe's son Lewis, also a carver, was a member of the Bahá'í Faith. The 1968 membership roster lists Annie M. Hillaire and Lewis G. Hillaire living on the Makah Indian Reservation, Washington. Lewis's son, carver Gary Hillaire, was a Bahá'í who served at a high level in the faith: he was appointed to the National Teaching Committee in 1968 and 1969. As regards Joe Hillaire's membership status, the National Bahá'í Center has no record of his membership; however, no electronic records were kept before the 1950s, and paper records were not well organized at that time. Many persons professed belief in the faith without signing a declaration card. Pauline recalls that her father did sign a declaration card as a Bahá'í. Thanks to Dr. Alvin Deibert of the Edwardsville Illinois Bahá'í Fellowship, who obtained this information from the National Bahá'í Center.

3. Don McQuade, press release for Joe Hillaire's national tour with the *Land in the Sky* pole carved for the 1962 World's Fair. From the archives of Pauline Hillaire.

4. Don Duncan, "Joe Hillaire Defies Paralysis to Carve," *Seattle Times*, July 25, 1965.

5. "Two More Tribes Bid for Job of Fixing Totem," *Seattle Times*, November 25, 1965. The article incorrectly identified Joe Hillaire as a member of the Queets Tribe.

6. Don McQuade, "World's Fair Sending Indian Totem Carver on Nationwide Tour," press release, March 18, 1962.

7. Harmon, *Indians in the Making*, 190.

8. Harmon, *Indians in the Making*, 199; Hillaire to Collier, March 15, 1935, Reactions to the Indian Reorganization Act, box 5, Record Group 75, National Archives, cited in Harmon, *Indians in the Making*, 326nn22, 25.

9. *Duwamish et al. Tribes of Indians v. the United States*, Court of Claims of the United States, #F-275, at Olympia, Washington, 1927.

10. Harmon, *Indians in the Making*, 210–11; Wesley D'Ewart to House Committee on Interior and Insular Affairs, "Washington State Indian Problems," unpublished U.S. House of Representatives Committee Hearings, 83rd Cong., 1953, HI-ni-T-549, cited in Harmon, *Indians in the Making*, 332nn48, 59.

11. "Indians Working at Naval Yard Form Bow and Arrow Club," *Seattle Times*, February 20, 1944, front page.

12. "Two Northwest Tribes Consider Alliance," *Seattle Times*, December 16, 1953, 33.

13. Randy Hart, "Joe Hillaire Hopes Weekend Festivities Will Grow into American Indian Day," *Bainbridge (WA) Review*, August 1, 1963.

14. Suttles, *Coast Salish and Western Washington Indians*.

15. Suttles, "The Plateau Prophet Dance," 360.

16. Stern, *The Lummi Indians*, 9.

17. University of Washington, Language Learning Center (online), Lummi Straits Salish, Joe Hillaire: http://depts.washington.edu/llc/olr/lushootseed/LUS_007/index.php.

18. Metcalf Coast Salish Audio Collection, 1950–61, Burke Museum of History of Culture, University of Washington. Also held by the Archives of Ethnomusicology, Department of Music, University of Washington.

19. The Evergreen State College (Olympia WA), "Mary Ellen Hillaire," http://archives.evergreen.edu/1976/1976-12/hillaire_m/hillaire_m.htm; "History of the Longhouse," http://www.evergreen.edu/longhouse/history.htm.

20. Hillaire, *Rights Remembered*.

21. Duncan, "Joe Hillaire Defies Paralysis."

22. Obituary of Joe Hillaire, "Rites Tomorrow for Lummi Chief," *Seattle Times*, December 30, 1967.

PART TWO

Coast Salish Art and Carving

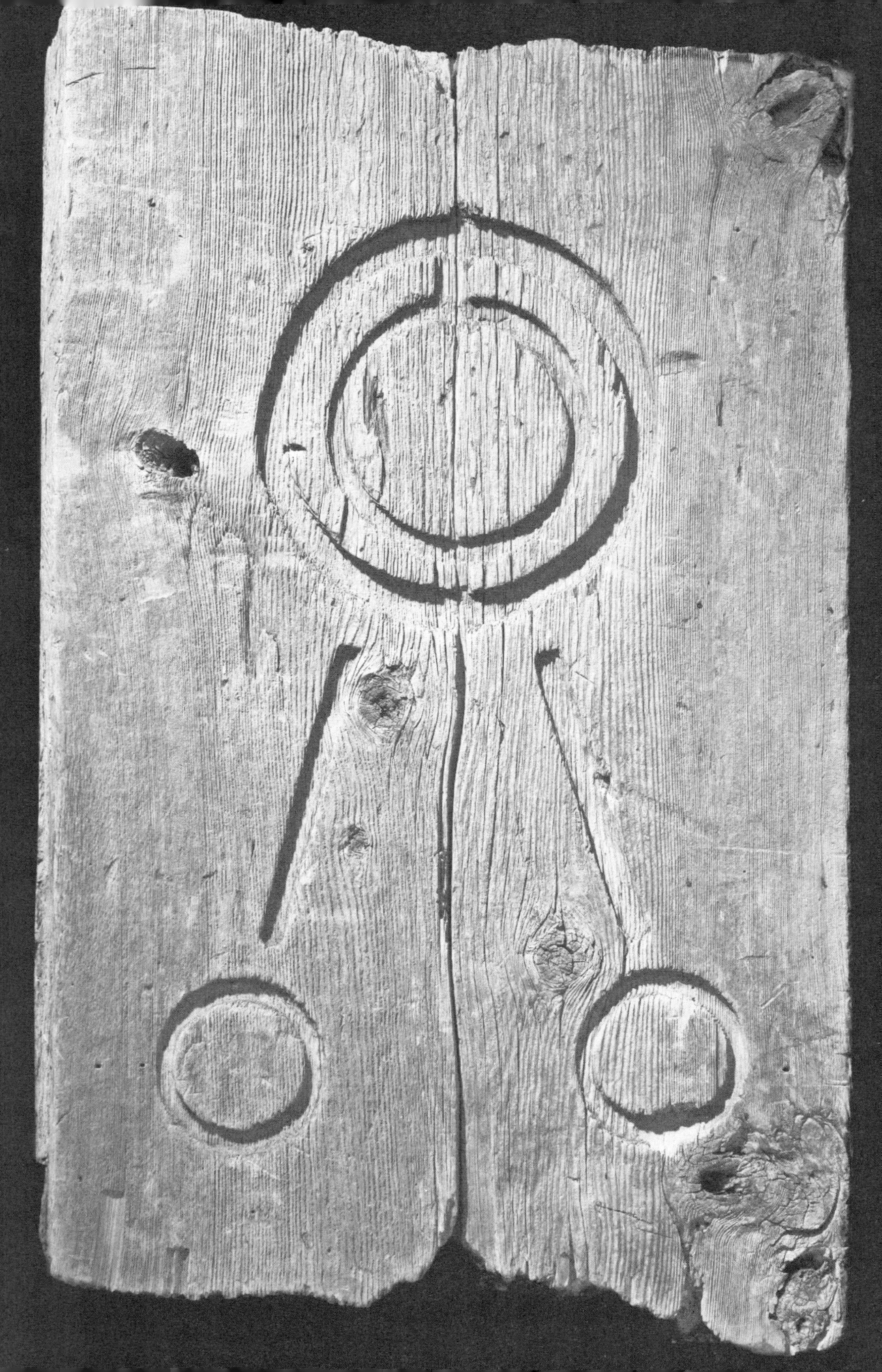

4 Straits Salish Sculpture

BILL HOLM

THE LUMMI PEOPLE ARE MEMBERS OF A GROUP OF tribes who spoke related languages called Coast Salish by linguists. These Coast Salish people live along the southern coast of British Columbia, including the south end of Vancouver Island, and the western part of Washington State on the shores of Juan de Fuca Strait and Puget Sound and stretching south as far as the Columbia River and the southwestern Washington Pacific Ocean coast. Within this broad Coast Salish region a number of distinct but related dialects were spoken. Lummi language belongs to one of these, called Straits Salish. The Lummi Reservation lies on a peninsula near the center of this area, at the juncture of Rosario Strait and the Strait of Georgia.

In common with other Indian groups all along the Northwest Coast, Lummi culture was heavily dependent on wood and its uses. The canoes that were arguably the central icon of Northwest Coast life were carved of western red cedar, as were the structural timbers of the frames and the split boards of the walls and roofs of Lummi houses. Among many

19. Chowitsut house post. Reprinted with permission from Whatcom Museum of History and Art, Bellingham, Washington, image number x.4242.1.

tribes the interior supporting posts were decorated with painted figures or sculpture. Although Lummi house posts very likely shared this custom, only a single example remains from an old traditional house. This one, now in the collection of the Whatcom Museum in Bellingham, has, incised in its flattened surface, an image representing the sun and two parhelia, or sun dogs, a celestial phenomenon caused by reflections of the sun's rays from ice crystals in the sky. This somewhat mysterious sight was viewed by many Indian groups with awe, and its representation on the Lummi house post was the prerogative of a mid-nineteenth-century Lummi chief named Chowitsut.[1] Although very few examples of Lummi sculpture from an early period remain in collections today, something of its character can be surmised from the work of neighboring Salish tribes surviving in museum collections or old photographs. A few small figures carved in bone and antler and stone figural bowls have been recovered from archaeological sites in Lummi territory, which offer information on precontact Lummi carving style.

Until the twentieth century, Coast Salish sculpture did not include any of the tall, carved columns we have come to call "totem poles." The making of those vertical monuments was confined to the northern tribes, particularly the Haida, whose villages sprouted literal forests of them in the mid-nineteenth century. Gradually, during the later years of the century, the custom spread southward, and by 1900, tall, free-standing poles had begun to appear in some Kwakwa̱ka̱'wakw villages around the north end of Vancouver Island. It may be that the custom would have continued its march southward into Coast Salish country had the forces of acculturation not built up so overwhelmingly in those years. Fully carved columns were being raised among the Northern Coast Salish tribes, but they were primarily structural house posts and shorter figural monuments and not the soaring poles seen to the north.

These Salish figures differed markedly in style from those on the northern poles, especially those from the Haida villages. The northern poles typically fitted the carved figures to the cylinder of the pole so that the heads of the men or other creatures represented were as wide as the shoulders, and legs, arms, or wings were compressed into the pole's cylinder. As the custom moved southward, the figures lengthened and spread outward to resemble the earlier, more naturalistically proportioned sculpture of the coast, including that of the Salish carvers. The proportions of figures on Salish carved house posts and grave monuments were not dictated by the shape of the log but were modeled in more or less naturalistic proportions. One variant of Northern Coast Salish sculpture was the positioning of the sculptured figures as high relief on a flattened surface of the log rather than carving the figure independent of the original cylindrical shape. None of these traditional Coast Salish sculptural figures was in the form of tall columns, or totem poles, as far as is known.

Coast Salish carving of story poles began in the early to mid-twentieth century. Probably the earliest and most prolific of the Salish pole carvers of that period was the Snohomish artist William Shelton (1869–1938). Shelton's poles usually followed the early Coast Salish sculptural style in carving the figures in high relief on the flattened surface of the log. Joe Hillaire's poles also resemble the earlier Salish style in positioning the represented figures singly, one above the other, in relief on the basic cylinder. Like Shelton, Joe Hillaire (1894–1967) considered his sculptured columns story poles rather than totem poles, emphasizing their function as illustrations of traditional narratives rather than crests or hereditary family prerogatives. The function of Joe Hillaire's story poles also differed, much as Shelton's did, from the early use of carved monuments in that they were usually commissioned by civic groups or organizations who wanted to express a relationship with Native culture or history of the area rather than family or individual traditions. But Hillaire usually included figures from Lummi myths, and even included, on his *Bellingham Centennial* history pole, a specific image from the lone existing Lummi house post, the Chowitsut sun dogs motif.

Joe Hillaire's legacy as a carver is being taken up by younger artists, some of whom are actively researching the traditions of Salish sculpture in museum collections and the photographic record.

NOTE

1. Suttles, "Productivity and Its Constraints," 79.

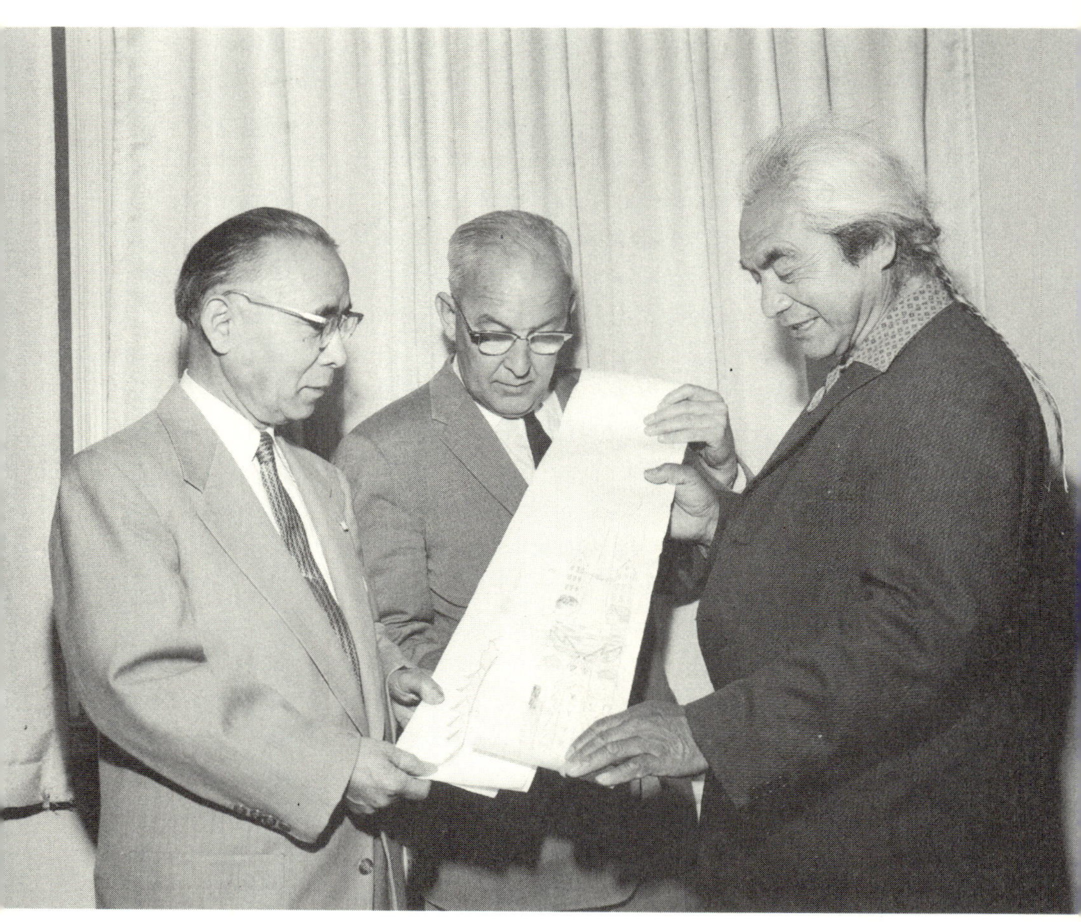

20. Kobe official Genji Mihara, Seattle's former mayor William Devlin, and Joe Hillaire look at drawings of the Kobe-Seattle Sister Cities friendship pole, ca. 1960. Reprinted by permission from Seattle Post-Intelligencer Collection, Museum of History and Industry, Seattle.

5 Joseph Raymond Hillaire

Lummi Artist-Diplomat

BARBARA BROTHERTON

JOSEPH HILLAIRE (1894–1967) WAS MANY THINGS: culture bearer, culture broker, artist, Native activist, and diplomat. He came of age in a tumultuous period, his generation having inherited the trauma of their parents' dehumanizing experiences in boarding schools and at the hands of missionaries and government agents. Theft of traditional lands meant an ever-shrinking resource base from which to carry on fishing, hunting, and gathering activities. Removed from lucrative properties and relegated to small plots of land, Lummi born in this generation had no choice but to gain a measure of success in the white world if they were to survive. Joe was fortunate to be under the tutelage of his grandfather and father, who maintained cultural practices, even bringing them into a public realm so as to project a positive image of Native culture. Blending Native and white traditions as his ancestors had done in their time, he enacted creative ways in which to elevate Native people: through public performances of song and dance, by providing cultural information to anthropologists, in carving poles that encapsulated authentic myths and legends, by collaboration with civic leaders to promote unity between diverse cultures, and as an advocate for the rights and needs of Native peoples of western Washington. This chapter provides an overview of the many roles assumed by Joe Hillaire, who was truly a man who walked in two worlds.

Hillaire's paternal grandfather, Salaphalano the Priest (of the Longhouse tradition), was a signatory of the Point Elliott Treaty of 1855. Salaphalano's son, Frank Haeteluk Hillaire (Joe's father), was a traditionalist whose Setting Sun Dance Group performed widely. Salaphalano and Haeteluk would have spoken the Lummi language, some Chinook Jargon, and some English. Before the official boundary between the United States and Canada was established in 1846, the Straits Salish–speaking Lummi, Semiahmoo, and Samish on the mainland and their neighbors on Vancouver Island (T'Sou-ke, Songhees, Saanich) would have moved freely around the Strait of Georgia and among the Gulf and San Juan Islands, setting reef nets in the saltwater channels in July and potlatching in cedar plank houses during the winter months (see map 3). Their permanent winter villages consisted of independent households inhabited by relatives and under the leadership of an influential man, although he was not called a "chief," a term used later by missionaries and Indian agents.[1] After the Lummi moved from the San Juan Islands to the mainland shore sometime in the eighteenth century, they established villages at Gooseberry Point and the Portage and, later, at Old Lummi Village.

The Lummi (xʷlə́mi) were united in their belief in a remote creator being (*xhals* [*x̣eʔəl's*]) and a powerful transformer who gave shape to the earth and the animals upon it. Origin stories told how and where the first Lummi appeared (see chapter 26). High-ranking Lummi families were descended from these First People and could trace their wealth and supernatural powers to these ancestors. Wealth consisted of tangible and intangible possessions, that is, material possessions (including food) and the more abstract and ephemeral songs and dances associated with guardian spirits, ancestral names, and ritual knowledge. Salaphalano would have heard stories about the first non-Natives — Spanish and British explorers who entered the region in the 1790s — and he likely encountered fur traders at Fort Langley (established in 1843) on the Fraser River or in Victoria.

A young Frank Hillaire no doubt heard Father Casimir Chirouse preach at Saint Joachim Church, built by the Catholic missionary in 1861 at Old Lummi Village. For a while, Joseph Hillaire attended Chirouse's school on the Tulalip Reservation. The elder Hillaires probably had ancestors who perished in the first wave of smallpox epidemics in the 1780s and direct family members who died in the epidemics of the mid-nineteenth century.

The establishment of a lumber mill on Whatcom Creek by newcomers Capt. Henry Roeder and Russell Peabody in 1852 (their meeting with the Lummi is commemorated on the *Bellingham Centennial* history pole; see figures 31–37) paved the way for white settlement and white-owned lumber, mining, and fish-canning industries. After the signing of the 1855 treaty, which promised food provisions, health care, education, and tools for building and for farming, Lummi continued to be engaged in traditional fishing activities as well as the recently encouraged agricultural practices. Women worked as domestics and in canneries, men worked as loggers and fishermen, and in the 1880s, families traveled to pick hops and berries for wages. Frank Hillaire and his family lived in the last traditional shed-roof-style house to be occupied in Old Lummi Village, a house owned by Jim Eldridge.[2] Although Eldridge's daughter didn't see spirit dancing take place in the house,[3] such dances, other demonstrations of spirit power, and Native healing practices persisted away from the watchful eyes of the Indian agent and Catholic priest. The picture that emerges is one of the blending of old and new practices and not wholesale assimilation. It is interesting to note that Frank Hillaire's Setting Sun Dance Group (figure 11) wore regalia and performed songs and dances that came directly out of the spirit-dancing tradition, thus making public something that had been private. In fact, there were many instances where older practices and beliefs found expression in activities that were acceptable to the newcomers in power.

In 1913 William Shelton, a Snohomish leader living on the Tulalip reservation, convinced the Indian agent, Dr. Charles Buchanan, to allow him to build a traditional-style house, with decorated interior posts, in order to stage a potlatch (and spirit dancing) on the anniversary of the signing of the treaty, January 22. Buchanan appears to have seen this as a moment of "historical comparison," wishing that the people, especially the younger generation, might view the ceremonies as "pageantry" from the past, compared to the progress of the present. Native people saw it differently and used this occasion as a springboard to expand religious expression. Buchanan and other bureaucrats realized that the apparent success of policies to assimilate Native people was tenuous and that the traditionalists amongst them could exert influence. Following this lead, smokehouses (the preferred name for traditional ceremonial houses) were built at Swinomish and Lummi for Treaty Day celebrations, thus opening the door for more expanded ceremonial and artistic practice. The house that was built at Lummi shortly after the turn of the twentieth century was in use until 1951, after which a new one was constructed. Today, there are several other active smokehouses, in addition to the Lummi Smokehouse, among Coast Salish groups. Treaty Day celebrations are open to the public, a rare instance when outsiders can observe Guardian Spirit dances.

If Frank Hillaire's generation can be said to have made strides for religious freedom, Joe's generation sought to use diplomacy and the legal system to advocate for social justice. Important legal foundations were laid by progressive Natives such as William Shelton and other men who had stature in their own communities and in the white world. The Northwest Federation of American Indians (NFAI), to which Joe Hillaire belonged, was established in 1914. Formed of representatives from tribal entities, its goal was to deal effectively with government officials on treaty rights issues.[4] There was a growing movement in the United States among Natives who believed that the provisions set out in the treaties and the promises of prosperity through assimilation had largely failed to advance Native people. Joe Hillaire's generation took it upon themselves to advocate for social and economic equality while maintaining their Native heritage. This twofold approach — social advancement and perpetuation of tradition — was one that Joe Hillaire enacted in his public life as an artist and as an ambassador. In the years between the granting of Native citizenship and the right to vote (1924) and the establishment of tribal governments under the Indian New Deal (1930s), pressing concerns of the Lummi were the loss of lands through the allotment process and the reconfiguration of the reservation boundary, and the incursion of white fisherman at Lummi reef-net sites off the reservation. The execution of sovereignty over tribal affairs became compounded by the necessity of tribes not only working with the federal Bureau of Indian Affairs but sharing responsibilities with state, county, and local governments. Throughout his life, Joe Hillaire used his considerable influence to further the aims of justice for Native people, including advocating in 1932 for legislation to provide old-age pensions for Natives and later campaigning for a National American Indian Day.

Shelton's actions at Tulalip in 1913 proved that demonstrations of Native heritage could both edify tribes and promote good relations between Natives and whites and served as an effective model for later generations. Even though reservations in Puget Sound were in close proximity to cities, before the 1950s there was limited interaction between Natives and non-Natives, except in the workplace (where Natives had inferior status). Indian summer festivals, commencing in the 1930s and expanding after World War II, initially organized by white service groups and tribal committees for the purpose of enhancing Native-white relations, brought outsiders to reservations and in direct contact with expressions of Indian identity. Joe Hillaire was an organizer, speaker, and performer at Stommish, Chief Seattle Days, Makah Days, and other festivals, promoting solidarity among Natives while providing a positive view of Native culture to outsiders. The Lummi Stommish Water Festival (figure 75), begun in 1946, included athletic events, games for children, salmon barbeque, Native singing and dancing, crowning of the Indian princess, crafts vendors, Slahál gambling games, and the popular "war canoe" races in fifty-foot racing canoes. Now organized exclusively by the tribe and still popular today (held annually during the third week of June), Stommish continues to be an effective presentation of Native pride and cultural goodwill.

MONUMENTAL SCULPTURE AMONG THE COAST SALISH

Coast Salish peoples did not traditionally have the large heraldic columns known as totem poles like those erected by the northern Northwest Coast Natives such as the Tlingit, Haida, and Tsimshian (map 1) to honor

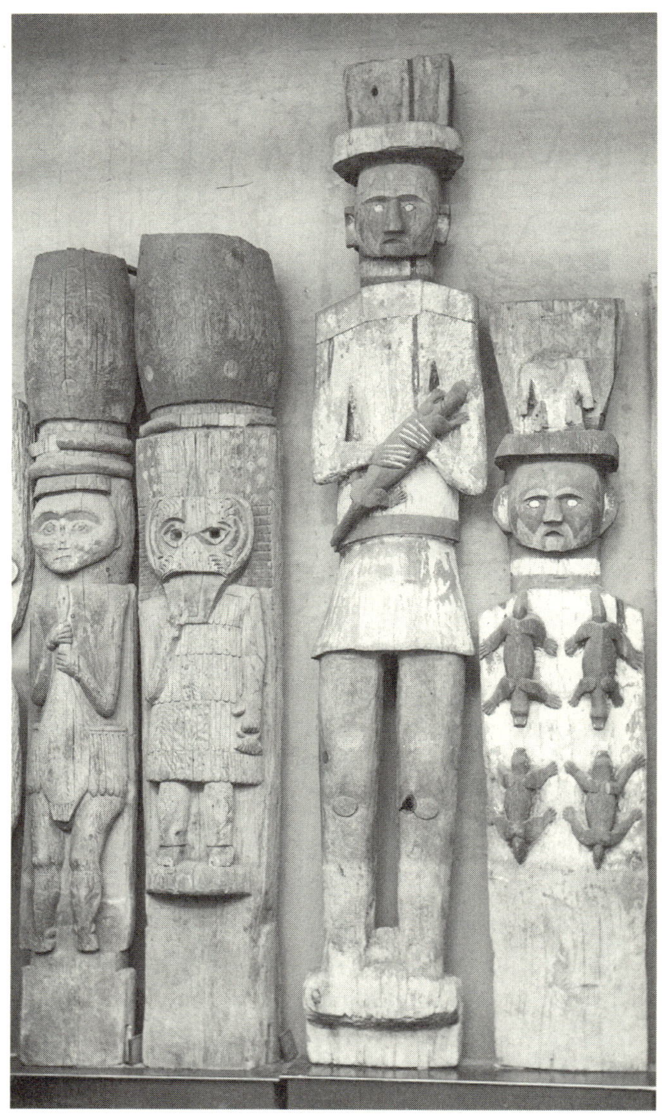

21. Salish interior house posts. Two posts on left: Cowichan house posts, red cedar, 11 feet 6 inches high and 12 feet high. Gift from the Department of Ethnology, World's Columbian Exposition, 1893. Two posts on right: Songhees house posts, red cedar, 7 feet 4 inches high and 6 feet 2 inches high. Collected by G. A. Dorsey and Dr. C. F. Newcombe, Field Museum Expedition, 1900. Reprinted with permission. © The Field Museum, Chicago, CSA17398.

deceased chiefs or to hold the remains of high-born people. The first recorded image of a totem pole was sketched by John Bartlett in the Haida village of Dadens in 1791, supporting more recent arguments that totem poles were precontact sculptures with established cultural significance. First Nations people south of these cultures — such as the Kwakwa̱ka̱'wakw and Nuu-chah-nulth of the central Northwest Coast — adopted this type of carving in the postcontact era, adding it to their aboriginal practice of carving large human welcome figures and interior house posts.

The Coast Salish of southern British Columbia and western Washington (to which the Lummi belong) carved large-scale interior house posts with images of spirit helpers and large human figures representing ancestors, which were used as grave monuments, such as those recorded by artist Paul Kane in the 1840s.[5] Ethnologist Harlan I. Smith and collector Charles Newcombe and others photographed and collected large interior house posts from Salish communities on Vancouver Island and the adjacent British Columbia mainland, some more than fifteen feet in height. James Teit, a Canadian ethnologist, photographed sculptures in the form of human figures at graveyards along the lower Fraser River. The Lummi are likely to have engaged in the making of large-scale house posts and smaller memorial sculptures, although no images are known from the early historic period, except a fragment of Chowitsut's house post now in the Whatcom Museum of History and Art, Bellingham, Washington (figure 19). Chowitsut (Pauline Hillaire's great-grandfather on her mother's side) was a wealthy and influential leader around 1850 who owned a large plank house at Gooseberry Point and also a house at the site of a fish weir on the mouth of the Nooksack River.[6]

Unlike their northern counterparts, whose sculptural traditions served to identify clans and their crests, Coast Salish image-making appears to be part of a larger complex of cultural expression that, according to Wayne Suttles, included visions, supernatural powers, and ritual words.[7] Stated more simply, living persons from high-born families inherited the powers bestowed on their ancestors by supernatural beings in a long-ago time; these power included abilities to cleanse, protect, and empower through ritual actions and words. Suttles points to the house post of Chowitsut, whose carved abstract images are said to "represent the sun carrying valises of expensive things," as an example of the esoteric associations between spirit helpers seen in visions or encounters and the powers that they confer on humans. For the Coast Salish, wealth is manifest both as powerful gifts from the spirit realm and in terms of tangible fortunes, such as resource wealth and trading prowess. Human, animal, and abstract imagery carved on house posts, masks, and rattles and pantomimed in guardian spirit dances forms a kind of sacred iconography that alludes to, but never directly reveals, the nature of individual and family powers. There were restrictions on the making of objects that outwardly expressed secret powers, and only those close to the objects would be privy to their meanings. Given this cultural constraint on art-making, the Lummi made and circulated far fewer examples, in contradistinction to their neighbors to the north, whose intertribal potlatches called for prestigious objects with identifiable crests publicly proclaiming family histories and supernatural associations. It wouldn't be accurate to state that Coast Salish art was more "sacred." Yet its primary examples — house posts, masks, and rattles — are elementally private in nature. As such, they were hidden from public view and not readily collected by outsiders, subjected to scholarly analysis, or displayed in museums. Indeed, the exhibition mounted in 2008 at the Seattle Art Museum, *S'abadeb, the Gifts: Pacific Coast Salish Art and Artists*, was the first comprehensive exhibition of Coast Salish art.[8]

In the heyday of museum collecting — the late nineteenth and early twentieth centuries — monumental works were removed from traditional villages after aboriginal people were forced to adopt European American life ways. Shed-roof houses and graveyards were emptied of the sculptures that memorialized Lummi ancestors. Of those carvings extant in museum collections, the predominant Central Coast Salish iconography is that of simply rendered human figures, often associated with a weasel-like creature, called *chieqen* (čəčiq'ən) in the Lummi language, that was believed to have the ability to cleanse and protect humans during life crises. The most important masks and rattles used in the Central Coast Salish region, the *sxwaixwe* (sx̣ʷə́yx̣ʷi) mask and the sheep-horn rattle, were brought out at transitional moments, hence spiritually dangerous states, such as puberty, illness, and death. As we will see, items and imagery associated with the winter smokehouse spirit dances and cleansing rituals migrated into a more public realm in the twentieth century.

Prior to the 1960s, *sxwaixwe* dances, spirit dancers in regalia, and smokehouse interiors were captured in photographs and were sometimes open to the public. Musicologists were able to record spirit power songs usually reserved for smokehouse activity. William Shelton carved figures of spirit beings (Puget Salish/Lushootseed, *sqəlálitut*) on his story poles. The type of regalia worn by Hillaire's Setting Sun Dancers — cloth and velvet shirts with carved miniature wood "war clubs" affixed to them, feather and hair headdresses, and knitted leggings (figure 11) — came directly out of the spirit dance tradition and traditionally were burned after the dancer had died. How is it that sacred items, imagery, and songs came to have such a public face? How were carvers like Shelton, Joe Hillaire, and Al Charles able to render what was private into versions made for non-Native audiences? In what ways might their actions constitute purposeful acts of resistance against decades-long oppression of Native cultures? Could such deliberate measures serve as a means of negotiating spaces of understanding between Natives and non-Natives while enacting strategies to keep culture alive within Native communities? These questions are not easily answered, but as the essays in this volume reveal, Native identities, and Lummi identity in particular, shifted as internal and external conditions exerted themselves throughout the twentieth century.

THE SOURCES OF JOSEPH HILLAIRE'S STORY POLES

Joe Hillaire's earliest sources for carving were his grandfather and father, who were mask carvers and canoe makers, and other Lummi artists. Some ceremonial arts, wool weaving, and basketry continued alongside carpentry and domestic crafts learned in the boarding schools. Regalia used in ceremonies in the postcontact era — sewn shawls and dresses appliquéd with beads for women, cloth tunics with wood paddles attached and knitted leggings for men, and a range of woven and feathered headdresses for both sexes — were requisite elements to accompany singing and dancing.

According to Pauline Hillaire, Frank's wife, Agnes, and other relatives made the beautiful clothing for the dance group. From an early age Joe would have observed handwork being executed for everyday needs, church and smokehouse functions, and public performances. While he was a young man, canoes were still used for subsistence fishing and gathering and for visiting relatives and friends at other locales. Joe would have had instruction in the use of tools (a mix of Native adzes and pioneer-style tools at that time; see figure 6), and according to Pauline, he was learning the art of carving by the age of sixteen. By all accounts, Joe had a semitraditional apprenticeship period during which he would have assisted his father before defining his own direction. Several members of the large, extended Hillaire family also became carvers, something that would have been common in earlier times.

Although surrounded by artisans of his grandparents' and parents' generation, Joe's work would depart from that of nineteenth-century artists in several ways, in what contemporary Puyallup/Tulalip artist Shaun Peterson describes as taking "a different direction."[9] The most significant change was the shift from creating carvings that were privately held and that represented personal or familial supernatural connections, as in the case of interior house posts, toward a monumental public form of carving story poles meant to appeal to a wide range of viewers, including non-Natives. Both Joe and his predecessor, Snohomish carver William Shelton (1868–1938), communicated that their story poles were to inform the general public about Native traditions and to teach new generations of Native children about the meanings and messages within the legends depicted on the poles. In the ever-changing arena of intercultural relations in the first half of the twentieth century, these carvers acted as culture brokers, engaged in mediating between the Native and white cultures with the objective of reducing conflict and effecting change. Thus, the story pole form was devised to operate in a kind of "collective arena," appealing to a population with little knowledge and more than a little skepticism about Native people while seeking to preserve the oral traditions and instill a sense of pride in young Native people. It was a risky terrain to enter because, on some level, it required that one overlook some historical realities. Yet both men possessed the skills of artistry and diplomacy, which caused the poles to be viewed as symbols of a shared history that, going into the future, might be defined by conciliation.

Shelton and Hillaire included on some of their poles "quintessential" Native imagery easily recognizable to outsiders, such as the Plains Indian man wearing the feather warbonnet (figure 32). Indeed, both men donned such headdresses in their public performances, partly for visual effect, but also as an authentic recognition of the intermingling of Coastal and Plateau traditions via the powwow and through participation in Native organizations. The stories rendered on the poles (and often recounted in pamphlets and news reports) were meant to invoke a common pride in family and a respect for genealogy and to appeal to the universal allure of storytelling.[10] In order not to trivialize these endeavors, it must be stated that the poles filled a perceptible void in the carving arts left by decades of suppression of Native art forms. Shelton's style was modestly related to traditional design aesthetics, but, more importantly, it was an expression of his own time. He was dedicated to gathering what was still remembered by elders — an undertaking for which he had to get governmental permission — and he creatively forged a visual vocabulary to convey that. Shelton's Tulalip story pole (1913), the Everett story pole (1922), and the Olympia story pole (begun in 1933 and finished in 1940 after his death) display human, animal, and supernatural creatures in singular arrangement on the front and back of the column in raised relief and accentuated with painted details. Shelton was purposeful in the choice of a totem format on which to place iconic images of mythic beings that could be clearly seen from a distance. These large monoliths are powerful and influential even today. Shelton's carvings prompted other artists to take up carving within their communities.

William Shelton is likely the source of the type of story pole that Joe Hillaire carved a generation later. Shelton could have seen the famous Seattle totem pole, erected in Pioneer Square in 1899, stolen from a Tlingit Tongass village by a group of Seattle businessmen.[11] It was a prominent fixture until 1938, when it was burned and a replacement was put up in 1940.[12] A popular speaker at civic events around Puget Sound, Shelton

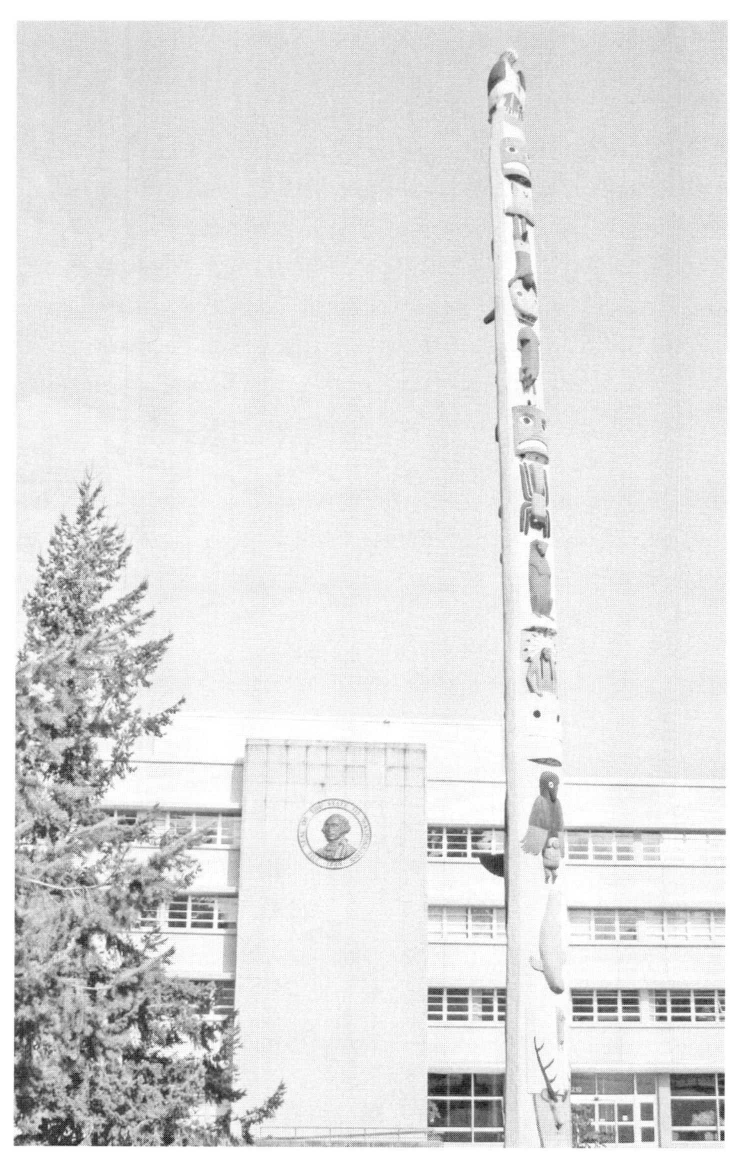

22. Totem pole carved by Chief William Shelton (Snohomish) installed at the Washington State Capitol, General Administration Building, Olympia, 1940–2010. The pole was removed because of deterioration, and in 2010 there were still no plans for replacement. Photo by Benjamin Helle. Secretary of State Photograph Collection, Washington State Archives, 029.

could certainly have seen the many totem poles for sale at J. E. Standley's Ye Olde Curiosity Shop on the Colman Dock in Seattle, where Standley commissioned local Native artists to create small and large carvings. Standley actively promoted the siting of poles in public places. In 1939 Shelton carved a major story pole for the state capitol grounds in Olympia, followed by another that was donated by the Daughters of the American Revolution and erected in Seattle's Woodland Park. The style imparted by Shelton was one of retaining the cylindrical form of the log and, in deep relief, carving individual figures related to family stories. Shelton garnered a respectable reputation as an artist and erected several more story poles for public settings.

Hillaire would surely have seen the sixty-one-foot Swinomish village totem pole, carved in the mid-1930s as a monument to the tribes living on the reservation: Swinomish, Skagit, Upper Skagit, and Samish.[13] His friend Martin Sampson (figure 18), a prominent Upper Skagit leader who was a fellow member of the NFAI, provided the interpretation of the legends depicted on the pole, many of them family stories, in a publication entitled *The Swinomish Totem Pole: Tribal Legends*.[14] A unique image on the pole is a rendering of President Franklin D. Roosevelt, who inaugurated policies of self-government for Native people.

A TALE OF TWO POLES: THE KOBE-SEATTLE SISTER CITIES FRIENDSHIP POLE AND THE *LAND IN THE SKY* POLE

By the time Joe was commissioned in 1961 to create two important story poles, he was already renowned as a liaison between the Native and non-Native communities. Hillaire used his considerable artistic skills, combined with striking good looks and a rousing gift of oratory, to challenge commonly held views of Native inferiority. His participation in Native organizations, like the NFAI, brought him into contact with the power brokers of the white world, and he was often called upon to be a spokesperson for Native history and culture. Often photographed in a buckskin shirt, feather bonnet, and bone-bead breastplate of Plains-Plateau origin (figure 17), Hillaire might have played into a romantic notion of

Indians, but he knew the value of projecting a sense of Native solidarity. Since the time of first contact, Native identities were on shifting sand, formed and re-formed by forces outside and from within, yet Hillaire and his cohorts never flagged in their objectives to gain social and political status for Natives. The full range of his contributions — to both to Native and non-Native people — cannot be recounted here, but a few important instances will be mentioned.

In 1933 Hillaire wrote a script for a reenactment of the 1855 Treaty of Point Elliott, sponsored by the American Legion of Kirkland, Washington, and staged at Juanita Bay (chapter 27). It was the main event of a weekend intertribal festival that included speeches by Shelton, Hillaire, and others, Native dancing, canoe races, crafts, and a salmon bake. Descendants of the original signers of the treaty stood in for their ancestors, with Joe representing the Lummi leader Chowitsut, and American Legion members played then-governor Isaac Stevens and his associates. To insure a good crowd of non-Natives, prior to the event Hillaire toured civic organizations and schools, providing lectures on the treaty's history and on Native culture. This promotional model would come into use again as Hillaire embarked on the Century 21 Seattle World's Fair project. In the 1950s he was a frequent feature at boat shows and at Seafair events, where visitors could observe him carving totem poles and recounting the stories they represented (figure 65).

A thoughtful and intelligent man, Hillaire was sought out by ethnologists as a consultant: by Bernard Stern, who wrote a monograph on the Lummi; Erna Gunther, director of the Burke Museum at the University of Washington; and Wayne Suttles, an eminent scholar of Salish culture. Joe permitted himself to be photographed on numerous occasions and to be audio-recorded by Willard Rhodes in 1950 and Leon Metcalf in 1953 telling traditional stories and singing songs.[15] Just before the Seattle World's Fair opened in 1962, Hillaire was an advisor to the tourist enterprise Tillicum Village, providing songs and dances to be used in the performances staged in the longhouse-style theater on Blake Island, a few miles from Seattle's waterfront. He instructed Boy Scout groups on Native arts, stories, and dances, thus creating a generation of enthusiasts, some of whom went on to become teachers and museum curators (chapter 17). Hillaire said, "It is only as Indian art is made available to the American people and they get familiar with it and use it in their homes that the Indian will be better understood." He also wished for Lummi children to learn about their heritage through the work of living carvers.

Hillaire's last major projects occurred in 1961; his carving was unfortunately curtailed by a stroke he suffered in 1964. Joe was a natural choice for a Native artist to promote goodwill among nations to which the Seattle World's Fair aspired.[16] It was the first international fair held since the end of World War II. Branded "Century 21," the theme was "Man on a New Frontier" and the promise of the space age. A traditional totem pole seemed an odd choice for a celebration of future technology and space exploration, yet Hillaire made the connection by choosing the story of two brothers who travel into the sky world and engage in battle with the Man Moon (figures 48–55). One wonders how he meshed the still-existent inequities experienced by Native people with the idealized future promoted by the fair's theme, but this was indicative of the contradictions he faced in his life. Before beginning the World's Fair story pole, Hillaire would complete a thirty-five-foot pole as part of the sister city affiliation between Seattle and Kobe, Japan (figures 43–47). The monumental sculpture was a gift to Kobe, meant to point out the commonalities of the two cities, promote commerce between Asia and the United States, and ease the memories of World War II.[17]

The pole's narrative was suggested by officials of the sister city association, yet Hillaire imparted a richly symbolic interpretation using the clarity of his carving style and his sense of a shared humanity. Two sisters (representing Seattle and Kobe) grow closer as they acknowledge things they share, like the salmon, the mountains, and the sea. One faces the rising sun, the other the setting sun. A hawk face represents freedom and the wolf represents strength, alluding to the leaders from both cities, who defend freedom. A monster blows a dark cloud, symbolizing the destruction of war, while the sun symbolizes the hope of peace. The pole was begun in Edmonds, Washington, then taken to Pioneer Square during Seafair Days in August. At that time Joe was artist-in-residence in Seattle (figure 44). Along with Seattle mayor Gordon S. Clinton, Hillaire served as an ambassador to Kobe when he traveled there to present the pole, representing the citizens of Seattle as well as the region's First People. Joe was sixty-six years old, an esteemed elder among his own people, and was respectfully welcomed and feted while in Japan. The pole had arrived via freighter before Hillaire flew to Osaka, where he met with foreign affairs officers, and then on to Kobe, where he would put the finishing touches on the pole. The dedication of the pole was the highlight of the Kobe Port Festival (similar to Seattle's Seafair). Black-and-white photographs show Joe in Native dress waving to a cheering crowd from the back of a convertible (figure 45). Other photos show Hillaire in a business suit and casual clothes making speeches, visiting schools, and sightseeing at markets, shrines, universities, artisan workshops, and rural farms. Hillaire made two small-scale replicas of the pole in order to explain the story and as gifts for officials. He also made carved and painted canoe paddles used by Japanese youth who performed for the ceremony. Interestingly, Joe appeared on a Japanese television show (*I've Got a Secret*) on which

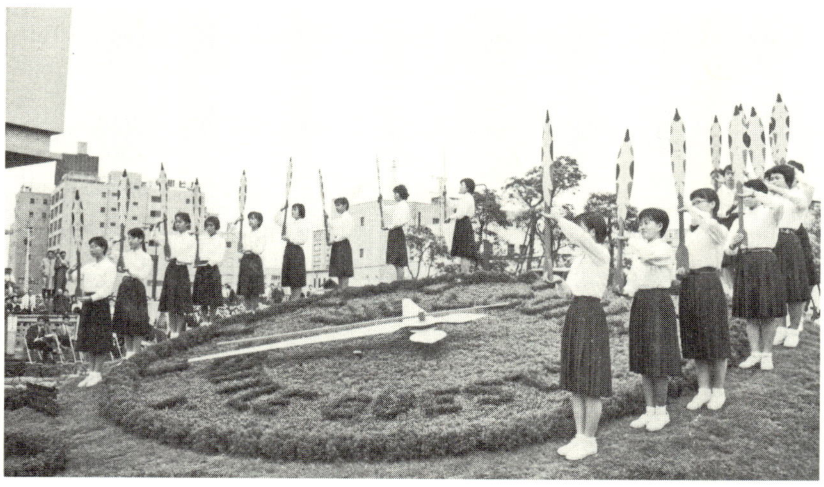

23. Students performing a paddle dance to Mr. Hillaire's song at the Kobe-Seattle Sister Cities friendship pole dedication ceremony, Kobe, Japan, October 20, 1961. Reprinted with permission. Courtesy of the Seattle Public Library, 327301.

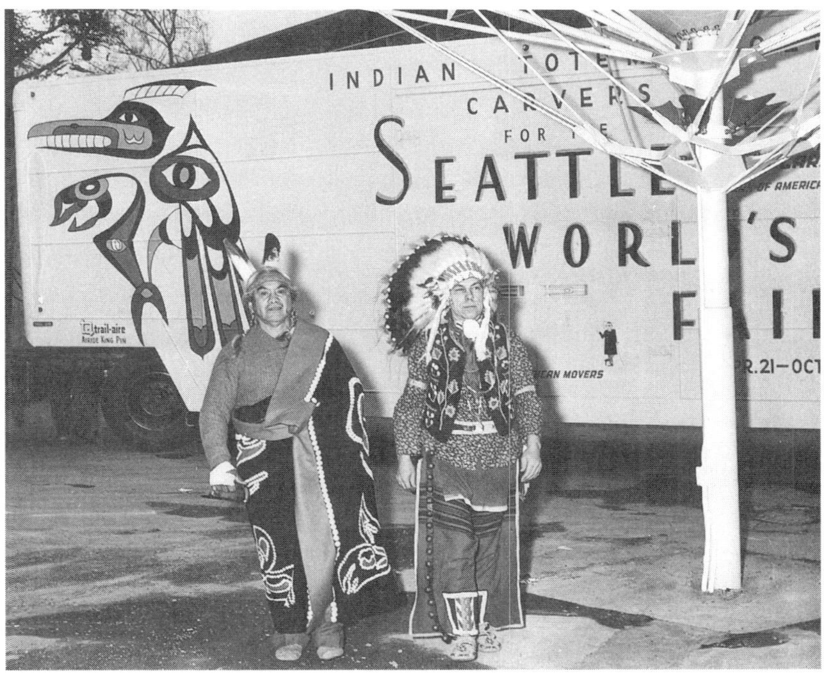

24. Joe Hillaire with Don McQuade (Anishinaabe) and the moving van used for transporting the World's Fair pole on its U.S. tour, 1962. Photo courtesy of the Seattle Times Archive, Washington State Historical Society, and the Archives of Pauline Hillaire.

the panel had to identify which contestant was "a chief of American Indians." Kobe's gift to Seattle was a friendship bell that was installed at the Seattle Center near the international fountain, where it is still a cherished testimonial of the region's strong ties to Japan.[18]

Hillaire must have returned to Seattle elated by the warm reception he had received in Japan and eager to embark on the Century 21 World's Fair totem, known as the *Land in the Sky* totem pole. A red cedar weighing more than thirteen thousand pounds was obtained from the Hoh Rainforest for the thirty-five-foot totem pole. A special truck trailer was outfitted to accommodate the log, with the side opening fully so that visitors could watch Hillaire at work and view Native artifacts from the Pacific Northwest. Don McQuade, an Anishinaabe Native and a World's

Fair promoter, accompanied Hillaire around the country as the van traveled along a route passing through twenty-five states and three hundred cities, stopping to promote the upcoming Century 21.

After returning, Joe was to be featured putting the finishing touches on the pole (with his son Ben) for fair visitors to watch in the "show street" area of the fairgrounds within a concession called the Indian Village, where Plateau and Plains Natives set up tipis and performed dances and songs. Located on the periphery of the fair — more as curiosity than culture — amid restaurants, show girl revues, a wax museum, personality testing, puppet shows, and Japanese pearl divers, the Indian Village was forced to close in August because of mismanagement and failure to pay the Native performers.[19] The original plan to raise the pole permanently on the fairground site was dashed, and the pole went into storage without being finished. Joe had remarried and, after that, lived on and off at the Port Madison (Suquamish) reservation in Kitsap County. After the debacle with the pole, the Kitsap County Historical Society, the Suquamish Community Club, and the American Legion embarked on a campaign to bring the pole to the reservation, where it was erected on a hillside above Chief Seattle's gravesite in 1963 (figure 51). When first raised, the pole was unpainted, but during the more than forty years that the pole stood at Suquamish, it was painted and the wings replaced. In 2005 the pole was taken down because of deterioration and brought to the Lummi Reservation (figure 29). Analyzed for restoration by conservation expert Andrew Todd and carver Felix Solomon, the pole is in desperate need of repair, and fund-raising efforts are under way. Traditionally, some poles were refurbished and rededicated with a potlatch, but usually they were left to let nature take its course. Today, there is a feeling that since Pacific Northwest Native peoples were forced to surrender, curtail, or even burn precious carvings, it is important to preserve what still exists.

THE LEGACY OF LUMMI CARVING TODAY

Shelton and Hillaire had no real models to follow as they devised their story poles. Perhaps growing out of an aboriginal predilection to depict spirit beings on house posts and masks, the narrative thrust of these new forms was completely unique to Coast Salish art. In part, the poles became a strategic invention to record fragile knowledge that had only been orally transmitted. Shelton's bold move in 1913 to display *sqəlálitut* images on a pole required the owner's permission and faith that exposing them would be all right. Susie Sampson Peter (Skagit), the mother of Martin Sampson, remarked that when Leon Metcalf arrived with a tape recorder she realized that treasured stories and songs would "be transferred to a different type of canoe," a modern vehicle for a new time.[20] A good story, by whichever means it is recounted or recorded, must suspend time and invoke the complexity of interaction between human and other beings. The success lies in the talents of the storyteller. Hillaire drew from a body of general myths, created an iconography derived from Hillaire family emblems, and, in some cases, invented modern narratives. His artistic style was similarly eclectic, reaching back to ancient carving traditions and supplemented by brilliant innovations. Hillaire's compositions are almost never static; figures appear in frontal and profile poses cut deeply away from the column of cedar and are captured in pensive thought or in purposeful motion. They wrap around the contours of the pole, crossing the planes of the sculpture, creating dynamism. The bright color palette signals modernity. Like the storyteller of earlier times, Hillaire had the task of synthesizing the salient actions of a cast of characters, conveying individual dilemmas and deeds, and imparting a sense of humanity (or its opposite). The stateliness and clarity of Shelton's style, where figures are isolated in stacked arrangements, give way in Hillaire's approach to passages of complexity and ambiguity. In the words of contemporary carver Scott Jensen, Hillaire's talent was in creating a feeling, and while precision is admired in art, an emotional connection is what lasts.

Joe's talent surely inspired other artists, as he was influenced by those around him. His grandson Gary Hillaire was a gifted draftsman, printmaker, and painter. Morrie Alexander (1915–73; figure 25) and Al Charles (1896–1984; figure 2), men of Hillaire's generation, made strong contributions to the arts of mask and totem pole carving, creating totem poles for the Lummi community and for public sites in Whatcom County and

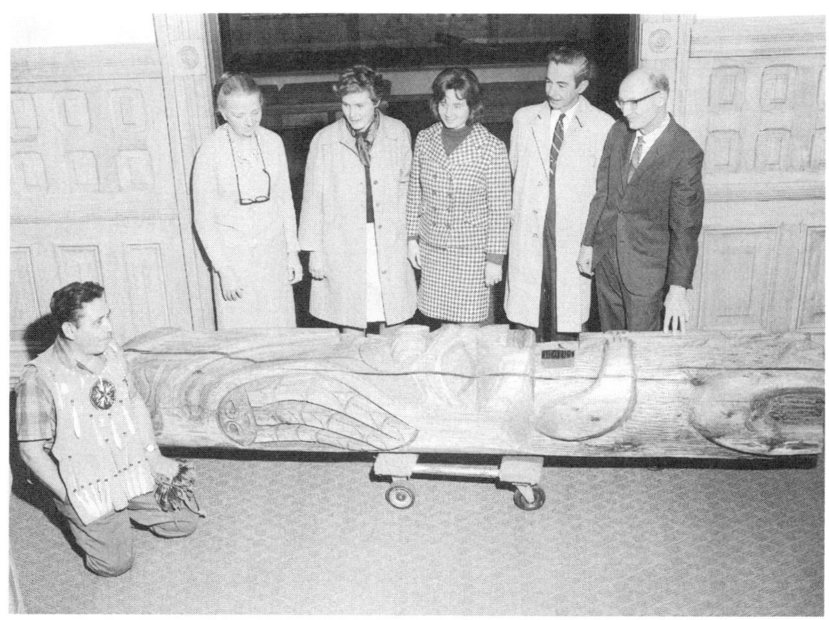

25. Lummi carver Morrie Alexander at the Whatcom Museum of History and Art, Bellingham, Washington, 1969. (*Standing*) Sue Barrow, museum director; Pat Fleeson; Rosemary Flora; Req Williams, mayor of Bellingham; Tom Glenn, Port of Bellingham manager. Photo by Jack Carver. Reprinted with permission from Whatcom Museum of History and Art, Bellingham, Washington, image number 1995-1.1.10930.

beyond. Alexander learned carving from his grandfather Jack Pierre. His totem carving style reflects his knowledge of northern Northwest Coast design systems, while his masks come directly from Lummi traditions. Alexander's work had a wide audience, including art gallery shows and participation in Expo 70 in Osaka, Japan. In 1971 he and Charles became master teachers under a project sponsored by the Whatcom Museum of History and Art and the Ford Foundation.[21]

Dale James (1955–96) was one of the young apprentices, and he went on to become a notable teacher at Northwest Indian College and a carver in his own right. Dale mentored his brothers Doug and Jewell James, founding the House of Tears Carvers, now under the leadership of Jewell James. Carving since 1972 while a student at the University of Washington,

Jewell James has distinguished himself with a series of monumental totem poles aimed at bringing attention to national issues, which is not surprising, given his decades of involvement in Lummi politics. After September 11, 2001, he carved three sets of poles to represent the three sites attacked and to honor those who perished and their families.[22] The ultimate goal has been to promote peace and healing as the poles journeyed across the country to their final locations (figure 3). In October 2011 another of James's totem poles made a journey across the nation, traveling 4,400 miles to the National Library of Medicine in Bethesda, Maryland, as the showpiece for the exhibition *Native Voices: Native Peoples' Concepts of Health and Illness*. The traditional symbols representing the sky, earth, and water, as well as the healing power of women, invoke awareness about the interconnectedness of life and the environment. Jewell James has created a new vocabulary of images meant to speak to contemporary events and issues.

Lummi carver Felix Solomon knows Joe Hillaire's art intimately, as he has restored, with carver Scott Jensen, the *Bellingham Centennial* pole and is the current steward of the *Land in the Sky* totem pole, with hopes that it too will be conserved. Solomon is a force in the revival of traditional shovelnose-style canoes and has completed three canoes of more than twenty feet in length after extensive study and planning (figure 26). He is currently working on a story pole for the Whatcom Creek Salmon Art Trail. It is a large, complex sculpture depicting two Native fishermen in a shovelnose canoe struggling to catch a salmon, which is being pursued by a giant serpent. Entitled *It's Mine*, the pole encompasses the social, political, and spiritually relevant issues that impact the Lummi and others, especially the loss of life-giving salmon and its habitat.

In July 2011 Pauline Hillaire made a call to Lummi carvers to create works rich in tradition but that are also relevant to today, a sentiment that Joe would certainly applaud. She says that once the carver puts his mark on the sacred red cedar, he becomes a storyteller and historian. She concludes by reminding artists of their responsibilities to their family, their community, and especially to the younger artists who will follow them. Although Joe did not live to see the resurgence of Coast Salish art and culture that began in the 1970s, he certainly understood that his life-long efforts to expose the rich history, deep spirituality, and expressive arts of the Lummi and Coast Salish people put the survival of these traditions on a secure foundation for future generations.

NOTES

1. Suttles, "Post-contact Culture Change," 33.
2. Suttles, "Post-contact Culture Change," 62.
3. Suttles, "Post-contact Culture Change," 73.
4. Harmon, *Indians in the Making*, 78–79.
5. Lister, *Paul Kane, the Artist*, 167.
6. Suttles, "Post-contact Culture Change," 53.
7. Suttles, "Productivity and Its Constraints," 69.
8. Brotherton, *S'abadeb, the Gifts*.
9. Peterson, "Coast Salish Design."
10. Native oral traditions provide people with the encyclopedia knowledge needed to live in the world and include epic tales of tribal origins, genealogical data, and practical advice about health and hygiene, knowledge of plants and animals, and vital information about interactions with spirit beings. As such, they were not seen as entertainment, although some stories were lighthearted and included humor.
11. The businessmen were an elite group of leading citizens on a goodwill tour of Alaska, and the ill-gotten totem became a civic symbol of the region's ancient past. When the pole was taken down, three Native communities submitted bids to carve the replica using funds from the Works Progress Administration (WPA). See Duncan, *One Thousand One Curious Things*, 165.
12. Garfield, *Seattle's Totem Poles*.
13. Averill and Morris, *Northwest Coast Native*, 131.
14. Shelton (Snohomish), *The Swinomish Totem Pole*.
15. Metcalf, who was trained in music education, recorded seventy-five reels of Northwest Coast stories, songs, and oral tradition material between 1950 and 1961. These materials are now located at the University of Washington. Willard Rhodes was a professor of music at Columbia University and made his 1947–50 documentation of Native music publicly available in vinyl record and cassette form as Library of Congress releases. *Northwest Coast (Puget Sound)*, released in 1954, features Joe Hillaire. For a detailed discussion of these and other recordings, see appendices 1–3 in Smyth and Ryan, *Spirit of the First People*.
16. Hillaire was not the first Native to carve a totem pole during a world's fair. According

to scholar Emily Moore, John Wallace, a Kaigani Haida carver from Hydaburg, Alaska, carved a totem pole at the 1939 World's Fair in San Francisco. His son, Fred Wallace, helped him. René d'Harnoncourt had invited the Wallaces to carve as demonstration artists for the Indian Arts and Crafts Board's exhibit, so they carved in the courtyard of the Indian Building to attract visitors and to show the laborious process of the art. The totem pole was later featured at the entrance to the Museum of Modern Art in New York for d'Harnoncourt's 1941 exhibit *Indian Art of the United States*. In addition, Charlie Tagcook, a Tlingit carver from Haines, carved at a world's fair in Oregon in the 1950s.

17. Although this pole was not the first to be erected in Japan, Hillaire's pole incited a "totem pole craze," prompting the making of totem poles by Japanese students. Previously, an Alaskan Native pole carved in 1922 was donated by the Alaska Steamship Company and shipped to Tokyo in 1951. Fifty Douglas fir trees were provided by the University of Washington to be planted around the pole. To commemorate the new sister city agreement in 1957, a totem pole (by an unknown carver) was given to Kobe and erected outside its new city hall. The pole Hillaire carved replaced this one, which had fallen into disrepair. It is a well-known attraction and is displayed in a beautifully landscaped garden.

18. I am indebted to historian Rob Ketcherside for sharing information and photographs about the sister city association and to him and his wife, Mai, for translating the plaque that accompanies the pole at the Kobe City Hall Park. I would also like to thank Dr. Yukiko Shirahara, curator at the Nezu Museum in Tokyo, for obtaining information from Japanese sources. In addition, Bo Kinney, special collections librarian at the Seattle Public Library, assisted me with Seattle World's Fair holdings in the library's collection, including two valuable albums of photographs taken of Joe Hillaire during his ten-day trip to Japan in 1961.

19. According to Pauline Hillaire, Joe was displeased by how marginalized the Native section was and the treatment he and others received. Adding further insult, a short distance away, as part of the fair's Fine Arts Exhibits, an extensive exhibition of Northwest Coast Native art, curated by Erna Gunther, an ethnologist and director of the Burke Museum, and drawn from historic museum collections around the world had been mounted. No modern or contemporary Native art was featured, and of the nearly two hundred works, only six were Coast Salish.

20. Hilbert, "To a Different Canoe," 254–58.

21. Whatcom Museum staff, *A Report*.

22. An interesting comparison is a symphony commissioned by Vi Hilbert (Upper Skagit, 1918–2008). *The Healing Heart of the First People of This Land* was written by Canadian composer Bruce Ruddell and performed by the Seattle Symphony under maestro Gerard Schwarz on May 5, 2005. Hilbert stated that the purpose was to help heal the grief caused by the tragic acts of September 11, 2001, by using the sounds and words of Puget Salish music together with classical music.

6 Coast Salish Carving

Our Work Is Our Identity

FELIX SOLOMON

I CAME INTO CARVING AROUND 1997. I STARTED OFF carving masks and bentwood boxes. With the help of master carvers who have taken me under their wings — they'll teach you if they see that you're a doer and not just a talker — there's absolutely nothing that these master carvers will not share with you. It is a blessing of mentorship, and now I'm in a position where I can teach and I can pass on this art form and teach protocol: how to bring a canoe to life, how to bring a mask to life, how to carve a spoon. You have to practice what you're taught. You can't just learn it or read about it; you have to do it. You have to have wood. You have to have tools. And you have to feel the form, you have to feel the carve. You have to know how the wood is going to act and react. Each piece of wood is different. Whether you carve identical spoons or two identical masks, each one is totally different. You're never done learning the process of the carve, relationships with people, your relationships with tools, your relationships with your spirit and your ancestors. It just goes on and on, and it gets deeper and deeper as you get into your art form.

In Coast Salish work there is just a very small number of pieces, so we're limited on what we can study. But I think that's a good thing, because it really gives us focus on who we are, and what we are, through our art. It's a different style of art than people are used to. People are used to seeing Northern work, the big totem animals, they're called nowadays. Coast Salish is a different style; it's a more three-dimensional style. It's something that came to my attention with having the opportunity to restore Joe Hillaire's work. Nobody is carving the Coast Salish style as in Joe Hillaire's work, or Morrie Alexander's work, or Al Charles's work. These carvers were very prolific artists from Lummi. Their work was carved at Fish Point, Lummi; it was carved on Portage Island. That's as Lummi and Coast Salish as you can get, and it has a specific style. These three carvers have a specific style to their work, and I want to bring this back to life, along with the canoes that were used by our river people.

Our Coast Salish people, from the Fraser River all the way to the Columbia River and every river tributary in between, had shovelnose canoes, and these shovelnose canoes were specifically Coast Salish style. This is very important to bring back, because they were overlooked. When canoes were brought back for the Canoe Journeys, starting with Paddle to Seattle in 1989, they brought back the ocean canoes, the big, wide ocean canoes that were steam bent, with the big prows on the front, and beautifully carved. And they brought back the racing canoes that were sleek and long and fast. They focused on these two types of canoes, but they overlooked the shovelnose canoe. That was one thing that I got a research grant for through the Whatcom Museum in 2003. So finding out about these shovelnose canoes opened my eyes to really wanting to carve this type of canoe and keeping this style of Lummi, Coast Salish art alive that Joe Hillaire carved. And you'll see that in the totem pole that I'm carving now in my studio. It's a three-dimensional form: the animals and the humans and the canoes are more lifelike. It's not two dimensional; it's a log that's carved in three dimensions, all the way around, to get the form of it. I'm also carving a shovelnose canoe as we speak. I started April 3rd of 2011. Today is July 1st, so it's roughly three months so far. I'm steaming it tomorrow, and then I have about another three weeks to a month of

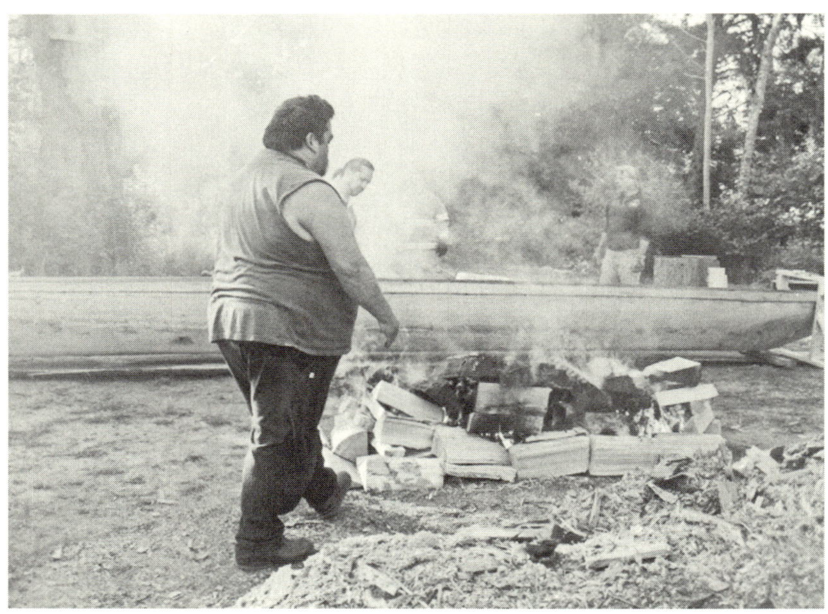

26. Felix Solomon steaming the shovelnose canoe he carved for the Sauk-Suiattle Tribe, 2011. Reprinted with permission. Photo by Melonie Ancheta.

carving after that. It's a thirty-foot, steam-bent, shovelnose canoe for the Sauk-Suiattle Tribe.

Last year I carved the first one. It was for Stillaguamish; it was a twenty-two-foot shovelnose canoe. It is important to be part of this revival to keep our Coast Salish ways and our culture alive. We're lucky here in Lummi because we have beautiful elders such as Scälla, and our chief, Bill James, and his mother, Fran James, and their incredible wealth of knowledge. We all want to do the same thing; we want to keep the art alive. We want to keep the carve alive. Bill and Fran weave, but they know about carving too, and they're excited about this canoe. They have followed this in our Lummi language. The shovelnose canoe is called a *t'ly'* (ƛ'ƚáy'), and they're so excited about this *t'ly'* coming back to life.

There is a big difference between Lummi Coast Salish–style carving and northern work. There's no such thing as "typical" northern work, but their totem poles are carved out of half of a log. They'll take a big log, and it's just carved out of one side, whereas Lummi work is carved from the whole log. If you look at all Joe's work, every piece of Joe Hillaire's work is carved 360 degrees. There's half of a story down one side and half of a story down the other side, and that's how it's read too. It starts on one side, it goes up one side, and it comes down the other side, and that's how you read the pole. If you hear Pauline's stories, you can follow the story as it goes up, and then it comes down the other side. The carving of a Coast Salish style is more three dimensional because it is carved 360 degrees, where the animals will be protruding out from the wood. From our region here in Lummi the story poles were created to identify times, they were created to identify peoples and culture and family and the time that we're in, they were created mostly for identity. The *Bellingham Centennial* pole, for instance, in front of the Whatcom County Courthouse, was carved in 1950, but the pole marks the time of a century prior to that, 1855, when our treaty was signed. In the canoe are Roeder and Peabody, the two white men, with the Lummi chief and his brother, Chowitsut and Tsi'li'x^w (Tseleq). It tells the story of when they came to Whatcom County; they wanted a piece of property so they could make their saw mill and start building this city. It tells of how they had to meet with the Lummi people, how they had to have the potlatch. All the symbolism is on the pole, of the potlatches that happened to bring this about. This is a story pole; it's just like you're writing a book.

We didn't write books; we did art. And back then, it wasn't art. Our boxes were used for a purpose, our bowls had purpose, our spoons had purpose, our gaff hooks, our canoes, everything had purpose, and they were all carved on, but they were carved on for identity. They were not "art" until the white man came and took our belongings; then they were in museums, and they turned into art. But when we had them, they were our tools, our utensils, our vehicles, our homes, our identities; that's who we were.

Lummi and Coast Salish are very well known for the house posts that built the huge community houses that we stayed in. There are records of houses on Portage Island that were two hundred feet long and sixty feet wide, and one hundred feet by fifty feet; they were massive houses. The corner posts were all carved. These were called house posts, and they were for identity, both personal identity of our families and clan identities and tribal identities of who we are. You walk into a house like this, you would see Hillaire, you would see Solomon. You would see carver or weaver, you would see a teacher; it would be identified by a carving. The freestanding poles evolved from that: for identity, for a story, to mark time, so it was created from a masterful art mind.

There's a way that Coast Salish people look at our own work; our work is our identity. The symbol and the symbolism mean so much. It might just be a circle. It might be just a circle with a couple of lines, and a couple of small circles at the bottom. But that is a sun dog, and a sun dog is a very powerful design. And each design, just a simple carve of a line, a simple cutoff of a corner, could mean something so deep to a family. It's what you put into that piece of work, what you think it's going to be used for. I want to put safety into this canoe. I want to put longevity into this canoe. I want to put good feelings in this canoe. I hope that travels straight into this canoe.

There are not a lot of carvers in Lummi. There's just a handful of us carvers; there are very few full-time carvers who actually make a living carving. There's a lack of material. You have to go outside and get what you need, to get your tools, get your knowledge, get your research, get your cedar logs. Even this last batch of cedar logs I got from Arlington. I know other artists have to go to logging companies and buy logs that come down from Alaska or northern British Columbia. But if we want to do our art, that's what we have to do. It's just something you do because you love it, because you have this vision. I always heard that from the elders: we are visionary people. I'm starting to feel what that means.

This opportunity that I've had to restore Joe Hillaire's work comes through Scälla. She chose me, through her heart, to do this work. The *Centennial* pole was the first pole that I got to restore. Joe was a very prolific carver. He carved many poles back in the late 1940s and early 1950s through the mid-1960s. He was probably carving a pole every other year. The *Land in the Sky* pole is a thirty-five-foot pole that is in deep need of restoration. It is a visionary and phenomenal piece of work. Joe did an amazing body of work, and the time has come when it needs to be saved or we're going to lose it. If we don't save this work, it's worse than tearing up a book, because we can reprint a book. You can't reprint a totem pole. You can carve one like it, but it's not going to be it. This is the original, and it needs to be saved with the technology we have today for conservation of totem poles and sacred wooden objects. I've taken on restoration as a big facet of my art business; restoring Coast Salish totem poles is very important to me. If we don't restore them, we're not going to have them; they are rotting, falling apart. And there are ways to fix them so they can last a bit longer. We can get another fifty years out of them with the technology we have nowadays and save the story, save Joe Hillaire's carve, save the face that he carved and the animals that he carved, that were done with his hands. We can restore that same shape. We could also take designs off it and carve a new one, but that's not going to be Joe Hillaire's work. So that's how important it is to keep the old work alive. Even if we don't stand it back up, it's important to restore it. Even if we have to lay it horizontally so people can look at it.

There are a lot of totem poles out there that need restoration, not just by Salish people but by many other artists up and down the whole coast. Some of the works you can restore. Public art, in my own heart and mind, can be restored back to being used and being seen again, because it is for the public eye. But then there is sacred work that cannot be touched. Cultural work, as compared to public art, has its own destination; if it is a grave marker, it just goes back to the earth. Art that was created for the identity of who or what the art is marking serves its purpose through its life, and then it turns to earth. It goes with the spirit.

With this art comes teaching, very spiritual teaching. And it goes beyond the physical. The physical carve comes through the human body. The art form that comes through in the wood — what you end up with is the spiritual work — it comes through in such a way that, when you're done with a piece of work, you set it there and you think, "Where did that come from? It couldn't have come from me." And I think that's part of the healing. That's why there's a cry inside. It's part of the healing that it takes to get this through, to get this work out so that people can see it. There's a strong teaching that still happens, and it still happens today, if you will let it happen, if you can be true to yourself and let it happen. The teaching is that you have to do your work. And there are no shortcuts to finishing. You have to do your work. I'll wake up in the middle of the night and have problems, figure it out. Then you have to wake up and do it. You wake up and just go straight to work, even before the coffee's done. When you're doing your artwork there are absolutely no shortcuts; you have to do it, all the work, to get to the final finished lines. And only you, as an artist, know when it's finished.

There are some up-and-coming carvers who are starting to show interest. There's always somebody who says: "I want to come learn. I want to learn that canoe. I want to learn that wood box. I want to learn how to carve a mask." And then they don't show up. They just kind of want to do it. But out of all those people, sometimes there's one who will come back and who really wants to learn, and it's not always who you expect. But there are lessons that need to be learned. And you can't be harsh with these people, because you want them to learn the art form. And it's not an easy thing to do, to become a carver, because it's a self-discipline. You have to sit there and do it. You have to do all your groundwork before you can carve a mask; you have to learn about tools, you have to learn about wood. You have to learn about asking for help. You have to learn about everything. You can't just learn how to carve; it's learning about everything, it's learning about life.

As a carver my mission is to bring back Coast Salish Lummi carving. And my work has reached out, too. I'm getting a little taste of what Joe got to experience: to have your work go out to different places, different tribes, different countries, and to have it recognized and to have it loved not only by our own people but by other cultures too. There's a feeling that carries, and it doesn't have words. It just feels like a very big honor. This art form creates so much energy, and it creates so much spirituality. It reminds me that people are spiritually hungry. It pulls people in for the spirituality of the piece, not just the piece of work.

Our work that was done, say, a hundred years ago or a hundred and fifty years ago, when it was being collected for museums — that work was done in secret by what they now call a secret society. So our work was very well kept. There is still a lot of our work that belonged to our people that never got collected and is still sitting in closets, wrapped in old towels and sheets. Now that I've learned a little bit about the world of museums and keeping the climate stable, I wish some of these old pieces could be taken care of better, because they are decaying. I know that there are very few pieces of Salish work to be studied. But I just think that they were very well kept. When I did my research in all the museums, there were only about seventeen pieces of Coast Salish work at the Smithsonian in Washington DC. But they have thousands of northern works, thousands of Eskimo works, and Athabascan works, and Aleut works. But Coast Salish: why only seventeen pieces? It was very well kept. All the healers had their own powers. There was the *sgwədíləč* or the *tusted* sticks or just their own power. They didn't have to have an object to have power. The true power is silent.

7 I Look to the Old People

Reflections on Joe Hillaire and Carving

SCOTT KADACH' ĀAK'U JENSEN

ONE SUMMER DAY I WAS SITTING AT MY KITCHEN table and a sudden thought came into my head: "I'm going to carve a totem pole." I was in my twenties, had worked many different jobs, and hadn't felt fulfilled by any of them. This thought about carving was odd enough in that I had no experience with it and knew next to nothing about Northwest Coast art. Even stranger was that I got up from the table that day and went down to the Bellingham Art Museum and bought Bill Holm's book *Northwest Coast Indian Art*, which at that time was a new book (now in its sixteenth printing). I went to the lumber yard and picked out some wood and then stopped by the hobby shop and bought some X-acto blades. First I tried carving some flat work with the inadequate tools I had chosen. I remember going up to the University of British Columbia, where Mungo Martin and Bill Reid were carving the beautiful totems that are still standing up there. I looked in the carving shed and saw their carving chips, which were as big as my hand, and it made me wonder, "What kind of tools are they using?" I went into the museum looking specifically at all the tools in its collection and then returned home to make the traditional adzes and crooked knives. Learning formline and carving has been that kind of self-taught process for me, which has been wonderful. It's taken me all over the place; I've met people I never would have met and had opportunities I never would have had. In Bellingham I had a little shop for a few years where I carved and sold my work directly to the public. A woman came into my shop one day, looked at all my carvings, and said, "Would you like to come to Craig, Alaska, and teach some Tlingit kids toolmaking and carving?" Two weeks later I was in Alaska, working with a small group of high school kids.

Around 1983, when the Northwest Indian College out at Lummi was starting to offer courses, Bob Lawrence called to ask if I would meet with him about teaching a carving class. I brought some of my carvings with me to the meeting. I remember when Sam Cagey arrived to the meeting, and the first thing he noticed was a bentwood halibut hook I had laid on the table. It reminded him of all the halibut hooks his dad had when he was a boy, and he hadn't seen others since then. They invited me to teach carving, which I did for three or four years. When I first began teaching at Lummi Community College, as it was known back then, I was teaching in the old vocational building. It had two sides, and Fran and Bill James were teaching basketry on the opposite side from my carving class. To increase enrollment in the early classes, the college had reached out to the non-Native community, and as a result the classes included both Native and non-Native students. On the first night, the Natives and non-Natives in both classes were sitting on opposite sides of the room. I usually bring food to events, knowing it is a universal icebreaker, and I did the same for these classes. It wasn't long before others began bringing food to class too. At each class, people increasingly mingled, until at the end of eight weeks all the people — all the weavers and carvers — were together, talking and sharing. We shared a common goal through learning and communicating, but it was the food that bridged that gap for the classes. That lesson is one that has influenced my teaching and my life ever since. I've been out to Taholah on the Olympic Peninsula to teach Quinault middle and high school kids to carve. I've taught up in Hatzic, British Columbia, at Xá:ytem, for the Stó:lō Nation, and in many other places. Anyone who comes to me, if they really want to know something, I want to help; to share and teach is as important to me as carving. Now I teach classes at my studio for all people who want to attend.

When I started carving, I tried drawing formline, the black-and-red two-dimensional design work particular to the Northwest Coast. I went to the local museum and looked at an old bentwood box, trying to copy those designs. I headed out to Lummi and saw Al Charles working on a totem in his front yard; I was totally naive. I stopped and said, "Excuse me, I see you're working on a totem. I'm interested in this, and I've done some drawings. Can I show them to you?" He looked at them, and he held them for a long time. He said, "There are not many people who can do this. Where did you learn?" and I said, "Well, I'm just trying to learn." After that talk with Al, I really started to notice the carving that was happening at Lummi. I remembered the totem at the courthouse, the *Bellingham Centennial* history pole, which had been the first totem pole I'd ever seen, and I remembered the totem out at the Ferndale Library that used to be at the Mobil Refinery. I went to look at them again; both are Joe Hillaire's poles. I visited the museum and looked at Morrie Alexander's poles. Over the years, living here all my life and being surrounded by all this, the legacy grew in my mind. It seemed to me that Joe was one of the few "visible" Lummi carvers in that there were (and still are) many of his carvings in public view. He carved during a time when there were few carvers working in the Salish style. Joe's entire family was creative in one way or another, and Joe was bringing their culture forward in his generation, focusing on woodcarving and his dance group. I realized that Joe Hillaire was practicing this art when it wasn't very popular, when it wasn't appreciated and was looked down upon as primitive. Many prejudices existed against Native people, and Joe worked to build understanding between different cultures.

There is nothing primitive about Northwest Coast Native art. Consider formline: with five basic shapes you can create anything, you can cover any surface. Give me a box, give me a canoe, a trade gun, a shirt, or a headdress. I can cover the entire surface and have control of all the negative and positive spaces with formline. This art rivals any art form

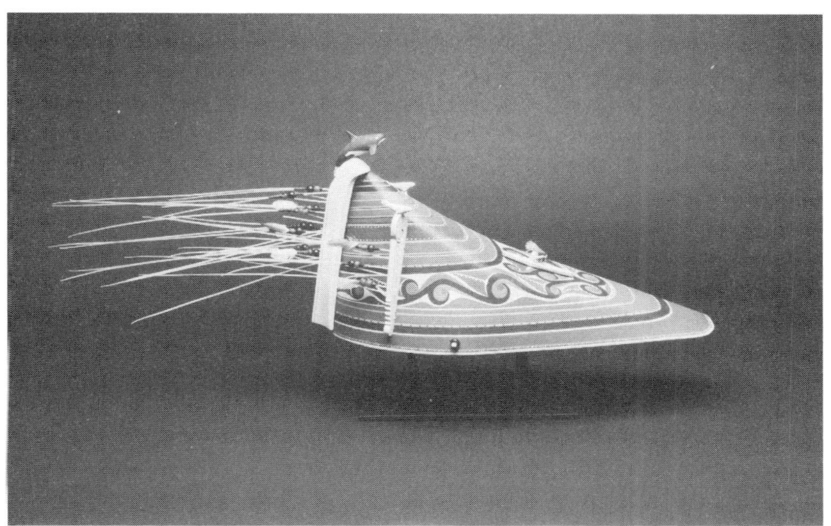

27. *Hunters on the Bering Sea*, Aleut-style chief's hat by Scott Jensen, 2011. Reprinted with permission. Photo by Carolyn Stone, the Stonington Gallery, Seattle.

that has ever existed in the world. One of the most complex and truly incredible man-made objects is an Aleut bentwood chief's hat. There are carbon-dated fragments of these bentwood hats from the Bering Sea that are two thousand years old. They are very difficult to make, even now with metal tools and specialized equipment. They consist of shaping a piece of wood, thinning it down in the correct places, leaving it thick in other places (in a very particular pattern), and if you do it all correctly, after steaming it, it folds up into an incredible hat-shaped form.

The art of the Pacific Northwest Coast is complex, diverse, and steeped in historical and cultural significance. A person can learn the techniques of these art forms; you can learn about totem carving, and you can learn about the flat two-dimensional design work, but I like to relate it to the alphabet or musical notes: it doesn't take long to learn the alphabet or the few notes that we have in music. They can be taught relatively simply, but what does it take to create art from those elements? How much talent and how many years does it take to write a great novel or to create a symphony? Joe Hillaire composed awesome symphonies.

Pauline Hillaire has followed in her father's footsteps through art, song, and storytelling, bridging a gap between cultures, promoting understanding, and sharing historical traditions with people outside of her culture. I know many others who have made this their life's work as well; it's been going on for generations, and yet inroads still need to be made. I remember the first time I met Pauline. I was teaching out at the Northwest Indian College. She wanted me to make some headdresses for her dance group. What I remember her saying to me was, "My dad always told me, if you want to get somebody to carve something for you, you need to get the best carver that you can find." I thought, "This is a wonderful thing," and I think it was at that point that I realized I had been studying the art and culture but that I really needed to focus on the culture to create the art. That was a big turning point for me.

I've been carving now for thirty-eight years and have begun to slow down and not struggle quite so much to earn a living. My reward is that now I have the time to get more in touch with the cultural part of my work. I carve mainly in the Tlingit style, though I am familiar with other styles as well. Last year at our wedding, my wife, Courtney, and I were adopted into the Tlingit culture and given Tlingit names. A Tlingit man who has carved with me, Fred Sat-Ka Fulmer, adopted me into the Chookaneidee Eagle Clan, and his wife, Ivy, adopted Courtney into the T'akdeintaan Raven Clan. I'm enjoying learning cultural traditions from my brother, Sat-Ka, and making pieces for their dance group, Língit Kustí.

I appreciate contemporary work, but when I look for inspiration, I look to the old people through their carvings. I tell people I am self-taught, but really my teachers were the carvers from the past. Looking at the old pieces and studying them closely, reading about them and studying the legends and the stories — they have been my real teachers. Even the tools themselves have been my teachers, because you can create this work with European-style tools, but it doesn't look the same. When I learned to make the knives — the bent knives and the adzes — the work took on a whole different form, look, and feeling. That was very important to me, because when I create a piece, I intend for it to be something that you might have seen here on the Northwest Coast three to five hundred years ago.

When I had been carving for just five or six years, I made ends meet working at a taxidermy shop, reconstructing the types of animals that I had been carving: the bear, the mountain goat, the deer, all the local animals. At first glance, when you look at Northwest Coast Native art, it seems abstract. I realized through taxidermy that there is realism within the abstract. I realized when taking apart a brown bear and putting it back together that the mask that I had just carved of the brown bear was very much the same: the curl of the nose, the shape of the eyes, the tilt of the ears. I thought that was one of the things that had been missing for me — and is missing for many people now — not knowing the animals intimately. To have the chance to be so close to those animals in their actual form was an education for me and helped my carving skills.

When I began carving and selling my work, I had to register a business name with the state of Washington, and I chose Speaking Cedar. That's what I feel; not so much that I'm speaking but that the history of cedar has been speaking to me. I've heard Lummi carver Felix Solomon speak about the lessons and the power of carving, and so many of these lessons I learned without elders like Pauline to help interpret them. For many years I asked, "Is it possible, if you're a carver, that you can just learn things from carving? Not being told or taught or having read it but to be carving and all of a sudden to understand things?" It turns out that it was like that for me with Joe's totems. The longer I worked as a carver, and the more I was around other people's carvings, the more I learned and was able to appreciate what I was seeing.

It was an honor to help restore Joe's *Centennial* history pole. It wasn't until we — Felix Solomon, Andrew Todd, and I — took the pole down and worked on it that I realized the real talent Joe Hillaire had not just as a carver but in his ability to create a character, to create a feeling. Over the years, the totem had been repainted and reworked to preserve it, but many layers of other people's interpretations of the piece had overlaid Joe's original vision. In restoring the pole it was important to us to uncover the original feeling Joe had carved into the piece. It's that spirit of tribal art — from all over the world — that draws people and has power. It is a way to make the unseen visible and tangible. If you are only looking at the craftsmanship and not the spirit of the work, you are not responding to the most important thing. You should be able to look at a piece, have an emotional reaction, and secondarily become aware of the artist's skill.

In my own work I try to keep a connection to the earliest pieces. This connection is very strong in Joe's work. Joe's style is very much connected to what I've seen in the old house posts, the very oldest ones from this geographic area, both here and across the Canadian border. Joe's work had his own style, it has its own spirit, and yet from looking at the few photographs of old house posts and the posts that exist in museums, one can see that, structurally, Joe's work is very much like the old pieces. When you look at the old Coast Salish poles, they look like a flat board with dimensionally carved figures placed on them, although they are carved from a single piece. This is very different from many of the contemporary Salish carvings you see, which are often carved more like the totems from the northern regions of the Pacific Northwest: deep relief carvings on rounded surfaces. The other thing that I've loved about Joe's work, which you can see in the *Man in Transition* pole at Northwest Indian College, is a sense of humor, a whimsy in the characters, in the faces, and in the things that are happening. Some of his works make me want to laugh out loud not necessarily because they are humorous but because they have spirit and attitude. His personality as an artist had many dimensions: psychology, politics, comedy, drama.

Another carver who was working in Joe's time was Kwakwa̱ka̱'wakw artist Mungo Martin. There's a video that was made by Barb Cranmer at the U'mista Cultural Society at Alert Bay called *A Slender Thread* that refers to an unbroken line of carvers carrying on their traditional art through the generations despite living through times of extreme oppression. I see Al Charles, Morrie Alexander, and Joe Hillaire as artists who maintained that slender thread in the Coast Salish region. That's the joy of watching Felix Solomon now, because he's someone who's very much interested in sharing what he's doing. He's interested in Lummi art, not just making art but all Lummi art, discovering what it is and what it means culturally, artistically, historically, personally. Years ago when I was living on Lummi Island, he came to me to ask about bending boxes. He asked, "Can I show you my boxes?" and so we talked about them. The wonderful thing about

Felix is that all I had to do was suggest a few things, and the next time I saw him, he had done the work. It is good to see him with all these people in the community, Native and non-Native, working with him, admiring what he is doing, being inspired by what he is doing.

The process of creating has a healing function no matter what that creation is. We all have the potential to gain satisfaction from whatever we do. My father was a butcher, which doesn't seem like an artistic thing or maybe even very important. I've been a deer hunter most of my adult life, but I remember the first time I went hunting, I didn't really know what to do with the animal I shot. I could field dress it, but I couldn't cut it up. When I got it home I called my dad, saying, "I've got this nice buck, and you know, I got it field dressed and skinned, but I don't know what to do from here." He said, "I'll be right there," and he came with all his knives, and I watched in amazement as he took this animal apart. He knew the location of every muscle, every joint, every bone, and it just came apart in his hands. It was amazing; it was an art. It made me appreciate the art of skillful action. So in the simplest terms, I think that skillful action is a healing thing, because when you feel good doing creative work, it's good for you. I have gone through many tough times in my life, as we all do. One of the anchoring things I found was to be able to carve, to focus on that, and to meditate while I was working, experiencing the smell of the wood, the feeling of the wood. Seeing wood transform into a new form is very healing.

For years Pauline has told me stories about her father and the achievements he made in his lifetime; the work he left behind is a monument to his dedication. I have always thought that one of the best careers a Native person can pursue is to practice his or her cultural arts. Not only can it be a financial success for them and their family, but it is culturally important, bringing pride, meaning, and respect to their traditions. Contemporary Native art perpetuates Native culture, keeping it current and relevant. As one who has spent a lifetime carving and teaching, I encourage all Native people, young and old, who feel the calling to follow the tradition of carving. The rest of the world is ready for the art form and looking to understand it, as awareness has been raised and attitudes changed over recent decades.

8 A Thin Red Line

Pigments and Paint Technology of the Northwest Coast

MELONIE ANCHETA

EVER SINCE THE EARLIEST HUMAN BEINGS CREATED charcoal and red ochre paintings deep in caves, every culture has used color in the forms of pigments, dyes, and paints to bring to life their dreams, their environment, and their experiences. Among Native people of the Northwest Coast, the application of mineral pigments and vegetable dyes to objects and to their own bodies has been one of the most enduring expressions of creativity, spirituality, and identity throughout millennia, and it still is today.[1] Prior to trade with Anglo-Europeans, the Indians of the Northwest Coast relied entirely on their environment for pigments and paints from a variety of sources, including colored earths, stones, burnt materials, and organic binders.

The first part of this chapter, "Coloring in the Northwest Coast," examines minerals and methods that Native artists of the Pacific Northwest used ancestrally to make pigments. The second part, "Trade Colors in the Northwest," is about the paints that became available to carvers beginning in the nineteenth century. The final section, "Paint on Joe Hillaire's

Totem Poles," offers observations on several of Hillaire's major works, their painting and repainting histories, their color schemes, and Joe's stylistic uses of color and form.

COLORING IN THE NORTHWEST COAST

Colors have universal associations; for example, blue evokes the calming sense of the vast expanse of sky and water, while green gives us a sense of vitality and harmony. At the same time, different cultures imbue colors with particular meanings. In the Northwest, specific culture groups associate deep meanings with particular colors. This is evident in the consistent palettes that have persisted throughout the history of particular cultures. Contemporary northern Northwest Coast and Coast Salish artists are still painting with colors used by their ancestors a thousand years ago. Among the northern tribes — Haida, Tlingit, and Tsimshian — the palette was and still is narrow, consisting of only three colors: black, red, and blue or green. In the North color schemes are based on a long tradition of design consisting of primary, secondary, tertiary, and negative space. Primary spaces are usually black and occasionally red. Secondary spaces are usually red. Sometimes black and red are reversed as primary and secondary colors. Only in the tertiary spaces are blue or green used. Among the Tlingit, prior to trade with Europeans, blue was apparently most often reserved for shamans and ritual work. The Haida used a pale green in tertiary fields. In the North there are long-standing rules about the design elements and about color use.

The Coast Salish have displayed more freedom in their carving style and in their use of color. They have used a wider palette of yellows, blues, greens, black, reds, and white. Yellows, reds, blues, and greens are earth pigments found as clays or stones. These pigments were ground and mixed with the proteins and oils from salmon eggs and a little human saliva, which provides an enzyme to help bind the oils and pigments together.

Black pigments were made from a variety of materials, including charred woods, soot, and burnt calciferous materials such as bone. The minerals magnetite and graphite were also used for black. White was made from calcium carbonate (chalk), gypsum, and soft white clay called kaolin,

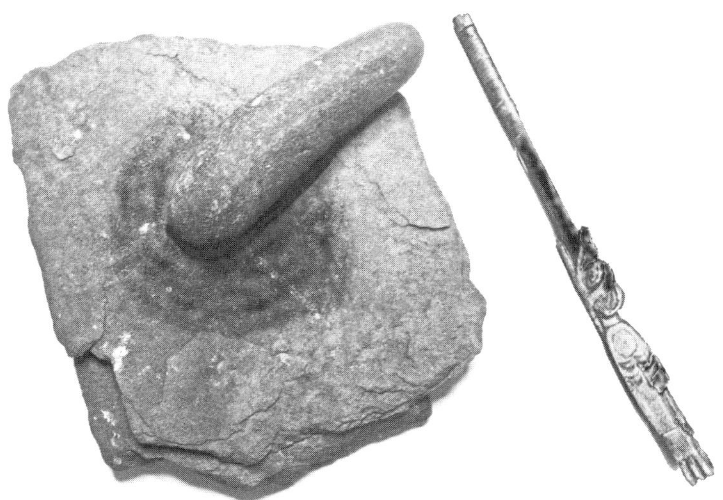

28. Flat mortar and small pestle; antique carved paintbrush. Reprinted with permission. Photo by Melonie Ancheta.

which has been used by Europeans and Chinese for making porcelain and china and is one of the most common minerals in the world. White was also obtained from roasting a particular species of clam shell. Greens were made from the mineral celadonite, which is an iron silicate found all over the world; it is often called green earth. For many years it was believed that greens and blues came from copper compounds, but research done by the Canadian Conservation Institute has qualitatively shown that there is no copper in these pigments, that the beautiful greens we see are celadonite.[2] Celadonite has the interesting characteristic of being able to be used with or without a binder like fish egg oil. It can be applied simply with water and is surprisingly durable. I have seen well-used objects painted with celadonite and water that are in excess of four hundred years old, and the paint is still intact. When water is used, the color tends to be powdery and pale but gives a good range of transparency (functioning more as a stain and letting the wood show through) to opacity (coating the wood so it is not visible). When mixed with oil, celadonite darkens, has a harder finish, and has a satin patina. Fish egg oils are not the only oils that can cause this alteration; spindle whorls painted with water-based celadonite have changed color and patina from contact with lanolin (oil) in the sheep wool spun on them.

The mineral vivianite provides a wide range of blue to dark blue-green hues depending on its state of oxidation and photochemical process. Vivianite is an iron phosphate, another "earth" pigment known as blue earth, and is widely occurring in areas of glacial deposits and other geologic conditions typical of the Northwest Coast. It can be found as friable (easily broken up, usually dry) clay, as heavy wet clay, as a medium hard stone, and in crystalline form. Among the northern tribes, vivianite appears to have been used almost exclusively by Tlingit shamans, but the Coast Salish and Nuu-chah-nulth on the west coast of Vancouver Island used it freely on a variety of objects. Like celadonite, it can be used with a water base or an oil base with similar results.

Yellow paint came from yellow ochres (a general term for clays used to make what are known as earth colors) and is now known as Mars yellow. Yellow ochre is hydrated ferric (iron) oxide. Red ochre is a variant of yellow ochre that can range in hue (hue meaning actual color, identified by a common name such as red or bluish green) from a golden yellow to a brown. Red ochre today is frequently called red iron oxide. There are many oxides; the earth's crust is made up primarily of solid oxides (along with sulfides, which are another chemical compound not addressed here). Oxides occur when an element such as iron is exposed to oxygen in the air. Red ochre can be obtained from yellow ochre by roasting the yellow to drive out the hydrogen, darkening the mineral to red in the process. Red ochre also occurs naturally as a loose earth, a clay, or a stone and is one of the most abundant minerals on earth. Hematite, although black or dark gray as a solid stone, was also used as red; ground hematite oxidizes and offers a variety of reds during the oxidizing process. Hematite is also found in a soft form. These ochres and hematite have a very similar chemical makeup, requiring only some manipulation, such as roasting or grinding (which exposes the molecules to oxygen), to achieve particular hues. Ochres and other mineral pigments are found and mined all over the world. Red and yellow ochre have been and still are used by virtually every culture in the world for a variety of purposes.

Celadonite (green earth) is an iron silicate found the world over and has also been used since prehistory. Celadonite paint has been found at rock painting sites in Argentina and on a Mayan temple in Honduras.[3] This pigment was used frequently by the Renaissance masters to tint (adding a small amount of another color to modify the base color) flesh colors and add depth to greens in landscapes. For hundreds of years, celadonite has been prized for use as a facial mask beauty treatment. I can walk into my local food co-op and buy it ground to a fine powder by the ounce or pound. These pigments have been used since prehistoric times by innumerable cultures and are still in use today among indigenous cultures. They are also used by high-tech cultures for a wide variety of applications, not just as pigments.

Native people of the Northwest Coast had such an intimate knowledge of their environment that they knew how and where to find these mineral pigments in the landscape. Over time they became masters at making paints, sometimes by trial and error, sometimes by process of deduction, sometimes by intuition and ingeniousness, and perhaps at times by happy accident. They also became masters of paint technology, learning which types of furs or bristles to use for brushes. (Almost all the brushes I have examined, and they number in the hundreds, use porcupine hair.) They used an ingenious method of laying the long bristles along the length of the brush and then wrapping it, sometimes in elaborate patterns resembling basket patterns, with spruce root. As the bristles wore out, they loosened the wrapping and extended the bristles, rewrapped, and went back to work. The majority of brushes I've examined all bear these same characteristics, and all have bristles worn down. Of the hundreds of brushes I have seen, all but about a half dozen were beautifully ornamented with carved, often highly detailed designs.

We can only make educated guesses about how Native people of the Northwest learned to obtain the minerals and what to use as binders, how they processed minerals by methods such as roasting, how they determined which minerals needed an oil medium and which were durable with only water as a medium, and how they manipulated the range of a color to achieve a desired shade (a full, definite degree of difference between two colors).[4] Their choices of colors and color schemes demonstrate mastery of how to manipulate the interplay of light and shadow with color to evoke particular effects. Details about the methods by which Native Northwest artists developed their science of pigments and paint technology are lost in history, but Native artists have carried on the use of traditional mineral pigments, methods, and materials down through the generations.

TRADE COLORS IN THE NORTHWEST

With the coming of the traders and explorers to the Northwest Coast, new pigments slowly became available to Natives. An analysis of artifacts from the eighteenth century to the present shows that the colors used historically are still commonly used today; the palette has not changed much with the passage of time or influence from other cultures. When commercial paints became available, Indians did not abandon their ancient methods of making paint; they have made use of both traditional and manufactured paints from contact up to the present, remaining true to traditional colors and color schemes. But the use of earth pigments became increasingly rare as fewer artists carried knowledge of traditional materials and methods and as manufactured paints of every conceivable color became more readily available. The availability of commercial paint colors must have been an exciting and inspiring advent for Native artists. It had to be an extraordinarily heady experience for an artist who grew up digging, cleaning, roasting, grinding, and mixing his own paint to walk into a store and trade for or purchase a premixed container holding an amazing and brilliant color like cadmium yellow, which became available in 1842, ultramarine blue (1828), carbon black (1864), or zinc white (1845). Vermilion, a brilliant orangey red in use for thousands of years in China, has been determined to be the first nonindigenous pigment used by Northwest Coast Indians and can be found on thousands of artifacts. Current research on the use of cinnabar among Northwest Coast Natives prior to trade provides some evidence that cinnabar was used as a pigment long before trade.[5] Cinnabar is the base mineral for vermilion and is frequently found mixed with commercially manufactured vermilion on postcontact artifacts. Cinnabar is mercury sulfide (common ore of mercury), which occurs naturally in the Northwest as a dark reddish-brown mineral.

Red lead (which was first manufactured in the fourteenth century) was the second significant trade pigment to reach the Northwest Coast, arriving on English sailing vessels in the nineteenth century. The English had used red lead paint for hundreds of years (and still do, although it no longer contains lead) to paint the decks of their ships. Unbeknownst to both Indians and Europeans at that time, red lead paint was highly toxic when it was used for body paint or was ingested, causing serious illness or death. It was banned in England in the 1940s and in the United States in the 1970s. The first trade-blue arrived in the nineteenth century in the form of laundry bluing packets. It was quickly adopted by Natives, and since there were no restrictions on using it, it became the blue of choice for a variety of objects. The synthetic ultramarine blue paint used today is a direct outgrowth of the brilliant ultramarine blue of laundry bluing.

Although there was a growing palette of new colors available, Indians still faced some of the same problems as with mineral pigment paints, such as having no way to prevent paint from drying out overnight, thus requiring that a fresh batch be mixed each day. This led to some variation in paint color, opacity (degree of coverage to hide the surface), and impasto (thickness and roughness of paint, or heavy layers built up with visible brush strokes) on pieces that could not be painted in a single day.

In spite of the availability of an ever-growing variety of colors, Northwest Native artists did not stray far or for long from their traditional palettes. It is rare to find an artifact or totem pole painted with colors that deviate from those customarily used. It is clear that Indians were receptive and quickly adapted to new tools, techniques, and materials introduced by traders and colonists, but their adherence to traditional colors is a clear statement of the cultural significance of color.

PAINT ON JOE HILLAIRE'S TOTEM POLES

In the twentieth century, Lummi carver Joe Hillaire and other carvers had a wide variety of oil-based paints to choose from to paint their totem and story poles. Until the 1960s, the only commercial paints available were oil-based paints. Linseed oil was the favorite oil among several oil choices, which included walnut, poppy, castor, and hempseed, used as binders for mineral pigments. Locally, Dutch Boy Paint, which was then a linseed oil–based paint, was available and was the most popular brand.[6] In the 1960s, acrylic paints were developed and quickly became popular because of their quick drying and ease of cleanup with water. The time required and the conditions necessary for oil-based paint to properly dry entailed a painstaking process that was alleviated by the new paints. Given the timing of acrylic-based paint becoming available to the public, it is obvious that Joe Hillaire's poles painted in the 1950s were painted with oil-based paints. It is clear from visual examination that those poles painted in the 1960s were painted with acrylic paints, as are the poles that have been repainted post-1960. Today an artist can go to the local artists' supply shop or hardware store and choose from thousands of colors or even have a color mixed. For totem pole carvers it is especially convenient, because they can obtain any amount, from pints to five-gallon buckets, of any color they need.

Close examination of the *Schelangen* pole, the *Bellingham Centennial* pole, and the *Land in the Sky* pole shows that each one has been painted at least twice and, in the case of the *Centennial* pole, possibly as many as four times. *Land in the Sky* shows evidence of having been painted three times: there are three layers of paint clearly visible in various areas. When the carving of *Land in the Sky* was finished, Joe Hillaire and his daughter Pauline agreed it should not be painted in order to allow chiaroscuro (the natural play of shadow and light) and the beauty of the wood to enliven the pole. Sometime after it was moved to Suquamish, *Land in the Sky* was painted using bold colors similar to those used on the *Centennial* pole ten years earlier. Later in its life *Land in the Sky* was again painted using flat, muted colors and pastels. Large parts of the pole, which the previous paint job had left as natural wood, were painted pale blue or white, and the pole was covered entirely with paint. The most recent paint is badly weathered, flaking away to reveal large areas of weathered and rotted wood and the earliest colors: rusty orange, scarlet, deep blue, and vivid blue-green. These original colors can also be seen in photographs of the *Schelangen* pole when it was first erected. It too has been overpainted with pastel colors, including pink, which has never been an acceptable color on the Coast Salish palette.

Joe Hillaire normally chose bold, bright colors to bring the viewer's attention to the various characters and elements on his poles. He thoughtfully chose colors that would enhance aspects of the story the pole is telling. At this time the only poles that bear colors that match closely those that Joe originally chose are the *Centennial* pole and the Kobe-Seattle Sister Cities friendship pole. When the *Centennial* pole was recently restored, a great deal of detailed cleaning, examination, and thoughtful analysis was done to determine what the original colors were. With each overpainting of the *Centennial* pole, the original color scheme was changed, with no regard to the original colors. The most recent restoration team for the *Centennial* pole, carvers Felix Solomon and Scott Jensen and conservator Andrew Todd, found archival photographs, and after digging through and stripping off layers of old paint, they were able to closely match the original colors that Joe Hillaire had used.

Joe knew that the use of red (or another bright color) as an accent can help the eye of the viewer immediately focus attention on a particular element. Joe used a red accent line around the eyes of the bear on his *Man in Transition* totem pole. Joe also used a little red in the nostrils and just a bit of red in the bear's mouth. The red is faded now, but when it was fresh, it would have been a distinct draw for the eye of the viewer. Even the smallest red spots and the thinnest of red lines help us focus not just on the features bearing red (in fact, most people do not even realize they are seeing the red) but on the entire design, by immediately orienting our perception of many features into a single cohesive picture. Red triangles beside the face of the Bear Dancer on the *Centennial* pole serve as visual signals to draw our attention to and to accent the dancer's face. The yellow details on the Wolf Dancer's regalia quickly inform us that his body is in motion, highlighting the positioning of his body in middance. The Flea in red and yellow stands out against the dark background, instantly signaling that he is a very deliberate and integral character in this story.

The *Man in Transition* pole is an aesthetically and visually interesting work that differs from Joe Hillaire's other totem poles both in the carving and in the painting. The paint job is understated and subtle, letting the carving take precedence. The black paint outlining the eye sockets and mouth, covering the cheeks, and running up into the spear headdress help emphasize the facial characteristics of this man who has struggled through the transformation from beast to human, from boy to man. The torso of the man is weathered bare wood, but the lower half of his body is carved to look like bear fur and painted black to reinforce this look. The green of the serpents and around the headdress spears is a simple contrast to the dark wood and black paint. The Eagle is also painted simply with a black background on which simple circles embellish the wings and chest. The Eagle's feet and head are painted naturally: the head is white, and the feet are yellow. Of all Joe Hillaire's poles, this is the least colorful and has the least paint. Yet it tells a powerful, archetypal story that is easily read and meaningful in any culture.

Joe Hillaire used color to emphasize the characters and creatures on his poles, bringing them to life and bringing oral tradition to visual life. Joe chose colors that complemented each other to help tell the story; he chose colors deliberately, thoughtfully, and with a sense of tradition and artistry to bring his visions and stories to life for thousands of viewers. Joe, like his ancestors, used color to bring visual life to traditional stories and characters and to bring life to stories relevant to the cultural, social, and political issues of his day.

NOTES

1. Vegetable matter was used for dyes (for wool and hides) and for staining objects (horn, wood, leather). When they are fixed by a mordant (i.e., made stable by an additive such as urine), most colors obtained from vegetation are long-lived in wool for weavings but are transparent and fugitive (they fade with time) on wood and leather.

2. Wainwright, Moffat, and Sirois, "Occurrences of Green Earth Pigment," 17.

3. Wainwright et al., "Identification of Pigments," 23–24; and Goodall et al., "Raman Microscopic Investigation."

4. Mayer, *A Dictionary of Art Terms*.

5. Melonie Ancheta, "Pre-trade Pigments of Northwest Coast Natives," article in progress.

6. Terry Peterson, interview by the author, Bellingham, Washington, September 16, 2011.

9 Maintaining Integrity

Totem Pole Conservation and the Restoration of the Centennial *History Pole*

ANDREW TODD

TOTEM POLES OF THE NINETEENTH AND TWENTIETH CENTURIES

PROJECTS TO CONSERVE TOTEM POLES HAVE BEEN motivated by many factors. In the early twentieth century, totem poles were restored and moved to new locations as tourist sights. Examples of this history border the rail lines through northern British Columbia. As landmarks, these totem poles were highly prized by the developers of tourist transportation routes. Even city parks were known early in the twentieth century to value totem poles as cultural attractions. Other conservation motivations came from well-meaning anthropologists in the museum field who believed for a long time that First Nations cultures were dying out and needed to have examples of their history saved in museums for the future. However, in First Nations communities, where totem pole art was practiced, people were suffering from illness, economic hardship, and displacement from their Native lands and ways of life. As a result, the work of carving and maintaining totem poles and other cultural works took second place to survival. Only a few artists, trained in the ways of the old carvers, managed to keep a thread of the past alive by making new totem poles in their Native communities and for customers in tourism, trade shows, and fairs.

Totem poles became highly valued collectibles for museums during the late nineteenth and early twentieth centuries. Museums acknowledged the value of these large, beautifully carved works of art and saw the potential for increasing visitor attendance. In many cases, totem poles were placed in stairwells of museums or outdoors on museum grounds or in public parks. Cities all over North America began to display totem poles as an attraction to their museums and as a form of cultural instruction in park landscapes. Artists who continued to carve totem poles sustained a thin line of cultural tradition in this field. Often they were trained by fathers, grandfathers, uncles, and stepfathers, and they continued the tradition of their ancestors as knowledge was passed down through the generations. Historians looking back at the period through the early twentieth century acknowledge that the continuation of the art form was very tenuous. Now, however, in the twenty-first century, the art form is thriving in many ways, and preservation of the old totem poles is being undertaken to try to preserve the record that was maintained through difficult times.

CONSERVATION METHODS

Although traditions of carving were being maintained by a small group of artists on the Northwest Coast, concern began to grow in the conservation field for the preservation of totem poles that had been collected and were on display in museums and parks. Many totem poles even remained in museum storage and were still in need of conservation steps for their survival. The field of conservation as a scientific method of analyzing and treating artifacts was growing during this same period. Conservators studied wood and factors of deterioration, and they began to develop techniques for arresting the process of deterioration and stabilizing the materials. Several standard methods were developed and shared among conservators who had responsibility for preservation of totem poles in the museum collections. Approaches to conservation treatment were first identified for particular applications to wood in indoor environments and then adapted for those totem poles that stood outdoors in parks and public spaces. Workshops dedicated to sharing this conservation knowledge among conservators and First Nations artists were developed by conservators, First Nations curators, and educators and conducted in several Northwest Coast communities. Over a fifteen-year span to 2010, a number of workshops and lectures have been presented on the conservation of Northwest Coast totem poles.

The conservation workshops have all emphasized fundamentals of conservation treatment, beginning with cultural research to identify and place the totem pole within its historical and social context. In each case, deeper research places the particular totem pole within the context of the total output of the artist. Then the material project begins with a focus on examination and documentation, creating records of the original forms and styles of carving, painting, and relationships of color and form within the style of the totem pole. The making of a record focuses on accurate measurements, sketches and photographs, and references to any changes and previous repairs. These standard methods of documentation are then followed by the steps of treatment, including cleaning, consolidation, and repair. The process concludes with application of a final protective coating or finish. All the stages of conservation treatment have been researched, and the methods have been compared and reviewed by peer professionals in the field. New materials used in conservation treatments have all been tested and are recommended by conservation science labs or by repeated practice in field situations. As in all conservation practice, procedures and ethical standards for the conservation of totem poles have been researched, reviewed, and published.[1] These procedures and standards are shared on an international level by conservators; this is important, since totem poles are now spread around the world. In museums, parks, and public spaces in many countries of the world, totem poles stand as cultural ambassadors of the arts of the Northwest Coast.

There are similarities and differences in the approaches to preservation taken by artists and those taken by conservators. Usually both wish to maintain the integrity of an original totem pole, although sometimes different methods are employed. An artist, through family connections, may feel entitled to proceed with an intervention using materials and techniques developed in the woodworking crafts traditions, which are often used by artists. A conservator, meanwhile, will wish to avoid intervention as much as possible and will use proven materials tested in scientific labs for their longevity and stability. Carvers, throughout the last century of totem pole history and possibly before then, have been known to replicate historical totem poles. Conservators, on the other hand, tend toward leaving old totem poles in a protected environment to remain as a record for historical purposes.

RIGHTS AND REPLICATION

Examples of replicated totem poles can still be found standing in public locations, sometimes now in need of preservation. The original totem pole, from which the copy was made, can be hard to find, often stored away from any public location. Museums have been asked to receive old totem poles and keep them for posterity. The replicated totem poles found in one community in British Columbia were copied from poles that had been acquired from abandoned villages on Haida Gwaii. The acquisition of totem poles from abandoned villages is a matter with serious ethical implications. Some recipients of these totem poles have obtained receipts to document the acquisition of the poles. A number of related ethical issues require serious consideration, which is beyond the scope of this essay. When poles are acquired from abandoned villages, the next-generation totem pole then contains its own record of legends and history, while the original becomes a mysterious archive of information, no longer completely fulfilling the purpose of representing the original legend and history. Added to the messages of past and present are issues surrounding the quality of carving in a replicated pole. The age and quality of the log that was used for a replica is also a factor in judging the final outcome of a replica totem pole. Even paint can have an important influence on the appearance, and therefore the record, of a totem pole that has been copied. The original, as regards the intention of its design, method of execution, and decorative finish, can be so unique that a replica really becomes a new interpretation of an old theme, and theoretical debate about originality and replication is truly unnecessary. These are all issues that affect the performance of conservation treatments for totem poles.

The right to perform conservation treatment is also a matter of controversy, especially if descendants of First Nations artists claim authority for any intervention or restorative treatment. In First Nations communities, the authority to permit treatment — or any change — often lies with the descendants of the original artist. Where these relationships are known and acknowledged, work on totem pole preservation can be delegated either to another (usually tribally related) artist or to a direct descendant of the original artist. Conservation work carried out by descendants or by a delegated artist is usually carried out according to the same fundamental principles and practices as those of a conservator. In many cases, artists descended from the original artist will work together with a conservator to develop and carry out a conservation treatment.

JOE HILLAIRE'S CENTENNIAL TOTEM POLE

In the case of Joseph Hillaire's totem pole known as the *Bellingham Centennial* pole, the artist's daughter Pauline Hillaire took responsibility for the care and preservation of the pole. Her decisions for treatment included her choice of an appointed artist, Felix Solomon (Lummi/Haida), as the designated artist to work together with a conservator to develop and carry out a conservation treatment. This project was successfully carried out between August 2006 and April 2009. Working together to preserve Hillaire's *Centennial* pole created a bond between myself as the conservator, Felix Solomon as the designated cultural artist from the Coast Salish Lummi Nation, and Felix's friend and carving teacher Scott Jensen, a master carver. Our project to conserve the totem pole required in-depth discussions and serious research, combing through disparate sources of visual and written information. Our discussions always revolved around the best practices of wood conservation while concentrating on the unique style and intention of Joe Hillaire's original work. Beyond employing

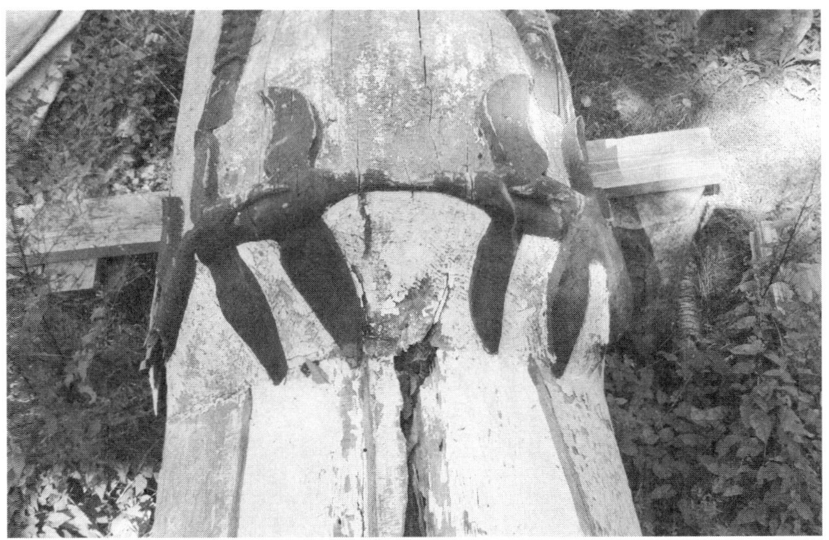

29. Condition of Joe Hillaire's *Land in the Sky* totem pole in 2010. Reprinted with permission. Photo by Melonie Ancheta.

the best possible practices, we strived to find and present Joe's best work in order to transform it safely from the state that it was in to a durable, long-lasting future. In a way, it was a rebuilding of his artistic achievements in order to set them into a protected space where this particular cultural record of his work could be observed, studied, and appreciated.

Other teams have dealt with preservation projects for totem poles, for example, the Gitxsan Nation, whose work has been developed in several villages within their territory. As these totem poles were delivered beyond the boundaries of Gitxsan territories into public parks, private and corporate collections, and museum holdings, the same need for care and maintenance has been required. The "northern" style of the totem poles from the Gitxsan, Tsimshian, Tlingit, and Haida Nations is often seen as similar to the "southern" style of the Coast Salish. The approach to conservation is a scientific method, but attention to and respect for the special nature of Coast Salish work, such as that of artist Joe Hillaire, are necessary conditions. As other writers have noted, the style of presentation of subject and ground is different in Coast Salish art, and dedication to these style distinctions requires a preservation plan that attends to details of how the totem pole was carved and painted.

Contemporary reasons for beginning a conservation project for totem poles differ from efforts in earlier history to re-create a cultural landscape for the sake of the tourist market. Yet the totem poles from that era are still in need of preservation. For example, the old totem poles along the railroads of northern British Columbia are in serious need of restoration and protection. The same is true for the valuable legacy of carved Coast Salish cultural objects. Hillaire's totem poles have reached an age in their lives when care is required in order to preserve them into the future. The totem poles of Joe Hillaire constitute a valuable record of Coast Salish cultural history and the traditions of the people of the territory.

NOTE

1. Cranmer-Webster, "Conservation and Cultural Centres"; Feist and Mraz, *Wood Finishing*; Florian, Beauchamp, and Kennedy, "Haida Totem Pole Conservation Program"; Rhyne, "Changing Approaches"; Rhyne, "Recent Approaches"; Todd, "Totem Pole Conservation"; Todd, "The Island of Impermanence"; Todd, "Painted Memory."

10 Archetypes from Cedar

Myth and Coast Salish Story Poles

GREGORY P. FIELDS

CARL JUNG BEGAN WORK ON HIS AUTOBIOGRAPHY four years before his death in 1961 at age eighty-five. His prologue to *Memories, Dreams, and Reflections* begins with the words "My life is a story." He speaks of his autobiography as the telling of his personal myth. The language of myth, not the language of science, Jung wrote, is the language that can be used to speak of the process of personal growth: "Science works with concepts of averages, which are far too general to do justice to the subjective variety of an individual life. My life is a story," he wrote, "of the self-realization of the unconscious. Everything in the unconscious seeks outward manifestation, and the personality too, desires to evolve out of its unconscious conditions and to experience itself as whole." In his autobiography, Jung reflects on his inner life and on his remarkable career of clinical and theoretical work, in which he founded the tradition of analytic psychology. He speaks as a person fluently conversant with the world's traditions of religion and mythology and as a person whose inner psychic life was a productive field for both his scientific inquiry and for the creating of his own life as art. Jung wrote the following, among the final conclusions that he articulated toward the end of his life: "In the end, the only events in my life worth telling are those when the imperishable world irrupted into this transitory one. That is why I speak chiefly of inner experiences, amongst which I include my dreams and visions. They form the *prima materia* of my scientific work. They were the fiery magma out of which the stone that had to be worked was crystallized."[1]

Jung and other thinkers have explored how the human process of transformation toward wholeness is provoked and supported by the psyche's engagement with symbols and archetypes encountered in dreams, art, and myth. This chapter considers how stories and myths can be transformative and healing, and how Coast Salish story poles function as a medium of archetype and myth.

Storytelling is one of the most ancient and universal of human activities. The reading of printed texts (let alone access to electronic media) is a relatively recent activity in human history. Since prehistoric times, people have gathered to tell and hear stories, and they still do. Many benefits are received in the hearing of stories, among them, companionship, instruction, inspiration, admonition, entertainment, and solace. One of the most important functions of stories is that they connect us with the wonderment of being. One kind of wonderment is the sense of *wondering* about questions concerning the universe and our human journey. Another kind of wonderment is a sense of *awe* at the greatness of the universe and the greatness of our human experience, wonderment in which we recognize our connection with that which is greater than ourselves. Even among the humble details that make up our lives, we can recognize the greatness of certain episodes of our life's journey. Myths can also redirect our focus away from our ordinary state of absorption in the details of our individual lives and limited perspectives so that we can, at least for a while, connect with important elements of our cultural traditions and common humanity. By participating in a myth, we can experience the vastness of the universe and presence of the sacred.

Response to a sense of connection with that which is greater than ourselves — God, the divine, the sacred, the Great Universe, or however it might be named — is at the heart of the human impulse toward spiritual life. On the side of the spiritual domain are principles of functionality, order, development, healing, and well-being, as distinct from, for example, dysfunction, disorder, lack of development, deterioration, and suffering. Myths provide powerful examples of healthy, constructive functioning and examples of destructive dysfunction. In so doing, myths help perpetuate insight and transformation, which are conducive to individual and community well-being.

STORIES AND MYTHS

The book *Life Lived Like a Story* contains the histories and traditional stories of three Yukon Native elders.[2] Each of the three Native women recounted her biography in her chosen way, including the traditional narratives that she regarded as essential to her life story. Our stories, personal and shared, are essential to our constituting and expressing our identities. Stories help us to understand and to lead our lives, to share our lives with others, and, to an extent, to create the journey that our lives become. The type of story that I would like to focus on here is myth and its transformative and healing power. Myth is a different kind of story from the kinds of stories that we tell about our lives, but myth is one of the means — one of the medicines — that we can use to create, and to cope with, the extended story that is our own life.

Stories, and myths in particular, are among humanity's most ancient and enduring ways of expressing and evoking patterns of meaning that help us to experience and respond to wonderment, to make sense of the tragedies of the human journey, and to cultivate our psyches and societies in the direction of functionality, order, healing, and health. There are many kinds of stories, including tales, fables, epics, myths, and legends. The distinctions between them are better understood in terms of gradations on a spectrum rather than in terms of distinct categories, but in order to point out some of the main purposes served by different kinds of stories, I'll say a few words about terms that are used for the various types.[3] In general, tales (including folktales and fairy tales) are told for enjoyment. Tales often give accounts of the origins and functions of natural phenomena, such as the story that Pauline Hillaire learned from her father about why the raccoon has curly feet (see chapter 30, "The Mink Family and the Raccoon Family"). But tales also teach lessons, as evident in this folktale of the out-of-control Raccoon family, who learn from the Mink family about parenting skills and respectful family dynamics. A fable is meant to be entertaining, but it has the primary purpose of instruction, often concerning moral life: "It is not, like myth, a revelation of transcendental mysteries, but a clever illustration of a political or ethical point."[4] An epic is a long narrative in poetic form, spoken or written in a ceremonial style of language. The word "epic" derives from the Greek *epikos*, from *epos*, "word, speech, poem." An epic may or may not be accompanied by music, but the oral presentation of an epic, even though it is not chanted or sung, is musical. Robert Bringhurst, translator of Haida oral epics, speaks of oral poetry as "a story carved in the air like spoken music, a voice in the dark that could only be stored as a light in the mind."[5]

The word "myth" carries two opposed meanings. Myth can refer to a belief that is not true, or not entirely true. But in the context of literature and oral literature, myth designates a story that is not intended to be literally true. Rather, myths are understood to embody important systems of belief and value and to express truths that are better expressed, and better understood, in a language of symbology. In ancient Greek philosophy, *logos* and *mythos* are two separate domains. In the domain of *logos*, logical analysis results in explanation. But in the domain of *mythos*, meaning is derived from observing the characteristics and actions of natural and supernatural phenomena, persons, and events. In myth, a variety of interpretations is possible. Explanation is not the goal, for interpreting meanings in a myth or story is a process of discovery and healing, understood here in terms such as gaining awareness and insight, wholeness and integration of the psychological self, strength and competence in one's functioning in the natural world and human community, and a vitally experienced spiritual self and relationship with that which is greater than oneself. Myth, writes philosopher Ernst Cassirer, expresses natural reality in the language of human, social reality and expresses social reality in the language of nature: "No reduction of the one factor to the other is possible; it is rather the two together, in complete correlation, that determine the peculiar structure and complexion of mythical consciousness." According to Cassirer, attempts to "explain" mythology in either purely sociological or naturalistic terms are, therefore, incomplete.[6]

Myths deal with issues that we can classify as religious, such as the ultimate origins of the universe and life on earth, and meanings and possibilities encountered in the human journey, questions that are not fully answerable, at least to the satisfaction of all individuals, by means of scientific observation and analysis or by philosophical reasoning. As regards the relationship between myths and legends, legends tend to give accounts of events that have occurred in a community's history, often its ancestral history. However, legends also incorporate mythological themes and symbolism. As compared to myths, legends are generally more rooted in particular details of a particular culture's history, practices, and important ancestors. Myths, on the other hand, tend to operate on a more cosmic scale: in other dimensions, such as the sky world or water world; in the deep past, before ordinary history; or sometimes in a suprahistorical future. When we say that an image or event is mythic, we mean that it has great power and significance; one implication is that its power and significance would be recognized universally by persons from other times and cultures. The universality of the tendency to constellate particular images, charged with meaning, was expressed by Jung in this characterization of the archetypes: "Pre-existent, innate patterns—the archetypes—can easily produce in the most widely differing individuals ideas or combinations of ideas that are practically identical, and for whose origin no individual experience can be made responsible."[7]

Mythologist and historian of religions Mircea Eliade wrote of how persons "live" a myth in the sense of being "seized by the sacred, exulting power of the events recollected or reenacted." Living a myth, Elide wrote, implies a religious experience:

> One is no longer living in chronological time, but in the primordial Time, the Time when the event *first took place*. . . . To re-experience that time, to reenact it as often as possible, to witness again the spectacle

of the divine works, to meet with the Supernaturals and relearn their creative lesson is the desire that runs like a pattern through all the ritual reiteration of myths. In short, myths reveal that the World, man, and life have a supernatural origin and history, and that this history is significant, precious, and exemplary.[8]

Myths provide understanding of the origins and the workings of natural and human processes. In Eliade's thinking, understanding origins in the context of myth does not mean accounting for the cause, or causes, of a particular phenomenon or event. Understanding origins encompasses understanding, for example, of how particular standards of behavior became established; thus, myths provide models for human behavior. Frank Morgan (Navajo) explains the following about Navajo narratives: "Blessing Way Teachings provide well-being, balance, and competencies in problem solving. The Teachings on each side come from traditional narratives about harmony and disharmony in the world. For example, the Protection Way Teachings may refer to a narrative (story) of a restricted behavior such as dishonesty. The narrative will tell about the consequences of the restricted act."[9] The knowledge that can be received by participation in a myth is a form of experiential knowledge. What do we mean when we speak of "participating" in a myth and the kind of experiential knowledge that can result?

To hear, to truly listen to a traditional story told by a master storyteller is to participate in ritual, to enter into sacred space and time, and potentially to experience a nonordinary state of consciousness that can permit attainment of transformative insights that are not ordinarily attainable. I'd like to say a few words about kinds of knowledge in order to further explore Eliade's view of the experiential knowledge available to persons who participate in the telling of a myth. In general, experiential knowledge is different from the kinds of knowledge that are gained without individual sensory experience by means such as logical inference or by the word of an authority. Experiential knowledge gained on the cosmic ground of myth and gained through participation in the myth differs from experiential knowledge acquired by individual sensory experience of particular events; it is experiential in a cosmic, comprehensive sense. In the context of the myth, events were experienced by important actors in a cosmic realm, whether ancestors, legendary culture heroes and heroines, supernatural beings, or deities. In myth, the patterns of how things function and the mechanisms of various types of action (both successful and unsuccessful) are understood to have been tested in ancestral time. Experiential knowledge gained from myth, Eliade observes, is conducive to the ability to work effectively with things and processes whose primordial origins myth helps us to understand. Frank Morgan speaks on Navajo philosophy and oral tradition:

> An understanding of this philosophy requires interaction with scholars and practitioners who practice it in their daily lives. Whether we know it or not, we are constantly living within its processes, powers, and effects: we are its child. Our being comes from it, and we think, feel, taste, see, hear, and move about purposefully by means of it. It is critical that we learn its principles and continuously be guided by the Teachings. In order to learn about the principles, one should be firmly grounded in the traditional stories of the evolution of the universe from a Navajo perspective.[10]

INTERPRETING MYTHS

The following words conclude Wendy Doniger O'Flaherty's book *Other Peoples' Myths: The Cave of Echoes*:

> The historians have demonstrated that there is no such thing as an even theoretically impartial observer, and the anthropologists have cynically undermined our hopes of getting inside the heads of other cultures, relativistically or otherwise. The linguists and philosophers have, finally, hopelessly defamed the character of language as a possible vehicle for mutual understanding. So we are stripped down to our naked myths, the bare bones of human experience. They may be our last hope for a nonlanguage that can free us from these cognitive snares, a means of flying so low that we can scuttle underneath the

devastating radar of the physical and social sciences and skim close to the ground of the human heart.[11]

Myth expresses and evokes meaning by using language as an intermediary instrument. Myths convey meanings and communicate scenarios and events with language that is symbolic; that is, the words in a myth create images and scenes that point to something beyond what the words refer to literally. A symbol, however, is not merely a sign that *points to* something beyond itself (if that were its only function, we would simply call it a *sign*). Symbols, Jung tells us, are "images of contents which, for the most part, transcend consciousness."[12] In the process of responding to symbols, symbols can activate meanings in a dimension of the psyche beyond the reach of what words can express.

Myths can be interpreted, and they can be compared across cultures and across versions of the same myth within a particular culture. Valuable insights can be gained thereby, but the deep and fundamental work of myths and traditional stories takes place not by a conscious process of rational analysis but through a more intuitive process. Intuition of the kind that is utilized to experience a myth is not a random, ill-grounded way of knowing; it can be an acutely sensitive mechanism of pattern recognition and the drawing of reliable inferences, but doing so below the threshold of consciousness of the steps that are involved. The psyche can intuitively recognize universal patterns and themes in a myth. The universal principles of order and functionality exemplified in the patterns contained in a myth can help listeners cultivate internal order and functionality and help them align themselves with the order and functionality of the natural and spiritual domains.

In cultures that convey ancestral teachings by means of oral and lived tradition (as distinct from traditions that rely mainly on texts), efforts at "analysis" or "explanation" of myths can be out of line in more than one way: adequate context for interpretation may be lacking to varying degrees. And significantly, the medicinal powers of the story, to be effective, must be derived individually through personal engagement with the story. Jo-ann Archibald (Q'um Q'um Xiiem, Stó:lō Nation) of the

University of British Columbia quotes Wapaskwan, mentor of storyteller Walter Lightning (Samson Cree Nation):

> Traditionally it has taken 40 years or so apprenticeship for an individual to work to gain the authority to tell the sacred class of story. That length of time is not required just to learn the texts of the stories, nor how to perform them. It takes that long to acquire the principles for interpretation of the stories.
>
> There is a "surface" story: the text, and the things one has to know about the performance of it for others. The stories are metaphoric, but there are several levels of metaphor involved. The text, combined with the performance, contains a "key" or a "clue" to unlock the metaphor. When a hearer hears that story and knows the narrative sequence of it, there is another story contained within that story, like a completely different embedded or implicit text.
>
> The trick is this: that the implicit or embedded text, itself, contains clues, directions — better yet, specifications — for the interpretation of an implicit text embedded in it. . . . A hearer isn't meant to understand the story at all levels, immediately. It is as if it unfolds.[13]

Dr. Vi Hilbert (Upper Skagit, 1918–2008) gives the following caution in her introduction to *The Clothes That Look at the People*, told by Johnny Moses, xʷistemǝni (Nuu-chah-nulth and Tulalip):

> Future scholars of the oral tradition are advised to remember that our people felt very strongly about not explaining the *meaning* of our stories. We maintain, as we were taught, that each individual has been given the unique and special ability to see and hear things in a way different from anyone else. The Creator has given each of us this very special gift, different from any other person in the universe. We are taught never to impose *our* way of seeing things on our listeners. They are to be given the courtesy of allowing a personal intellect to interpret meaning. How enlightening then to invite each reader to express what they interpret the stories' teaching to be. How rich the experience can be for individuals, students, for scholars.[14]

Hilbert speaks here of different ways of responding to stories, ways that are appropriate in two different and interrelated domains: the inner, psychic landscape and the realm of human community. The topic of interpretation of myth points to other pairs of interacting domains: another pair is the world of ordinary experience and the mythic world of supraordinary experience, whose semipermeable boundaries can be experienced through participation in myth. A very important idea for interpreting myths, which can also be conceived in terms of a pair of interacting domains, is Jung's concept of the archetypes and the collective unconscious. But before examining that topic, here are a few words about myths and archetypes.

MYTHS AND ARCHETYPES

Mythic forms in both stories and art can be interpreted at multiple levels. As mythologist Joseph Campbell wrote in one of his illustrated works, *The Mythic Image*, mythic forms "may be regarded either as pointing past themselves to mysteries of universal import, or as functions merely of local ethnic or even personal idiosyncrasies."[15] Campbell analyzed countless myths from across the world's cultures and periods of history. One of his contributions, which awakened untold numbers of people to the contemporary and personal relevance of mythology, is the universal pattern in stories of the hero's journey.[16] Let's look at major stages of the hero's journey. The hero receives a call to adventure. He responds to this call; to accept it sets him on a path to integration, integrity, and strength, but to refuse is to take a path of dissipation. The hero must survive threats and succeed in challenges in order to cross into new dimensions of being. He is confronted with obstacles and temptations. He overcomes the temptations, but the challenges are beyond his initial capabilities. In facing those challenges and obstacles, he connects with powers within and beyond himself. He becomes something greater not so much by gaining new powers but by realizing his inner potentials and connecting with the divine or sacred power within and beyond himself. He cannot do this alone; he has one or more helpers along the way. His helpers do not solve his problems for him; they provide guidance, encouragement, and insight about how he can use and develop his resources. The helpers may, however, assist him once he begins to take the lead. After successfully surviving ordeals of body, heart, mind, and spirit, the hero is initiated into a higher state of accomplishment and possibility. He attains reconciliation with a figure of sacred power. He may be united in a divine marriage. He may or may not return to his place of origin. If he returns to his people, he brings a new power to help and protect them that only the journey and its ordeals could have made possible.

As an example of the hero's journey, consider the life journey of Moses, who received from God the foundational teachings of the faith of Judaism. Moses received the scripture and the law through the course of a long ordeal in leading the Children of Israel in an exodus from Egypt and bringing them finally to the Promised Land after forty years of wandering in the desert (although Moses himself was not permitted to enter because of a transgression). From India's many traditions, the story of the Buddha's enlightenment also aligns with this model of the hero's journey, beginning with the young Siddhartha's renouncing his comfortable life to go on a six-year journey of intense study, self-deprivation, and spiritual practice in search of solutions that no teacher or tradition could offer. His extreme effort culminated in his attaining enlightenment. He chose to take his newly acquired understanding of the Four Noble Truths and the attendant teachings of Buddhism back to his community. For the rest of his life, until age eighty, he gave these teachings to the people as a spiritual medicine for their suffering. The hero's journey need not be so large-scale as to found a world religious tradition. Consider, from ancient Greek literature, the ten-year odyssey of Odysseus to return home to Ithaca and, in the George Lucas *Star Wars* films, Luke Skywalker's becoming a Jedi knight in his phenomenal journey to preserve good over evil in a futuristic universe. The hero's journey-story can be everyone's story, however profound or humble our life events may be.

The word "hero" literally means protector, from the Greek *hērōs*. If it seems out of place to call the journeyer a hero or a heroine before she has succeeded in her quest, thereby acquiring the ability to protect her people, consider that in order to succeed through all the ordeals of the journey, she had to protect herself. Learning to do this successfully required her to cultivate self-knowledge, strength, integrity, and means of skillful action. To succeed in the journey is to heal oneself, in the sense of gaining wholeness of capacity and confidence to act, such that one *can* help oneself and help one's people. Characters in a myth (whether human, animal, supernatural, or divine) receive and exemplify teachings concerning these matters in the course of their mythic adventures. Here in the earthly world, the participant in a myth receives teachings as she integrates what she gleans from the story and then interweaves these insights (of which she may be more or less conscious) with the elements that populate her internal mythic landscape. This internal landscape is not a static place; it is the inner psychic world that a person inhabits and within which she travels as the story of her life unfolds.

Mythologist and historian of religion Wendy Doniger has observed that the application of a "monomyth" model, such as Campbell's model of the hero's journey, if employed with uninvestigated presuppositions about the universality of myths or mainly for the purpose of identifying similarities between myths from different traditions, falls short of attaining many kinds of insights that can be revealed by comparative analysis. Although I cannot do justice to the ways that Doniger's many contributions — or the contributions of the other thinkers referenced here — can illuminate our current topic, I would like to mention one of her ideas that is very illuminating. Doniger has provided a model for understanding myths that suggests three levels of lenses: "the big view (the telescope) is the universalist view sought by Freud, Jung, Eliade; the middle view (the naked eye) is the view of contextualized cultural studies; and the small view (the microscope) is the focus on individual insight."[17] The microscopic view permits a very subjective experience of the meanings of a myth. The telescopic view can both provide a broad view of myth in relation to universal themes that exist in similar myths of other world cultures and shift our focus from the minutiae and banality of our daily lives.[18] At least at moments — as can happen through participation in a myth — we are moved by the greatness of the universe and the commonality of our humanity. Both the microscopic and the macroscopic views, Doniger says, allow us to see beyond our personal views; a myth can deepen our connection with the environment and with persons in other cultural and political circumstances.

Psychiatrist Carl Jung had wide-ranging and deep understanding of the world's cultures, religions, mythology, and art. Jung elucidated many ways in which meanings that illuminate the human journey toward wholeness can be evoked by engagement with symbols in dreams, art, and literature. Although Jung pointed to the uniqueness of each human psyche as a reason why mythological — not scientific — knowledge and language are necessary for exploration of human subjective experience, one of Jung's central ideas is the *collective unconscious*. Jung's concept of a collective unconscious is inseparable from his idea of the *archetypes*. The unconscious, for Jung, has two dimensions. First, the unconscious includes the personal, which contains memories of experiences that are not accessible to a person's awareness because those memories have been forgotten or repressed. More significant, according to Jung, is the second dimension, the collective unconscious, which contains universal patterns of interpretation, patterns that Jung called archetypes. The archetypes arise in states when the intensity of conscious mental activity is reduced, such as dreams, delirium, reveries, and visions; thus, the origin of archetypes is the unconscious, rather than the conscious, aspect of the psyche.[19] A common set of mythological types exists across cultures, evident in art, mythology, and other expressions of cultural life. Jung designated the ground of these mythological types or archetypes *collective*, rather than individual, because of their universality across cultures and because the human inclination to recognize and respond to them is not necessarily traceable to individuals' life experiences. Jung's discussion of archetypes in the context of myth speaks of archetypes in terms of mythological components with a typical nature that we could call "primordial images" or "motifs."[20] To attempt to characterize a motif, such as the child-motif, as "a vestigial memory of our own childhood" does not, Jung says, suffice. A more adequate but still incomplete statement would describe it as "a picture of certain forgotten things in our childhood," for this characterization embodies the unconscious nature of archetypal material. But the best characterization embodies both the unconscious and the collective aspects: "The child-motif represents the pre-conscious, childhood aspect of the collective psyche."[21] The archetype, Jung says, "does not proceed from physical facts, but describes how the psyche experiences the physical fact."[22] An archetype is perhaps better characterized in terms of process rather than structure; we could say that an archetype is a patterning mechanism within which particular universal meanings are constituted.

A major archetype is that of the Earth Mother, or Mother Earth. When the two brothers in the "Land in the Sky" myth encounter her, they recognize her, and those of us who may participate in the myth also recognize her by her actions, as she provides the journeyers with nurturance and wisdom. There is a difference between the archetype and the *manifestation* of an archetype: an archetype is not the mythic image itself; rather, it is a psychological pattern by which the psyche identifies and responds to a particular symbol or image. Neither the image of Mother Earth portrayed by the storyteller's words nor the visual image of her portrayed on the totem pole by the carver is the archetype. The image of Mother Earth that is experienced in hearing the myth or seeing the carving is a manifestation of the archetype of Mother Earth; the archetype itself is a universal human function that identifies the particular manifestation. The title of this essay, "Archetypes from Cedar," would not be correctly expressed as "Archetypes *in* Cedar," because the medium (whether cedar, a story, or another medium) expresses only the manifestation of an archetype. The archetype itself is not in the cedar; the artwork contains a symbol or mythic image that permits a person to experience the archetype. The archetype itself is internal to human beings who experience the art; the archetype makes possible a response in the experiencer's psyche, which is, in part, a universal human response. The response is occasioned by the experiencer's engagement with the figures and symbols expressed by the artwork. Cross-cultural comparisons can yield insights about both differences and universality. The moon has associations with the feminine in many traditions, but many ancient traditions regard the moon as masculine.[23] What kinds of insights might we receive from engaging with the symbol of the moon as presented in the Lummi myth "Land in the Sky" as a cold, mean old man? And what archetypal patterns might be common across cultures in universal human archetypal responses to the moon?

In Jungian terms, the collective unconscious is the ground of psychological development and health. Healing, in the psychological sense, is an increase of wholeness and functionality that is supported by bringing archetypal material from the unconscious into the light of conscious awareness and integrating it with the psychological elements that compose one's conscious life. In Jung's view, the natural inclination of the psyche is to seek wholeness, which may be described in terms of integration on two different planes. In one of these planes are the poles of the individual and the universal. Progress toward health and wholeness consists in expression of creative individuality, which functions in dynamic relation with the universal aspects of one's humanity. In the other plane are the poles of the conscious and unconscious. Attaining wholeness on this plane entails self-development in the direction of an increasingly functional relationship between the conscious and unconscious aspects of the self. Unintegrated aspects of oneself (that is, elements that function within the psyche but that are not within one's conscious awareness) can contribute to various forms of psychological sickness, suffering, hostility, lack of development, and unrealized or misdirected creative energy. In order to bring forth the hidden contents of the unconscious and to integrate them in functional dynamic unity with the conscious self, the unconscious needs engagement; it needs, so to speak, food and medicine. Art and myth are two of the greatest sources of material for such engagement.

COAST SALISH TOTEM POLES AS A MEDIUM OF STORIES

Art and myth are ways of awakening human insight, evoking transformative experience, and activating the realization of higher potentials. Among the art forms of the world, Coast Salish story poles stand out, along with mosaics, as one of the few forms of visual art that express extensive and detailed narrative not in language but in symbology. As carved works of art and as media for recording and telling stories, Coast Salish totem poles function to bring about learning, healing, and transformation for individuals and communities. A Coast Salish story pole, such as those of the style developed by Joe Hillaire and other early Coast Salish carvers, portrays tribal symbols and motifs (*visual motifs* are recurring designs that have symbolic significance), commemorates historical events, and conveys myths and legends of the culture. The history and symbols carved in Coast Salish totem poles serve purposes that include the commemoration of important events and beings (both natural and supernatural) and the transmission of important events, stories, and teachings so that they can provide insight and strength and be carried forward into the future.

Stories connected with particular poles may be given voice by a storyteller, or a person can silently experience a story by viewing the pole. As with myths and legends in general, variants of a totem pole story may arise when a person who has heard the story later recounts it in memory or retells it aloud. Each of these variants of the story may have different details and emphases. When stories associated with story poles are told and heard (or read), the story proceeds in time from beginning to end. In the tradition conveyed by culture bearers such as Lummi carver Joe Hillaire and his daughter Pauline Hillaire, the story portrayed on a Coast Salish story pole is read first on the front of the pole, from the bottom up, then on the back of the pole, from the top down. Similar to a written or narrated version of the story, a story "read" in this manner proceeds in time from beginning to end. But much more than that is occurring simultaneously. The viewer is also experiencing the component parts of the totem pole simultaneously and, at the same time, experiencing the carved work as a whole. The story in its carved form is not experienced in the medium of language; rather, it is experienced visually. The simultaneous visibility — in both time and space — of the figures and symbols carved on the pole permits the viewer to experience multiple meanings and levels of meaning simultaneously. When a person hears — or reads — a story, the sequential nature of language directs her attention to the current point in the narration while she holds in memory what has transpired, and her powers of imagination and inference can leap ahead to what may transpire. If she has heard or read the story before, her memory allows her to anticipate what will transpire. And, as Doniger points out, every new hearing of a story that a person has heard (or read) before is, in a sense, a new variant, for the listener (or reader) experiences new meanings made possible by developments in her own history and psyche.[24]

A remarkable feature of totem poles as a vehicle of stories is the way that carved images do what is also done by the language of myth; however, story poles do this even more directly, in that the carved images present mythic material without the intermediary vehicle of words. Jung tells us that "what an archetypal content is always expressing is, first and foremost, a *figure of speech*": "If it speaks of the sun and identifies it with the lion, the king, the hoard of gold guarded by the dragon, or the force that makes for the life and health of man, it is neither the one thing nor the other, but the unknown third thing that finds more or less adequate expression in all the similes, yet — to the perpetual vexation of intellect — remains unknown and not to be fitted into a formula."[25] A myth uses words to express and evoke images that are beyond the literal meaning of the words. A story pole is even closer to the images of the myth, in that visual images convey the elements of the myth without the extra representational step of using words to signify meanings. Jung's colleague, mythologist Carl (Károly, Karl) Kerényi, in comparing the nature of music, poetry, myth, and art, writes that a process of pictorial shaping takes place in mythology: "A torrent of mythological pictures streams out. . . . Various developments of the same ground theme are possible side by side or in succession, just like the variations on a musical theme, for, although what 'streams out' always remains pictorial in itself, the comparison with music is still applicable, certainly with definite works of music, i.e., something objective, that has become an object with a voice of its own, that one does justice to, not by interpretation or explanation, but above all by letting alone allowing it to utter its own meaning."[26]

A Coast Salish story pole is a uniquely powerful medium of myth and story by virtue of its simultaneously presenting (1) a narrative, (2) the specific visual elements that represent the components of the narrative, (3) the total presence of the entire artwork, and (4) cultural associations regarding the setting, the purpose(s), and the history of the pole. The meanings that may be received from viewing a totem pole and experiencing its associated narratives depend on factors including the experiencer's understanding of the cultural figures and symbols incorporated in the carving as well as meanings expressed in the accompanying stories. Stories that have become important and that have therefore been carefully transmitted through centuries, and even millennia, of a culture's generations are part of larger, interwoven patterns that constitute the culture's full mythology. When we hear a particular version or variant of a story, we hear only a small part of a large complex of myths, legends, history, geographical knowledge, genealogy, and spiritual teachings. Persons within the culture from which a story originates can experience greater range, depth, and shades of meaning in experiencing a story. Persons within a culture are familiar (to varying extents) with the comprehensive mythology, history, and teachings of which the story is a particular instance. For instance, the "Land in the Sky" myth invokes the power of the stars, which was gained by the brothers who journeyed to the sky world and back; this is part of a larger complex of ancestral star teachings.

For outsiders to a culture from which a story pole or other totem pole originated, tremendous meaning can be derived in experiencing the carved artwork. However, many levels and connections of meaning expressed within the artwork's carved symbols, characters, and events are largely lost on an outsider. Even the medium of the artwork, cedar, has deeper significance to a member of the culture from which the artwork originates. For Native people of the Pacific Northwest, before the major changes that resulted from the arrival of Anglo-Europeans, the cedar tree provided the material for shelter, clothing, transportation, cooking utensils, storage, music, ceremony, and art. Cedar objects for all these purposes are still made and used today. Cedar trees themselves are recognized as living beings integral to a familial ecological system, and they possess spiritual personhood. An individual who encounters a totem pole with an understanding of these dimensions of cedar has a more extensive context within which to respond to the medium of the artwork. Consider the experience of the carver: as he carves, his very breath and blood are infused by molecules of pungent cedar, as compared to someone who works mainly indoors for a lifetime and for whom trees may be experienced more as abstractions, landscape elements, or lumber.

VARIANTS OF THE "LAND IN THE SKY" MYTH

My aim in this concluding section is not to interpret the "Land in the Sky" myth, a process that is, of course, for each participant in the myth to do for herself. Rather, I will close with some remarks on variants of the story presented in this book and its media companion. I'll begin with describing the skeletal structure of the "Land in the Sky" totem pole myth as told by the pole's carver, Kwul-kwul'tʷ Joseph Hillaire (Lummi, 1894–1967) and by his daughter Scälla Pauline Hillaire (Lummi, b. 1929). The "Land in the Sky" myth aligns with the pattern of the hero's journey-story.

Two brothers are impelled to journey to the Land in the Sky. Upon arriving, they must first overcome the distraction of some calling geese, which are actually young women, who might tempt them from their mission. Mother Earth appears to the brothers and gives them food, rest, and pearls of wisdom. She advises them to find the Daughter of the Sun and the Daughter of the Moon; together the four ascend into the Land of the Moon. The cruel Moon sets potentially fatal traps, and he demands that the brothers meet the challenges he sets, but the young men act skillfully, according to the teachings they have received, and their successful efforts exasperate Man Moon. Intent on killing them once and for all, Man Moon summons them to a battle against his fearsome animal warriors. Along their journey the brothers have followed Mother Earth's advice to collect what they have found along the way: a broken lance, a bent harpoon, and other items whose value is at first unknown to them. Faced with Man Moon's warriors, who viciously attack, dozens against one, the elder brother begins a medicine song and dance and calls upon his spirit power and the spirit of Mother Earth for help and strength. The broken weapons and other items that the brothers had collected coalesce and transform into enormous weapon-creatures, with limbs like those of a grasshopper and the ability to jump long distances, each limb a deadly blade or barb. With spiritual integrity and focus, the brothers' army defeats the army of Man Moon. The brothers thereby attain spiritual maturity and reconciliation with the Moon, a figure of cosmic power. The young men also attain a plane of existence that bridges the cosmic and earthly worlds; this is represented by the marriage of the younger brother to the Daughter of the Sun and the marriage of the older brother to the Daughter of the Moon. The two couples descend to earth, bringing with them a special healing oil that was created with the help of the Daughter of the Sun during one of the brother's ordeals. On arriving in the Earthworld, the first act of the Daughter of the Sun is to restore life to a little minklike creature, a *chieque* (*čəčiq'ən*) who had grown old and died while guarding the brothers' possessions during their absence. The powers gained by the brothers in their journey to the Land in the Sky, which from then on they use to help their people, are the power to heal sickness and the power to provide food.

A myth is an art form, whether it is conveyed as a text or told as a story. I have described the main events in the "Land in the Sky" myth, and although the elements of the plot are conveyed, my bare-bones account clearly shows that relating a sequence of mythic events is not equivalent to the telling of a myth: the elements of performance art inherent in the storyteller's oral versions of the story are entirely lost. Audio and audiovisual recordings of Pauline Hillaire's telling of the story demonstrate many artful features of language, drama, and musicality. A verbatim transcription of the story as told live (as appears in chapter 15) is an instance of textual literary art. Of course, the live performance of the story is the ultimate medium for the art form of myth: in the live telling, the storyteller employs a range of narrative techniques, including gesture, facial expression, intuition about the knowledge that would be valuable to listeners, along with a human connection with them and the ineffable ability to transport them into the world of the myth — and into a transformed frame of mind — where healing transformations within the psyche may take place.

This book and its companion media contain five versions, or variants, of the "Land in the Sky" story. First, there is an audiovisual presentation given by Pauline Hillaire in 2008 concerning the major totem poles carved by her father (including the *Land in the Sky* totem pole) in which she provides commentary about the interpretation of each pole along with samples from the stories that accompany them. Audio CD vol. 2 contains a second variant of the story told by Pauline Hillaire that was recorded in 2008. Doniger's examination of the many variants and voices in which myths are told includes observations about the gender of voice. One aspect of this issue concerns the fact that one cannot presume to identify "women's texts" or "women's voices" on the basis of subject matter.[27] For example, in her 2008 audio recording of the "Land in the Sky" myth, Pauline Hillaire describes in considerable detail a feast that was held for the young men who journeyed to the Land in the Sky and met the Daughter of the Moon and the Daughter of the Sun. This episode is not mentioned at all in Joe Hillaire's version that appears here. Joe's version emphasizes the gruesome battle that takes place between Man Moon's warriors and the warrior-creature helpers who fight in behalf of the two young men, finally vanquishing the animal-warriors that Man Moon had sent to destroy them. If considering only these two variants, one might draw faulty conclusions about women's or men's voices or topics as regards this myth. However, in another variant told by Pauline Hillaire — an audio version that we recorded in 2010 — she too describes the gruesome battle in detail. This is just one example of many points of comparison that can be fruitfully considered within the several variants of the myth that are offered here.

A third variant in this collection is a short movie narrated by Pauline Hillaire telling the "Land in the Sky" myth. (The movie's narration is the audio version mentioned above, recorded in 2010.) This audiovisual version is illustrated by photographic images of the *Land in the Sky* pole. The fourth variant is the textual version of the story (chapter 15), which contains a transcription of Pauline Hillaire's 2010 audio recording. Additionally, in order to provide the textual version of the story in a form that represents all the carved figures on the totem pole, we have incorporated selections from Joe Hillaire's telling of the story as published by R. O. Bishop (portions of the story from Joe's version are shown in italics).[28] So a fifth variant consists in printed selections from a version told by Joe Hillaire. Interested readers can consult Bishop's publication for the entire story told by Joe Hillaire as prepared by Mr. Bishop. It is not known whether the story was prepared from a recording or from notes alone, so we can't know how close Bishop's version is to Joe's original telling. Pauline had hoped that we would locate some of the recordings of her father that she believes Mr. Bishop made, but none had been located by the time this publication went to press.

The short movie of Pauline Hillaire telling the "Land in the Sky" story, with images of the totem pole, constitutes a new kind of variant of this story. The format is not a live storytelling, a text, an audio recording alone, or an audiovisual recording that shows the storyteller. In any of these formats, participants in the myth would create their own visual images as they listened (or read). In this particular audiovisual production, images appear along with the narration. There are disadvantages to providing images along with the voice of a storyteller, a main one being that the images prevent or interfere with participants' deriving their own images. In this case, however, our aim was to provide views of the totem pole as a participant might see it if she were in the presence of the pole. Granted, the images are views as seen by particular photographers, and as editor of the production, I have made decisions about which images to place at which points of Pauline Hillaire's narration. So, granting the limitations of the medium, we have provided a variant of the story that suggests how a totem pole can tell a story. In so doing, we have offered an audiovisual version of the myth that may be of interest in future discussions of the limitations and potentials of electronic media to portray oral literature. We have also provided a way for participants to see one of Joe Hillaire's masterworks that is not currently available — and that might never again be available — for viewing. And we have preserved for future generations the voice of his daughter, storyteller Pauline Hillaire, an ancestrally trained master of an art that allows us a great gift: participation in myth. Finally, we have offered all these variants of the "Land in the Sky" myth with the hope of inspiring interest in the study of traditional stories and commitment to the ancestral disciplines of memorizing and storytelling.

Two main topics stand out for ongoing dialogue: What is possible, transformative, and healing in the experiencing of Coast Salish story poles that may be universal to human beings across cultures? How might the experience of Coast Salish story poles and their symbolism differ for a member of the culture from which that artwork originated, as compared with the experience of a person from outside that culture? As regards the first question, I have offered some thoughts about the transformative and healing power of story pole art and its associated oral tradition. As regards the second, it is a question whose answers cannot be fully known by persons from outside a story pole carving culture, but I believe that engaging the question can be illuminating. Engaging such questions can encourage comparative work that is grounded in living intercultural dialogue, which can not only expand our insight but provide another way that working with stories can be healing.

In his dedication to his book *Lushootseed Culture and the Shamanic Odyssey*, anthropologist Jay Miller quotes Vi Hilbert: "Write all you want because you can never learn culture from a book."[29] There is no substitute for being in the presence of a storyteller — for participating in a myth. Similarly, seeing images of a totem pole is not the same as being in the presence of that carving. Writing is another kind of art and medium for preserving, expressing, exploring, entertaining, and generating further insight and dialogue. Beyond the transformative possibilities inherent in experiencing totem pole artwork, there is insight and inspiration to be found in exploring totem poles as a medium of stories. The force of Coast Salish story pole art goes to the heart of what myth is and what myth does: using a language of symbology to carve and paint stories of life, that we may better live the story that is our life.

NOTES

1. Jung, *Memories, Dreams, and Reflections*, 4.

2. Cruikshank, *Life Lived Like a Story*.

3. General distinctions between types of stories are drawn from Campbell, *The Flight of the Wild Gander*, 15–20.

4. Campbell, *Flight of the Wild Gander*, 19.

5. Bringhurst, "Introduction," 230. See also Bringhurst, *Masterworks of the Classical Haida Mythtellers*.

6. Cassirer, *Mythical Thought*, 192.

7. Jung, *Symbols of Transformation*, 313 (#474).

8. Eliade, *Myth and Reality*, 19.

9. Frank Morgan (Navajo). "A Central Principle of Navajo Philosophy," ed. Gregory P. Fields (unpublished manuscript, 1996).

10. Morgan, "A Central Principle," 5.

11. O'Flaherty, *Other Peoples' Myths*, 166.

12. Jung, *Symbols of Transformation*, 77 (#114).

13. Wapaskwan, quoted in Lightning, "Compassionate Mind," 229–30. Cited in Archibald, *Indigenous Storywork*, 83–84.

14. Vi Hilbert, in Moses, *The Clothes That Look*, ii.

15. Campbell, *The Mythic Image*.

16. Campbell, *The Hero with a Thousand Faces*.

17. Doniger, *The Implied Spider*, 10.

18. Doniger, *The Implied Spider*, 21.

19. C. G. Jung in Jung and Kerényi, *Essays*, 99–103.

20. Jung, *The Archetypes*, 42–43 (#89), 153 (#260).

21. Jung in Jung and Kerényi, *Essays*, 110–11.

22. Jung, *The Archetypes*, 154 (#260).

23. Jung, *Symbols of Transformation*, 318 (#487). Along with the Lummi, the Aleut is another Pacific Northwest culture in which the moon is masculine. See, for example, Berglands, "The Moon's Sister."

24. Doniger, *The Implied Spider*, 41–42.

25. Jung in Jung and Kerényi, *Essays*, 105.

26. Kerényi in Jung and Kerényi, *Essays*, 4.

27. Doniger, *The Implied Spider*, 113.

28. Bishop, *Land in the Sky Totem*.

29. Vi Hilbert in Miller, *Lushootseed Culture*, dedication page.

11 Artists Were the First Historians

Spiritual Significance of Coast Salish Carving

CHIXAPKAID (MICHAEL PAVEL)

Artists were the first historians.
— SUBIYAY

THE AUTHORS IN THIS BOOK HAVE SPOKEN ABOUT what I have been taught about as the immortal spirits, whose purposes for being are to preserve and perpetuate. These profound intentions were known so well by Kwul-kwul'tʷ, as his life was filled with art that preserves and perpetuates sacred teachings. To honor such dedication and humility, this essay seeks to convey the cultural and spiritual significance of Coast Salish carving. It is important to begin by quoting my uncle, subiyay (Bruce Miller, Skokomish, 1944–2005), because he was a renowned spiritual leader and an extraordinary traditional carver. This single sentence, *artists were the first historians*, says so much that to interpret its entire significance would be beyond the scope of this essay. So as artists do when they bring something to life, I will create some boundaries by conveying a brief interpretation in these words on the cultural and spiritual significance of Coast Salish carving. This interpretation will be embellished

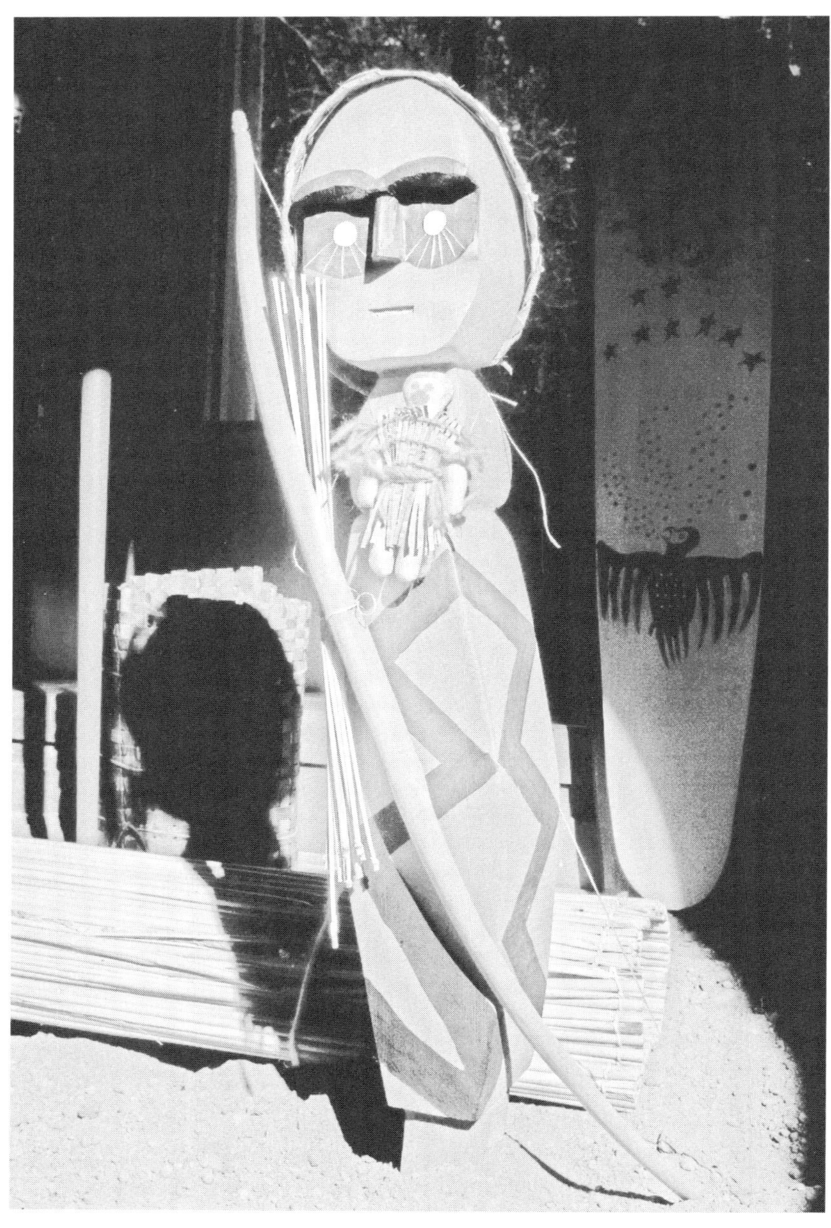

30. *Soul Recovery* by subiyay Bruce Miller (Skokomish) and CHiXapkaid Michael Pavel (Skokomish), 2005. Reprinted with permission. Photo by Martin Kane, the Evergreen State College.

by personal stories so that Coast Salish carvers of all ages and abilities may be inspired to embrace the possibility to preserve and perpetuate all things that are ancient, profound, and beautiful. The development of a Coast Salish carver should be informed by indigenous ancestral wisdom because that is what makes us who we are and what we should strive to be as Coast Salish people.

The first section invokes the wisdom of our ancestors by embracing the ancient aspect of being a Coast Salish carver. It invokes this wisdom by recognizing the existence of powerful elemental forces and the Plant and Animal people that preceded the coming of Human people. The second section addresses the profound nature of the work that takes place when we embrace the significance of becoming a highly trained Coast Salish carver. The important thing to remember while reading this chapter is that the physical act of carving is far less important than the intellectual, emotional, and spiritual dimensions. The third section shares some thoughts about why a Coast Salish carver must embrace the nature and meaning of beauty and the essential aspect of bringing forth the beautiful life that Coast Salish carving can help achieve.

ANCIENT

To be ancient is a dynamic experience. It is not a concept simply constrained in the past and held in some fanciful notion of being static (that is the way it was) and unchanging (that is the way it will always be). The notion of the dynamic (evolving, changing, growing, etc.) is compatible with the necessity to maintain traditions, to follow sacred teachings, and to be faithful to our ancestors. To embrace the ancient aspect of being Coast Salish is full of movement, growth, and evolution, and it emulates the very ancient world that we still live in as Human people. This is part of why art forms vary from tribe to tribe and why art forms can and will change.

Our oldest teachers consist of the elementals: fire, water, earth, and air. These elementals are truly ancient, yet they are constantly in motion and rarely, if ever, the same in any given moment in time and space. Yet they maintain traditions that are familiar over time and within different spaces. This familiarity conveys stability, and stability provides an environment where balance and harmony prevail, which in turn feels better than chaos. On a fundamental level, even as time expands outward, I was taught by my elders that there will be a place when time reverses itself. Having finished its journey, time will return to its birthplace. It will do so by following a different path, but it will return to the birthplace it calls home. Yes, a Coast Salish carver can anthropomorphize time, fire, water, earth and air, for they were alive before humans; they taught humans how to be people, and they will live long after humans are all but forgotten.

Coast Salish carvers can be at peace, knowing that when they pick up a carving tool, they will be doing something that their ancestors did, just as the ancestors of those ancestors did, since the beginning of time. It is silly when our Coast Salish carvers are looked upon with disdain or misguided contempt when challenged about the "traditional nature" of our art when we use steel knives, chain saws, and other so-called modern tools to create physical testimonials conveying the sacred teachings of our people or the desires of people who commission some form of our art.

So many times I heard my uncle laugh at such an inane question ("How can you call it traditional when you use modern tools?"), and he would say, "They [our ancestors] would have used them if they had them." That realization is so true, because to embrace the ancient is to evolve with a sense of knowing where you come from. The consequence of not knowing is to drift and to have no emotional foundation upon which to create, cultivate, and appreciate a shared identity within a community. In many ways, among the Lummi, this is called *schelangen* (sčəláŋən), a way of life that must be preserved, protected, and taught in order to achieve a sense of peace within one's being.

I had long conversations with my uncle, late into the night, because he rarely slept, and he would relish dialogues that explored the deepest crevices of our imaginations and primordial memories. One early evening I innocently asked, "How can we, as artists, learn from fire, water, earth, and air as well as the Plant and Animal people?" He took a deep breath and then began to talk. He finished when the sun rose and saw that I was finally nodding off to sleep. Neither time nor space permits me to tell you all the teachings that were conveyed, but essentially he explained, metaphorically and quite literally, that humans saw that water was an efficient carver of earth in its liquid state as well as in its solid state (ice), so they thought of using different knives to make different kinds of cuts. Although water, in whatever form, could create a smooth surface, the wind also could put a finish on the carved earth when utilizing small particles like sand (think of sandpaper, or the abrasiveness of shark skin, which can be used as sandpaper). Fire was able to provide color by changing the very chemical structure of compounds that made up the earth.

Plants and animals learned from all that existed prior to their creation. One might not think of plants as being able to teach humans about carving. However, imagine the roots of a plant slowly making their way through even the toughest terrain; the plant is patient, determined, and persistent in doing what is necessary to live. Every traditional carver knows that our ancestors worked with tools that might be more difficult to use compared to the "modern" tools that make it easier to carve, but they still achieved a high form of art. Why? Because the type of tool we use really is neither the point of being a Coast Salish carver nor the purpose of the core values embraced in learning how and why to carve.

Nobody is going to have the perfect tree or piece of wood. Plants don't strive to grow that way, to be perfect. They grow to survive and to hold true to charges given to them by the Creator. One charge was to hold the earth together to prevent the omnipresent forces of air and water from eroding the topsoil away, leaving it devoid of the nutrients necessary for plants to grow so that animals and humans can live. So a Coast Salish carver must be patient, determined, and persistent while being respectful, kind, considerate, and generous. If a Coast Salish carver maintains these kinds of core values, then there is a chance to become a great carver who will be highly respected by the people. To strive for anything less is not *siem* (high-class) training.

One time Uncle watched me struggle (there were many times) while carving, and he heard me blame it on the knife — it was too dull, it wasn't the right curve, the handle was too short. "Did you bother to pray and thank the life from which that board came?" he asked. "No." "Do you understand the nature of the life that that plant lived and conveyed in the grain of the wood?" "No." "Are you happy with the little progress you made?" "No." "Then don't blame the knife. Find a way to take personal responsibility for making sure that carving is about the way you are being as a human and not about the tool." He then went on to talk about Beaver and Woodpecker (and other Animal people that carve) to explain that they carve to survive and to keep the teachings alive, not to complain or feel anything less than the appreciation they have for doing what they are able to do as a means of survival.

PROFOUND

When I think of the word "profound" it reminds me of the need to be reflective, thoughtful, and philosophical. Kwul-kwul'tʷ's work is profound. To be profound is the kind of yearning that a Coast Salish carver should strive for in life. We should want to look back on the historical record we leave and, if completely understood by the viewer, trust that it will have an enduring influence with regard to the message we left behind. It doesn't always have to be an extremely large, monumental figure to achieve a profound learning experience. One morning, Uncle came up to me and handed me something. It was a small (about two inches long), crudely carved, lizardlike figure. "Burn this with me when I die," Uncle said, as he wanted to be cremated, and continued, "It is the first thing I ever carved as a child. I saw it crawl underneath my mother's bed, and then it turned to talk to me in Indian. It asked me to carve something in its image and keep it with me all my life." So much reflection took place while holding this tiny object, and I was lost in deep thought for such a long period of time. I could not even remember what I thought about it until months after my uncle had passed away.

Where Coast Salish carvers go to achieve the mindset to believe that they will produce something profound begins early in the process and involves other people. In the beginning it might be the family that touches and admires, with a sense of appreciation, every piece first created. There is no place to be critical of a beginning carver's work, because the beginning will invariably look a lot like the last pieces a carver produces later in his or her life, if the carver lives to become an elder. It is a profound connection that we regress to our childhood memories as we become elders, that the last memories we remember are from our childhood. What this means is that to become a Coast Salish carver is a journey through life that we take with other people.

Some of the people we connect with might be the relative who keeps the things we produce as children, the master who has the discretion to keep something from the apprentice, to signal that the apprentice has made the master proud, or the buyer who sees that budding talent and skill and purchases an item, knowing that the carver will only get better. This articulates the reality that a Coast Salish carver must have the fortitude to keep at carving to get better, to discover hidden talent and abilities, and to realize that carving is a journey in which we make connections to other people to improve ourselves as good human beings.

This became very apparent to me in the early days of my carving career, when I was instructed to give everything away and keep nothing for myself. Uncle told me not to keep it but give it away. He said, "Your early pieces are like seeds, and they will eventually sprout and continue to grow, if you let the seeds grow. This is to embody the teachings of the Plant people, whose seeds are dispersed in so many ways. Some fall to the ground, others blow in the wind, still others need the Animal people to spread the seed and create the initial environment for it to sprout. You influence the environment that enables these seeds to grow."

Remember everything you give away in the early days, whom you gave it to, when you gave it to them, and occasionally use this as a reason (but not the only reason) to go visit them. These visits will enrich your human emotions and feed your spirit, and, in turn, your spirit will reward you even more. It is a profound experience to spend countless hours bringing something to life and then give it away freely with no expectation other than to embrace the sheer joy and pleasure of being generous. This was important to the ancestors because it keeps at bay the greed that is destroying our world today. You see, the act of being a Coast Salish carver presents the opportunity to live the life of our ancestors, the good life filled with *siem* behavior in terms of being generous, dedicated, determined, and respectful. It is important to foster a sense of thankfulness for the gifts that we receive in our lives. It is a profound experience to be kind and considerate and then receive the blessings of the spirit and, in turn, to give and receive the blessing and admiration of your people.

BEAUTIFUL

It is important to let emerging and established Coast Salish carvers know that everything they create is beautiful. As Coast Salish carvers, we want to achieve a state of consciousness to see beyond the external form that we gaze upon, to see and feel the life within, which we bring forth. Everything we make will have a life and should receive a name, and those so named are recognized. This is the value of having your traditional/ancestral name called on the ceremonial floor. Without such recognition we become lost in the fog, where there are no bearings to define our rightful existence. Kwul-kwul'tʷ, as a Coast Salish carver, was obedient to the charge that each piece brought to life would have a name (*Land in the Sky*, *Bellingham Centennial*, *Man in Transition*, and so on). Not having a name results in an empty feeling.

For example, one afternoon I was visiting a place that had two welcome figures out in front of a building, one a male and the other a female figure. A person walking by who obviously worked for the establishment said, "Beautiful, aren't they?" I replied, "Yes. What are their names?" He replied, "They are welcome figures." "Oh," I said, continuing, "what are the welcome figures' names?" He was puzzled and stammered, "Uh . . . they don't have names . . . they're just welcome figures." The person's answer left me empty. I felt compelled to ask them — the welcome figures — their names. This I did by closing my eyes to touch them, and I felt what they had to say, and it was Protection and Love. I felt better. That was a beautiful moment.

Beauty is, it is often said, in the eye of the beholder. For the Coast Salish carver, beauty is what we see and what we feel. Anger, hatred, and ugliness are not emotions and behaviors conducive to instilling prayers and blessings upon the people. That a Coast Salish carver can instill prayers and blessings upon the people is what Jewell Praying Wolf James does when he leads an effort to bring forth a gift like the *Liberty* and *Freedom* totem poles with the *Sovereignty* crossbar to help honor those who lost their lives in the 9/11 attacks. "Well, what about the shame totem poles carved by our northern relatives?" someone reading over my shoulder asked me to explain. I replied, "They do a beautiful job of expressing themselves in a way that is traditional instead of holding resentment and negative feelings in the heart, where they will only erode a person's life in the end."

Watching an art piece being finalized, to see it finally finished and come to life, is such a beautiful experience. It is like watching the birth of a child who then gasps its first breath; that is a beautiful feeling. A Coast Salish carver can see and feel these things by having a kind and sensitive heart that can think a good thought before a bad thought, to see the virtuous life before seeing the awful, to think positive before being negative, and to pray for the well-being of others instead of for their demise. This is the ultimate choice of the Coast Salish carver, and it is a choice, because he or she doesn't "have to" see his or her work as being beautiful. Nevertheless, please note that the choice of how we see our work is also indicative of how we see and treat ourselves. So we might as well think of ourselves as beautiful people who are strong, resilient, and faithful to the opportunity to become carvers.

The purpose of this essay was to reinforce the need to preserve and perpetuate Coast Salish carving. There are ancient, profound, and beautiful reasons for embracing the possibility that being a carver is a good thing for oneself, for our families, and for our communities. To have faith in entities that existed long before Human people is a blessing in our lives, and their ancestral teachings are needed now more than ever. The profound nature of being a carver is to create a form that carries an identity, a purpose, and a meaningful existence. Whatever we as carvers create is beautiful to behold. There are so many virtues and values that are part of being a highly trained Coast Salish carver, among them generosity, skill, perseverance, and love. Our communities need us more than ever. Every Coast Salish community needs artists to record our history in the pieces we bring to life. In doing so, we did what our ancestors did: we carry forth a profound and beautiful way of life.

PART THREE

Totem Poles of Joe Hillaire

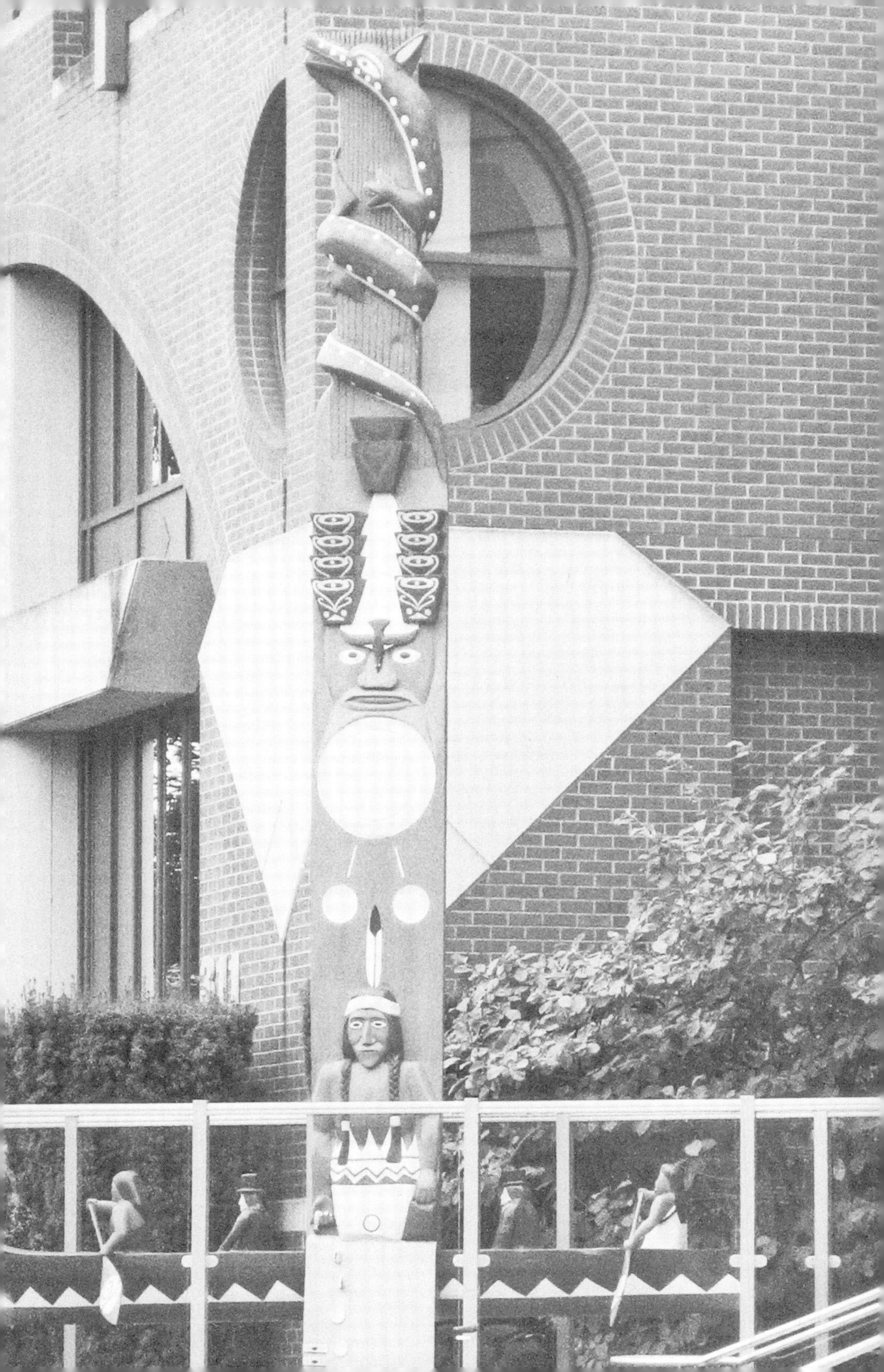

12 *Bellingham Centennial* History Pole

PAULINE HILLAIRE

The *Bellingham Centennial* History Pole was carved for the 1952 Bellingham Centennial Celebration and installed near the Bellingham, Washington, Post Office. It was restored by Felix Solomon, Scott Jensen, and Andrew Todd at the Chulh tse X'epy (čə́ɬ cə x̣əpáy') Tradition of Cedar Carving Studio, Lummi Reservation, and installed at the Whatcom County Courthouse in 2007.

THE *CENTENNIAL* POLE EXPLAINS IN GREAT PICTORIAL detail the historic culture of the Lummi people and commemorates the first meeting of white settlers and Lummi leaders in 1852. It is a twenty-two-foot history pole, first dedicated in 1952.

The canoe carries two Indians and two white men. Only the Indians in the canoe are using paddles, which represent their generosity and the trust they received. They are traveling the nearby shores, showing the white men their land. Seated from front to back are the subchief Tsi'li'x^w, Capt. Henry Roeder, Russell Peabody, and Chief Chowitsut. Below the

31. *Bellingham Centennial* history pole, Whatcom County Courthouse, Bellingham, Washington, 2011. Reprinted with permission. Photo by Melonie Ancheta.

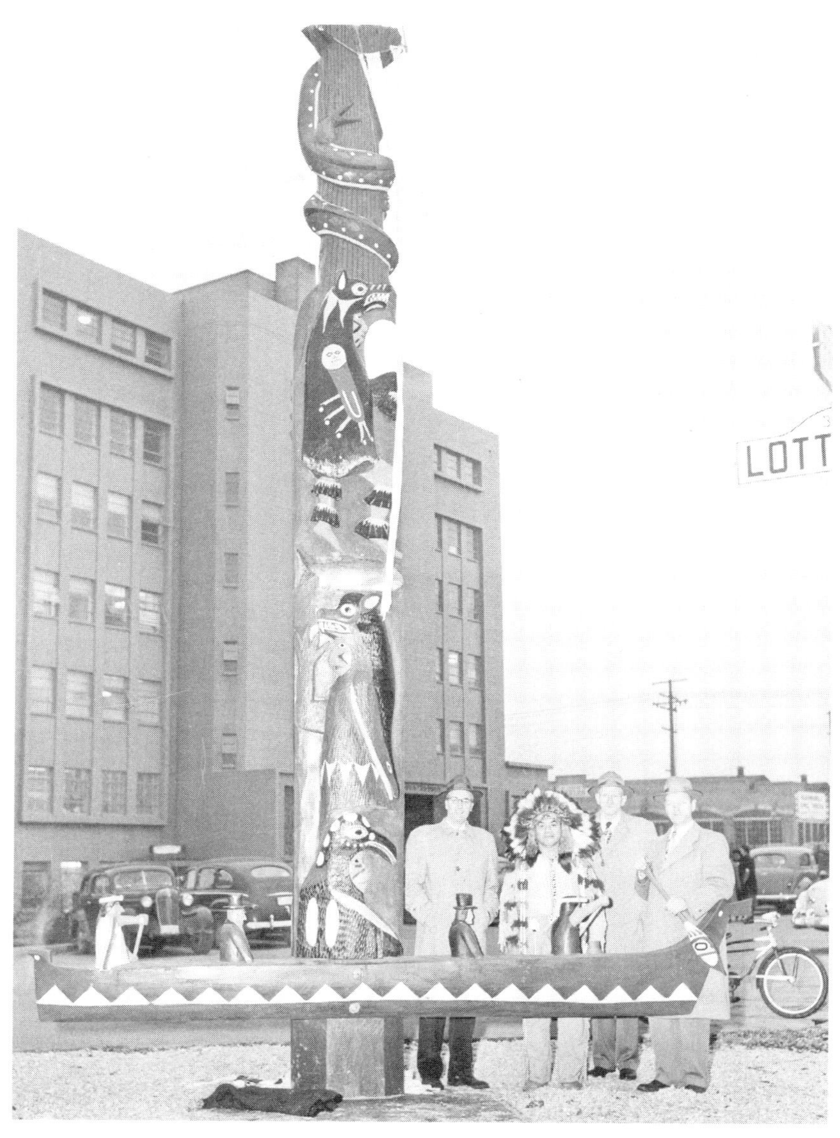

32. *Centennial* history pole dedication, 1952. Committee with Joe Hillaire includes Rev. Carl Calhoun, William Breuer, and Harry O. Loft. Photo by Jack Carver. Reprinted with permission from Whatcom Museum of History and Art, Bellingham, Washington, image number X.4928.007a.

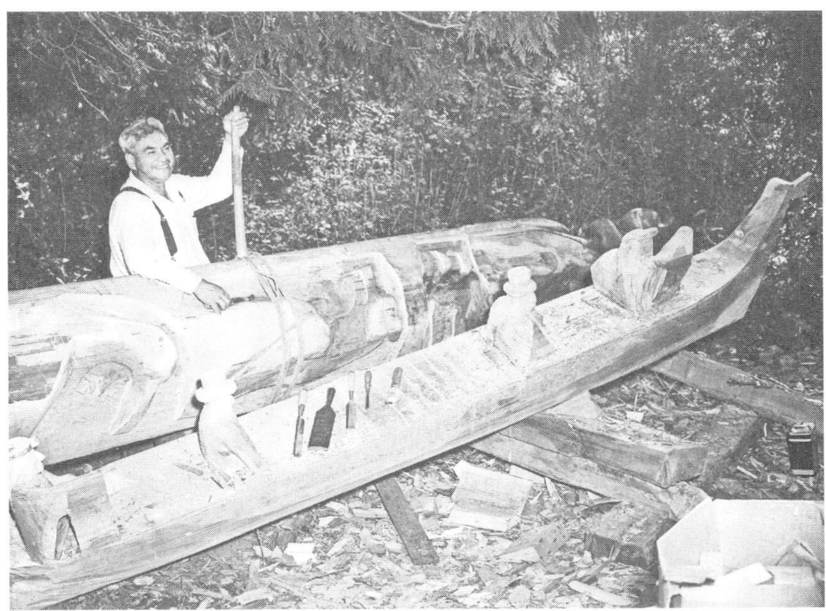

33. Joe Hillaire carving the *Centennial* history pole, 1952. Photo by Jack Carver. Reprinted with permission from Whatcom Museum of History and Art, Bellingham, Washington, image number X 4928.012a.

canoe is a single clam, showing the viewers that there were clams on the beaches of the Lummi homeland.

Above the canoe symbol is someone we recognize as a Watcher, a witness, a negotiator, who tells the stories of the Lummi people as he travels. He wears the blanket and headdress of Raven, whose importance in legends is shown by his placement at the base of the pole. Above the Raven, the story shows the power of the Black Bear Dancer. The Bear is his guardian spirit. Very long ago, Bear introduced spirituality to everything. And as a person grew, his common sense and the logic in his behavior showed his elders what Guardian Spirit he might receive when he deserved it. Above the Bear Dancer is the fish, representing the most bountiful resource, the salmon.

Above the salmon is a Wolf Dancer, holding a moon. Above the second Wolf Dancer is the *say-nilh-xay* (sínəɬqiʔ), a most feared giant beast and

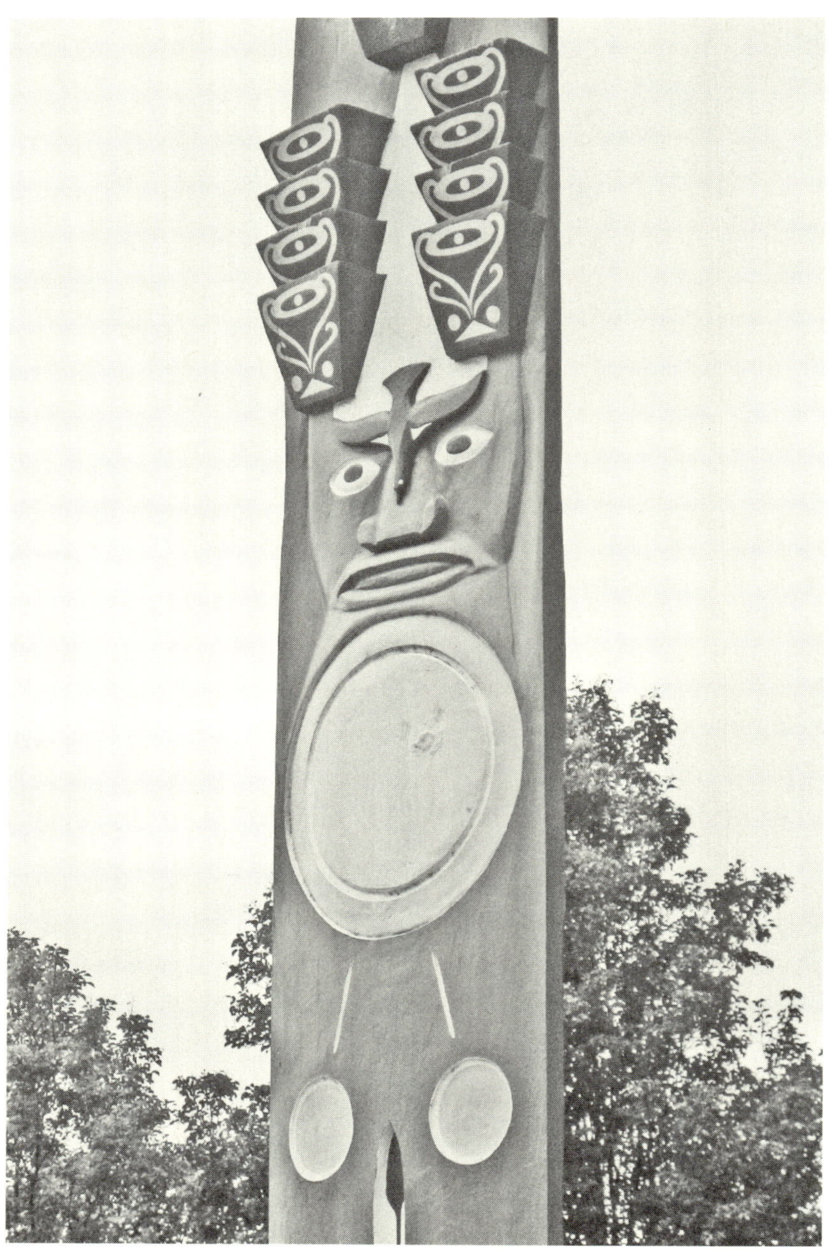

34. *Centennial* pole detail: eight potlatch baskets, Man of Vision, and sun dogs, 2011. Reprinted with permission. Photo by Melonie Ancheta.

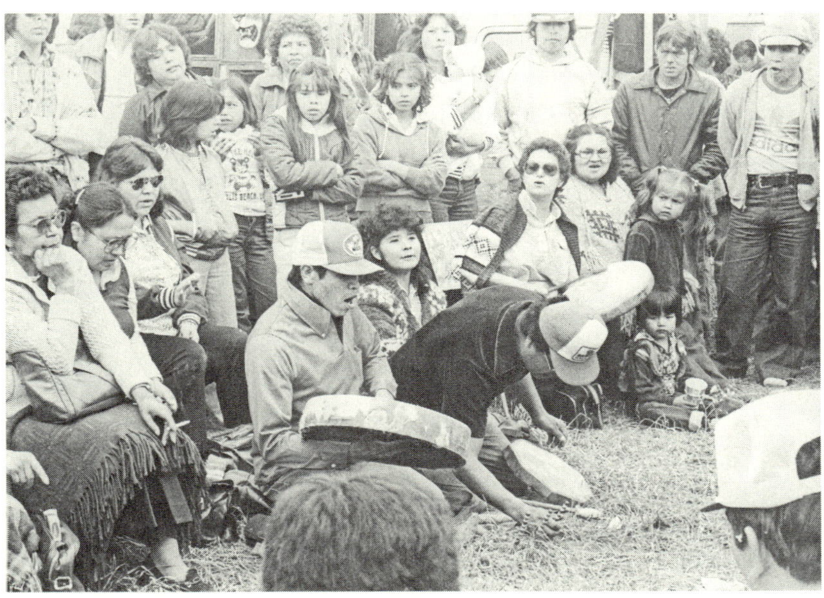

35. *Slahál* game at the Lummi Stommish Water Festival, 1980. Photo by Jack Carver. Reprinted with permission from Whatcom Museum of History and Art, Bellingham, Washington, image number 1995.1.044033.

protector of the people who, with one arm, holds the entire tribe together. This, of course, shows the viewers that legends are held in high esteem by the entire tribe, represented by the cattails, which are many and are never-dying, like the Lummi. Progressing down the back, the story pole continues the story of the tribe that was held together by myth, vision, and legend. Below the cattails and the *say-nilh-xay*, the pole shows that women prepared the eight ceremonial potlatches that were held by the tribe before the signing of the Treaty of 1855. From the number of potlatches held by the tribe, one can easily understand that a great deal was considered in a ceremonial and serious manner before the tribe signed the treaty. Eight baskets contained food, and the baskets were given as gifts of thanks. Below the potlatch baskets is a Man of Vision, who displays the sun dogs, a rare vision of the sun as it is setting. The sun dogs are the two circles below the design of the sun.

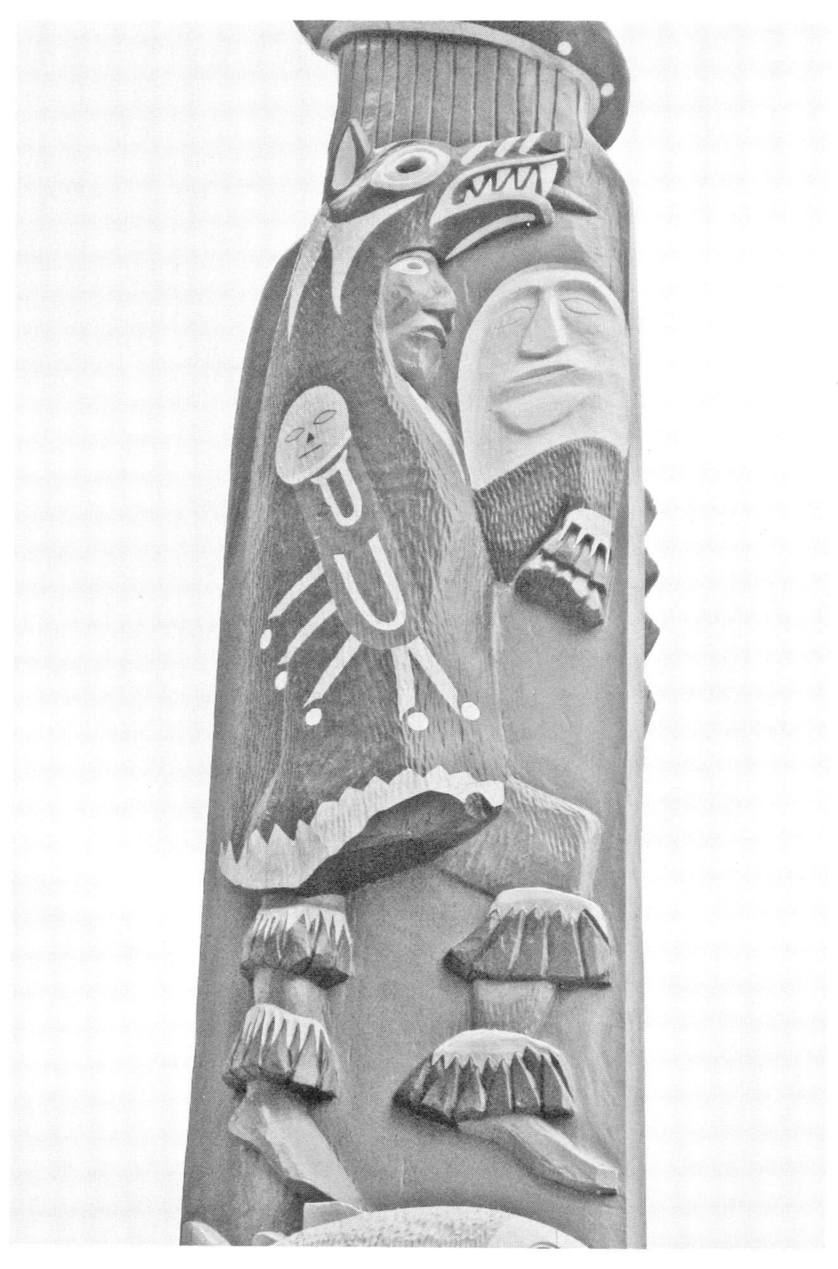

36. *Centennial* pole detail: Wolf Dancer with Flea, Moon, 2011. Reprinted with permission. Photo by Melonie Ancheta.

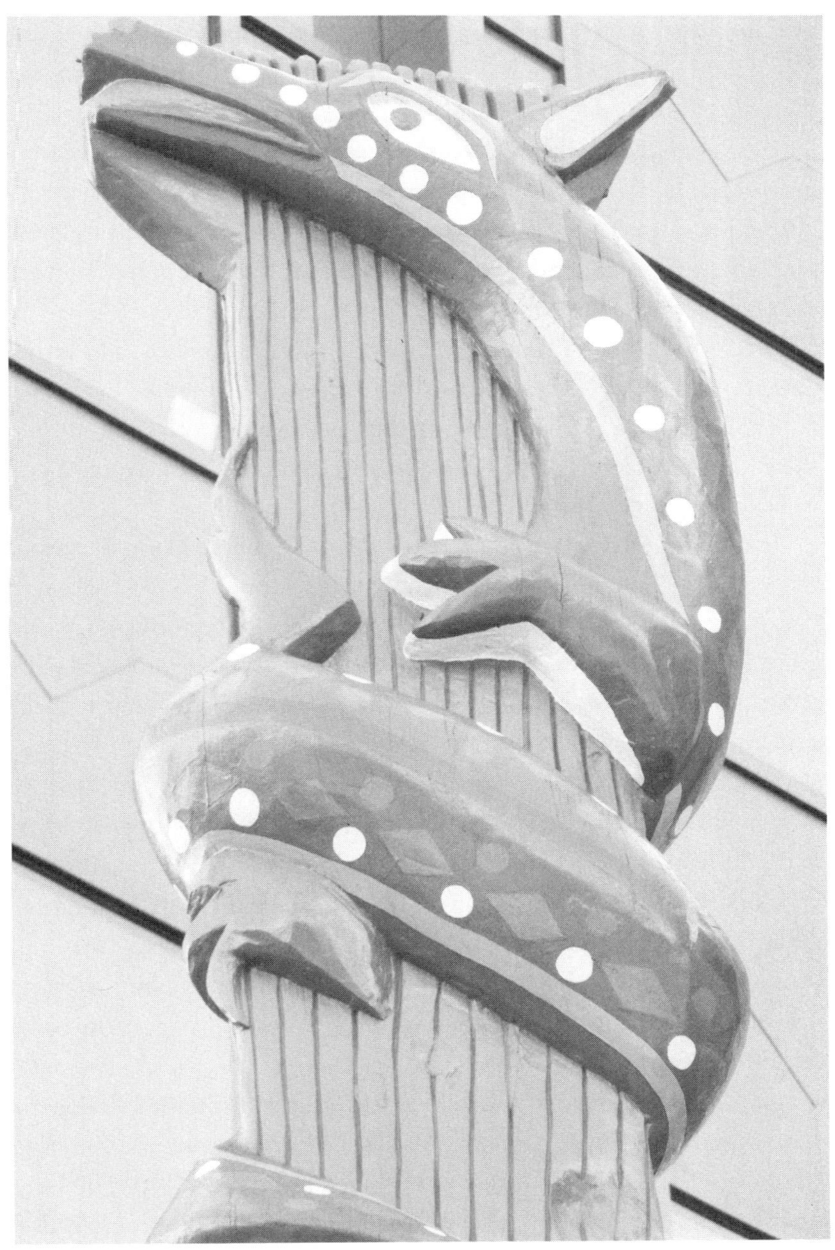

37. *Centennial* pole detail: the *say-nilh-xay* (sínəɬqiʔ) and cattails (*front*), 2010. Photo by Gregory P. Fields.

Below the sun and sun dogs is an Indian in regalia playing the game Slahál, or the Bone Game, as it is more commonly called today, showing that life wasn't always serious.

The Raven disks below the Indian are part of the score-keeping mechanism. The Slahál dancers and singers have such skill with the drum and rattles and clappers and the voices of all. They never sing in tune with each other, and that's the magic of their sound; they're not in tune with each other. They all have a different note but the same beat.

The Wolf Dancer upholds the universe. Notice the Flea, a beautiful design on the Wolf Dancer. This shows the viewers that we lived with both the good and the bad. It shows you that we have both the good and the bad in our country, both the pestilence and the abundance. That's what the artisan is saying.

And then, right up on top, is the *say-nilh-xay*. The giant serpent at the very top of the pole is not an eagle, so therefore it's not a victory. In 1855 we were ordered off of that ground, so it's not victory. But we're held together by fear, by the serpent, and what's inside, representing us, is the cattail. Why did the artisan choose a cattail? It never dies, and so that's why he chose the wrapping of the cattail.

The cattail never dies, and the *say-nilh-xay* represents fear, that we were held together by fear. Every art piece that I've ever known — white man's, Indian, Chinese — has more than one single explanation. This *say-nilh-xay*, the serpent, can also represent control by the Bureau of Indian Affairs. The Lummi have legends of the five Terrible Beasts that hold people together with fear while nurturing good behavior by encouraging one to confront "the beast within." The beast has one serpent-arm and one frog-arm.

The *Centennial* history pole, which was originally installed during the Centennial Celebration in 1952, was a Bellingham landmark, standing across from today's post office near Whatcom Creek, where Roeder and Peabody, Bellingham's first white settlers, had built a sawmill that was a center of early Bellingham life. Over time, the pole needed to be restored and relocated, and the Bellingham County Council led efforts to ensure its preservation. In 2007 carvers Felix Solomon and Scott Jensen, in consultation with art conservator Andrew Todd of British Columbia, completed two years of work to restore the totem pole at Felix Solomon's Chulh tse X'epy (Tradition of Cedar) Studio on the Lummi Reservation.

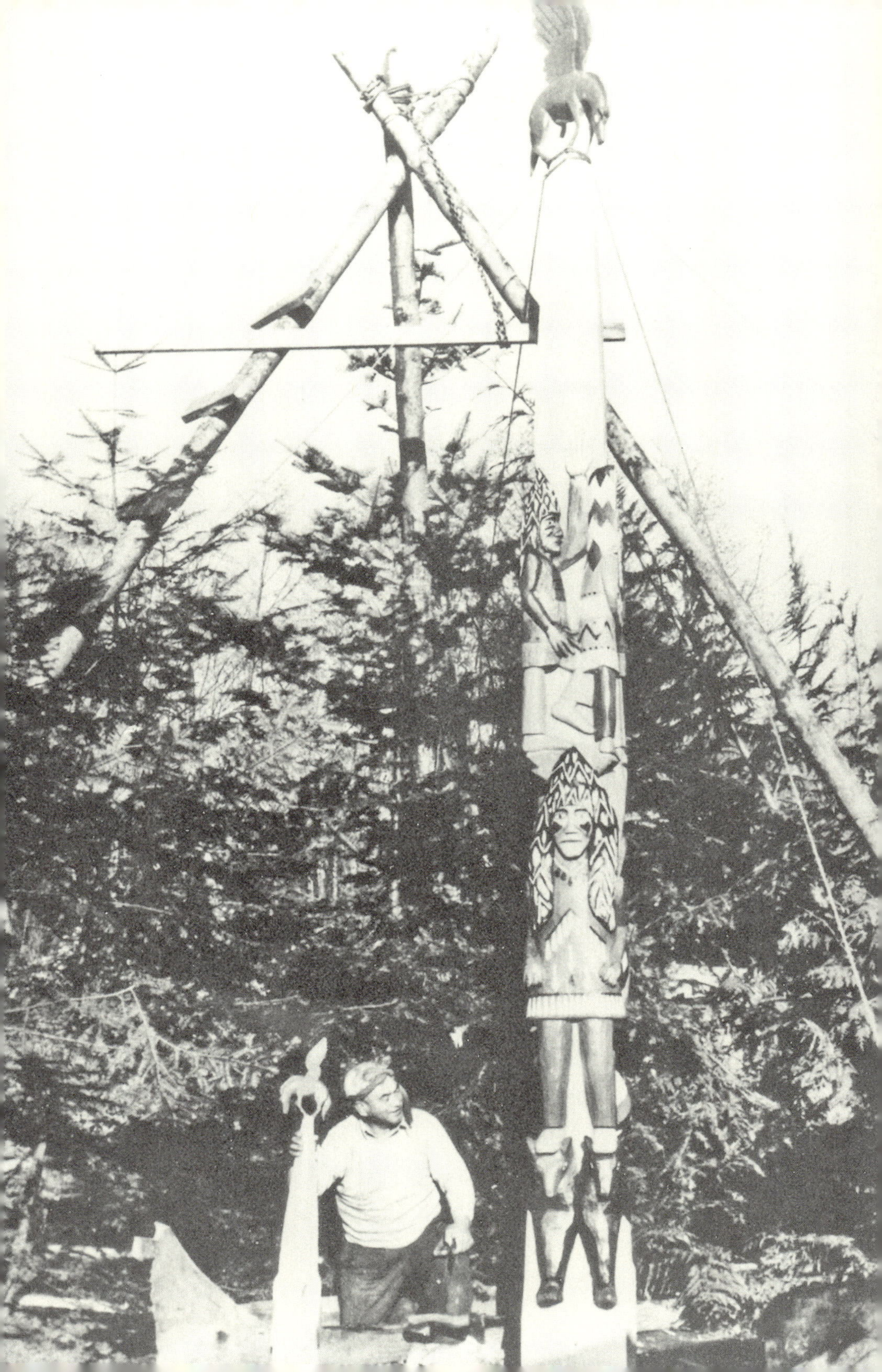

13 *Schelangen* Story Pole

PAULINE HILLAIRE

The Schelangen (Mobil/Ferndale) pole was carved for the General Petroleum Refinery in Ferndale, Washington, to represent the close relationship between the Lummi Tribe, industry, and the Ferndale community. The pole was installed at the refinery from 1954 to 1992. Restoration was undertaken under the sponsorship of the Mobil Annuitants Group, and repairs were funded by the Mobil Foundation. Restoration by Dan Thomas and Sean Siner was completed in 1994, and the pole was donated to the city by the Mobil Annuitants Group. It was installed at Ferndale Public Library from 1994 to 2011. As of 2011, the pole has been in storage, awaiting restoration and reinstallation by the city of Ferndale.

THIS TOTEM POLE WAS ORIGINALLY INTENDED TO show the mastery of the Mobil Oil Company of years ago, but time changes everything. One of the biggest compliments my father ever received was the dignitaries' surprise, voiced directly to him: "That Flying Horse looks

38. Joe Hillaire carving the *Schelangen* (sčəláŋən) pole, 1954. Photo by Mobil Annuitants Group. Reprinted with permission from Whatcom Museum of History and Art, Bellingham, Washington, image number 1995.0081.931.

great, even if it was done by a canoe master." My father always smiled so big every time he heard mention of this compliment.

On one side, at the base of the pole, is a Lummi tribal crest. It consists of the serpent, *say-nilh-xay* (sínəɬqiʔ), a protector of the people. He is entwined around a clump of bulrushes, sə́naʔxʷ, symbol of productivity. The Lummi aspired to be so great that ducks would fall to the ground by the shock of the Lummi's united voices. On the other side at the base is one of the crests of the House of Haeteluk, a man dressed in the traditional Lummi regalia. Miniature war clubs and deer hooves decorate the tunic, and the headdress is made of split eagle feathers, a symbol of humility in a great leader. He is standing on a Two-Headed Wolf. One of the heads is black and the other is brown, representing male and female (see chapter 21).

The upper half of the pole is the theme of the carver, "Call of the American Indian for Equality in Industry." In the middle are four human figures, dressed in different headdresses. On the west side is *sxwaixwe* (sx̣ʷəy̓x̣ʷi), the mythic mask. On the south is a man wearing the headdress of the mighty wind. On the east is the warbonnet. On the north is the headdress of humility. The four are dancing, calling to the Flying Horse, Pegasus, which was the symbol of the Mobil Oil Corporation at that time. The horse is standing on the pinnacle, looking down, and listening to the call of the Indians for equality in industry. This was the carver's plea for his people.

As a viewer, I can hear the shells, the little red cedar paddles, and the shattering sound of the clubs in rhythm with the beat of the drum and song as they introduce the flying horse above them. What a fantastic spirit.

This pole is also known as the *Mobil* pole and the *Ferndale* pole, but the original name given by the carver was the *Schelangen* (sčəláŋən) pole. *Schelangen* refers to the Lummi heritage and way of life and all that must be preserved, protected, and taught. The space between the horse and the culture of the Lummi people dancing around the pole — the space is there. It's not one of anger, it's not one of frustration; it's just a peaceful spot between us, and so it represents the Lummi way of life.

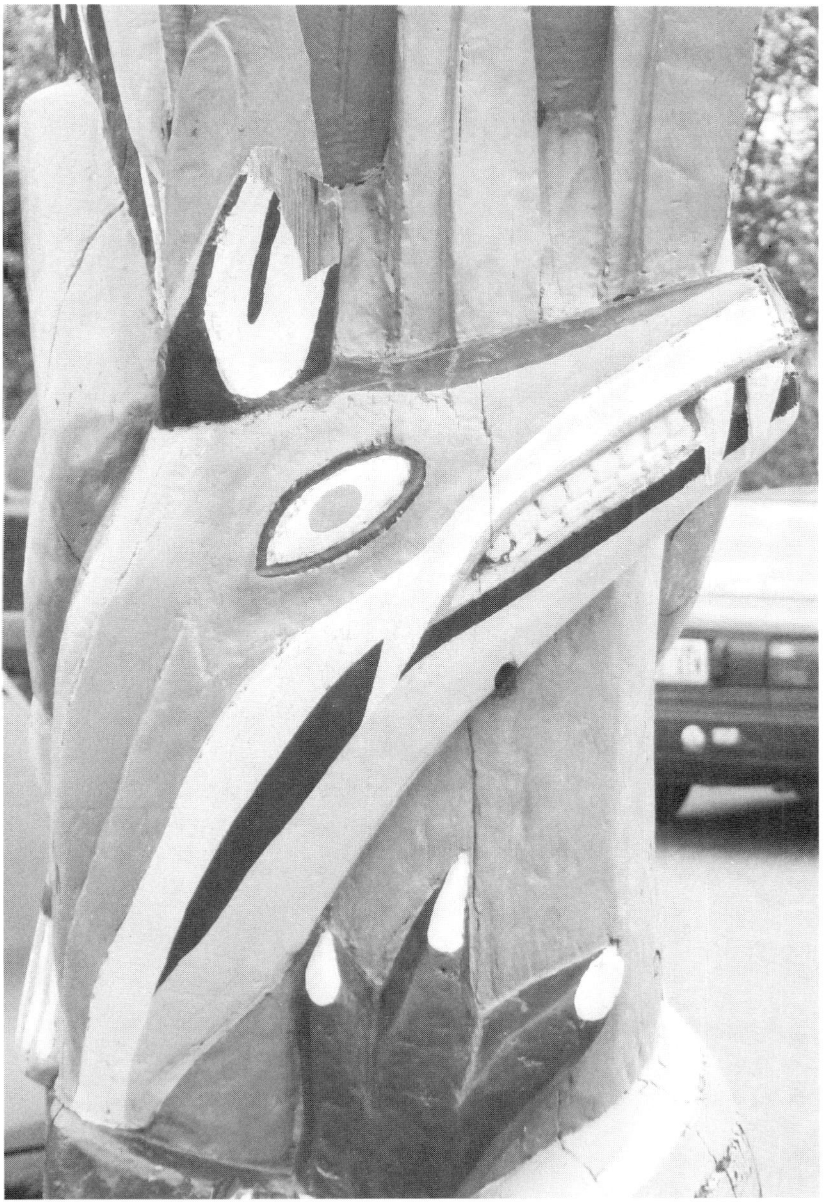

39. *Schelangen* (sčəláŋən) pole detail: the *say-nilh-xay* (sínəɬqiʔ), 2009. Reprinted with permission. Photo by Scott Jensen.

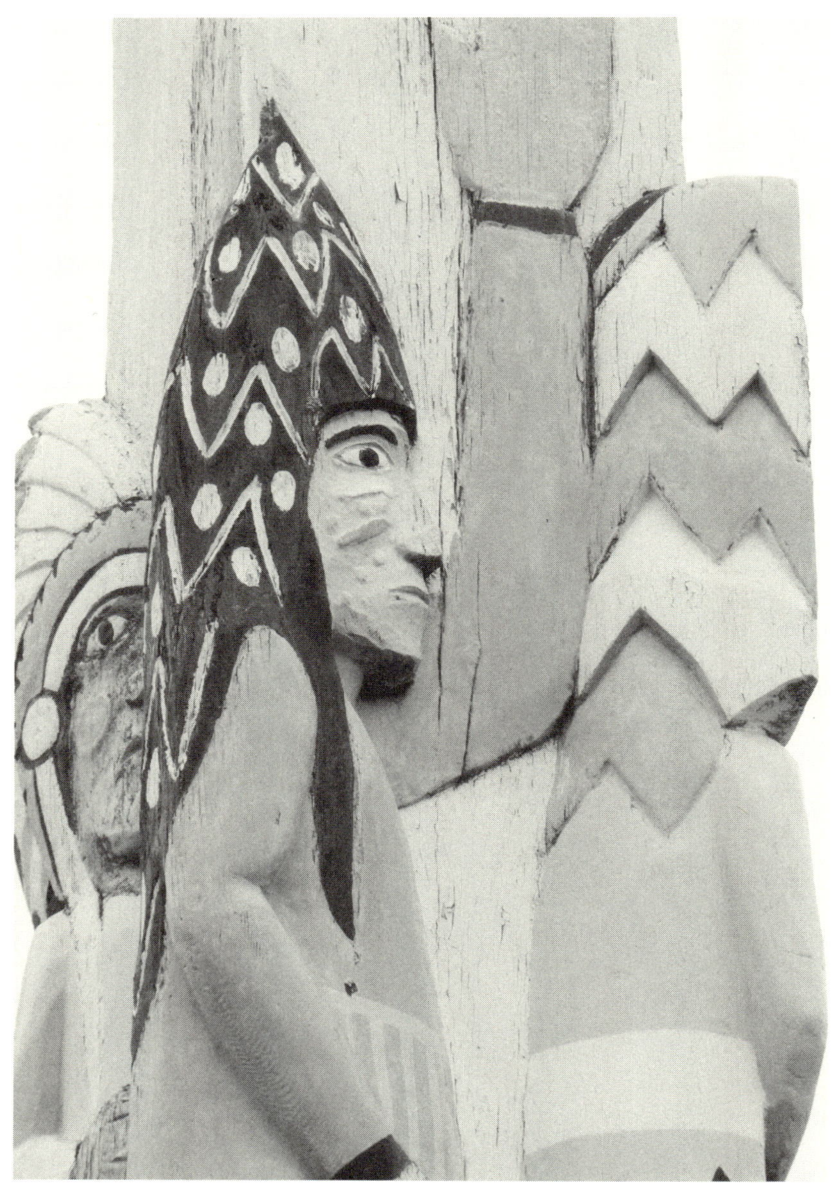

40. *Schelangen* (sčəláŋən) pole detail: potlatch dancers, 2009. Reprinted with permission. Photo by Scott Jensen.

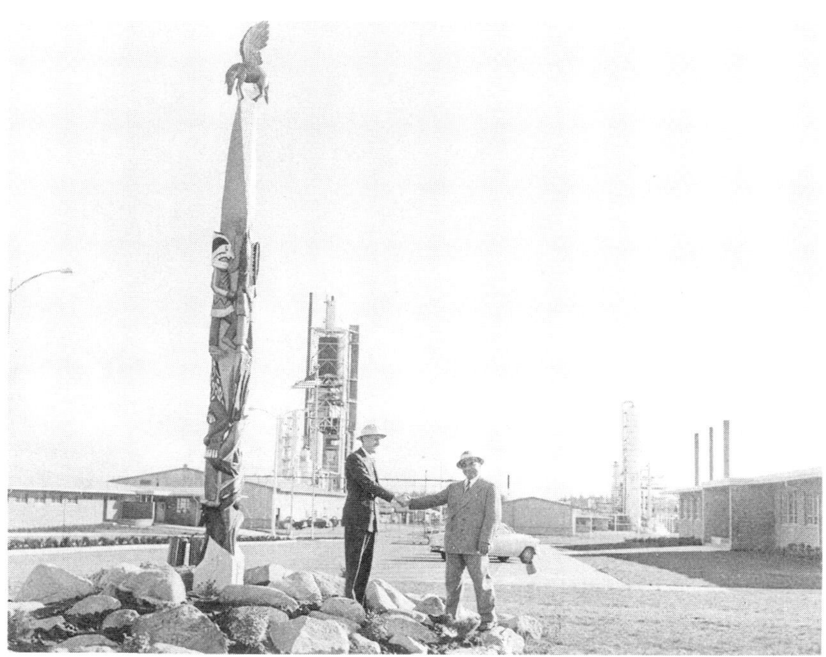

41. Joe Hillaire and Manager Curt Cortelyou with the *Schelangen* (sčəláŋən) story pole at the General Petroleum Refinery, Ferndale, Washington, 1955. Photo by Jack Carver. Reprinted with permission from Whatcom Museum of History and Art, Bellingham, Washington, image number 1995.1.473.

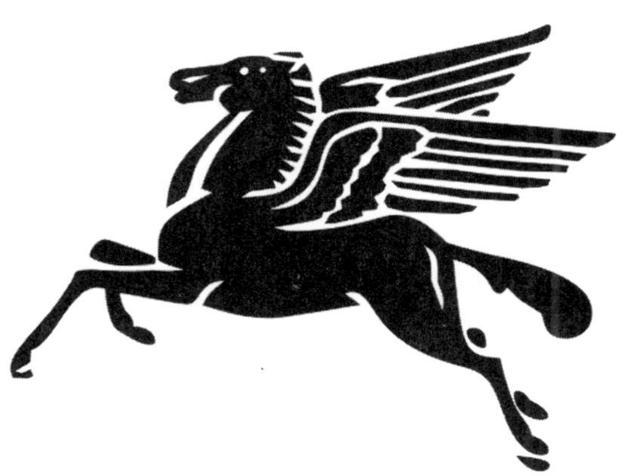

42. Pegasus logo. Courtesy of Exxon Mobil Corporation.

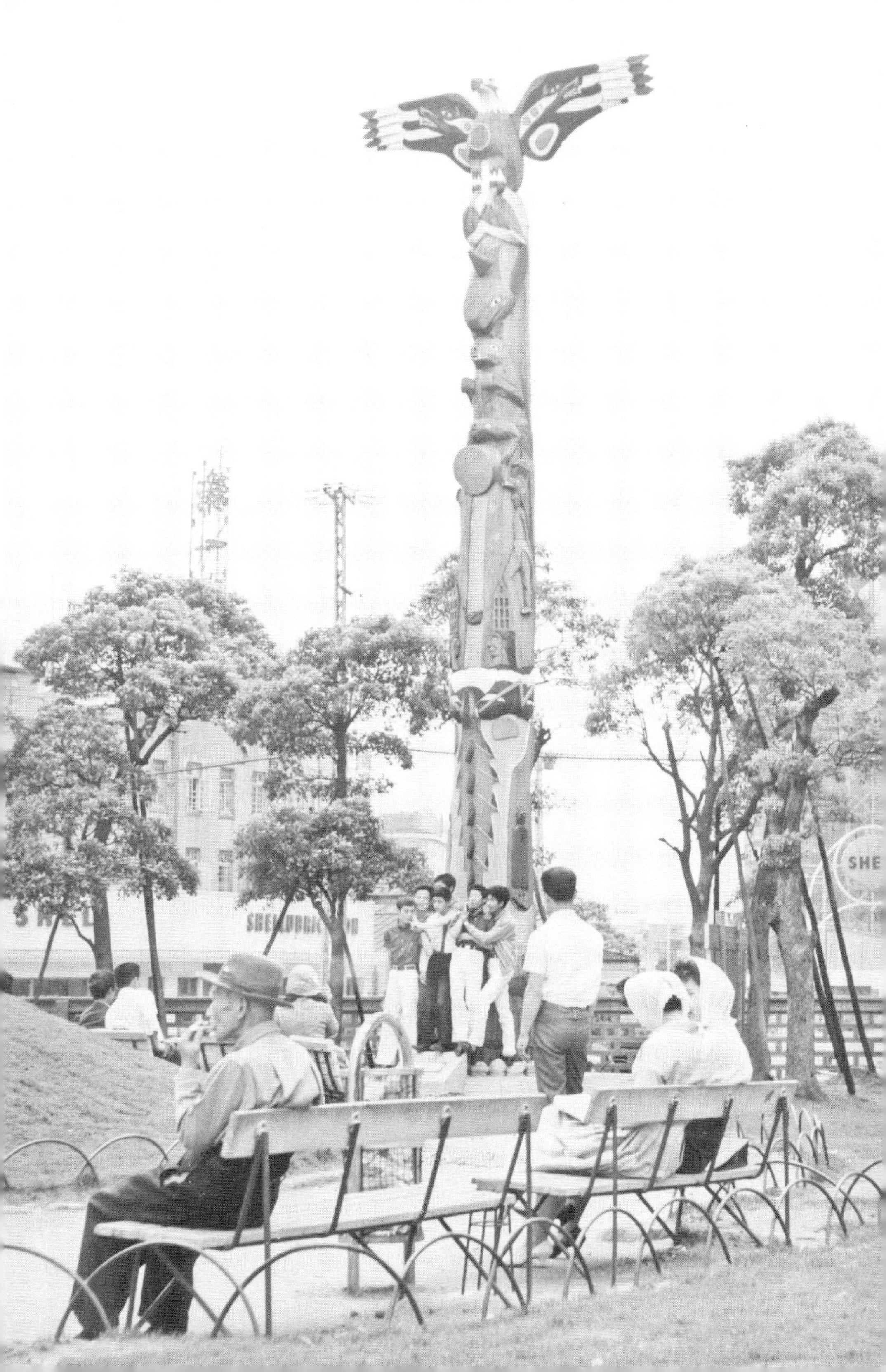

14 Kobe-Seattle Sister Cities Friendship Pole

PAULINE HILLAIRE

Joe Hillaire was commissioned by the Seattle-Kobe Affiliation Committee to carve the Kobe pole as a gesture of international friendship after the devastation of World War II. Like some of Joe's other carvings, the Kobe pole reflects important historical events and community relationships. These works also reflect the spirit of intercultural fellowship that infused Joe's work as an artist and a diplomat. Joe carved the pole in Seattle's Pioneer Square, where local residents and visitors could watch him carve and learn of the Kobe-Seattle friendship initiative. For the installation of the pole Joe traveled to Kobe, Japan, where he conducted ceremonies and addressed community groups and schoolchildren.

43. Japanese citizens taking pictures at the Kobe pole. Engraved on the brass plaque at the base of the pole are the words "Presented in friendship to the people of Kobe, Japan, from the people of Seattle, U.S.A., Sister Cities, October 20, 1961." Courtesy of the Seattle Municipal Archives, 1960s.

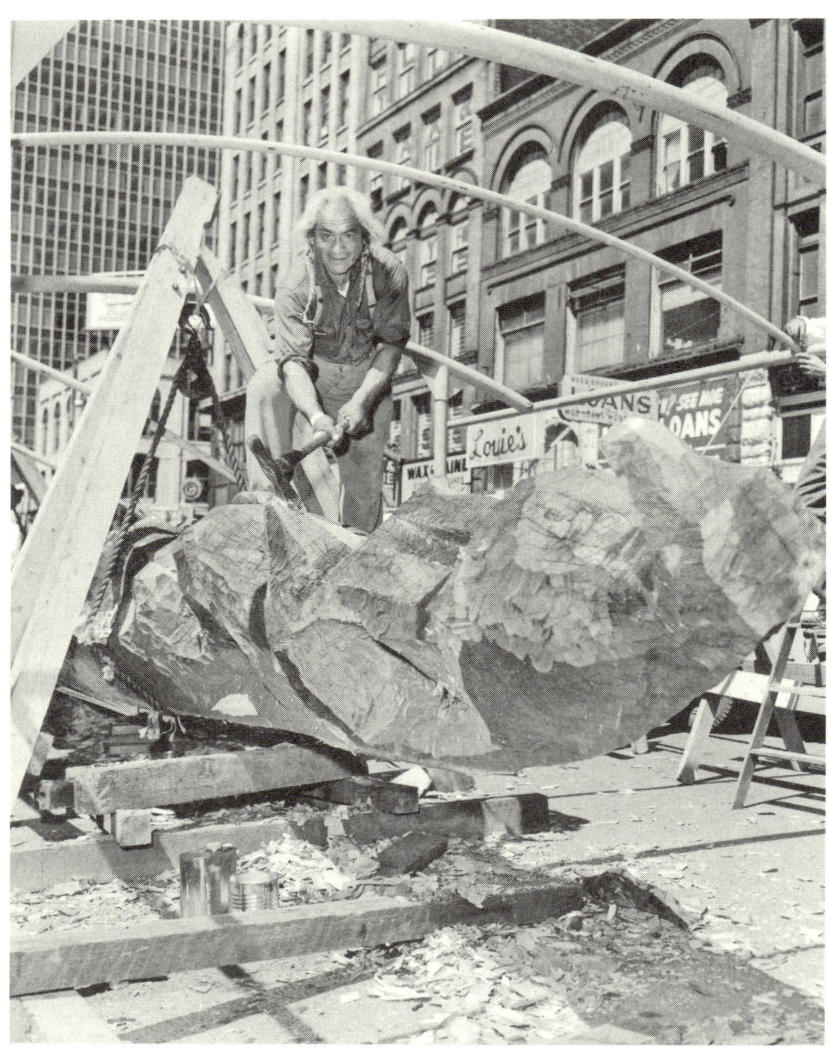

44. Joe Hillaire carving the Kobe pole in Pioneer Square, Seattle, 1961. Reprinted with permission from Seattle Post-Intelligencer Collection, Museum of History and Industry, Seattle.

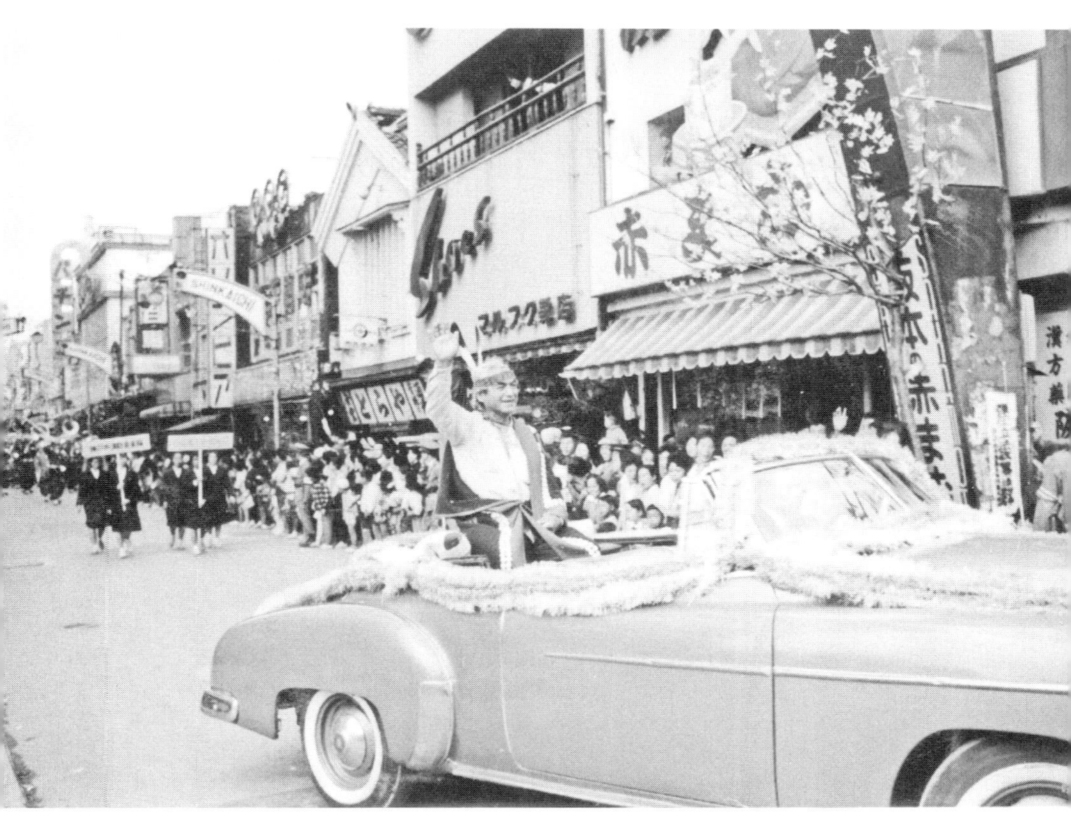

45. Joe Hillaire in the parade held for the Kobe-Seattle Sister Cities friendship pole. Totem pole dedication ceremony, Kobe, Japan, October 20, 1961. Reprinted with permission. Courtesy of the Seattle Public Library, 327301.

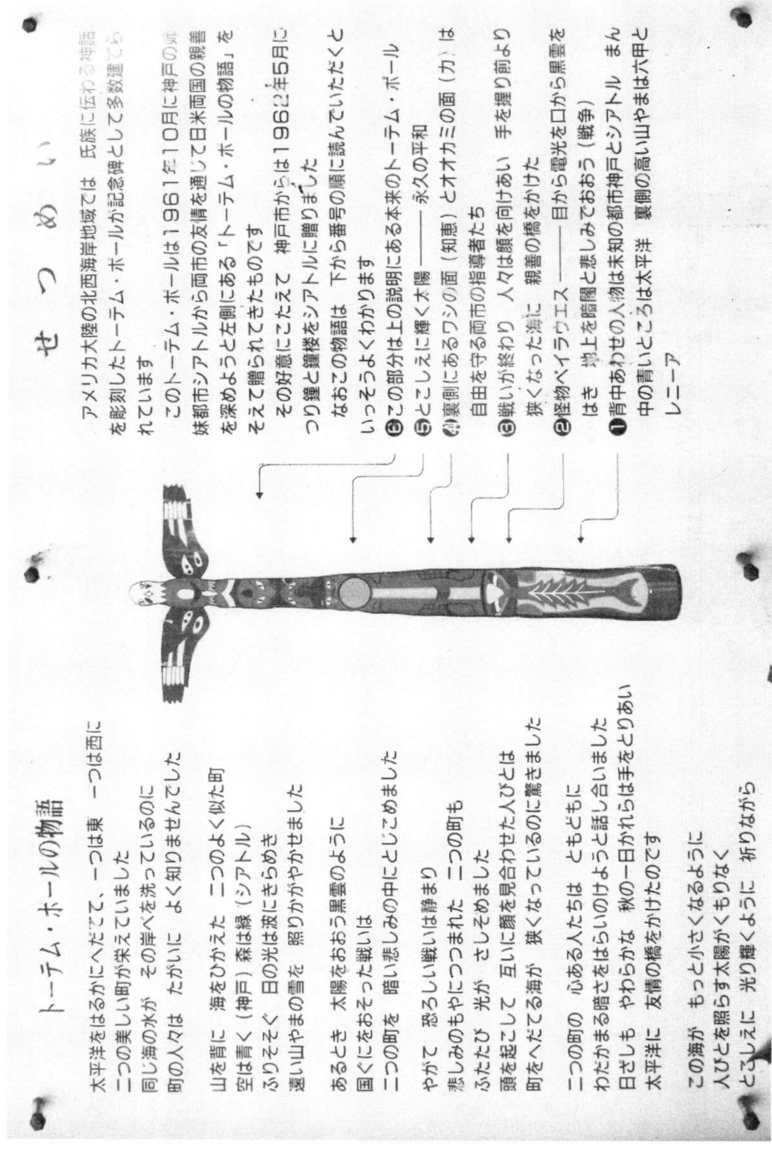

46. Kobe totem pole interpretative plaque with the explanation of the figures carved on the pole, 2009. Reprinted with permission. Photo by Masaharu Onishi.

TRANSLATION OF THE PLAQUE

In the Pacific Northwest of North America, you can see many totem poles, which are monumental sculptures carved from large trees, and they often illustrate Native American legends. Along with the "Totem Pole Tale," this totem pole was sent by our sister-city, Seattle, as a goodwill gift in October of 1961. In return we presented them a friendship bell and its accompanying structure in May of 1962.

Read the following story from the bottom up to better understand the "Totem Pole Tale."

6. This part represents the traditional Native American totem pole.
5. Forever shining sun = everlasting peace.
4. (On the back side of the pole) mask of hawk (= wisdom) and mask of wolf (= force) represent the leaders of each city, who defend freedom.
3. When the war ended, people greeted one another with a clasp of hands, and built a friendship bridge over the Pacific, which no longer divides the two cities.
2. Monster ペイラウエス – its eyes a streak of lightning and its mouth blowing a black cloud – overcasts the earth with darkness and sorrow (= war).
1. Persons, facing one another, represent the future of Kobe and Seattle. The blue section in the middle represents the Pacific Ocean, and the mountains in the back represent Mount Rokko and Mount Rainier.

トーテム・ポールの物語

太平洋をはるかにへだてて、一つは東　一つは西に
二つの美しい町が栄えていました
同じ海の水が　その岸べを洗っているのに
町の人々は　たがいに　よく知りませんでした

山を背に　海をひかえた　二つのよく似た町
空は青く（神戸）　森は緑（シアトル）
ふりそそぐ　日の光は波にきらめき
遠い山やまの雪を　照りかがやかせました

あるとき　太陽をおおう黒雲のように
国ぐにをおそった戦いは
二つの町を　暗い悲しみの中にとじこめました

やがて　恐ろしい戦いは静まり
悲しみのもやにつつまれた　二つの町も
ふたたび　光が　さしそめました
頭を起こして　互いに顔を見合わせた人びとは
町をへだてる海が　狭くなっているのに驚きました

二つの町の　心ある人たちは　ともどもに
わだかまる暗さをはらいのけようと話し合いました
日ざしも　やわらかな　秋の一日かれらは手をとりあい
太平洋に　友情の橋をかけたのです

この海が　もっと小さくなるように
人びとを照らす太陽がくもりなく
とこしえに　光り輝くように　祈りながら

A TOTEM POLE TALE

Divided by the Pacific Ocean, two beautiful towns were flourishing,
one on the east, and the other on the west.
Although the same sea water flows from one coast to the other, the
townspeople didn't know much about each other.

Two very similar towns, each with an ocean and a mountain in the
back. The sky was blue (Kobe), the forest was green (Seattle).
The radiant sun glistened on the ocean waves and shone upon the
snow-capped mountains.

One day, as if black clouds covered the sun, a war erupted.
The two towns were entombed in bleak sorrow.

Soon the dreadful war ended. Once enwrapped in the gloom of
lament, the two towns were now flooded with light.

Raising their heads and looking at one another, the townspeople
marveled at how the dividing ocean began to feel like a narrow
body of water.

Thoughtful people from both towns began conversations in hopes
of banishing the smoldering darkness.

On a serene autumn day, hand in hand, they built a Friendship
Bridge over the Pacific,

wishing that the distance between two towns grows even smaller
and that the sun forever shines upon people without casting a single
cloud.

Translated from the Japanese by Mai Ketcherside

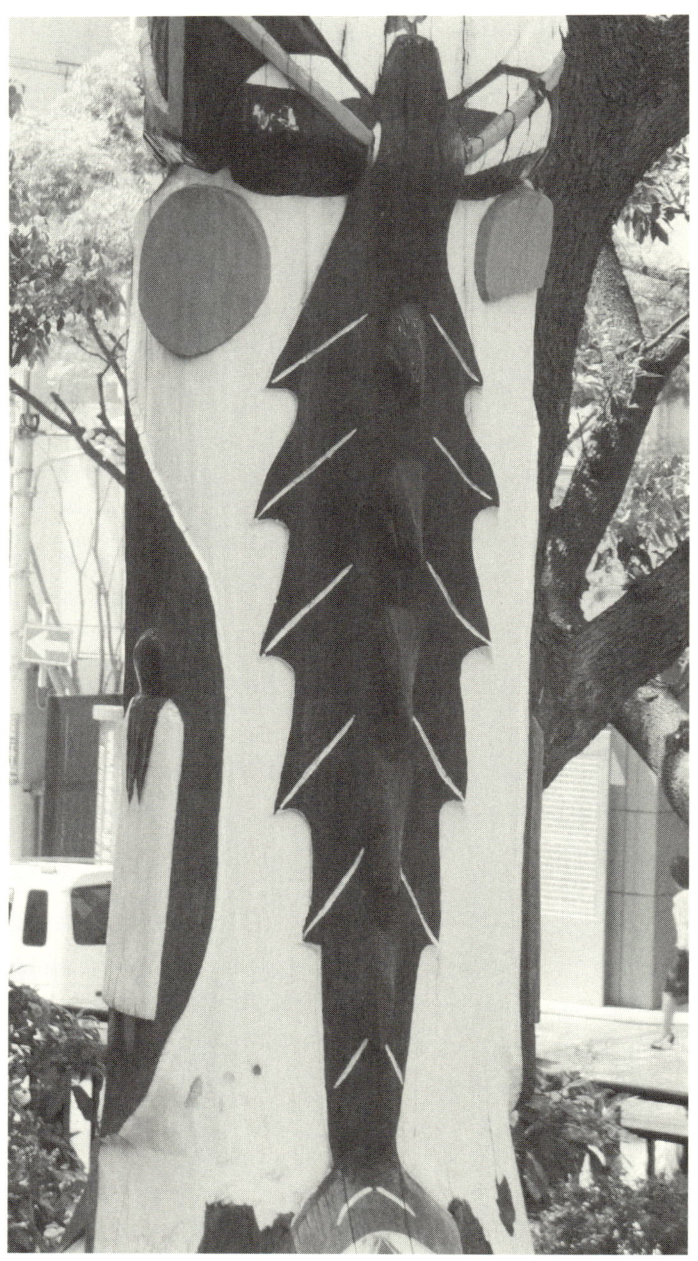

47. Kobe, Japan, totem pole detail: one of the two sisters and the monster representing war. Reprinted with permission from Kobe Trade Information Office.

As I have understood the story of these two beautiful cities after hearing my father tell it to dignitaries from Seattle and Kobe as well as in the city where he last lived, Suquamish, Washington, I related the story of these two cities to sisters in general. They grew up together from infancy, and they became more and more beautiful. Every now and then, on a very clear day, and especially on a clear, starlit night, they got glimpses of each other. For you see, the Pacific Ocean separated them. They began to nurture their understanding of each other. Father Sea freely allowed each his best and tastiest food.

Time passed happily, and each sister heard of the myths the other shared, listening to every word about the Dragons and the Thunderbirds. The excitement grew as their populations grew; city lights expanded as though in competition. But seriously they pondered all that they shared, not just the salmon, not just the mystery of the myths, but also the clouds and sun, freely floating through the sky to each side of the ocean. Kobe, of the east, had the strength and courage of the rising sun. Seattle, of the west, had the beauty and the blessings of the setting sun. And from each, each sister's people spoke spiritually of their good fortune.

As sister cities, Kobe and Seattle have so much in common. Both have the beautiful lights of the city and the setting and rising sun. So they share these common denominators every day of their lives. The women at the bottom of the pole are on either side of the ocean. And so when they once get to know that the other in fact exists, they begin to share the things they have in common: the creatures of the sea, the creatures of the sky, the spirit of the land as it was held together by the Great Spirit. And when they numbered so many common denominators they said: "After all, you must be my sister." And they were both blessed with the spirit of the Eagle at the top of the totem pole. The bottom of the pole represents all the similar things in the ocean that Kobe and Seattle have in common: the salmon, the monster, all the things in the ocean. And they share the same sun. The Bear is telling who the artisan is — that's my father. The Eagle represents victory. That is what Seattle and Kobe share: the ocean and the sky, and the victory.

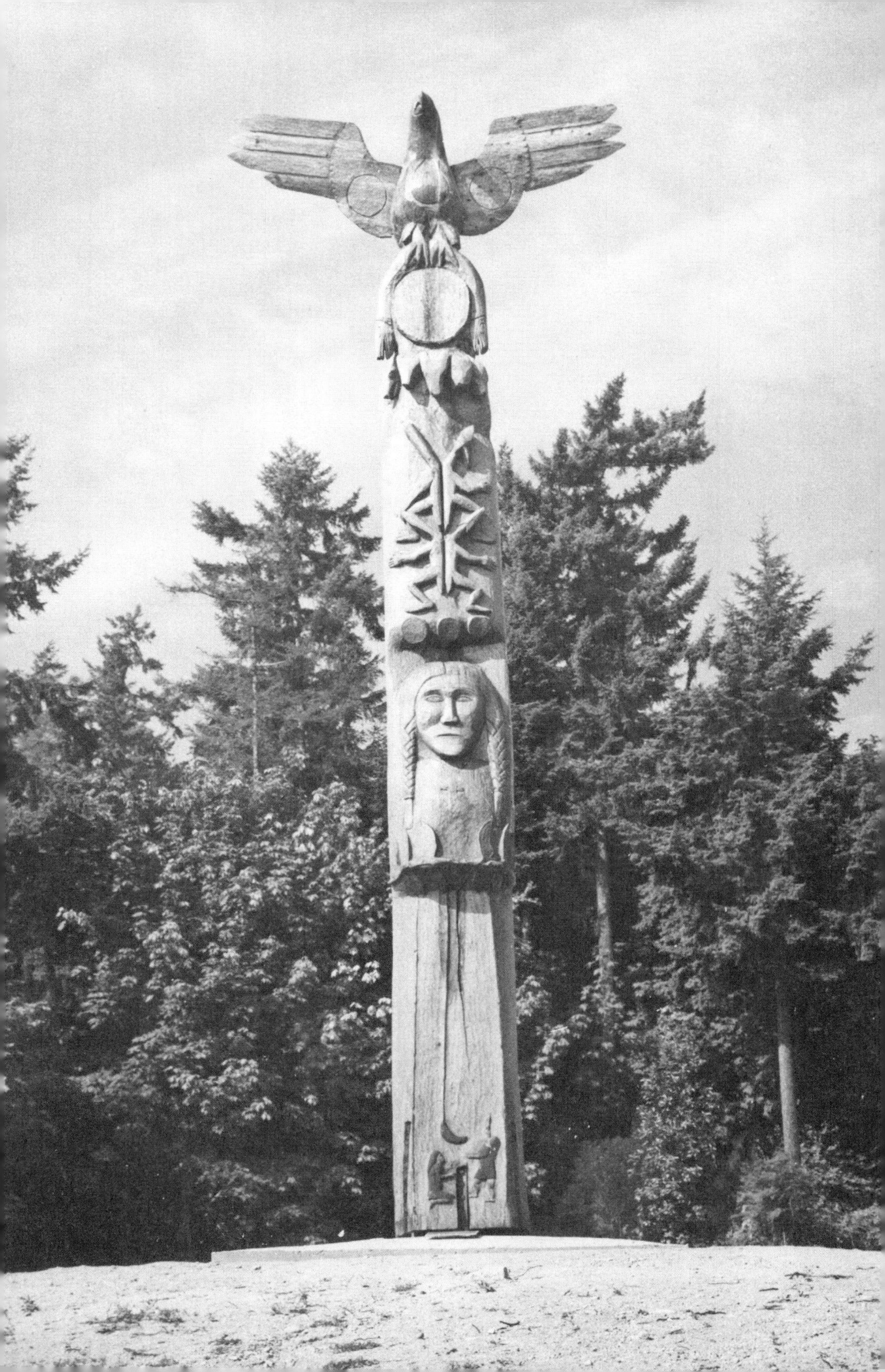

15 *Land in the Sky* Story Pole

PAULINE HILLAIRE

In 1963 this pole was installed in Suquamish, Washington, by the Washington State Pioneer Association, Kitsap County Historical Association, and American Legion Post No. 60. Dedicated to Chief Siʔaɬ (Seattle) and Chief Kitsap, it stood until 2005, when it was taken to be stored on the Lummi Reservation, with hopes of restoration. The myth that follows was told by Pauline Hillaire. The portions of the story in italics are from *Land in the Sky Totem, from Tales Told Me by Joe Hillaire*, by Robert O. Bishop Sr.

JOE HILLAIRE CARVED THE *LAND IN THE SKY* TOTEM pole for the 1962 World's Fair in Seattle. This was just after Sputnik came out from Russia in 1960. It's a thirty-five-foot pole, three and half feet in diameter, weighing 13,240 pounds, and carved from a red cedar tree about a thousand years old, harvested in the rain forest near the Hoh River on the Olympic Peninsula. It is carved on both sides, showing two

48. *Land in the Sky* totem pole, Suquamish, Washington. Photo by Lawrence D. Lindsley. Reprinted by permission from University of Washington Special Collections, Lindsley 1638, 1963.

brothers' ascent to and descent from the moon. While Joe was carving it, he traveled with it in a specially equipped moving van around the United States on an 8,470-mile goodwill tour, with stops in twenty-five major cities, including Washington DC.

"LAND IN THE SKY," A LUMMI MYTH

The legend of the totem concerns two brothers, one of them a medicine man. Their figures are located at the base of the pole. One boy is pointing toward the sky, which indicates a boy with vision who can see the Land of the Moon. The other boy is in a stooping position and is unable to see what the other can.

The two boys, after securing enough food for their people so that they might be safe in the boys' absence, went to an isolated island, where they saw a little worm suspended in the sky. The younger brother, who had vision, could see that there was a web emitting from the body of the worm. The idea formed that they, too, could go up in the sky by making a chain of arrows. The younger boy then shot the first arrow up in the sky until it fastened, then shot a second to connect to the base of the first. Thus, the chain began.

The Medicine Man said, "My brother, we have lived on the sandbar, pondering our lives and what to do with our future. Our village is secure against all foes. There is food for all; they need us not. Our future? The answer hangs before us. Let us accept this challenge. Come; let us take the path the little worm so laboriously points out." They began to prepare for the journey. Realizing that they could not climb the slender chain of tufted arrows if they carried anything with them, they stored their bows under their canoe and left a pet mink, chiequen (čəčiq'ən), *to guard their belongings. The little mink, not yet full grown, watched them begin the long climb. Like all travelers who aspire to the heavens, they took only their persons. As they climbed, the slender arrow chains swayed, making a tinkly, crackling sound like elfin crystals or pond ice breaking. After some time they reached the underbelly of the sky and found an opening near them. They pulled themselves through, and like prairie dogs, emerged to find themselves in the middle of a great green grassy*

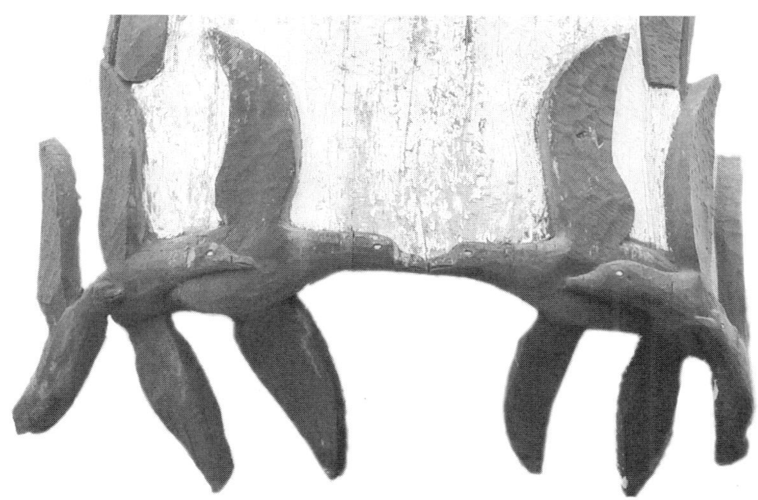

49. *Land in the Sky* totem pole detail: geese, 2002. Reprinted with permission. Photo by John Aitchison.

meadow. A soft wind was blowing and the lush grass and rushes moved like the waves of the Whulge (Puget Sound) far below them.

To their ears came the sound of geese gabbling, calling to them. Walking the lush prairie, they approached a little lake and the noisy geese came out of the water. To the young men's surprise, the geese were really young women dressed in feathers. The carefree women beckoned to them and enticed them, promising them delights if only they would come to the women's camp for a little while.

The younger brother was tempted and started to follow them, but the Medicine Man called him back. "Pay them no heed. Yield not to them, for they are all those things that stop a man from completing his mission. We will be like the wind with no direction if we go with them." The younger lad pondered this and finally replied, "All right, from now on, you lead and I'll follow." Immediately after he said this, Mother Earth appeared before them in the guise of an old woman. "I have been here all the while waiting for you," she said. Then in the manner of a mother she cared for them, giving them food and resting them. "I know the trail you are traveling," she said, "but you will find the Moon a mean host. He considers himself above the Sun and certainly above all mortals. He will destroy you if he finds you unprepared for him." So saying she gave the brothers three round flat stones. "Keep these stones with you. They will make your strength as ten, and in other ways protect you. Remember, on the trail should you see any weapon your old people might have used, pick it up and keep it. It may save you from the Moon Man."

The brothers were now rested and ready to move on, but Mother Earth counseled them further, "The trail is ancient and must be followed with care. Just over the next mountain is a small lake. There, each day, come the Daughter of the Sun and the Daughter of the Moon to bathe. You must find some way to get them to help you." Taking their leave of Mother Earth, the brothers began again their journey across the wide plain. The call of the wily geese was behind them and bothered them not. The trail was indeed faint but the whole of their lives had trained them for such a trek. The Medicine Man broke trail and kept his senses alert and stayed them on their course. The younger brother was able to look around and observe the land and listened to

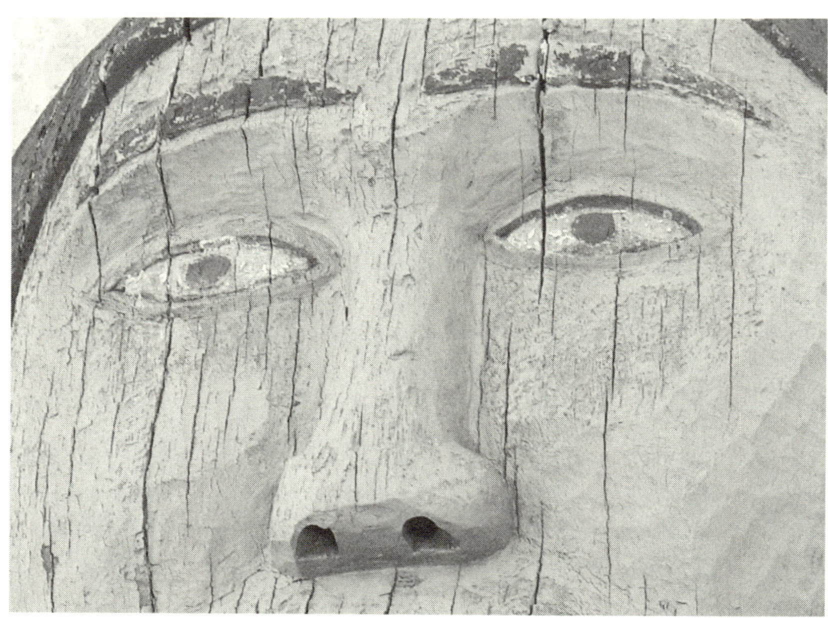

50. *Land in the Sky* totem pole detail: Mother Earth, 2004. Reprinted with permission. Photo by John Aitchison.

the sounds of the country. As the day wore on he found an arrowhead laying in the grass and near it a spearpoint. "Look, my brother," he cried, "what I have found along the trail."

"Remember what Mother Earth told us," replied the Medicine Man. "Save them; put them in your bag. They may be of use to us." Now the prairie was behind them and they found themselves in the low pass leading through the mountains. The day was nearly gone when the younger brother spoke, "My brother, in the grass along the trail, I have found a harpoon head and a broken war club. Shall I save them too, as Mother Earth told us?" "Yes; do that," replied the Medicine Man, "none of us know what things will aid us in life." But now the day was over and they rested in the rushes alongside a little lake. They were richer by their finds of weapons and rested secure because of the little stones given by Mother Earth.

The night passed overhead and when morning arrived they were awakened by gay voices in the sky over their heads. From their hidden beds they watched the Sun's Daughter and Daughter of the Moon above them. Dressed in flowing garments, each wore a fine golden bracelet on each wrist. They faced one another, clasping hands as they descended slowly to the ground. Landing gently they looked around. Seeing no one they disrobed and dove quickly into the clear water. Breaking the surface they looked around again. Seeing no one, they swam to the center of the lake. The young men then rushed out of the rushes and seized the girls' clothing.

The girls were very frightened and the Daughter of the Sun berated the Moon girl. "You should have been more careful where you took us to bathe." "Now, stop that kind of talk," replied the Daughter of the Moon. "These are not ordinary travelers. I have a feeling that we could not avoid this meeting. We will just take them to my father's land. That should satisfy them and my father will know what to do with them." The girls swam to the edge of the lake and pulled watercress around them. "If you give us our clothes, we will take you to my father's land," said the Moon girl. Upon hearing this, the young men reluctantly withdrew, leaving the clothes on the shore. After the girls dressed, the Daughter of the Moon divided golden bracelets among the four of them. Clasping hands in a tight circle, they soared swiftly upward and approached the high plateau where the Moon awaited them.

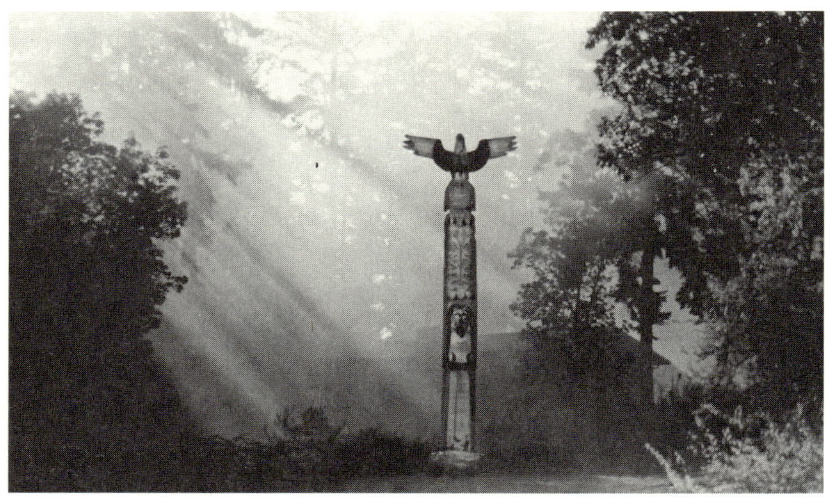

51. *Land in the Sky* totem pole, Suquamish, Washington, 1992. Reprinted with permission. Photo by Tony Hayden, Aloha Studio, Lebanon, Oregon.

When they arrived at the home of the Moon, they were greeted somewhat haughtily—scornfully—but were invited to enter his house. The younger brother jumped in quickly, because the Moon intended to kill him with icicles hanging from the roof, which only crushed against the door. When this failed, the Moon told the boy to put on his hat, which had an icicle in it to pierce the boy's head. The boy put on the hat and pulled it down, and the icicle crushed on a flat stone, which the boy had prudently placed on his head. The Moon praised the boy and then went out and split open a tree. He put props into the tree to hold it apart and then dropped his wedge into the jaws of the split tree. Then he called to the boy to prove his greatness by retrieving the wedge. The boy jumped quickly and dropped past the log, took some white substance, and put it onto the jaws of the tree. The Moon pulled out the props, and the great jaws came together. The white substance splashed into the air, and the Moon thought this to be the boy's brains and that he had finally killed him. But the boy suddenly appeared, saying, "Here is your wedge." And the Moon, acknowledging defeat once again, then told the boy to stay with him.

A while later, Man Moon wanted some salmonberries, but they were out of season. The older brother offered to get some for him. He went into the woods and found some bushes and blew upon them until they bore fruit. He took the fruit and gave it to the younger brother to give to the Moon. The younger brother was happy and gave the berries to the Moon, and Moon started eating them. Suddenly, salmonberry bushes sprouted from Man Moon's head.

After Man Moon was full he wanted fat ducks to eat. This was a challenge to the young boy. The older brother again went out to get them. He got his canoe ready, and the girls warned him to be careful, because this was another plan of Man Moon to destroy him. The boy said he would be careful. He got his bow and arrow prepared and was ready to depart when the winds started to blow from the Moon's house and blew him hard out to the sea. The older boy then shot a seal and laid it over the bow of the canoe. The Daughter of the Sun descended upon the seal and melted the oil in the skin. Thus, when he paddled the canoe through the water, it hit against the oil, the water became smooth, and the roughness went away.

The boy got the ducks and headed back toward land. When he reached land it was right where Man Moon was standing. He gave Man Moon the ducks, and a great feast was prepared. With this task completed Man Moon told the brothers that he wanted them to match his strength, and then they could be his friends. The boys agreed to even this. The Man Moon's power was all of the animals in the prairie, and he summoned them to kill the boys.

Never had mere mortals been able to thwart him. It was intolerable and he decided to end it once and for all. He called the brothers to a high spot and showed them his weapons. On the prairie below stood his warriors: a grizzly bear, the great cats, the wolves—pack after pack, as far as the eye could see. "These are my servants," boasted old Man Moon. "They do my bidding. You must survive against them before I will accept you as my equal."

Then it was that the Medicine Man spoke. "Younger brother, where are those objects you found along the trail?" Reaching into his bag, the younger man laid on the ground before them the broken lance, the shaftless arrowhead, the broken war club, and the bent harpoon. "Hah," exclaimed the Moon.

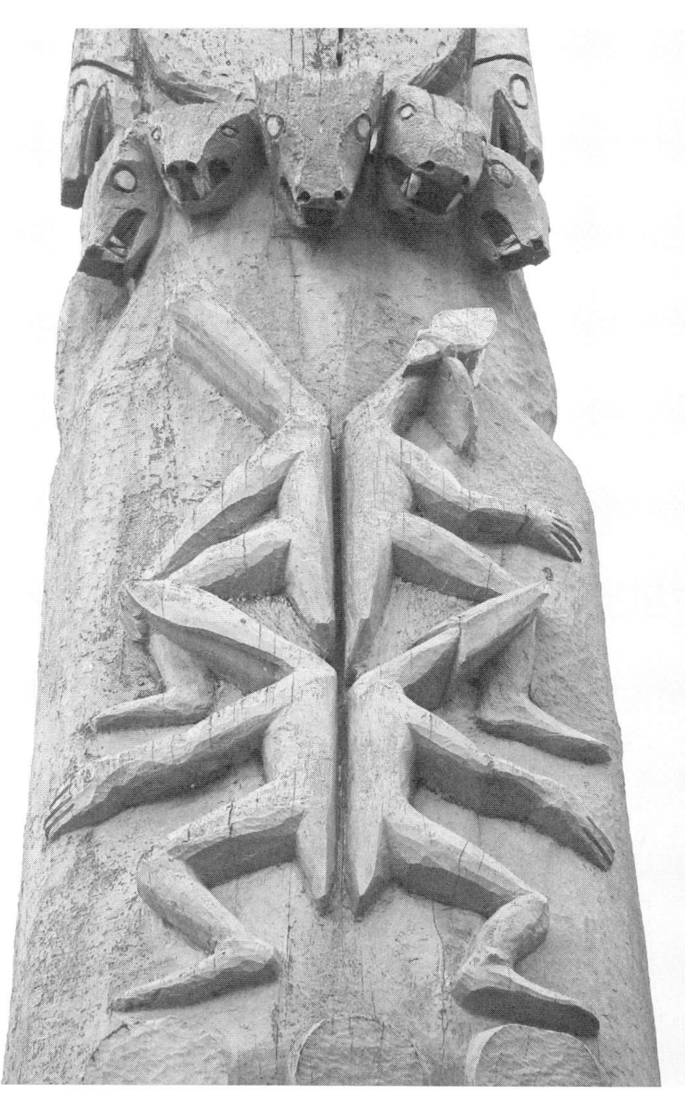

52. *Land in the Sky* totem pole detail: warrior helpers of the two brothers, 2004. Reprinted with permission. Photo by John Aitchison.

"Great as you both are, you cannot hope to live with these poor weapons. My lodge will not see you tomorrow!" He then retired to a nearby hill to watch the coming battle. When they were alone, the Medicine Man began to sing and dance. He called on his tamahnawis *or kindred spirit for aid. He urged Mother Earth to give them further help. So strong was his medicine that his brother was released from the bonds of youth, and came to know at once the secrets of all Medicine Men.*

The older brother started an Indian song, and these weapons started to become creatures, with arms and legs like grasshopper arms and legs and with the ability to jump a long distance. The harpoon was a slow killer because its barbs would get tangled in the flesh, and the lance was a smooth, rapid killer.

The boys gave orders that when they told the weapon creatures to quit and give up, they were to fight harder and more fiercely until they killed anything and everything in sight.

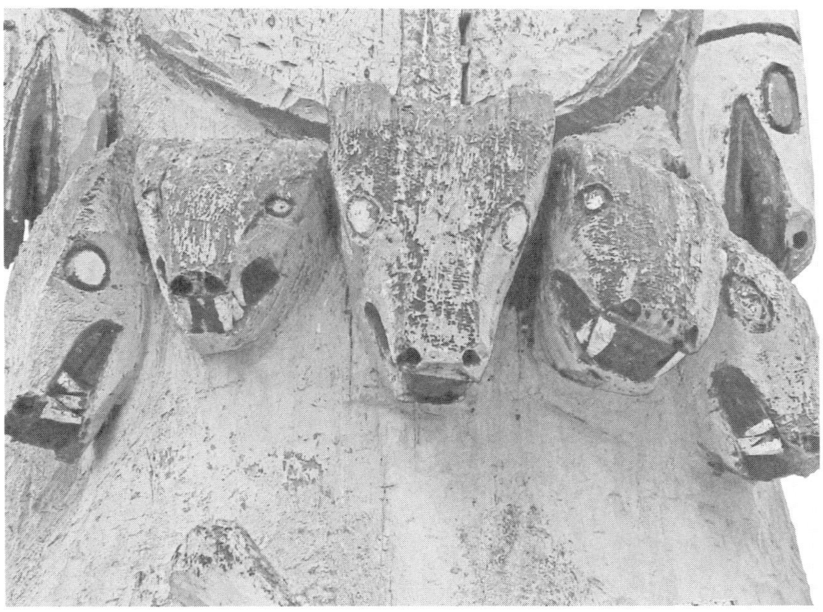

53. *Land in the Sky* totem pole detail: Man Moon and his animal warriors, 2004. Reprinted with permission. Photo by John Aitchison.

Now, together, they worked and felt that Mother Earth was with them. Before them on the ground, the broken weapons stirred and seemed to grow larger. They quivered and then rose together in the air to the height of a tall man. They floated there, changed. Sticklike bodies appeared, with arms and legs not unlike those of the giant grasshopper. The head in each instance was the weapon the younger Medicine Man had found along the trail. These strange creatures, part weapon, part animal, part spirit, moved with sudden spurts of motion so fast the eye was strained to watch. The older brother spoke to them, "Now arrowhead, you are a slow killer, so you must always stay back to back with the lance, because he is fast death. He will be at the front of the battle. Harpoon, you stay back to back with the war club, who will also face the front with the lance." The younger brother said, "We have to prove ourselves better than the Moon's weapons, so he will accept us as equals." "Yes," continued the older brother, "keep the positions I have given you until I call on you to stop. When I tell you to stop fighting, then and only then you must leave the square and fight and slay the more, until the animals are swept from the plain." The two Medicine Men then retired to a high hill and the battle started.

First the great grizzly bear charged the fighting square of earth weapons. The ferocious wolves leapt high above and the great mountain lions slashed and bit at their flanks. But the lance flashed like lightning and a cat or bear was dead. The wolves were knocked out of the air by the arrow and the harpoon. Soon a pile of carcasses surrounded the fighting weapons. Together, as if on signal, they gave a great bound and alighted in another section of the battle. The great weapons of the Moon kept coming at them and soon the dead encircled them again. Four times the stick weapons leapt and four times there were great piles of dead. The Moon saw he could not prevail, that his weapons were not equal to the fighting weapons of the earth. "Enough!" he cried, "Enough! You are my equal! Stay your weapons."

The brothers called out, "Fight no more, oh arrow and lance. Kill no more, harpoon and club." At this command the weapons left the square and began to leap crazily about the battlefield, leaving death wherever they touched. In fear and panic the animals fled and the Moon knew that weapons and trickery were of no avail to him. Of course the Daughters of the Sun and

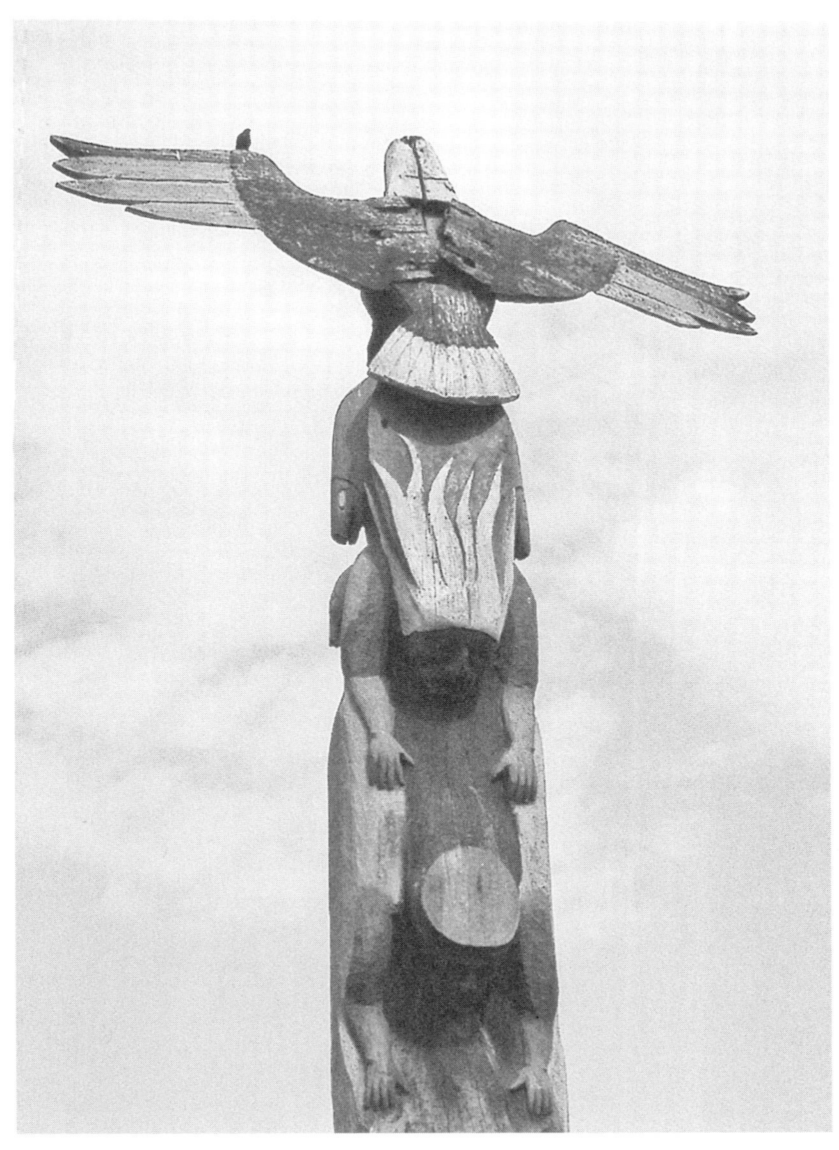

54. *Land in the Sky* totem pole detail: descent from the Land in the Sky (*back of pole*), 2001. Reprinted with permission. Photo by John Aitchison.

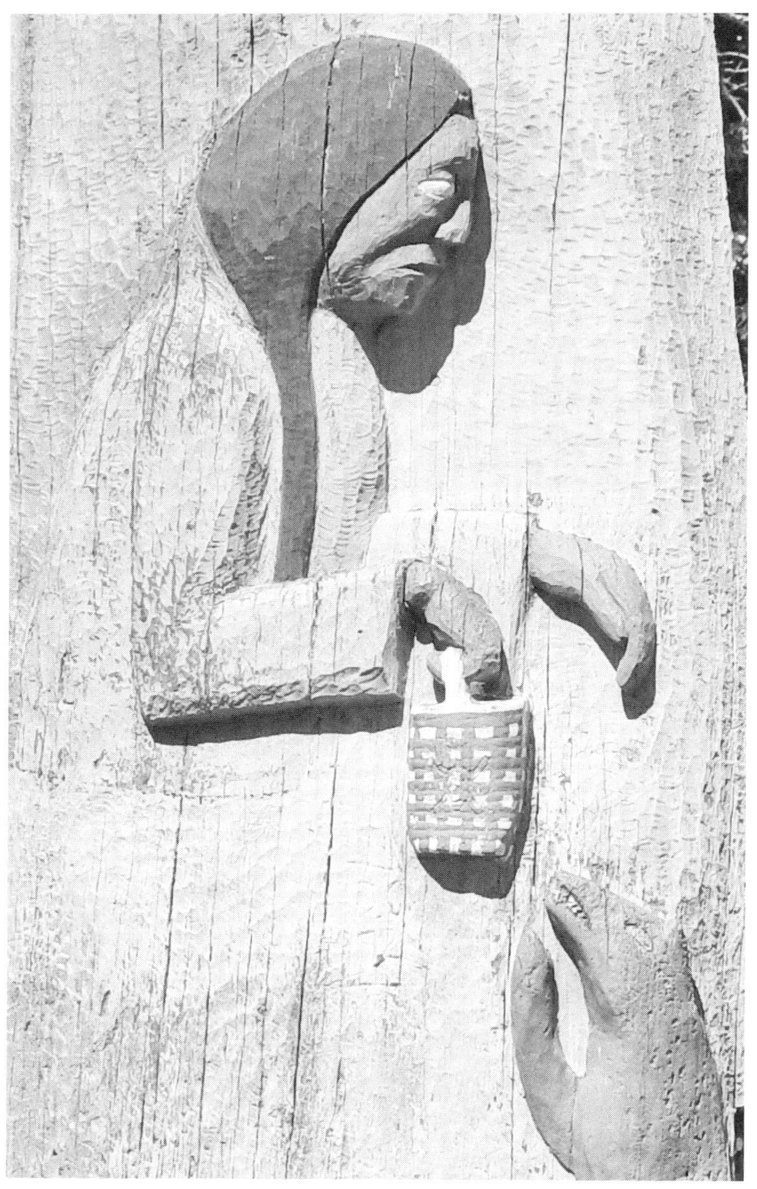

55. *Land in the Sky* totem pole detail: the Daughter of the Sun uses the healing oil to restore life to the little mink who had guarded the possessions of the two brothers while they were on their journey to the Land in the Sky, 2004. Reprinted with permission. Photo by John Aitchison.

the Moon were very impressed by the young earth men, as was old Man Moon himself.

The younger brother then took the Daughter of the Moon in marriage, and the older brother took the Daughter of the Sun. When preparations were made, the older brother and the Daughter of the Sun started down to Lummi first.

The Daughter of the Sun had a basket that contained a special healing oil. The younger brother and Daughter of the Moon also came down. When the party reached Earth where their canoe was waiting, they found the little mink, which lay dead in his bed. The Daughter of the Sun sprinkled the healing oil on him, and the mink awoke.

The mink opened his eyes and exclaimed, "Oh! Oh! I must have fallen asleep." But the Daughter of the Sun told him that he had died and the oil had brought him back to life. The party then journeyed to their own people. When they reached their people, the news of the healing oil had spread before them, and their people came to them to be healed. The brothers healed all and any sick people who came to them for help.

From then on, the older brother would always point to the constellations of the stars, to Orion — the Greek hunter — whose power he had used to obtain the ducks for the Moon, and he would say to his people, "I will get you food. You need never fear starvation, for my power, which comes from the stars, is great, and I will always help you." Thus was the experience of the two brothers who traveled in the sky to the Land of the Moon and came back to their people with healing power and power to get food, so that their people would never know sickness or starvation.

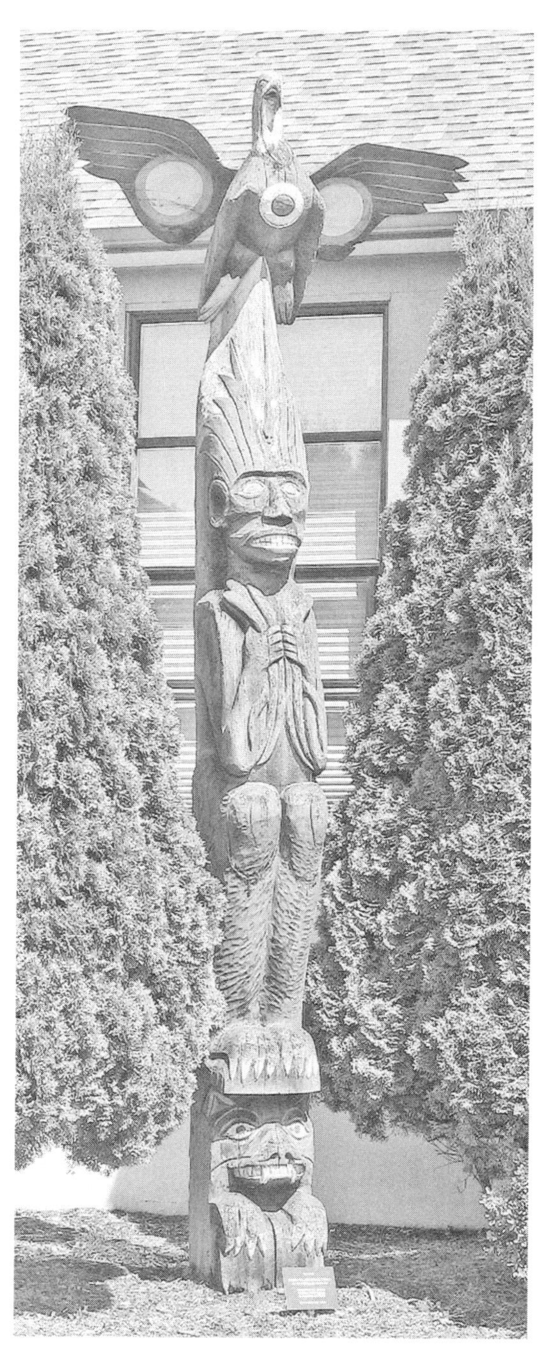

56. *Man in Transition* pole, 2011. Reprinted with permission. Photo by Melonie Ancheta.

16 *Man in Transition* Story Pole

PAULINE HILLAIRE

The *Man in Transition* Totem Pole was carved for the 1962 Seattle World's Fair. It was restored by Dale James and donated by Craig Cole and family to Northwest Indian College, Bellingham, Washington.

MY DEAR ONES, I'D LIKE TO TELL THE STORY THAT goes along with this particular totem pole. We must take the lesson from the painter that we used pastels, but we should use sharper colors for all totem poles. The story of this totem pole is called "Man in Transition." The *Man in Transition* totem pole has a great story that goes along with it. We'll start with the bear, at the very bottom.

Once the bear's jaws are open, you see those powerful teeth. And this means to me and all people looking at this totem pole that it takes a strong person to decide to make the change that they must make in their lifetime.

The spear ferns that he is wearing look like real spears. They represent the *komquoyot* headdress that the dancers wear. *Komquoyot* is not a name; it's a form of dancing with specific regalia: pointed helmets. But above this beginning, the bear rises out of his viciousness only to show that he is a man, rising higher and higher. The spear ferns that he is wearing look like real spears, and, gripped in his hands, he is showing us that he holds

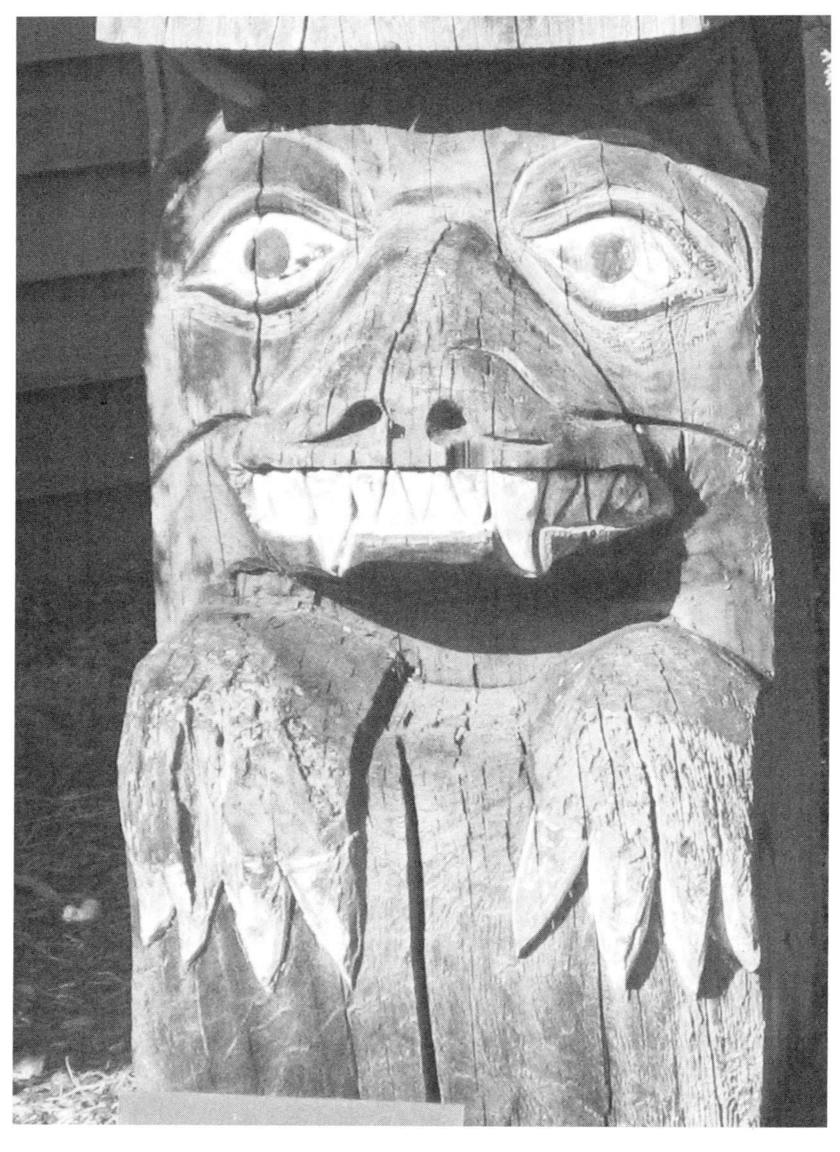

57. *Man in Transition* pole detail: Bear, 2011. Reprinted with permission. Photo by Melonie Ancheta.

the power of snakes. Wow, and we had better watch out for him, for once in his power, those snakes will do his bidding. He has found his power, and he has all the training that goes along with this power. What can he not do as a master now?

Man in Transition in my way of thinking shows the story of a man growing up from boyhood to manhood, but this is represented in the Indian way of life. Down at the bottom is a bear. Halfway up the pole is half-bear and half-man, half-animal and half-man. The man chose the power of the snakes; that's his Guardian Spirit. He has snakes in his hand, a hat of spears, and then victory, because he has now graduated from school, or graduated from the Smokehouse Way of Life into old age. You see, much training goes along with mastering a power. The bear has turned into an Indian, who then trained for this power, and the snake shows it. The eagle above the Indian reminds us that this Indian has graduated and now has a master's degree in his Quest of the Spirit. Wonder of all wonders. And now we've translated *Man in Transition* from the Spirit Quest to Education. Just like us: human beings who went to school, to college, and trained to become a master in one or more skills. Can you do it?

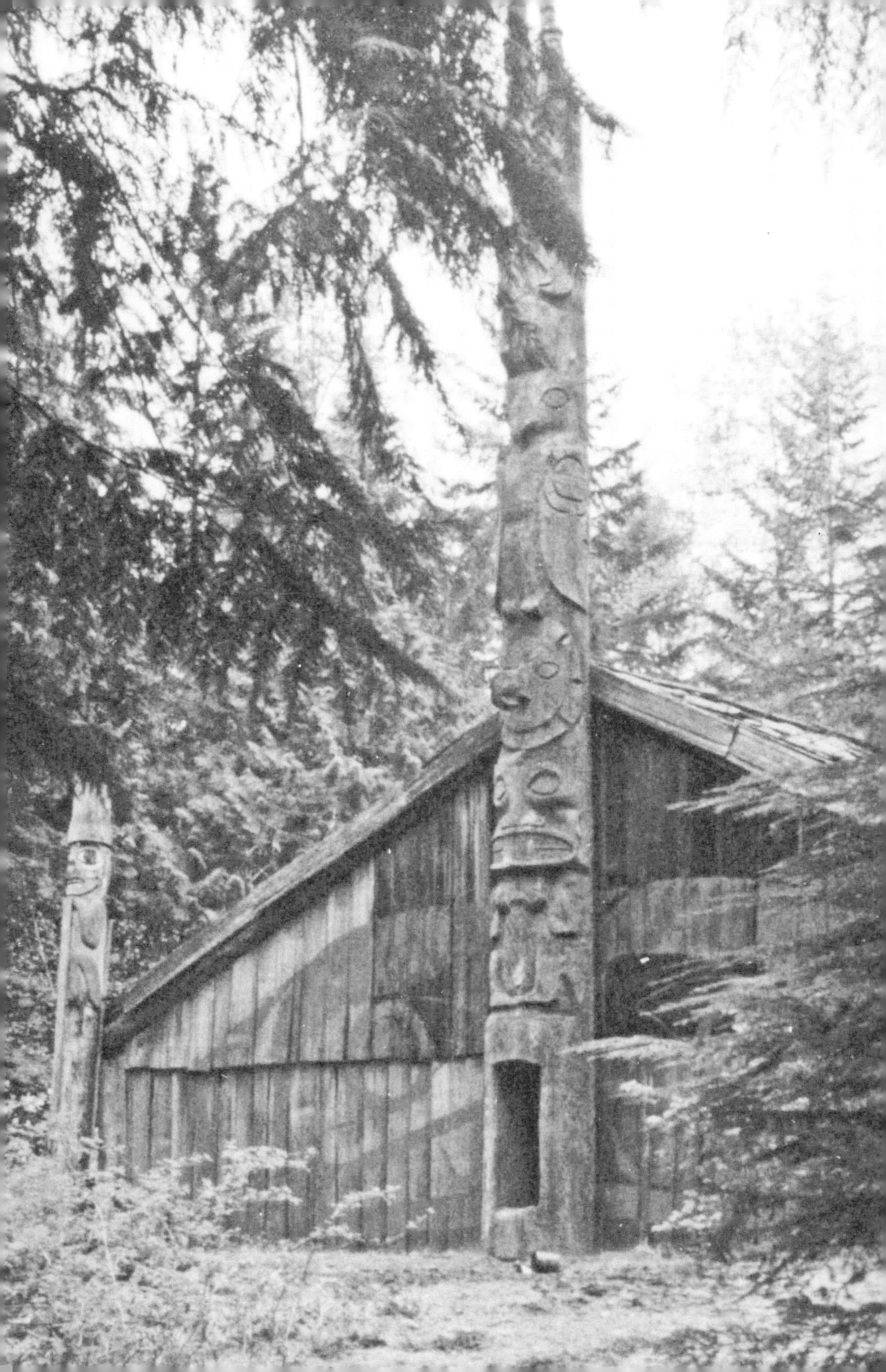

17 T'Kope Kwiskwis Lodge Entrance Pole

PAULINE HILLAIRE

The T'Kope Kwiskwis Lodge Entrance Pole was designed by Bill Holm and carved by Joe Hillaire and his son Ben Hillaire. It was installed in 1962 by the Chief Seattle Council of the Boy Scouts of America at Camp Pigott (formerly Camp Omache), Snohomish, Washington.

UP UNTIL THE MID-1960S, IT WAS NOT POPULAR TO be an Indian. Therefore, some Indians tried to pass themselves off as Mexicans, others invented the name "Smoked Irish," and if they happened to be "breed" (half-breed), they would not claim their Indian side. There is no end to counting the things that Indians were totally banned from doing daily. But the Boy Scouts proudly claimed an invisible Indian side or characteristic. Some young men who had met Joe Hillaire through his work with the Order of the Arrow ended up working for Mr. Bill Hewitt at Blake Island's Tillicum Village (The name Tillicum is from a word in

58. T'Kope Kwiskwis Lodge and entrance pole, 1999. Reprinted with permission. Photo by Matthew Kahn.

Chinook Jargon meaning "friend." The name was chosen from Chinook Jargon, rather than from any particular language or dialect, to show inclusivity.) Joe Hillaire gave them permission to use the Lummi paddle song, a Lummi Slahál song, and a blanket song. And they proudly announced where the song came from. Joe also showed and taught the dances.

I, Joe's daughter, worked at the cash register. Joe carved totem poles on the side. He had completed the design of the building and shared Indian history, all of which the Boy Scouts learned, looking so proud of what they were learning. In fact, I was extremely proud of their performance of the gambling or Slahál song, even to this day. Today still I maintain contact with two of the former Boy Scouts, Thomas Speer and Joe Tougas.

> Tom Speer (lakw'a̱la̱s) is an honorary member of the Duwamish Tribe, and for many years he has served the tribe in capacities including as a member of the Duwamish Tribal Services Board of Directors, as an advisor to the Duwamish Tribal Council, and as an educator for the cultural heritage group tilibsədəb (Singing Feet). He reflects:
>
>> *siʔáb* [Puget Salish/Lushootseed, masculine for "respected, honorable"] Joseph Hillaire gave us a glimpse into another universe, a different perspective of all that we thought we knew, a culture with ancient beliefs and traditions, living in ancestral homelands that had sustained First Nations communities for untold centuries.
>
> Joe Tougas, a member of the faculty at the Evergreen State College (Olympia), comments:
>
>> I first met Joe Hillaire while he was doing the carving at the longhouse at Camp Omache. I clearly remember watching him use a razor-sharp, double-bitted axe to rough out a cedar mask to be used in a killer-whale dance. I learned the basics of carving as I watched him carve several large pieces over the next few years. I continue today to teach those same skills to my students at the Evergreen State College.

For centuries the Native people of the Pacific Northwest Coast built large gathering places called longhouses or smokehouses. Traditional

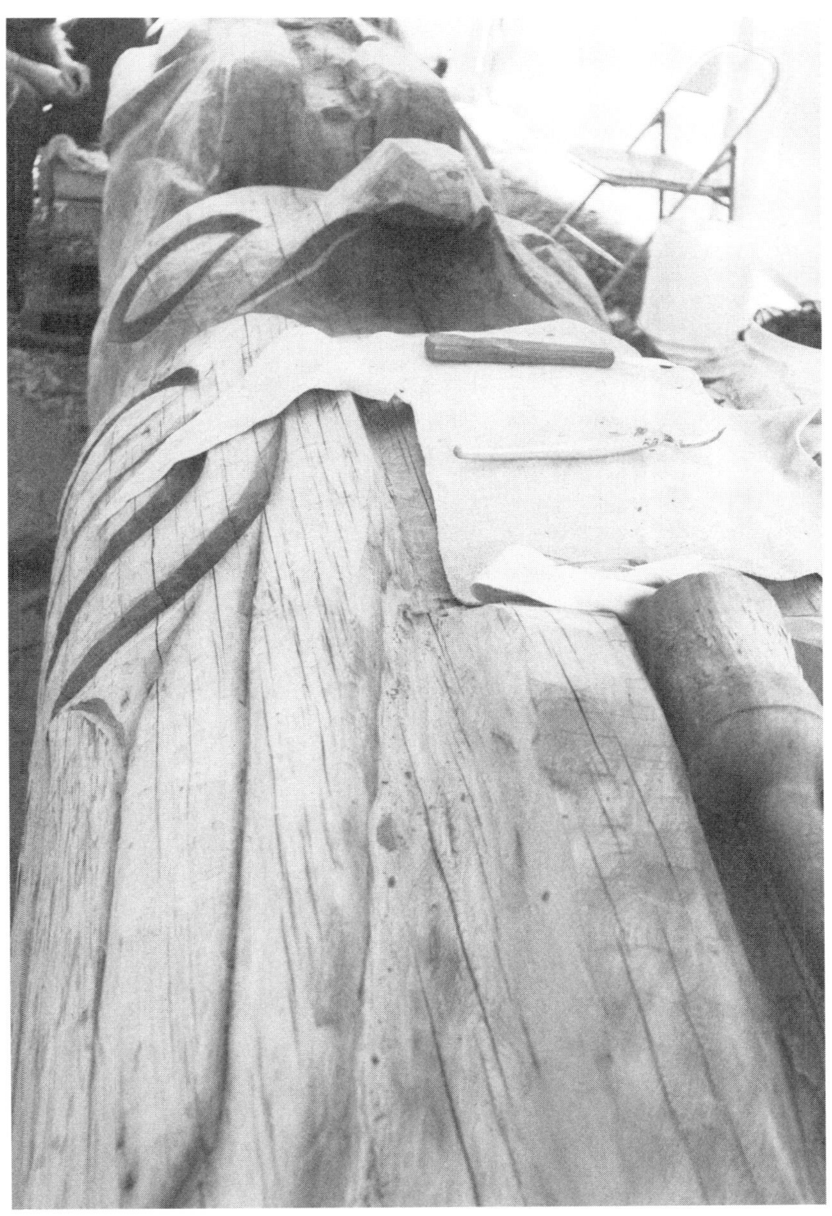

59. T'Kope Kwiskwis pole under restoration, 2006. Reprinted with permission. Photo by Paul Tankovich.

longhouses were constructed of cedar logs and planks and lasted at least thirty years. During the cold, damp winter months, the longhouses hosted elaborate ceremonies and enormous gatherings called potlatches. These events allowed clans from various places along the Northwest Coast to gather in fellowship and share family traditions. This lifestyle existed solely on the Northwest Coast. In recognition of this way of life, the Chief Seattle Council of the Boy Scouts and T'Kope Kwiskwis Lodge (northwest of Mount Rainier National Park) chose to help preserve the culture at one of the council's summer camps. (The words *t'kope kwiskwis* are Chinook Jargon for "silver marmot.") In 1962 Chief Seattle Council and T'Kope Kwiskwis Lodge completed a replica of a Northwest Coast–style longhouse on the edge of Camp Omache (now called Camp Pigott). The pole was designed by Bill Holm, then professor and curator at the Burke Museum at the University of Washington. Holm designed the forty-two-foot pole in the Haida style as an entrance pole. Later, Joe Hillaire was commissioned to carve the pole. The pole and longhouse were dedicated in 1962. The pole has been restored, and in 2010 the dedication was done by Pauline Hillaire's daughter Debra Covington Paul and Lummi master carver Felix Solomon.

18 Bronson Story Pole, 1957

FROM THE ARCHIVES OF PAULINE HILLAIRE

The Bronson Story Pole was commissioned by the Richard Bronson family, Gig Harbor, Washington. Joe Hillaire completed it in 1957. It was restored by Larry Ahvakana and Ed Carriere at the Carriere Studio, Suquamish, Washington, and installed at Indianola Park, Port Madison/Suquamish Reservation in 1992. It was later installed on the Lummi Reservation. When Joe Hillaire delivered this story pole to the Bronson family, he gave them the following story, written in his own handwriting, along with a sketch of the pole showing the paint colors so that it could be maintained in the colors he intended. The current colors are not the same as the original ones. The mink is the bottom figure on this totem pole. It has been separated from the pole and is at a different location.

BRONSON STORY POLE

By Chief Joseph of the Lummi Tribe

This pole is carved of Alaska Yellow Cedar. The Lummis called it *pa-shel-aqu.* The two figures at the base of the pole is a story of the Bear and the Raven when they were people.

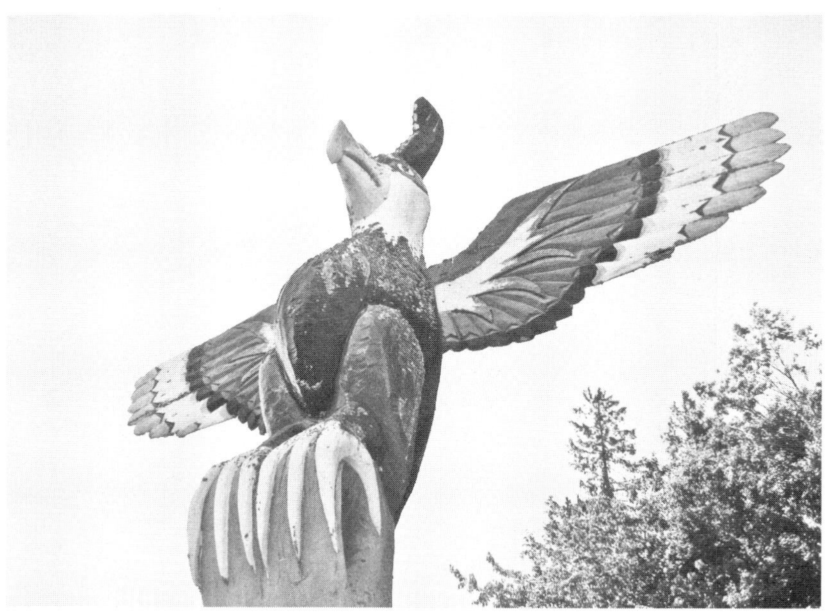

60. Bronson story pole detail: Eagle, 2011. Reprinted with permission. Photo by Melonie Ancheta.

The Bear was a very busy man. He made provision for the winters by having good food to keep himself fat and fit for his long sleep through the winter. The Raven was not like the Bear. He was neither a hunter nor fisherman. He liked to call upon people when they were preparing food for a meal. He would have jolly things to talk about until the meal was ready and the host would end up inviting him to eat with the household.

One day the Raven called at the home of the Bear. The Bear said, "Here comes that glutton. I will tend to him and be rid of him quickly." He greeted the Raven and the Raven said, "O! I smell the scent of dried salmon toasting by the fire. That is what chiefs like when they are gathered at the big potlatches. But what I like is toasted dried salmon dipped in good rich oil. That, I say, is good and pleasing to a big chief."

The Bear listened to all that the Raven said and in his heart he wanted to show the Raven that he, the Bear, could provide a dish fit for a big chief. When the Bear finished toasting the dried salmon, he placed a large

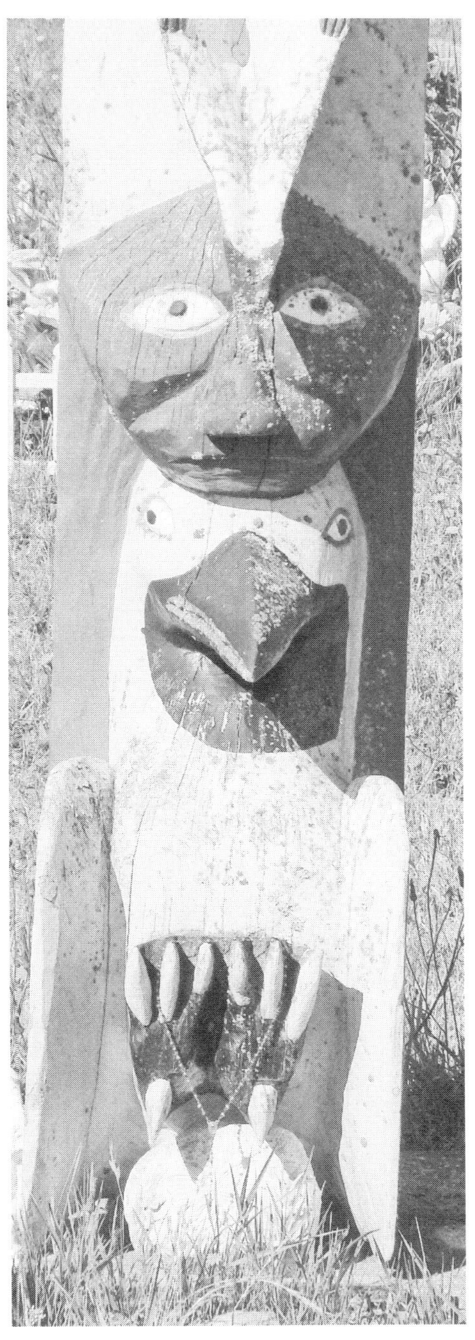

61. Bronson story pole detail: Bear and Raven warming his hands, 2011. Reprinted with permission. Photo by Scott Jensen.

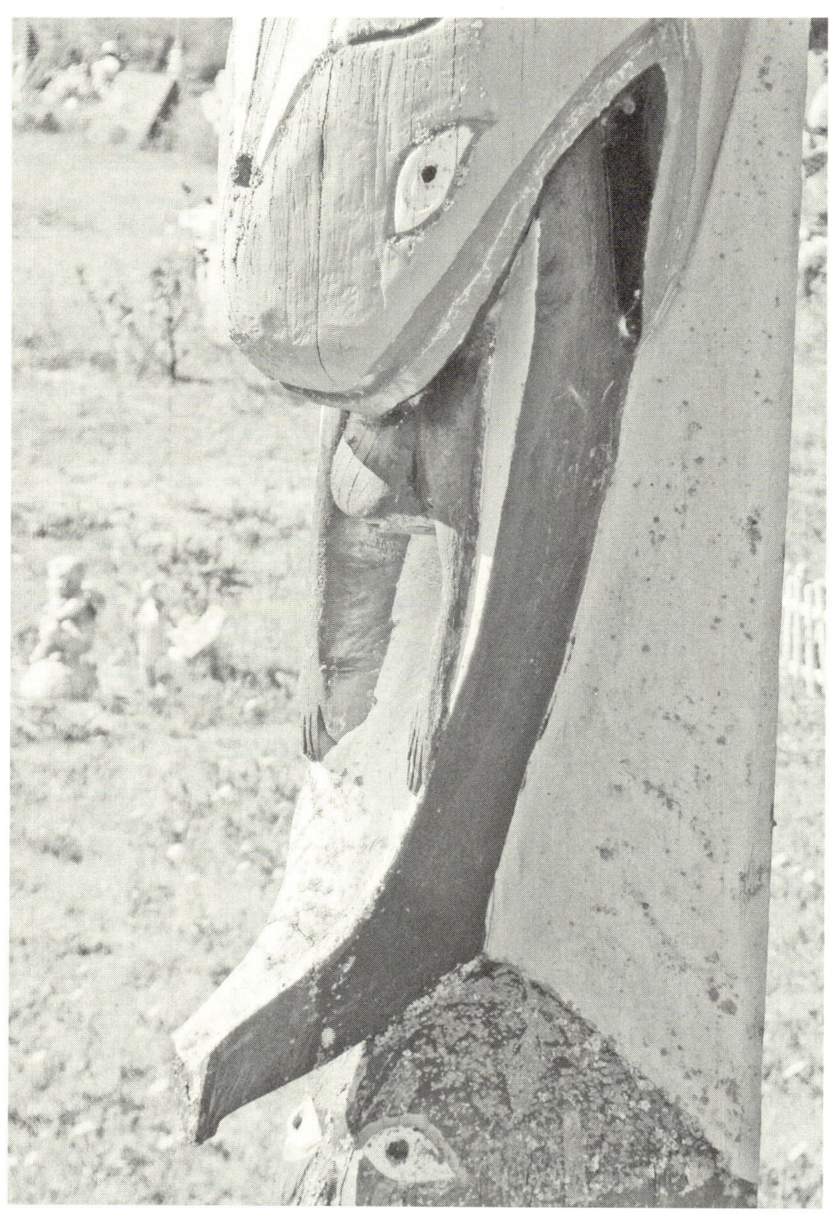

62. Bronson story pole detail: Mink in canoe being swallowed by Whale, 2011. Reprinted with permission. Photo by Scott Jensen.

clamshell by the fire and he sang his Medicine Man's song, as he held his front paws out like a man warming his hands.

Soon the fat began to drip from his paws into the clamshell, and in a little while the shell was full, and the Bear offered it to the Raven. The Raven ate until he was so full he could hardly move. He said to the Bear, "My cousin, I like to eat well in the house of a man like you. We all enjoy feeding our guests the best we have. So you must come to my home someday." The Bear listened to the boastful words of the Raven and he was glad when the Raven went away.

Soon afterward the Bear called at the Raven's home. The Raven sent his wife to the neighbor's to borrow some dried fish so he could feed the Bear. The neighbors were tired of lending food to the Raven because he seldom returned the food he borrowed, but they pitied his wife so they gave dried fish. But it was not a fat one. When she got home Raven told her to hurry and prepare a meal for the Bear. She did and when she finished toasting the dried fish, it was burned in places and lacked the natural oil that comes from fat salmon.

The Bear sat quietly while the Raven scolded his wife, hurrying her with the work. Raven wanted to prove himself an equal to the Bear, so when the fish was toasted he placed a large clamshell by the fire and raised his feet up to the fire, hoping that grease would come as it did for the Bear. The fire was hot but his feet had no fat. He squawked and flapped his wings in pain but no fat came. His boney feet got black and curled up in knots, but still there was no oil.

The Bear sang his song, raised his paws to the fire, filled the clamshell with oil and left the Raven to learn his lesson.

The third figure on the pole is just a dividing point between the two stories. The figures in the upper half of the pole tell the story of the Mink, then a Whale and the Thunderbird. In the mythology of the Lummis, the Whale swallowed the Mink.

They call him *S-what-what-us*. Long time ago when Mink was a man, he was forced to fight the battle of life, like all people. He tried hunting, trapping, canoe building and warfare, but in all of these things he was a misfit. He even failed as a fisherman. One day he was trolling for halibut.

He tried every trick, but failed. And all the time he would blame something other than himself for his bad luck. He was paddling along, his hook trailing in the water, while he was feeding. Mink looked at Whale and said, "You stink, old Whale. You make so much noise and you spit all over the water. That is why I cannot catch any halibut. You stink, Whale; you go away."

The Thunderbird, who is the Spirit in the sea, heard the Mink and was displeased. So he commanded the Whale to punish the Mink. So the Whale turned and caught the Mink. The Whale swallowed the Mink and his canoe, as shown on the pole. When Mink stood up in the Whale's belly, he bumped his head on some object dangling above him. He was so mad he struck at it, but it swung and hit him again and again. In angry rage he broke his canoe into firewood and lit a fire under this troublesome object. Storytellers say that it was the Whale's heart. The heat made the Whale sick, so he swam to the shore and in the morning the people of the village found it, and they said it was a gift from the great Thunderbird, so they had a ceremony and divided the Whale among all the people of the tribe. Great chucks of blubber were cut away and given to members of the village. Soon only a thick tissue covered the bones; then Mink noticed daylight showing through in the thin places. He shouted frantically as he beat on the thin places saying, "Here is a thin place; cut here."

The people did not hear him, but they saw the thumping on the carcass. Soon some cut a hole there and out popped the Mink and all the people were amused at him. The children laughed at him, and he asked why they did. He was told that he was bald headed, and when he felt his head and learned that he was bald headed, he ran off into the woods in shame. Ever afterward when a Mink was trapped, the trapper would look at him, and if he showed his teeth, they would say the Mink was still grinning in shame.

19 *Halibut Fisherman* Story Pole I

PAULINE HILLAIRE

The date and location of this pole are unknown. While completing the research for this book, Pauline Hillaire concluded that the pole shown here does not entirely correspond with Joe's carving style and was probably a replica of his *Halibut Fisherman* story pole I carved by another carver. As research continued, we discovered that photographer John W. Thompson noted that this pole was carved by Joe Hillaire, likely with his son Lewis Hillaire.

ALTHOUGH THIS TOTEM POLE CARRIES SIMILAR symbols as my father's totems carry, such as symbols that look like sun dogs on the wings and the transition symbol of the bear in the middle holding a giant serpent, the carving isn't familiar. The carving style doesn't quite match. I need to relay the message that many people copied totem poles and learned in that manner how to read them. The story is very familiar, similar to totem poles carved by Joe Hillaire. Therefore, showing it amongst Joe Hillaire's carving seems acceptable. Any carver would be proud of this work.

This is a story pole. This is the lazy fisherman; he's being swallowed

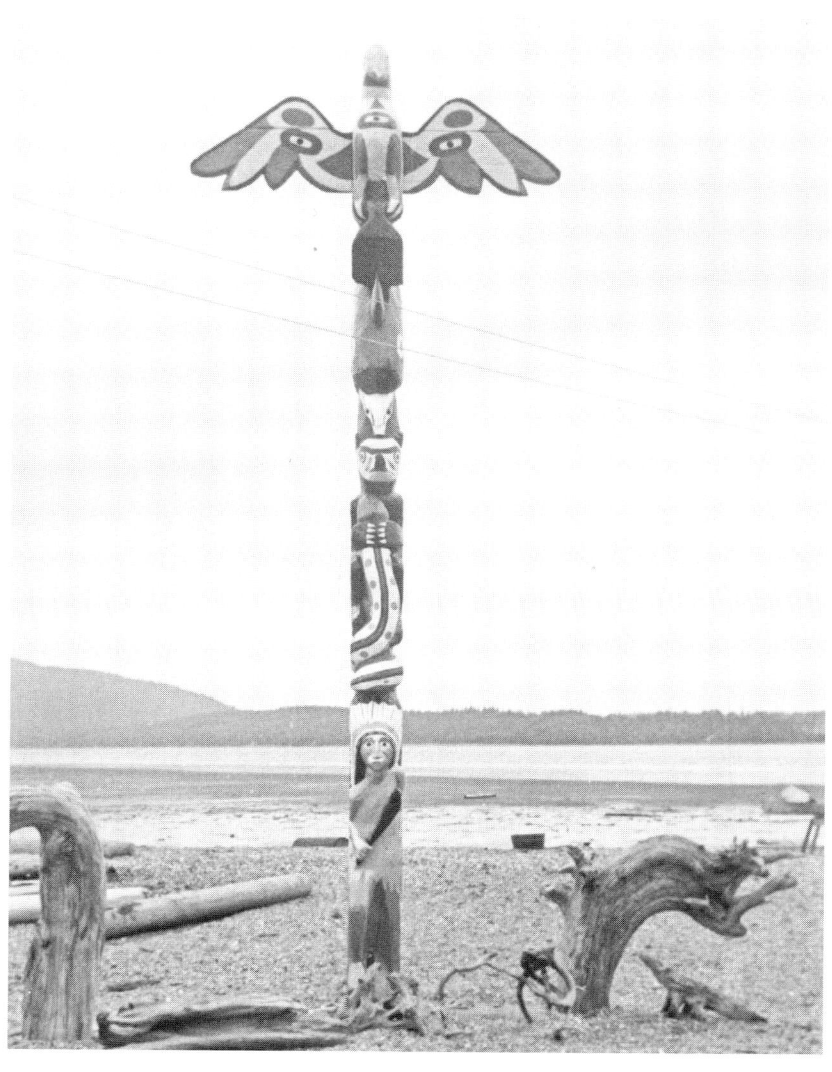

63. *Halibut Fisherman* story pole I, carved by Joe Hillaire, likely with his son Lewis, ca. 1955. Photo by John W. Thompson. Reprinted with permission from University of Washington Special Collections, UW29810Z.

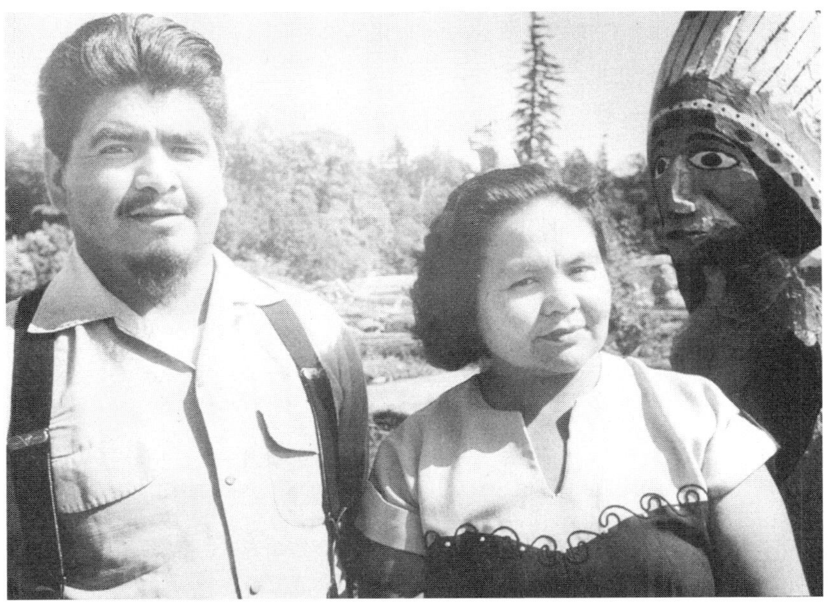

64. Lewis Hillaire and his wife, Helen, standing with the *Halibut Fisherman* story pole I, ca. 1955. Photo by John W. Thompson. Courtesy of the Pauline Hillaire Archives.

by the whale. The whale swallowed him because he wasn't behaving, and this is what happens when a fisherman is lazy. It's a story of a young boy who didn't know how to behave; he didn't know how to listen. He was on the wrong path; he didn't listen to the voice of authority.

Down below you'll see an Indian man in a chief's garment. This Indian chief is speaking with authority, and he is telling the people that this is the serpent. It is a serpent that has possessed one of the members of their tribe, and that member of the tribe is being swallowed. He's being swallowed by the whale. And these four figures are telling the story of the young man who was possessed, who had not any of the qualities of a fisherman. And this story is speaking with authority. It's a story pole of what happens to a young man if he permits himself to go that route. And in those days it wasn't drugs or alcohol; it was just the wrong path, the wrong path that they took. And this young man who is being swallowed by the whale has received his punishment. He was possessed by the wrong of the serpent, and the chief who spoke with authority no longer had anything to do with the young man being swallowed by the whale.

Every figure, from the man, to the serpent, to the man who is being swallowed by the whale, to the whale, and then the victory, belongs to this man down here. The victory is the eagle. And the eagle always represents victory. It doesn't ever have to look the same. You're going to see many eagles, because this is eagle country, and they are the most artistic of all the birds, and the most historic, as far as legends are concerned. So this is a story of the young man who was possessed, who was told by the voice of authority of the chief never to do this, and he never listened. He never minded, he didn't do anything he was told. Therefore, he's swallowed by the whale as he tries to fish. And these are showing all at once, not on a panorama picture, but on a cedar tree.

20 *Halibut Fisherman* Story Pole II

PAULINE HILLAIRE

Halibut Fisherman story pole II was carved by Joe Hillaire in 1956. Its location is unknown.

THE SCIENCE OF CATCHING HALIBUT INVOLVED THE art of making the hook with which to catch the flat fish of the sea. Our story begins with the difficulties of two young men whose mother was unable to teach them the art of making the halibut hook. The boys' father had died, and the mother, being a member of a distant tribe, chose to remain with her departed husband's people, which was the prudent thing to do. It was very common for a widow to be wed a second time into the same tribe. But it was not so with this widow. She had the goodwill of the people, but she was left to raise her two boys, and the season of halibut fishing was at hand. Every man in the village was prepared, and early every morning they launched their canoes and paddled out to the halibut fishing grounds. At the end of the day the canoes came home with no fresh halibut for the camp. For many days this state of affairs continued, and the village provisions began to run low.

The supplies in the widow's home suffered most because she was dependent upon the goodwill of her people and her two boys were very young,

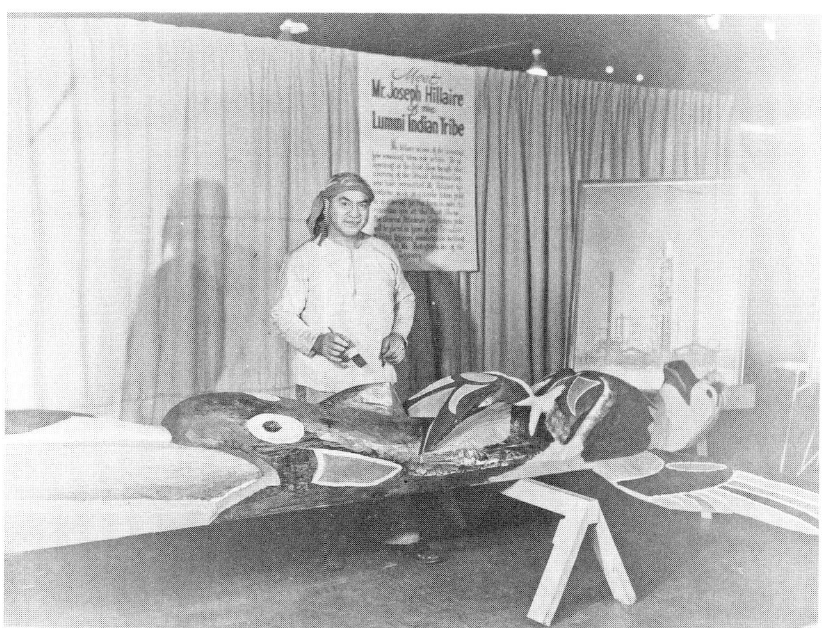

65. Joe Hillaire painting *Halibut Fisherman* story pole II, Seattle National Boat Show, 1956. Courtesy of the Pauline Hillaire Archives.

but they were eager to help. They told their mother they wanted to try their hand at fishing halibut. The mother said, "Your uncles and their friends are all good fishermen, and they will all do their utmost to land a halibut, and their combined efforts will be our reward. Why should we hope to do better than they?" But the oldest boy said, "Mother, I can feel the spirit of the men talking to me. All I need is a canoe and halibut hook and tanks, and I will be able to help you and our people." The little boy said, "Mother, will you ask our uncles to lend us a canoe and hooks, and we will try to fish with them when they go out again?"

The mother was timid, but hunger was stronger than her feelings, so she did ask for the canoe and hooks that her boys needed. The boys followed the rest of the fishermen out to the fishing grounds. The oldest boy handled the fishing tackle. They were so unfamiliar with this work that while they were arranging their equipment, the wind had gently blown them toward the shore, and the other fishermen were amused at the plight of the boys being blown ashore. But when they finally got set to fish, they were startled when the line began jerking. With mingled feelings of fear and joy the lineman began to haul it in. There was weight in the line, but it yielded to the boy's strength as he hauled. Suddenly the line began pulling the little canoe with it as the boy continued to haul in the line. By the time the boy was ready to land his catch, they were close enough to the shore to make it safe, so he struggled to land his first halibut. The moment the halibut ceased to struggle with him, he began with his killing club. The boy killed the halibut and hauled him into the canoe.

The day was far spent, and many of the younger fishermen paddled near to see the boy's exciting first experience. It was too easy to have a sense of calling it a day to go home. But the older fishermen were reluctant to admit that the widow's children should have to share their only catch with them, who were veterans of many years in fishing halibut.

That night was a great moment for the widow and her boys. As the custom was, a young man's first kill was to be served as a feast for the people. This was not only a young man's first kill but also a deliverance from certain hunger among the people. The widow requested that her boys be permitted the canoe and fishing tackle the next day, and again, they were the only ones that caught a halibut. A feeling of jealousy began to grow among the people, and the uncle who loaned out the canoe and tackle changed the ones he had loaned the boys to an old set. But still the boys continued to catch halibut, and always they brought their halibut near the shore.

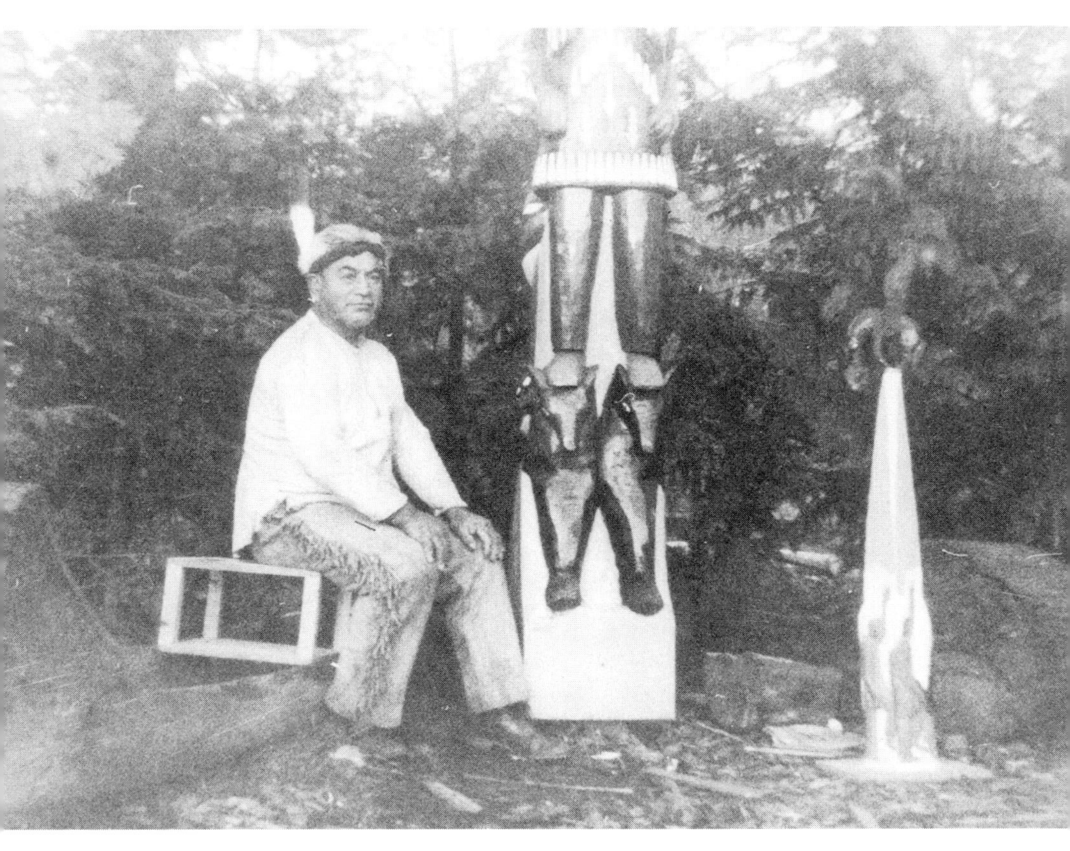

66. Joe Hillaire carving the Double-Headed Wolf section of the *Schelangen* totem pole. Courtesy of the Pauline Hillaire Archives.

21 Double-Headed Wolf Totem

PAULINE HILLAIRE

The Double-Headed Wolf totem is at the base of the *Schelangen* story pole, carved in 1954 (see chapter 13).

EVERY NOW AND AGAIN, SOMEONE APPROACHES ME and asks me, "What is the crest of the Hillaire family? What are the symbols of the Hillaire family?" And then I go through a list of, say, half a dozen or a dozen, and this is one: the Double-Headed Wolf.

This is a Double-Headed Wolf: two heads, one body. And there is a man above; that's his power, and when he dances, he has two wolf heads. When seen in a vision, he is carved on this totem pole. And the one who carved it is standing above him in the paddle shirt. It is identifying the power held by the man who mastered the power, the vision of the Two-Headed Wolf. What an awesome name once mentioned. What if it stood before us in full reality? After all, we see much worse than that in movies and television these days. So a Double-Headed Wolf in all reality would be just another horrible curiosity as any of those we see on-screen.

But on a totem pole, and with all that we know about totem poles these days, is it really just another curiosity? Remember what my dad said when he was hunting for a tree: "Stand back, and I shall see what I will be." Is it the person with an artist's eye, or can every tree talk? We're left with these questions, and they're only answered when you're by yourself on a vision quest, or when you've been told about one. They're not supposed to share their vision when they're in the longhouse, but you can see it demonstrated in their dance. And then you can see without their talking.

If they did talk, we would hear stories beyond imagination of all the animals that rove our forest and of all the people too. Let me see, what kinds are there? They sneak, they hide, they hop, they run, and they stare. Oooooh! They stare!

But the Double-Headed Wolf on the totem pole that my dad carved represented a very real creature, a creature that reminds us that Wolf is considered to be the very best teacher, the very best of trackers. The man standing over him is there to remind us that he obtained the spiritual power of the Double-Headed Wolf. Once you have spent the time to earn that, you could conquer your world's worst fear. The viewer then must take warning, turn around, make tracks, and run, of course, to see things as they really are.

PART FOUR

Lummi Oral History and Tradition

22 Some Place-Names from Lummi History

FROM THE ARCHIVES OF PAULINE HILLAIRE

The following is a composite of information stated told by Al Charles, Mr. and Mrs. Peter Victor, Johnny Julius, August Martin, and Mr. and Mrs. Julius Charles during a meeting with Norbert James and Joseph R. Hillaire. Joseph recorded these testimonies (no date).

JULIUS CHARLES SAID THAT HIS PEOPLE LIVED IN A village called Xxe lel kuut, north of the present town of Friday Harbor on San Juan Island. Near this village was a cemetery; his uncle is buried there. Patrick George's father is buried there, and so is Johnnie Tom. "All these people are my relations; they are Lummi. The name of the island was Ei'əlyxw," Mr. Charles said.

There was another village called Peqwielwet, west of Roach Harbor. Johnnie Tom's father was named Sye kwetitmetvw. Billy Sepass is from this family, and so was Martin Sepass. On the south end of Henry Island, Xw te tin kwel, is a reef-net site. Mitchell Bay was called Smax; this is where the army camp was built. Charley French operated reef nets there. His wife's father's name was Sehenep. This island is the scene of the Lummi origin story of łe legemec. Sweten is the name of the first man. Xhals (x̣eʔəl's), the Transformer, showed him how to make a reef net and when and where to use it. Halibut, cod, salmon, deer, berries, and ducks were plentiful there.

Waldron Island was called T's xeni; this place was noted for small deer. Orcas Island was called Swe'lex. This was also the given name of some of the people as it appears in some of the government reports.

Coal Point was called Tt gwə legs, where Boston Tom operated reef nets. There was a village at East Sound called Ts'el wesey. There was a village at West Sound called El e'ley, and the place is marked by great heaps of clamshells. The Indian name of the place signifies the place to cook clams.

Xwlə leg'w, the father of George Warbus, had a reef-net location on Shaw Island. Whatcom was a village. Qualliqum was where the Lummi caught and dried dog salmon. The Semyamoo (Semiahmoo) were allies of the Lummi Tribe, and they occupied the area round about Blaine. Marietta was called E'leq.

Once, the Lummi were attacked, but they were prepared, because messengers told them an enemy was coming. The men helped the women and children to go to a place of safety, and while they were doing so, the enemy came to the village. Finding the place deserted, they thought the Lummi were afraid and had run away, so they began robbing the village. They were busy when the Lummi warriors came upon them. The first shot was fired by a man named Syg wə neq. The arrow struck a post near one of the enemy, and he let out a scream. This sent the pillagers running out of the big houses. The waiting Lummi warriors came at the doors and slaughtered the enemy with spears. Sex wem ken (Sa hum kun?), a Lummi leader, was wounded in the arm. Very few of the enemy got away.

Yi'q wet tex is the name of the island in Chuckanut Bay named after the Ya'quul'tah from the North who were killed by blackfish (minke whale) while they were pursuing a band of Lummi. As the fleeing Lummi entered the mouth of the bay, they cast stones into the water. This stirred the anger of the blackfish, so they attacked the pursuing Indians and killed them, saving the Lummi.

23 Canoes

PAULINE HILLAIRE

I WATCHED MY FATHER, JOE HILLAIRE, CARVING THE canoe pictured here with the two boys in it. When he was finished, the two boys, Willy and Charlie, got in it, and my husband raced them, swimming, to the dock of the ferry landing. And my husband beat them, but they were new at canoe pulling. The boys paddled for all they were worth to get to the ferry dock before my husband; my husband was in the navy, and he was a good swimmer. And so he was swimming along just easy, and they were just pulling so hard, trying to get their canoe to do right. Oh, they tried, and by the time they got to the ferry landing, they knew just exactly how to handle a canoe, because they were so determined to beat my husband.

The carvers carve the outside first, and then they burn out the middle. And they use gut, or what they call tendons or sinew; they stretch them, and they use that as a string, a straight line, and they burn out the center in three spots — the center and each end — and then they carve with an axe. When this particular canoe was carved, I watched the carver balance the canoe. And it takes an artist, it takes an inventor, it takes a scientist to figure out how to perfectly balance any canoe. There are different ways, and my father used water. And so this is one way, and there are other ways also. So we don't limit ourselves in the world of Indian people.

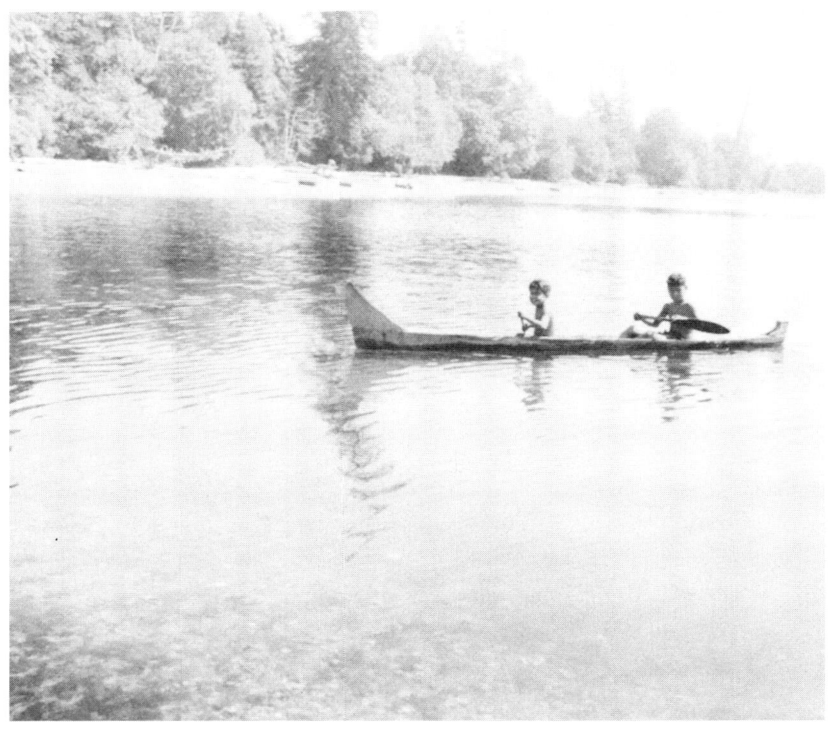

67. Willy and Charlie in a canoe made by Joe Hillaire at the site of Pauline Hillaire's childhood home. Courtesy of Pauline Hillaire Archives.

My father carved so many things, and I'll just go on with one of the things that fascinated me. It was like a loom, a beading loom; it had many strings. And attached to each end was a carving, and like a loom, the string could be strung across. Each carving of the various species of fish had something like a bead, with a hole right through it. And so when he'd put a fish into this mechanism that he made, it turned into a school of fish — two dozen or more. And every time I would touch it, the fish would move, like they were swimming. It was so fascinating to be next to a person who's an expert carver. So it wasn't just dreams, it was reality.

The science that goes into the work of the reef-net fisherman is one of the highest forms of engineering I've ever seen. When they made the nets they used nettle peelings: the nettle skin. They take that skin and they pick

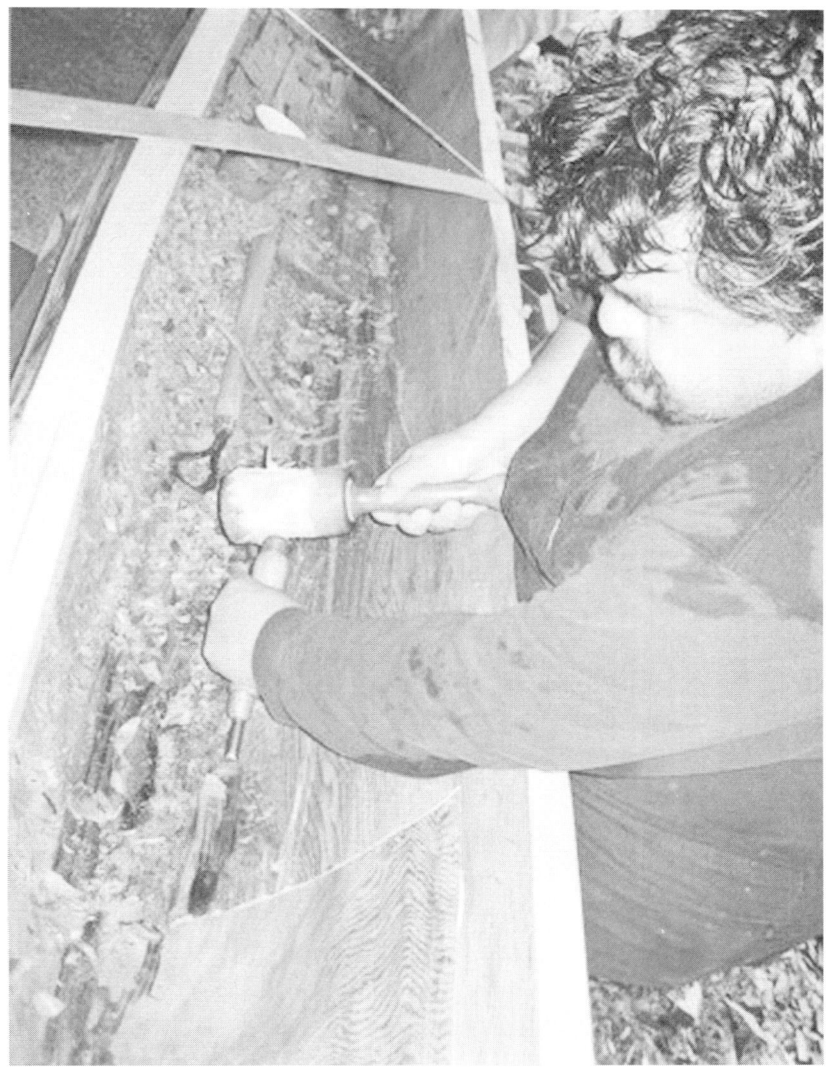

68. Felix Solomon chiseling the shovelnose canoe he carved for the Sauk-Suiattle Tribe, 2011. Photo: Melonie Ancheta.

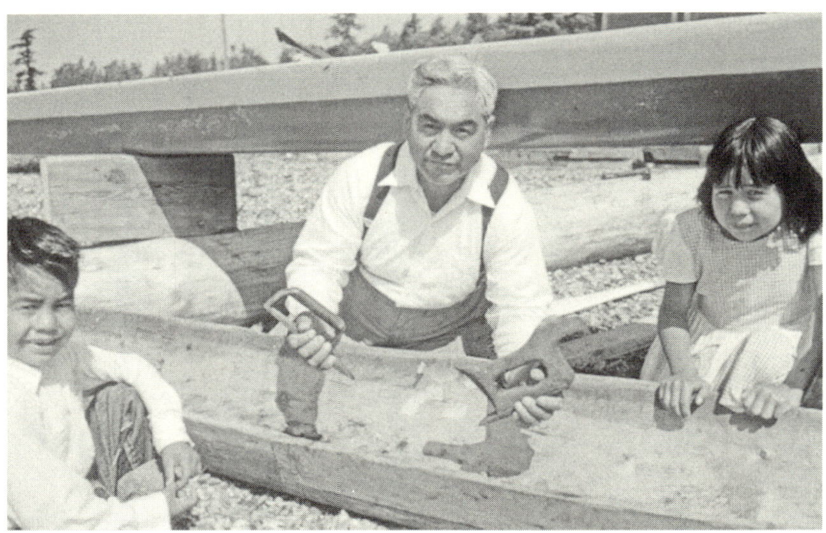

69. Joe Hillaire carving a canoe with two grandchildren observing, ca. 1955. Photo by John W. Thompson. Courtesy of the Pauline Hillaire Archives.

it from the very bottom of the nettle growth; they pick it with gloves. And then they break the roots off, and then they peel and lay, peel and lay, and then they take the center and let the two sides hang, and then they twist it. They twist and twist — one side goes this way, the other side goes the other way, then it twirls into a strand, and it's the toughest material you could ever ask for. And that's what those nets are made of. They also had cedar bark braids that could hold thousands of pounds.

To prepare the salmon for the First Salmon Ceremony, the women were not allowed to use regular knives. You can almost see through the stone knife that they used; when you put it up to the sun, you could see through it. They left the salmon's head on, and they left the tail on. It takes an expert, someone who really knows how to butcher salmon: slice it down the back on both sides of the head, turn it over, leave the head and the tail on the backbone, and just fillet the meat of the salmon so you have the slab of salmon.

They put that salmon on a stick, on a very narrow stick, and they put sticks through, weaving back and forth, weaving in ceremonial prayer until the whole salmon is on the stick, and then they place it at the fire, flesh first. And then they turn it around, back and forth, until it's done. Once it's cooked, the children don't eat, the men don't eat, the old women eat. The old women prayerfully show the children just how to eat the salmon. Every bit of it is gone. Take away the bones, eat it carefully: teach the children just how to eat their salmon so that they don't choke, so that they don't waste. They never wasted; it was a sin to waste food. And so when the old women finished eating, then the table was spread. The beautiful blankets and mats, cedar mats and cattail mats, were spread on the ground, and everyone sat down to eat. They had boiled potatoes that were slow cooked in a wooden box, and they'd fill it with water, and they'd keep it by the fire, turning it, turning it, then adding hot rocks, putting the small potatoes in there. Wild potatoes are small, and they're good tasting. That's how it's cooked, slow-cooked food always. Slow-cooked or sun-dried berries, or sun-dried whatever — deer meat maybe — but they laid the table with their feast. And the prayer songs were sung.

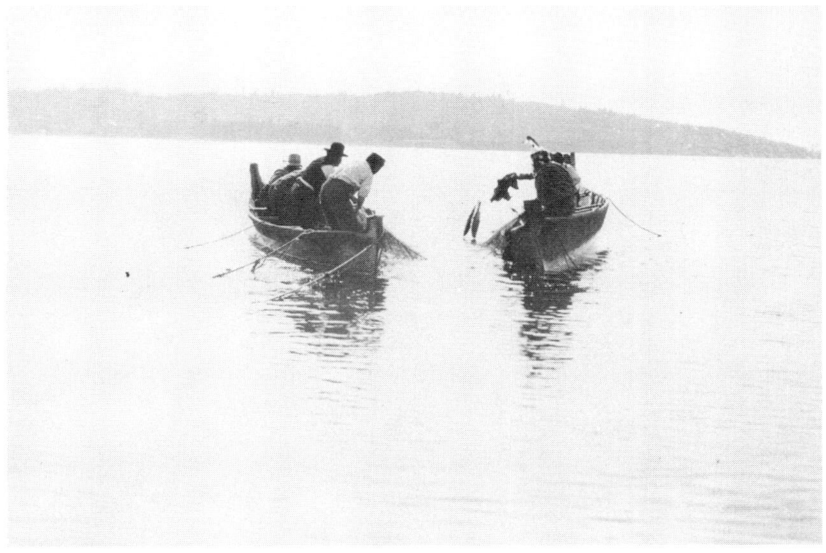

70. Lummi fisherman setting a reef net between two canoes, ca. 1930–33. Photo by Eugene H. Field. Reprinted by permission from University of Washington Special Collections, NA1813.

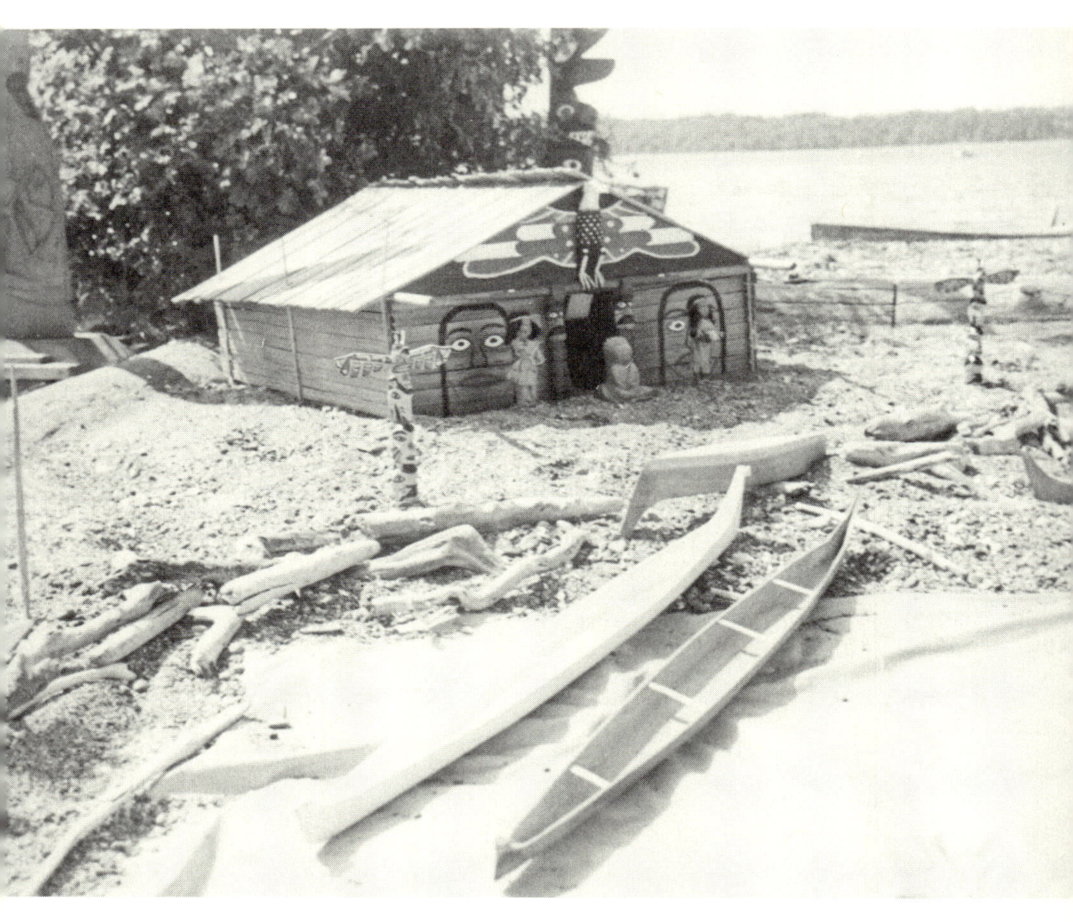

71. Smokehouse replica built by Joe Hillaire, showing cedar dugout canoes with a reef net, ca. 1955. Photo by John W. Thompson. Reprinted by permission from University of Washington Special Collections, UW29812Z.

24 Longhouses of Long Ago

PAULINE HILLAIRE

THE LONGHOUSES OF LONG AGO WERE STURDY structures, and because the Indians who built them were colorful, the longhouses were colorful. They were usually built where drinking water was convenient. There were several freshwater springs in the Lummi area. Not only were the longhouses colorful, but with the wisdom of the ages, they were built comfortably and wisely. I was born in a square longhouse. We just had one fire. The benches were all trunks, and we could lift up the lids and store our clothes in them.

The men used sharp stones fastened to a yew-wood handle to chop down the trees, cut off the branches, and peel them of their bark layers. When they had enough to make a longhouse, which could measure from eighty to one hundred feet long, depending upon the desire of the leader or the architect of the band, they dug holes with long sticks that were made especially for digging. After digging the holes in preparation, they placed sturdy and prepared logs into the holes, after which they tied log after log up against the standing and partially carved poles. Each pole told a story; entrance poles were elaborately carved (see figure 21).

The ropes were made of various materials: specially treated animal innards, shredded bark ropes, the sinew of an animal, or whatever the builder chose. To make their structure more comfortable and free of unnecessary draft, they brought wet clay or pitch and plastered as close in as possible between the horizontal logs, using a suitable-sized stick. The roof was made of cedar shingles, which were very long compared to shingles the white brothers used on their houses in later years. These shingles overlapped each other, but the significant design that they used on the very peak of the roof was ingenious in that the building planner considered fires, for which pits were dug. These fires were always to be burning in single file down the center of the longhouse for warmth. Usually there were three fires, and the roof openings were arranged to allow the escape of rising smoke from each fire. The roof had a steep pitch, and smoke was vacuumed out by the design of the roof openings. The opening was formed by rough-hewn shingles pitched like the roof itself, with one side slightly higher than the other and extending toward the lower side and over the opening to prevent rain from entering.

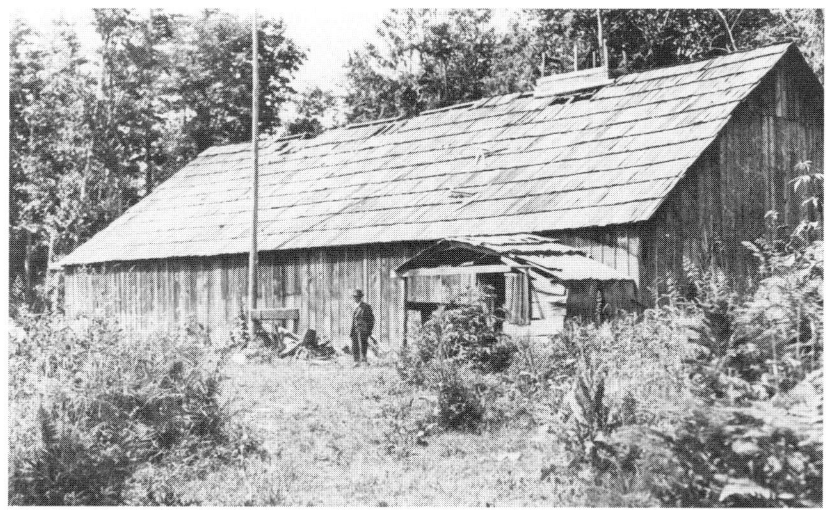

72. Lummi potlatch house, ca. 1930–33. Photo by Eugene H. Field. Reprinted by permission from University of Washington Libraries, Special Collections, NA1824.

Inside the longhouse, the men built platforms such as the leader desired, which could be either small timbers cut or split in half or large logs cut every three feet or so to create a platform, usually about three feet high. They filled the inside of these platform walls with insulating dirt and made flooring to cover the ground; women spread their cedar bark or cattail mats. Blankets of goat wool and dog wool hung on these platforms, which were against three walls of the longhouse, the two long sides and the farthest end wall. There was one large door and, at the rear, a small entrance door. Because the Indian was wise as to human nature, he built his own type of entrance, and in Lummi, this was a dip, with a depth set by the leader, so that when someone entered the building, he would suddenly and unexpectedly step into this dip, and, therefore, the wise leader and Lummi folk could tell whether the visitor was friendly by how he reacted upon entering the house.

The kitchen, with one long window to ventilate cooking odors, was near the entrance, and the women were always busy with something there. They had woven baskets of cedar roots or bear grass. The black cherry root baskets were woven very tightly and were the strongest. With these the women cooked, stewing meat, fish, or vegetables. Berries, meat, and fish were prepared outdoors and in their special places, such as smoking houses and drying racks. When the oppression of winter set in, the leader of the bands would send out their messengers to the other friendly tribes, inviting them over for an Indian get-together, like a potlatch. The evil spirits were driven out by their fellowship, friendship, and goodwill. Their drums could be heard for miles around. The Indian dancers each took their turn singing the special song of their Guardian Spirit, a spirit of the creatures of the earth or of the sky or water. They would sing powerful songs of the Great Spirit, for they knew spiritually that there was someone greater than mankind. There were feasts, which the women made very efficiently and generously while the men exchanged views and stories. Thus these warm-hearted people made their homes, building the interiors according to their needs. Contrary to popular opinion, these wise people were industrious year-round and very, very friendly up until they were told they were wrong.

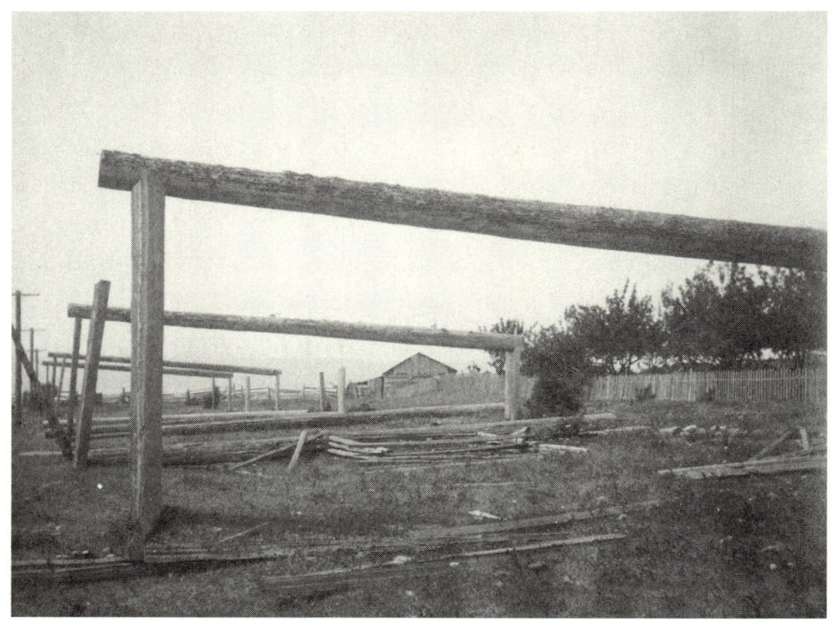

73. Ancestral Lummi potlatch house in ruins, 1905. Photo by Edmond S. Meany. Reprinted by permission from University of Washington Special Collections, NA1237.

Their canoes took them to other islands that were free of boundaries, where they picked foam berries for ice cream, three kinds of blackberries, wild strawberries, salmonberries, elderberries, black caps, wild cherries and plums, and sprouts: the smallest tender salmonberry sprouts, thimbleberry sprouts, celery sprouts, and water sprouts. These were tender and tasty; they quenched thirst when sometimes water could not. The people also picked wild crab apples. Canoes were very handy for gathering berries and other foods. There were tiny wild potatoes and tiny wild carrots to be harvested. A jubilant song was sung when Mother Earth was good to them or when Father Sea allowed good fishing.

25 A Wedding in Lummi History

Plans for a Play by Joseph Hillaire

FROM THE ARCHIVES OF PAULINE HILLAIRE

ORIGIN OF THE ISLAND TRIBES

Long ago there lived upon Lummi Island a young man named Switunk. The Great Transformer came along and told him how to get the salmon for food and how to care for himself. By and by, the young man became lonely, for he wanted company. The Great Transformer had said nothing of such, so the young man had to fashion his own company. He made himself a small idol, fashioned by his hands from rotten wood. This, Switunk would talk to whenever he became lonesome. By and by, the Great Transformer came again. When he saw the idol, he was much vexed at Switunk, for he had given Switunk all he had need for when he was there last. After Switunk explained, the Great Transformer changed his mind and afterward waved his hands and made a woman of the idol. That is the origin of the island tribes.

PROLOGUE

From the top of this great mountain,
across the great and mighty water,
a land I view of lakes and rivers.
Wooded hills of pine and cedar
stretching over to the eastward
toward the rising of the sun.
Food is there in great abundance
in the lakes and in the rivers.
Broad the plains where game is plenty,
in the hills are roots and berries,
cedar's there to build our houses.
Would that we might share the plenty
with our brothers in that great land.
Must we stay here on this island
at the foot of this great mountain
as my people grow more mighty?
How can we enlarge our borders?
Would we gain or lose in war?
A northland people have I heard of.
Even now they're looking toward us
with envying eyes at this great land.
Do we want them here among us?
Would they not make trouble always?
If this tribe across the waters
and my tribe could be united
in a quiet peaceful manner,
could we not drive back this people
when our lands they try to conquer?
A way there is in peace and honor
whereby tribes may be united.
Industrious and fair are their daughters,
young and brave are our sons.

Might we not make some agreement
whereby our young ones would be wedded?
Thus would our tribes be united
and become one mighty people
strong enough to guard our loved ones
and drive back all who would harm us.

SCENE 1

FIRST OLD MAN enters the village and sees a group of boys playing at wrestling; he calls his son from the group. He talks to him thus:

Son, wrestling is a good pastime. I am glad that you enjoy it. It will give you a strong and agile body. Young braves must always be strong and agile, full of courage and quick-witted. We have lived at peace for many years, but in the future, I see our young braves guarding our lands from all invaders. My son, you will be one of the strongest and most courageous, enduring hardships and braving danger for the honor and safety of your people. Return now to your wrestling, but never forget that someday you will need all the strength and courage you have.

FIRST OLD MAN to the other old men of the village:

Brothers, we have lived here long and in peace, but I feel troubling times are before us. The Northland people are moving toward us.

SECOND OLD MAN:

We are not afraid of them. They are over on the mainland. We are here on this island. Surely they could not disturb us here.

FIRST OLD MAN:

Yes, it is true; they are on the mainland, and the mighty water is between us. But if they should form a league with our neighbors, would they long leave us in peace?

SECOND OLD MAN:

Why talk about what may happen? After we are dead, we cannot help then. We are old now. They will be old men then, too old to solve their problems, and will need strong, young braves to fight their battles. Why talk about that now?

FIRST OLD MAN:

I was wondering, as I stood on top of yonder mountain, if we could not form a league with our brothers on the mainland that would so firmly unite us that we would be as one people. Then we could help each other when the Northland tribes come upon us.

SECOND OLD MAN:

How shall this come about? Shall we go to war and compel them to join us? Could we conquer them if we tried? We are now old men, you must remember. Will not their young braves outnumber ours? I believe war would not help us any. We do not hate our brother. Is there not a peaceful way to bring the tribes together and make them want to help each other?

THIRD OLD MAN:

In times past, tribes have been united through the marrying of their young people.

FIRST OLD MAN:

Your young brave Wh ta'thum is a leader now among our sons. Will he not someday be their chief? Could we not find a wife for him of the maidens from the mainland? Yes, the uniting of tribes through the marrying of their young people is one of the most honorable of ways. It may be that our brothers on the mainland would consent to bring the tribes together in such a way.

THIRD OLD MAN:

Let us seek to make arrangements for a wedding between the tribes, if our brothers will consent to such a plan.

SCENE 2

Indian men test the boys for bravery and as runners by taking coal from the fire and sending the boys on an errand to a given place, sometimes after dark or through the forest, to see if they can return before the coal burns out. A messenger comes from the mainland and invites them to contests and a potlatch on the mainland.

The boys ask their mothers what their fathers meant when the fathers talked to them and told them that they would have to be brave and strong and someday help to guard their land and homes.

SCENE 3

Proposals of marriage come after the wrestling on the third day of the potlatch. At the potlatch, the best wrestlers sit back and do not wrestle until the others have been thrown. Wh ta'thum is finally drawn into wrestling (back-hold wrestling) and comes out a winner.

Young men to be married sit in the streets of the village covered with a blanket. When the girl's father agrees to the wedding, two old men, selected by the father, take a young man a blanket and take him to the part of the building occupied by the father. He is accepted, and the date is set for the wedding. The groom then spends from three days to a week getting food for the feast. He also takes food to the family of the bride. This food is often thrown away. It usually consisted of deer, duck, halibut, salmon, clams, and berries.

SCENE 4

When food is accepted, the friends and relatives are invited to the feast. On the last day of the feast occurs the wedding. There were usually from two to twelve masked dancers. The chief men of the tribes compliment the father of the girl and relate the history of the young man and his accomplishments and those of his people for the bride.

The bride is taken to a secluded part of the building by magic people. Each morning at sunrise, magic words are spoken. Her hair is plaited. A doll is made of cedar bark. At sunrise, the girl is hit in the face with the doll to get her to not blink her eyes. This was to develop fortitude and stoicism so that she should not be hasty in answering when someone did something contrary to her wishes. The Great Spirit would tell her what to say when she was at her wit's end.

Masked dancers are in a place curtained off from the rest of the people. The women chant songs for the masked dancers. At sunrise, the old man who directs the wedding climbs to the roof of the building and makes a loud noise with a plank; he waits for one half hour. He then assembles the singers and dancers. The bride is led out by two leading men from among the visitors. She sits on a pile of blankets or in a hammock with a goat hair blanket. The dancers dance around the place where the bride is and fan her with cedar boughs. If she is in the hammock, they swing her three times.

They retreat to the curtained place and then repeat the action. The dance rhythm is slow, and the dance is a crow hop. The old man takes the girl from the blanket and gives her a broom and a bucket of skin or alder. The leading men of the masked dancers on each side of the bride take her to a waiting canoe. Old men from the groom's tribe receive her into the canoe. If the groom wishes to, he hires men to carry the canoe into the house, which is filled with gifts. The bride's relatives receive the gifts. The canoe, with the bride in it, is carried back to the water. The bride and groom then go to the house he has prepared for her.

26 How the Lummi Came to Their Present Abode

Told by Joseph Hillaire

FROM THE ARCHIVES OF PAULINE HILLAIRE

AMONG THE S'WAL-LAK PEOPLE, WHO LIVED ON Orcas Island, there was a widow with two sons. The oldest boy's name was Wh ta'thum. The widow decided to have her son marry a girl from among the S'kalakin Tribe, who lived on the mainland. After due preparations were made with the help of some friends, the widow secured the hand of a young maid from the mainland to become the wife of her son. This being the first marriage relationship between the two mighty tribes, the young couple was esteemed very highly.

Wh ta'thum, then a young man and enjoying the best of health and strength, became a victim of pride and credited to himself all that his young wife enjoyed. He would taunt her about her great fortune in having married him. The girl tolerated this abuse with bravery, and her forbearance was praised by the people. The kindness shown by the people to Wh ta'thum's wife kindled the fire of jealousy in his heart. His mother cautioned him against such behavior, but this advice only made him worse.

One day the wife's parents came with some of their near relatives to visit their daughter. They brought food with them, and according to custom, the girl prepared this food and invited some of the oldest people of her village to come and eat it and to meet her parents.

The topic of conversation was principally the expression of goodwill and admiration of the daughter who came as a stranger in their midst but who had won their respect through her untiring kindness to all who came to her home. The visit lasted for two days, after which they returned to their homes laden with food, which was given them at their departure. Wh ta'thum had enough respect to behave while his wife's parents were there, but after they went away, his old moods returned with greater intensity. In the course of one of his outbursts, he took a basket of elderberries, which had been part of the food that was brought by the girl's parents, and threw it out, saying, "They even bring their dung to me."

Looking at his wife, he said, "Go! Get out of here!" The girl's patience was exhausted, but her mother-in-law begged her to stay for her sake. She remained, but her husband persisted in his cruel treatment in spite of his mother's pleading. Finally one night, when Wh ta'thum sent her away, she took a canoe and departed alone for her home. When she arrived at her parents' village, she revealed how she had been abused.

The people could hardly believe the story, for they had received such a warm welcome, and all seemed to be so well pleased with the girl. When they heard of Wh ta'thum's disposition, they were angry and determined to kill him at the first opportunity. They decided that if he were such a man, he would soon come to them, for his people would convince him of his folly, and in order to restore himself in their favor, he would try to get his wife back.

Wh ta'thum tried to convince himself that he had a right to act as he had done, but every time he discussed his behavior with anyone, his position was weakened. He began to inquire among his people if they had seen his wife, but no one gave him any encouragement. His mother only told him that his wife's desertion was his own fault. She cried and warned him that great wars were often the result of such conduct as his. Wh ta'thum saw his mistake.

There was nothing now for him to do but to go to the parents of his wife and see if she were there, and if she were not there, to confess what he had done and take the consequences in order to prevent a war between the two tribes.

One day, he asked his young brother to accompany him on a trip. It was early, and the day was warm and calm as they paddled swiftly and silently through the oil-like surface of the waters. As they came around Sho-wahes (Point Migley), they could see the blue smoke curling up from the village, far up on Lummi Bay at a place called Momley. It was early afternoon when they started across Hale Passage and followed the shore along the mainland north of Tanwhay-kizn, or Gooseberry Point.

The tide was running out when the two men reached a place called Tala-pey, where their canoe went aground. A young man on the shore noticed the two as they stopped. He saw the man in the rear of the canoe step into the shallow water and, after making some motions toward the camp, start off alone toward the village. The young man rushed up to warn the people of the coming stranger. It was Wh ta'thum who stepped from the canoe.

As he stood in the water by his younger brother, he told his brother of his sorrow. He repented his conduct, and he told his brother that he would try to reconcile himself to his wife's people if they would accept him. He feared, however, that they would not forgive him, and he told his brother to be careful and not permit the canoe to get lodged on the sandbar but to keep it in the water by following the tide out. He said, "If I see any danger, I will warn you by running out on the sandbar in front of the canoe. If you see me do that, do not wait for me, because it will mean sure death. You must go right home and take care of Mother."

So Wh ta'thum started away from his brother unarmed, hoping to right the wrongs of the past. The people were all on alert as soon as the young man brought up the name of the coming stranger. Wh ta'thum's wife recognized him and told the people that this was her husband. Her brother told her to go down to the beach and work on a mat, and when he came, she should be peaceful with him so that he would not suspect any danger until they could surround him. They knew his strength, and they wanted to make sure to get him.

Sitting on the almost finished mat on the warm sand, her long hair bathed in the afternoon sun, she was very attractive to Wh ta'thum. He recognized her at once, and in his eagerness to make up with her, he did not sense the danger before him. She seemed agreeable in every way. So in order to see what she would do, he lay down on his stomach on the mat and said, "Will you see if there are any bugs in my hair?" The wife, who had been so wronged for so long, had only one object in mind, and that was revenge.

Now was her chance. She started to fondle his head and pretended to be looking for lice, but all the time she was tangling her fingers in his long, coarse hair. When her hands began to tighten against his head, he jokingly asked, "What are you doing?" She did not answer but screamed for help. He rose to his feet, but his wife held firmly to his hair. He saw the men coming with spears ready to kill him.

His only thought now was to warn his younger brother so he could leave and save himself. Wh ta'thum, like the stately bush deer of his mountain home, raised his hand and summoned all his power in one desperate effort to get far enough out on the sandbar for his brother to see him. His wife held onto his hair with all her might, and as he ran, she dangled behind him like a blanket.

The young boy in the canoe, who was destined to become Skalaxt, the great conqueror, saw his brother running with an object clinging to him. Directly behind him came a band of warriors that quickly gained on their victim. Then he saw them mercilessly kill his brother. Broken-hearted, he stepped into his canoe and started for home. When he arrived, he told his mother of his brother's fate and cried out, "They have killed my brother! I have nothing to live for but revenge."

So he left his home and friends for the more friendly stillness of the great forests and lake of Orcas Island. He lamented the loss of his brother, and he bathed and fasted for many days. Only occasionally, he would chew a little bit of licorice root. He came to Mountain Lake, where he stayed for several days, bathing in its cool water, scrubbing his body with cedar boughs, and diving down in different places along the shores in hope of meeting the Spirit of the lake. He did not experience any strange thing until he had gone clear around the lake, when he heard a hidden voice say, "I am no good for you. Go to a little lake at the foot of Mount Constitution. There, they will give you what you want."

Nearly a year had been spent in the quest of the Spirit, and the young man was getting weak from fasting and exposure. As the voice gave him directions, it seemed to him that the whole island on which he lived was placed before him, and he could see just where the lake was to which he should go. Weak and worn, he started out for the lake. It was early in the morning when he found it, just as he had seen it in his dream. There was a little steep bluff overlooking the little lake from the east, and as he examined the water, it looked strange. Fine seaweed lay hanging downward in the water along the edge. He threw a stick in the water, and a whirlpool appeared and drew the stick out of sight. He decided that this would possibly happen with him when he would dive in the water. So he made a rope of cedar boughs long enough to reach the center of the lake. This he fastened securely to a little tree, and the other end he fastened around his waist. He went into the water and swam out to the center. Suddenly he was drawn down by a whirlpool until the rope tightened. The current drew him downward so forcibly that he was unable to turn and reach for the rope. The strain was so great that he fainted. The suction in the lake ceased, and the water of the whirlpool gushed out, overflowing the banks of the lake. When the water of the lake settled back to its natural level, the body of the young man lay high and dry upon its banks. While still in a faint condition, the young man heard a voice say, "Go down to the Matase (Point Lawrence) and you will get what you want."

When he arrived, he swam out some distance and dove. A war club was handed to him by an unknown hand and a voice said, "Take this and go. When you use it, all living things around you will become dazed and helpless. When you show it to people, a heavy fog will enshroud you. Your name will be Skalaxt."

So the young man's cry for vengeance was heard. He prepared some cedar bark covering, wrapped the club up, and carried it toward home. When he neared his destination, he hid his treasure and then went to his home. He was weak, but with the care of his mother, he quickly recovered.

But he told no one about what he had gained. As he went about, he would try his arm to see how much of a blow he could give, and the result was amazing.

His brother had a dog that he used while hunting. This was now Skalaxt's keepsake. One day a group of young men went out to Deer Point to use the deer net. While they were setting the nets, the dogs began to fight. Skalaxt's pet dog was getting the worst of it, so Skalaxt took a stick and struck one of the dogs to stop the fight and killed it. His Guardian Spirit had given him the power in the use of the arm that was to wield the club, and as a result, without much effort on his part, the blow was fatal. The owner of the dead dog looked at Skalaxt and sneered, "For dogs you are brave. Why don't you think of your brother?" The hunt was abandoned as the young men heard the bold reply, "All right, let's go! I must wipe away my sorrow for my brother."

When Skalaxt came to the village, he announced his decision to attack the S'kalakin Tribe. He said, "Dry your canoes and singe the roughness from the bottom. Tomorrow we shall go." The whole camp was astir; groups here and there were discussing the possible outcome of such a step. They knew that the S'kalakin were a mighty people. But they also remembered Skalaxt's long absence and the possibility of his getting some great gift that gave him the courage to take such a step.

The next morning, several canoes were carried bodily from their place on the shore and met on the water. When all were ready, Skalaxt said, "Wait until I return." He went up where he had hidden the club and brought it out, leaving it still wrapped in the cedar bark. He stepped into the landing canoe and gave the word to start.

Men who were skilled in the use of the paddle sank them deep into the green water, and with even strokes, the canoes were carried swiftly out through Obstruction Pass and around Point Lawrence. It was evening when they reached Point Migley. The old men who were along called a halt and said to Skalaxt: "Why are you bringing us to such danger without showing us what your strength is? Kindly show us a little." So Skalaxt unwrapped his bundle, and as he lifted it, a heavy mist came up, so much that the men in the same canoe could hardly see one another. This act brought approval from the leaders of the several canoes, and the party moved on across Hale Passage under the cover of this heavy fog. When they came to the place where Skalaxt had stood some years before and had seen his brother killed, he stopped the party and gave these orders: "I shall do all the fighting. There must be a trail along which the people are accustomed to travel to go to the woods. I will locate the trail and guard it while you people approach the village from the beach. Give me a little start, then follow up quickly and give a war cry."

With the speed of a deer, Skalaxt bounded off through the night and heavy fog. As he expected, he found a well-beaten trail behind the camp that the people used in leaving the village during an attack. No sooner was he ready when he heard the war cry of his comrades from the beach.

There was a stir and a rush in a house near the trail. He could hear the heavy breathing of the people as they made their way up the trail. As they would come groping their way through the fog, he would club their heads and let them fall to the ground. The people seemed to be in a stupor, and they did not seem to notice what was happening to those ahead of them. When the bodies were heaped in a great pile in one place, Skalaxt would move down the trail a little and continue to slaughter the people as they came. Each time he moved he would get a little closer to the houses, until finally he came upon the warriors attempting to keep back the enemy while the rest of the people got away. These men he also killed. The slaughter was so great that it is said that very few, if any, escaped from that village.

Skalaxt and his party returned victorious, but he was not satisfied, because he knew that the S'kalakin Tribe lived in many different villages. Sometime afterward, with a few men, he returned to satisfy his revenge. This time he landed at Portage, and there they found a man fishing for flounders at night. They silently drew close to him. When he saw them he was frightened, but Skalaxt told him not to fear, that if he would tell them where the village was and where the grounds lay, they would not harm him and his family. After he told them, he took Skalaxt's advice to hurry home, bar his door, and keep the fires well lit in his house.

That night Skalaxt crept into one of the houses and hid. The people were all busy preparing meals of fresh flounder, which had been caught that evening. While a woman was cooking, a dog came near her, and she drove it away, saying, "You long-faced thing like Skalaxt." Skalaxt stepped up to the woman, pushing her to the ground by her hair. Taking the flounder that she was cooking, he slapped her across the face with it, saying, "Yes, here I am! Take that!" Then another slaughter took place.

In the spring, Skalaxt decided to come the third time, but this time he wanted to get a wife. He came with two men to Sandy Point, now Red River, to a place called Quk kus. There they pulled their canoe into a little slough and waited to see what would happen. There was a *siʔám'*, a rich man, living up the river. He decided to go out net fishing. The rich man said to his friends, "It may be that Skalaxt will be waiting for me somewhere along the river. I will take my daughter along and offer her to him so that he will spare the few of us living. I will also give our river and land to him so that he will come and live with us." While he was fishing he would loudly repeat his promise to Skalaxt if he would only spare him. When they came near Skalaxt's hiding place, Skalaxt pushed out to him and said, "I am here all right, and I will be glad to take your offer." The *siʔám'* told Skalaxt to take his daughter, accept the river as a gift, and move his friends to the mainland and become friends again.

Skalaxt took the girl as a wife and moved his friends to the mainland, thus enlarging the territory of his people. From that time the Lummi grew to be a mighty tribe, roving not only along the mainland but all over among the islands.

27 The Lummi at Treaty-Making Time

A Play by Joseph Hillaire, Performed by the Setting Sun Dancers

FROM THE ARCHIVES OF PAULINE HILLAIRE

In 1933 Joe Hillaire wrote this script for a reenactment of the 1855 Treaty of Point Elliott. Joe hoped that the play and related activities planned in observation of the upcoming centennial of the treaty would afford an opportunity for both Indian and white citizens to reflect on events of the past century and on their future coexistence. The play was staged at Juanita Bay in Kirkland, in the Seattle area, and was sponsored by the American Legion of Kirkland, Washington. For more information, see the essays by Alan Stein at HistoryLink.org: The Free Online Encyclopedia of Washington State History, and see chapter 5, "Joseph Raymond Hillaire: Lummi Artist-Diplomat."

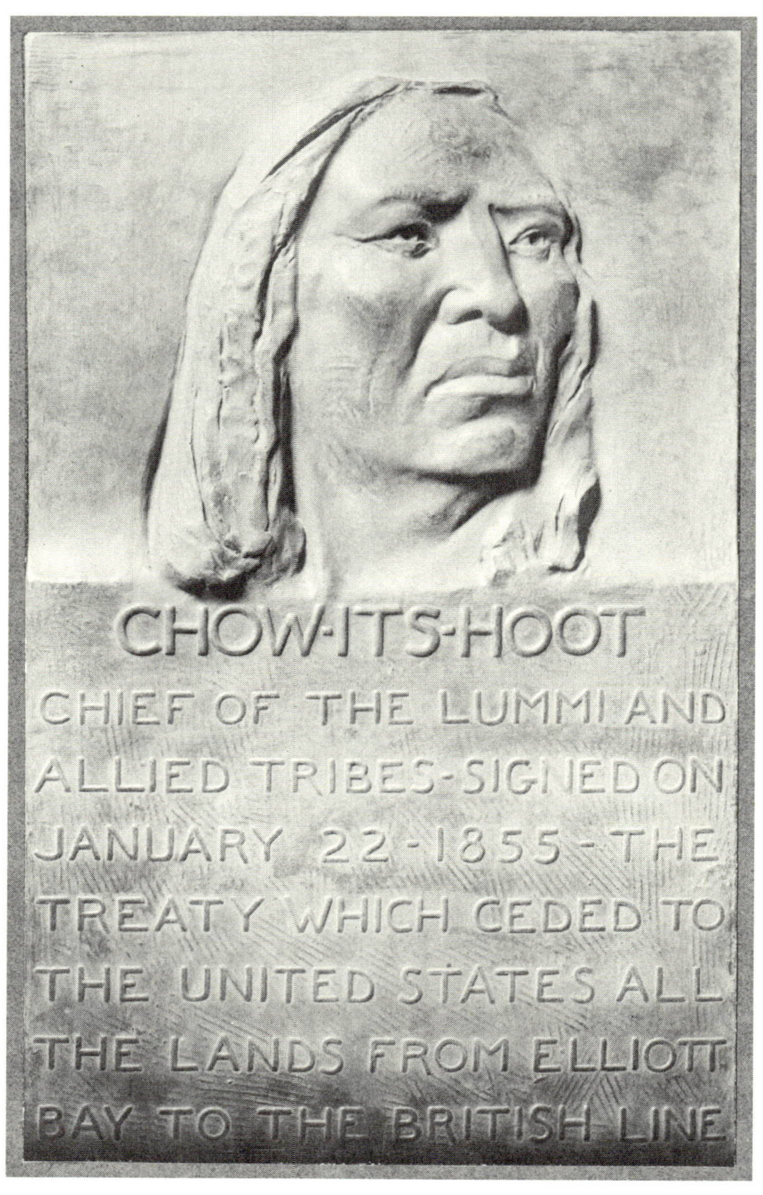

74. Lummi and Allied Tribes Chief Chowitsut (brother of Tseleq, great-grandfather of Pauline Hillaire's mother, Edna Price Hillaire Scott). Bas-relief with inscription, ca. 1915. James A. Wehn Collection, no. 532. Reprinted by permission from University of Washington Special Collections, NA4028.

SCENE I

Winter of 1855, Lummi Village

Cast: Old Woman, Chief's Wife, four Children, Old Man, Hunter, Fisherman, Sea Lion Killer, Clam Digger, Berry Picker, Messenger, M. T. Simmons (Indian Agent), John Taylor (Snohomish), two Indian Guides.

The Old Woman is alone in the great Smokehouse of the Chief, doing her work of basket weaving, but her main concern is to care for the baby grandson who is in the cradle. She sings a lullaby as she rocks the cradle with her foot.

Enters the Chief's Wife and their children, packing baskets of food, which are for a feast to be held that night. She and the children move about, arranging the house for the feast.

Enters the Chief, carrying a heavy load of food. He places the food down where his wife can prepare it for the feast, and he goes about and makes a fire. He then addresses the Old Woman.

CHIEF:

I see that you have cared for my little son. I want him to be a great man. Let your old age be the beginning of his youth, so that he will be wise. I will give him the name of your father, who was a great chief. Tonight the young leaders of our tribe will sing their songs. Guard my son carefully so that the Great Spirit will walk close to him.

Enters the Old Man. He is the first of the guests to arrive, and he walks about the house, nodding to show his approval.

When the other guests arrive, the Old Man assumes the role of host, greeting each one and directing them to their places in the house of the Chief. Then, when all the guests are seated, the Old Man speaks:

OLD MAN:

I am an old man; my days are spent in waiting. But my inner mind is open so that I can see. An evil day is about to fall upon us. I see strange things: people speaking strange languages. They ride in strange canoes that neither stop for the winds nor change course. They come in great numbers from the rising sun, they move like the incoming tide, taking all that is before them. But beyond the meeting of the tide, I see a brighter day. I see our people joining hands with those strangers. Our children see eye to eye. Their fears and their joys are one.

This change takes place like the seasons of the year; the bloom of one year makes way to changes that give birth to a year that is grander than the first one. The prevailing of the first will smile at the birth of the second.

My children, there is a part of life we must take by faith, like when we ford a stream and we near the center: the momentary depth will not stop us, because we see the other shore. Only the Great Spirit can guide us now. Come, let us sing and dance in the Spirit.

The Hunter rattles his staff of deer hooves, and he is in the spirit.

OLD MAN:

Ah! Great Hunter, you open the way for us all to sing in the spirit. Mind your way so that no evil will come to our people. Let us sing, my people; let us sing.

The Hunter sits, and the Fisherman rattles the staff of deer hooves.

OLD MAN:

Now we have the mystery of the swift creatures of the sea. Let us sing the song of the hordes of the sea.

The Fisherman sits, and the Sea Lion Killer rattles the staff of deer hooves.

OLD MAN:

Arise my people, and join us in the song of the sea. The mighty sea lion is but the toy of the mighty sea. The sea will give the sea lion to whom he will. Dance the great killer dance.

The Sea Lion Killer sits, and the Clam Digger rattles the staff of deer hooves.

OLD MAN:

Oh, the joy of the weak and humble members of the people when the sun catches up to the moon in the pathway to the sky, the waters gather in the center of the sea, and the shore is laid out to feed the people, for all to share. Beat the drums and sing the song; sing.

The Clam Digger sits, and the Berry Picker rattles the staff of deer hooves.

OLD MAN:

Pride of the village, joy to the weary, is the girl who is willing to pick the berries. Sing, my people, sing.

After the Berry Picking Dance, the Old Man sings his song. The song is a prophecy song of the coming of the white man.

CHIEF:

My dear friends, you have pleased the spirit of our forefathers. This house has resounded with the songs of the Great Spirit. The drums have set our hearts in tune to better things. The smoke of our fires has linked us with the Great Spirit. We are ready to move forward.

Enters a Messenger.

CHIEF:

A stranger has come, guided by our friends from the Snohomish Tribe. See, here they come.

Enters Mr. Simmons, Mr. Taylor, and two Indian Guides.

CHIEF:

Stranger, we do not know who you are or why you come, but we are full of the songs of the Spirit. Your guides from the Snohomish Tribe understand. Come forward and speak the words of your message.

Turning to his people, the Lummi Chief says:

We will hear the message of the stranger.

AGENT SIMMONS:

I come in the name of the Great White Father in Washington. He has placed a white chief at Olympia who is chief of all white people. This white chief has sent me to give you this message. The Great White Father who lives toward the rising sun wants the white man and the red man to live as brothers. The white chief has set a day for a great council for white and Indian leaders. He will put the words of the council on a paper and send the paper to the Great White Father.

JOHN TAYLOR, SNOHOMISH:

All the words of the stranger are true. I have traveled with him for many days. We have talked with every tribe in this island country of ours. Even the mountain people, like the Snoqualmies, have heard the word. I want you and your people to believe this word and follow. I have spoken.

CHIEF:

My friend of the Snohomish, I have heard your words. You have set a trail for us to follow, and I am glad. Tell the stranger to finish the message that he brings.

AGENT SIMMONS:

I am no longer a stranger; I am your brother. The message that I bring is also for me. The white chief wants us all to meet at Mukilteo when the next moon has passed its youth and the winter is getting ready to leave. We will join our words and our hands in a treaty of peace.

OLD MAN:

My son, I have listened to the words that have been spoken. This is the time for decision. I cannot let you stand alone. Let me speak to the white brother.

The Chief faces the Old Man with a firm gaze. He turns and goes to his seat.

OLD MAN:

White brother, our Chief has listened to your words; his mind cannot be moved like the dust of the earth. He carries the good of all his people; he cannot speak hastily. I am an old man; I have seen many things: victories, defeats, years of plenty, and years of want. I have seen many chiefs, good and bad. In your words I have seen the heart of your white chief. You may go now, and we will prepare our plan. We will come to Mukilteo and speak to your white chief. Then we shall know how the white man and the red man shall dwell in peace.

AGENT SIMMONS:

Chief of the Lummis, I see that you trust in your elders. Many winters have brought wisdom very close to them. I will tell my white chief that you will come to the council. But before I go, I want to leave a word for the Nooksack Tribe. We planned to go up the river and see them face to face. But the river is frozen, and we must hurry back to my chief and tell him that all the Indians are willing to come to Mukilteo. You tell the Nooksack leaders that we want them to come to the council. They must learn the plan of the Great White Father.

There is silence as the Old Woman moves to the center of the stage.

OLD WOMAN:

Let the white brother and his guides sit down with us at the feast.

The cast forms a semicircle and sings as the curtain closes.

CURTAIN

FISHERMAN:

I am the fisherman for my people the Lummis. I have listened to the council of the old fishermen before me. I know the season for every kind of fish in the waters of our domain.

The great king or *tyee* comes in the spring of the year. He yields to the two-pointed harpoon that I wield.

Sometimes he drags the duck-shaped float before he dies, and the reef net — masterpiece of all our appliances — is for the sockeye, eldest of all creatures in the world. We used the reef net in the waters at Point Roberts, Lummi Island, Orcas, Lopez, and San Juan. These are old and accustomed fishing grounds of the Lummis; we caught the silver salmon, the humpy and dog salmon, the steelhead, the cod, flounder, and the skate fish. The halibut was enticed by the bait of our ancient hook; we prize this heritage of abundance.

SEA LION KILLER:

I am the Sea Lion Killer for my people the Lummis. My work is masked with the mystery of many generations. My prey is one of the mightiest creatures of the sea. No ordinary man can hope to be master of a duel with him.

My harpoon, canoe, and helper must be clothed with the protection of the ceremony which is as old as our people. When the new moon and the morning star come together and the flower of the camas plant is in full bloom, the mighty sea lion will bask in the sunshine on top of a rock, where he served as sentinel for his kind while they fed.

This is the time of the great venture: man against beast. Here we tested the strength of our leaders; this too is the heritage of our people.

BERRY PICKER:

I am the berry picker for the Lummi tribe. I roam the woodlands on the mainland and the islands. I venture out to the marshlands for the cranberries. I climb the mountains to gather the red and blue huckleberries. Our harvest of berries brings refreshment and cheer to each household. This is the work of the maidens of the tribe, and their worth is determined by the good they can do. So the berry lands of our nation are a heritage that we must guard.

CLAM DIGGER:

I am the clam digger for my people the Lummis. Mine is the humblest calling among all the people. The weakest of our people find subsistence in this line, but where are the nations that have not the weak?

One thing we learn from the life of the clam is that time and tide wait for no man. As we ply our trade from one shore to another, we follow the Lummi leaders as they make use of the land, which is the heritage of the weak as well as the strong.

SCENE 2

January 1855, Point Elliott (Mukilteo), Site of the Treaty Signing

Cast: Washington Territorial Governor Isaac I. Stevens, Stevens's Clerk, Messenger, Lummi Chief Chowitsut, five Soldiers, Chief Seattle

(Duwamish and Suquamish), Chief Pat Kanim (Snoqualmie), Chief Goliah (Skagit).

Governor Isaac I. Stevens, alone and in the spotlight, thinking about the letter he has written to the U.S. Congress, asking permission to make treaties with the Indians of Washington Territory. There are portions of the letter he repeats out loud, as if to emphasize the meaning.
CURTAIN

The Governor is seated at a table, and his clerk is writing down the proceedings. Some members of the Governor's party are seated, and some are standing. Chief Seattle of the Duwamish and Suquamish is seated to the left of the Governor. Chief Pat Kanim of the Snoqualmie and Chief Goliah of the Skagit are seated beside him. A group of Indians is onstage at the left.

GOVERNOR STEVENS:
The chief and head men of the Lummi Tribe should be here soon. We have been in council here for two days, and the question of our agreement is clearly understood. We want each of you to help make the agreement clear to the Lummis. We must finish this work of making these papers today so we can send them to the Great White Father.

MESSENGER:
The Lummis have landed, and the chief is ready to come to the council.

The Lummis enter stage right; the Governor meets them and shows them their places. The Governor returns to his place.

GOVERNOR STEVENS:
We welcome the people from the Lummi Country. We have waited for them, and now we will hear from the Lummi Chief.

CHIEF CHOWITSUT:
I am the Chief for the Lummi Tribe. Your messenger came to our country nearly two moons ago. He told us of your plans for this council

and asked us to come. I see that my friends from Swinomish and Skagit are here. I and my people are ready to hear your plans.

GOVERNOR STEVENS:

Chief of the Lummi, I am glad that you and your tribe are ready to hear. The Duwamish, Snoqualmie, and other tribes have counciled together for two days with me and your friends from the Swinomish and Skagit Tribes.

We have agreed that there is room in this great land of yours for the white men and the red men to live peacefully together as brothers. We have made papers to show our faith in each other, and we believe that you will help us finish these papers today.

CHIEF CHOWITSUT:

White Chief, we have seen some of the white people that you talk about. We can trust them to live with us on the land. Put there on the paper some things that are sacred to our people from time immemorial: our home sites, our fishing and hunting grounds, and the ground where the bones of our departed friends lie at rest. These places are different from other parts of our vast domain. Our children must have land for their homes in the future. And here are the ones who are the leaders and counselors that my people trust. They will speak.

The Lummi Chief moves closer to the Governor.

GOVERNOR STEVENS:

I have listened to the words of the Lummi Chief and his people, my heart full of the meaning of life. My eyes are open: I can see the needs of the Indian people and those of the white people too.

I want the Lummi Chief to understand all that I have told your people. The Great White Father wants the Indians to keep some of their lands. We will call the land of the Indians the Indian Reservation. And each Indian will have eighty acres of land for his home. They will have their right to hunt, fish, and pick berries and roots on accustomed grounds. These will be further secured to them by the name of the Great White Father, together with the right to dig clams on the tidelands.

So I tell the Lummi Chief and his people as I have told the rest of your people, that as long as the sun rises in the East and sets in the West, as long as the tides rise and fall along the shores of your land, this is how long you will have land for your homes and the right to hunt and fish on all old and accustomed places together with the right to pitch camp and to dry roots and berries. This great heritage is yours by your birth, and it is further secured to you by the pledge of the United States.

CHIEF SEATTLE:

I have listened to the Lummi Chief and his people; I have heard again the words of the white chief. I want our good friends from the Lummi Tribe to know that I believe that the words of the white chief are true. He will keep his word as long as the signs remain before us.

CHIEF PAT KANIM:

My mind is like the mind of Chief Seattle toward the Lummi people. The word of the white chief is true, and we have signed the papers.

The white people are here, and they want the land, and more will come, but the promises of the Great White Father will be true forever.

CHIEF GOLIAH:

You have heard Chief Seattle of the Duwamish and Pat Kanim of the Snoqualmie. I too will speak. And if everyone could speak, they would say the same. I believe the words of the white chief. I think he will keep his word.

CHIEF CHOWITSUT:

My mind is crowded by the words of many chiefs. The white chief is only the son of the Great White Father. And he needs land for the rest of the white people. White men have married our daughters; we cannot deny their children, who have some of our blood. So I cannot turn to the right or to the left. I will take the word of the white chief and sign the papers today.

All the people show signs of relief as the Lummi Chief goes to the table to place his mark on the treaty papers. Each of the leaders do as their chief does.

As the curtain falls, all the people shout:

HURRAH! HURRAH! HURRAH!

SCENE 3

August 1856, by the River on Clark's Place

Cast: Herald (Crier); Agent M. T. Simmons; Chief Chowitsut; group of Indian Men, Women, and Children; seven Soldiers; Old Indian Man; White Boy; Indian Girl; Indian Warrior; John Taylor (Snohomish); B. F. Shaw (interpreter); Priest.

The Crier enters and calls out as he crosses the stage.

CRIER:

Si-wa-shum si-wa-shum si-wa-shum [he turns to go back] si-wa-shum!

Enter all the Indian cast.

Enter M. T. Simmons, Indian Agent for Washington Territory. He orders his men to count the people.

AGENT SIMMONS:

You, count the old men. You, count the young men. You, count the old women. You, count the young women. You, count the boys. You, count the girls and the babies. You, go find out how many are absent.

Agent Simmons proceeds to arrange his papers and the items that are to be given for presents. Report of the count: 45 old men, 137 young men, 57 old women, 166 young women, 117 boys, 57 girls, 42 female babies, 77 male babies, 26 absent. Total: 724.

AGENT SIMMONS:

One year has passed since you signed the treaty with the Great White

Father. The papers we made have been sent, but the way is long and hard. Many days passed before the Great White Father saw the paper; he has sent us money to buy you these presents that you see. I have seen all the other tribes, and they are pleased with the presents. I have counted your people, and I will tell the white chief. In the name of the Great White Father, I give you these presents [he gives presents to all].

The Old Man helps by calling the people to receive their presents. A clerk keeps a record of what is given to each one. When the gifts are all given away, the people cheer:

HURRAH! HURRAH! HURRAH!

CHIEF CHOWITSUT:

Mr. Simelus [Simmons], my heart trembles as I look at my people. They take the presents you give like a child takes a new toy. Yet it is the price of our land, Mother Earth. This land where we stand is part of the homeland of the Lummis. The white man has taken it by paper, which was made before our treaty. It takes up to one half of the Nooksack River where we used to fish. When will the Great White Father do as he promised on the way of the treaty?

There is a rustle as the Women and Children leave the stage. The Men gather by their chiefs, and Mr. Simmons and his men enter the stage.

OLD MAN:

Is this the quiet before the storm? Must we forget so quickly the words that came from our hearts? There we see the great mountain, and up here the sun.

Flowing beside our camp is the river, whose living waters continue to flow into the placid waters of the sea, where the tides continue to rise and fall, signs to remind us of the treaty we made with our white brothers.

A white child and an Indian child enter, skipping along; they sit down to play at center stage.

AGENT SIMMONS:

Chief of the Lummis, I speak for the white chief who is in Olympia. We know that it is high time that the Great White Father should keep his word. But he is a father over a large country and the father of many people more. I say to you as I have said to the leaders of the other tribes: "Let us wait yet for a while and learn to work together like these children who have learned to play."

The Indian Warrior tosses his blanket aside to reveal a musket.

WARRIOR:

We have learned to use the musket in place of the bow and arrows. We kill wild game with ease, like we could kill an enemy. But the word of the white man is hard to understand. While we wait for the good word, the white man takes more land, and half-breeds are becoming more and more.

JOHN TAYLOR:

My friends of the Lummi Tribe, I have been with Mr. Simmons from the start. I was with him before the treaty, at the treaty, and I am here today. I have been with him as he met with the leaders of the other tribes. I have heard the words from both sides, and I think that our white brother will do well for us all. We cannot stop the white men from coming west. If we kill any of them, more white men will take their places. It is better for us to be friends than to be master or slave.

AGENT SIMMONS:

John Taylor is my friend and helper. He knows your people better than I do. He is a witness to all that we have said and done. There were more than eighty Indian leaders who signed the treaty papers; there were twenty-nine tribes under the treaty. We cannot hide away from so many people. All we can do is to try and fulfill the words of the treaty. And that is what Governor Stevens will do.

CHIEF CHOWITSUT:

Mr. Simelus [Simmons], you are a great leader and a brother to us. My friend John Taylor has made that very clear to me and my people. We want our land marked out so that our white brothers will know the line and let us live in peace.

AGENT SIMMONS:

My heart is glad to know that we'll wait to hear from the Great White Father. And I want you to know that I will come again next year with more presents. I want to know what articles you need most so I can bring them to you.

Enters a Priest. All cast onstage, and everybody present kneels as the curtain falls.

THE END

28 Tsats-mun-ton

A LEGEND TOLD BY PAULINE HILLAIRE

The teachings in Indian Country remain the same. Only the faces of the people change. The teaching on this family totem pole is, as the elders say, "Never go alone." Whether you are hunting, berry picking, fishing in the deep waters, or gathering basket materials way up in the mountains, "Never go alone" echoed the words, one generation after another.

LONG AGO, ONE YOUNG MAN IN OUR FAMILY WAS known for his strength, his courage, and his hunting skill. He was also an early riser. His name was Tsats-mun-ton. One morning he awoke very early. Everyone else was asleep. The day started out quiet and very beautiful. How he loved the land, looking at the water, the mountains, and the beach. He knew exactly why he loved the land: it held mastery among his people far and near. Everyone knew Tsats-mun-ton, the hunter of our family. His mind began to wander. He was thinking, "Why do the elders say over and over again, 'Don't go wandering anywhere alone'? Didn't everyone know of his hunting skills? Hadn't he proven that over and over again?" And today was such a beautiful and peaceful day.

He knew what he would do. He'd go to the Forbidden Cove. He quietly and quickly got into his best canoe and started out bravely. Once at the

Forbidden Cove, he secured his canoe and looked all around. He saw the beautiful flowers (now called rhododendrons), the cedar tree limbs reacting to the quiet breeze, the sand and beautiful rocks on the beach, and he inhaled the air gratefully. His thoughts rolled out of him in a great sigh filled with wonder and admiration for Mother Earth and Father Sea.

Suddenly he understood the elders in his own way. No wonder they didn't want anyone to come here; they wanted it all for themselves. With that thought he stepped in the blue, clear water and gazed at his village across Hale Passage. Everything was quiet — not a cricket chirped, no birds were singing, only the cedar trees were wafting in the soft breeze. Deeper and deeper he walked, feeling the fresh coolness of the water. Suddenly, he felt what he thought was seaweed tangle his legs. He simply shuffled it off. But all too quickly the twining of what he thought was seaweed tightened, creeping around his waist. Quickly he drew his knife and began slashing.

All too suddenly he knew that the giant squid had him entangled in its many arms. His knife became useless. His thoughts quickly turned home as he looked one last time at his village at Gooseberry Point. His mind and his spirit called to his wife and family. The miracle was that his mother heard him call out to her and to all who had bird Guardian Powers, as she did. Quickly they all arose together in flight to the Forbidden Cove. Looking down, they could each see the trouble that Tsats-mun-ton was in. There was a fluttering of wings and the screams of eagles, ravens, and hawks; even the crows and seagulls helped.

The birds clawed at the horrible beast and ripped the flesh apart. With each bite-full and claw-full, they dropped the meat of this terrible beast, and they dropped those pieces all over the area. A very grateful Tsats-mun-ton was freed by the help of his family, loved ones, and relatives. To this day we are reminded of his violating the ancient teaching — never wander off alone — by the false clam meat now growing on the rocks along the shores. Tsats-mun-ton was also reminded of the teaching. His great mind added that he would never again meet evil all at once, for there is false flesh of the Terrible Beast scattered on the rocks at the Forbidden Cove.

29 Four Generations of Medicine Men

A LEGEND TOLD BY PAULINE HILLAIRE

This story was recorded by Gregory Fields at the Center for Spirituality & Sustainability, Southern Illinois University Edwardsville, June 26, 2008.

THIS STORY IS ABOUT A MEDICINE MAN AND HIS little son. The son was a little tyke; he'd follow his father all around to each house. He'd go from house to house and house to house, and he'd see how everybody was. The little boy watched like a hawk. He wanted to be just like his massive, smart father. Every time he'd find someone who was ill — mentally ill, physically ill, angry, addicted — he would go to them, and he would listen all around. And then he would go to the wilderness. There was an altar in the wilderness; it wasn't a man-made altar, it was just a natural rock that formed an altar. He would go up and he'd say a specific prayer; if it was for illness, it was one kind of prayer; if it was for anger, it was another kind of prayer; if it was for any kind of trouble, there was a specific prayer.

And so he'd utter the sacred words that put it all in its right place, like the words today, "Forgive me O Lord, for I have sinned." He would say, "To all the stars above, to all the trees in the mountain, to all the rocks and pebbles, to all the flowers that visit every season." And then he'd feel like all was put in its place. He's small now. All the mountains made him small, so he felt like he was in his place, and then he'd say the prayer that was meant for the illness that he had observed. He said the prayer at the sacred altar, the sacred words, the specific prayer. Then, once those three were done, he'd sing. And there's magic in song, because when we sing, we have a rhythm, and that rhythm establishes a good mindset, and that good mindset allows your viewing of anything to be more accurate. And so he sings and sings and sings to the Great Spirit, he opens his heart to the Great Spirit, and then he goes home. He sits in his cabin, and it's only a matter of time before that one that he prayed for is well. He did this throughout the Pacific Northwest in many villages. Every tribe had many villages, and he was popular, and when he died, the little tyke had grown up and taken over for him.

We earn our positions in that way. And so the next generation did the same thing at every house, the same thing: inquiring, being told what's wrong. But then the underbrush hid the altar; he couldn't find the altar. He couldn't find the altar; he looked everywhere. So then what did he do? He made another one. The underbrush had hidden the altar that his father used. So when he found another altar, he said his sacred words, maybe his sacred words were for all the people, or all the horses, or all the dogs in the world, or all the chiefs, or all the shamans, but it put him in his place. It put him in his place. And then he was permitted to say the prayer for whatever it was that was happening during this time.

He came back, and it was just a matter of time, and the prayers were answered before his very eyes.

The third generation came along. The little boy who had tagged along with his father followed him, and when he learned everything that his shaman father had done, then he was put to the test. "Go and talk to this woman over here, she's very troubled. Find out what it is. Talk to everyone around her." And so he would go. That was the third generation. But when he went to the wilderness, he couldn't find the altar. He couldn't remember the sacred words. "Oh my, what am I going to do? I'm losing it, I'm losing it. I don't want to lose it."

And he was determined in his heart that he was going to succeed in spite of lack of memory. So he sang the song, sang it until the mountain, all the trees in the mountain, could hear his breath. He sang until his heart was totally free of thoughts of that woman he had talked to, the one who had such great trouble. He sang and sang, and then he came down and went to his house. It was just a matter of time before the woman he had prayed for was healed. In this next generation of shamans, it was the same orders, same ranks, same attitude and attention. So he went up to the mountain, but he forgot the altar, he forgot the sacred words, he forgot the special type of prayer for the special types of things. But he remembered the song. And when he sang, he sang louder and harder than anybody in his tribe, and when he came home, it was just a matter of time before he noticed that everything was fine in the home of the troubled one.

The medicine man of the fourth generation — with the same orders to watch over the village and the people — went to the mountain. He couldn't find the altar, couldn't remember the sacred words, couldn't remember the special prayer. He couldn't remember the song, and he sat there. What to do? "I must face my people." He came back down, and he remembered the story, and that saved his people. The storyteller, no matter where that storyteller comes from, is an important person in your life. They remember sacred things; they remember that healing does happen, it does and it can. And that's a story of the changing generations, the four generations that changed.

The little kids would come up to me and say, "Are those true stories? Are they true?" And I'd have to tell them, "Just as true as your spirit exists, just as true." And that means that I challenge them to have a spirit; I challenge them to have a spirit. Oh, that makes them feel so good; they're special then, you see.

30 The Mink Family and the Raccoon Family

A FOLKTALE TOLD BY PAULINE HILLAIRE

This story was recorded by Gregory Fields at the Center for Spirituality & Sustainability, Southern Illinois University Edwardsville, June 26, 2008.

THIS IS A STORY FROM LONG AGO, WHEN THERE were no people on the land, just animals. Only the creatures that creep around were here. Can you imagine not a single human being? Not a single human being, no matter where you looked. But the animals were happy. There was a little inlet bay. Over here lived the raccoons, and over here lived the mink. Well, the mink had a good reputation. They were sleek, their fur was just sleek. Oh, every day they went to the water, and they brushed their hair, and they washed their eyes, and they washed the food from around their mouth, and their mother said, "That is what will keep you young. You keep the food away from your mouth." And so they did that every day, and they'd splash four times. That was a sacred number. Then they'd come in and sit at their table, and they'd eat the breakfast that their mother cooked. They sat down and thanked their mother for the food, and they were so happy to eat the sweet porridge that she had mixed for them. They eat wild things — berries, sprouts, clams, crabs — that's what was placed before the mink babies.

Well, over on the other side of the bay were the raccoons, and they were mischievous, oh, they were mischievous. Every day you could see them tossing and turning, and bouncing in the air, and sassing their mother, and sassing their father. Oh my, it was a riot when you looked over there, but over here at the home of the mink, everyone was peaceful and quiet. After the mink ate, it was time for them to go out to the beach, to go onto the beach and walk softly. They were ordered, "You walk softly on the beach, because if you run and jump on the beach, you're going to scare every clam, you're going to scare every crab, and you won't have anything to eat if you scare them away." And so they'd walk just normal and soft all along the beach, and suddenly they'd get a clam; oh, it was a nice fat clam. So they fed it to the mother, and they fed the other one to the father. And the children were happy, going and looking, looking all over for something to eat. You know how animals are: their heads are down, always down, looking for something to eat. Then the father mink said, "Come over here, come over here; there's a rock over here with lots of mussels on it. I want you to learn these trails. Here are the clams over here, and here are some mussels over there." And the mother mink said, "Oh, mussels are so sweet and juicy this time of year; they're sweet and they're juicy." And so the young mink went and ate their fill of mussels, and they had a little basket, they put some spare in there for supper, and they covered it with thimbleberry leaves. They kept on going: they ate the clams, they ate the mussels, they ate the crabs, and not one of them ate in a sloppy manner.

Mink have good reputations, so they ate dainty. They went and they got a fish, and the little mink said, "I can catch fish." You know what he did? He stuck his toe in the water. There was a pool because the tide was out. Some water was caught in this little pool, and there was one fish in it, and they could see it under the seaweed. It was trying to hide, but they could see it. And they said, "Well, we just have to be real quiet. It will get used to us, it will get used to us." And the little boy mink stuck his toe in. Every now and then he'd stick his toe in again, and the fish got curious; they're curious creatures, you know. He'd stick his toe in, and pretty soon the fish got closer and closer. There was seaweed that the fish could hide in, and the mink waited, and they'd just look at each other and signal each other what to do with their eyes. And so the fish got under there and the bigger of the two mink said, "I'll get it." The big mink caught the fish. And so they had something to eat; they eat things raw, you know. And so they had a feast on the beach. By that time they were done with the clams, they were done with the mussels, they were done with the crab, and they even caught a fish, and they shared it. Their basket was getting fuller and fuller, and they put some cedar on the top. The cedar would protect it. On the way home, more lessons, more lessons to learn: "Go and get that frog leaf over there. You put it in here, and if you get hurt, we'll put it on you so that you will heal; that frog leaf will heal you." They call it plantain now; we called it frog leaf. So they put the plantain in their basket, lots of it.

They went a little farther, and the mother said, "You're the only one that catches a cold in our family; you go and pick the light green ends of the tree, you see? It has dark, dark branches, then right at the tip they're light green; go get the light green." And they call it *yella*. They went and got it, and they put it in there, and they covered it in fur for a cold. As they were going home, the father would tell a little story, and the mother would tell a little story, and they'd get home. They'd store the food in the rocks — in between the rocks — they'd store the food there.

Well, the raccoons over there were watching like hawks. "Where are they going to put that food?" They had little knowing looks on their faces, and when the mink went to bed that night, the raccoons sneaked over there, got between the rocks, and ate all the food. No more food for the mink. Days went on like this. The father mink said, "Where is our food disappearing?" He thought it was the mother mink who took it in secret, but he talked to her. "No, it wasn't me," she said. "It must be the kids." And the kids looked at their parents and said, "We thought it was you." So who was taking the food? And so the father was starting to get mad. He was going to go over there and confront the raccoons. They're mischievous, you know; they didn't have a good reputation at all. And so he was rolling up his sleeves and going to go over there and tell the father which way to go. There were some cockle clams — they sit on the surface of the sand, and they're not as edible as the ones you dig. And so the cockle clams were sitting on the beach; a long time ago there were no people to pick them up and carry them away. When cockle clams walk, they put their nose out, and they drag their shell. They walk, and they can walk quite a ways. And so there was a big clam out there, and he called to the mink father, "Hey, hey, where are you going? You look mad." "Yes, I'm mad that somebody's been stealing all our food, and I want to find out if it was the raccoon family."

The clam said, "Don't fight. You know, they're happy." They say "happy as a clam," you know; when you're happy you're smiling like a clam, ear to ear. And so the clam said, "I'll take care of it for you. I'll do everything that you wanted to get done; I'll get it done." The mink father said, "How are you going to do that?" "Just watch and see. This is going to be something that will last forever. Everyone will know." So the father mink went back home, and the chief of the clams lined up all the cockles by the food. They hid in plain sight on the beach, and they waited. What's going to happen? Well, along comes the raccoon, sneaking up to get the food again. He was just about there, and the cockle shells slammed on his little feet. Raccoons have little feet, you know. And the clams hung on for all they were worth; they hung on to the tips of the toes of the raccoon. And the clams pulled, and they pulled, and they pulled — as much as they could — trying to get back into the sand. And they trapped the raccoon. Out comes the mink father; he looks and he says, "Oh, good; look, the clams have saved our food." So he thanked the clams and said, "Forever, forever, we'll take care of your home. We'll do everything in our power to make things peaceful. Thank you for doing what you've done about our food, you saved it, and I'm going to go teach those raccoons a lesson. They're naughty — you should hear them holler at their mother. You should hear them cuss at their father. You should hear them fighting in their bed. You should hear them." "No, no, just leave them alone, just don't bother them," the chief of the clams told the mink family. "Don't you bother the raccoons, even though you know they did all the wrong things, and they're wrong, wrong, wrong, no matter how wrong they are."

So it took everything in the mink's power to keep their tempers down, to keep from screaming at the raccoons. They stayed at home, they tried to sing their little songs, but they were thinking about their stored food. The next morning, the mink mother woke up, and she had more compassion than the father. She had compassion. The father was mean; he was going to confront them in anger. "No, no," she said, "I'll go over, and I'll help that mother become a better mother."

The raccoon mother tells her children, "Get up, lazy." "No, we don't want to get up," the raccoon children say. "Come on, get up, let's go; let's go gather like the mink family gathers food." The raccoon children cover their heads up and say, "No, no, I want to sleep; I'm not hungry." And oh, everybody hears them, and they're cussing, and they're mean to their father, and meaner to their mother. And one day, the parents just took off and got a lot of food, and the children just poured it on the food from the day before. They kicked it around and didn't care. Those children were not respecting their parents, so their parents didn't respect them, and kicked at the food. The raccoon children finally got up. There was no food where the mink had stored food anymore. The raccoons had learned their lesson, and so what were they to do?

The mother mink came over and taught them how to make mattresses. The father raccoon said, "All my kids ever do is stink up their bed. They don't get up and clean it out like the mink family does. They don't do anything. They don't get up and wash the sleep out of their eyes, or wash the food away from their mouth; they're going to get old fast." And so it happened, the mink father came over and taught the raccoon father just what to do, how to gain the respect of his children, how to have them have a clean sleeping bed, and how to have clean food. "Don't kick it around like this, feed them clean food, let them appreciate clean food." And they did.

That was the lesson of the cockle clams, and that's why today the raccoon's feet are curly, just like the lips of a cockle shell: wavy. That's how their feet are today. They walk funny, and they can be heard by anybody because their claws get stuck and they look crippled and ugly, but that's the mark of a thief. The thief has a mark, and they leave it behind or it's put on them. And that's what my father learned, long, long ago, is how to behave.

31 Stommish

Revival of the Water Festival

PAULINE HILLAIRE

ALL INDIAN CEREMONIAL DANCING STOPPED IN 1917 when the Lummi Indians went into mourning over lost sons in World War I. This silence continued until 1946, when Indian boys returned from World War II. Then began the Stommish Water Festival (*stommish* is a Cowichan word meaning "warrior"). The celebration was patterned after the old potlatches, still fresh in the memories of tribal elders. Events include a salmon bake feast with war canoe races, bone games (gambling, also called Slahál), and the Lummi celebration dances.

The Lummi Indian Stommish is now usually held during the second weekend in June. Many war canoes converge at Gooseberry Point, cutting through the choppy, tide-tortured waters of Hale Passage, in a competition as old as Lummi history. The Stommish is one of the few authentic Indian ceremonials open to public view. It has become a display of one of the finest aspects of Lummi culture. The Lummi Stommish Water Festival was begun in 1946 by the John H. Kittles American Legion Post 196, which was one of the first, if not the first, all-Indian American Legion Posts. The initial purpose of the celebration was for social gathering of

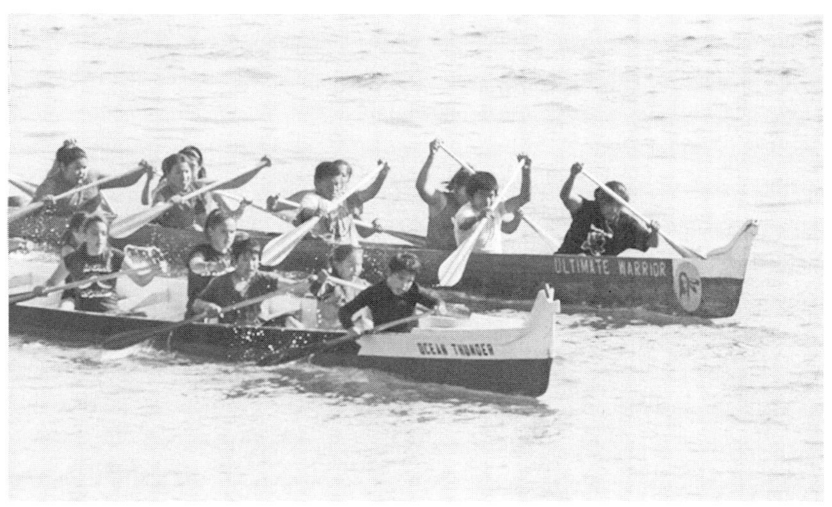

75. Canoe paddlers at Lummi Stommish, 2010. Reprinted with permission. Photo by Lummi Tribe Archives and Records.

goodwill to the neighboring tribes and also to raise funds for an American Legion Building. The building was completed and is now being used for the Head Start school program for Lummi children.

The Stommish has long been a solid tradition for the Lummi people. It is a time for all to come together once a year to socialize, feast, and compete in various events. The annual celebration attracts people from Washington State, northern Oregon, Idaho, and western Montana and many people from across the Canadian border in mainland British Columbia and Vancouver Island. People came to take part in events such as field sports, boxing, Indian dancing, Slahál bone games, and the main event: the eleven-person canoe races. Approximately twenty canoes participate in the four-mile race.

The Stommish is a fitting exchange of old and new cultures. You will see the Lummi people fillet the spring salmon and place them on ironwood sticks over an open barbeque pit, a delicious Indian dish prepared the way the Lummi ancestors have for many generations. Many people return to this celebration every year to visit with old friends, meet new friends, and just have a good time.

32 Signs of the Seasons

PAULINE HILLAIRE

The white butterfly introduces sockeye season.

The orange-and-black butterfly means the springs are running.

When the grunter grunts, the clams are fat.

In the fall, when the caterpillars are mostly orange, we'll have a good winter. When they're mostly black, we're in for a bad winter.

If the trees in the fall have lost all or most of their leaves, we're in for a bad winter. But if they kept at least half their leaves when fall winds quit fighting, we'll have a milder winter.

Bald eagles appear, and they harvest grunters, smelt, and herring.

When snowbirds gather in the fall, snow will follow in a week or two.

When blue jays appear nearby, watch for rain.

When the frog croaks for the last time in late fall, it's time to prepare for the Winter Dances.

When the frog croaks for the first time in the spring, it's time to stop the Winter Dances.

Appendix

Selected Sources on Totem Poles and Coast Salish Art

Averill, Lloyd J., and Daphne K. Morris. *Northwest Coast Native and Native-Style Art.* Seattle: University of Washington Press, 1995.

Barnett, H. G. "The Southern Extent of Totem Pole Carving." *Pacific Northwest Quarterly* 33, no. 4 (1942): 379–89.

Brotherton, Barbara, ed. *S'abadeb, the Gifts: Pacific Coast Salish Art and Artists.* Seattle: University of Washington Press, 2008.

Carlson, Roy, ed. *Indian Art Traditions of the Northwest Coast.* Burnaby BC: Archaeology Press, Simon Fraser University, 1983.

Duncan, Kate. *One Thousand One Curious Things: Ye Olde Curiosity Shop and Native American Art.* Seattle: University of Washington Press, 2000.

Garfield, Viola. *Seattle's Totem Poles.* Bellevue WA: Thistle Press, 1996.

Garfield, Viola, and Linn A. Forrest. *The Wolf and the Raven: Totem Poles of Southeastern Alaska.* Seattle: University of Washington Press, 1948.

Halpin, Marjorie M. *Totem Poles: An Illustrated Guide.* Vancouver: University of British Columbia Press, 1981, 2002.

Hansen, Kenneth C. (Samish). *The Maiden of Deception Pass: A Spirit in Cedar.* Anacortes WA: Samish Experience Productions, 1983.

Holm, Bill. *Northwest Coast Indian Art: An Analysis of Form.* Seattle: University of Washington Press, 1965.

Jonaitis, Aldona, and Aaron Glass. *The Totem Pole: An Intercultural History.* Seattle: University of Washington Press; Vancouver: Douglas and McIntyre Press, 2010.

Lister, Kenneth R. *Paul Kane, the Artist: Wilderness to Studio.* Toronto: Royal Ontario Museum Press, 2011.

Malin, Edward. *Totem Poles of the Northwest Coast.* Portland: Timber Press, 1986.

Peterson, Shaun (Puyallup). "Coast Salish Design: An Anticipated Southern Analysis." In *In the Spirit of the Ancestors: Contemporary Northwest Coast Native Art,* edited by Robin K. Wright and Kathryn Bunn-Marcuse. Seattle: Bill Holm Center for the Study of Northwest Coast Art and University of Washington Press, 2013.

Sampson, Martin (Swinomish). *The Story of the Totem Pole: Early Indian Legends, as Handed Down from Generation to Generation*. Everett WA: Kane and Harcus, 1923.

Shelton, William (Snohomish). *The Swinomish Totem Pole: Tribal Legends*, accounted by William Shelton to Rosalie M. Whitney. Bellingham WA: Union Printing Company, 1938.

Stewart, Hilary. *Cedar: Tree of Life to the Northwest Coast Indians*. Seattle: University of Washington Press; Vancouver: Douglas and McIntyre Press, 1984.

———. *Looking at Totem Poles*. Seattle: University of Washington Press, 1993.

Whatcom Museum staff. *A Report: Master Carvers of the Lummi and Their Apprentices*. Photographs by Mary Randlett. Bellingham WA: Whatcom Museum of History and Art, 1971.

Wright, Robin K., ed. *A Time of Gathering: Native Heritage in Washington State*. Seattle: Burke Museum and University of Washington Press, 1991.

———. *Totem Poles: Heraldic Columns of the Northwest Coast*. University of Washington Libraries Digital Collections. http://content.lib.washington.edu/aipnw/wright.html.

Selected Sources on Lummi and Coast Salish History and Culture

The first expeditions by ship to the Pacific Northwest provide, from a European viewpoint, records about geography and Native life in the Northwest during the eighteenth and nineteenth centuries.

1776–80. Cook, James. *The Journals of Captain James Cook on His Voyages of Discovery, Edited from the Original Manuscripts*. 4 vols., edited by J. S. Beaglehole. Cambridge: Cambridge University Press for the Hakluyt Society, 1955–67; Rochester NY: Boydell Press, 1999. *James Cook: The Journals*, selected and edited by Philip Edwards. London: Penguin, 1999, 2003.

1784. Cook, Capt. James, and Capt. James King. *A Voyage to the Pacific Ocean, for making discoveries in the northern hemisphere to determine the position and extent of the east side of North America, its distance from Asia and the practicality of a northern passage*. 3 vols. plus folio atlas of plates and maps. Madrid: Complutense University; London: A. and S. Strahan, 1784; New York: Columbia University, digitized 1999, http://www.columbia.edu/itc/mealac/pritchett/00generallinks/kerr/.

1789. Portlock, Nathaniel. *Voyage Round the World, but more particularly to the Northwest Coast of America: Performed in 1785, 1786, 1787, and 1788, in the "King George" and "Queen Charlotte," Captains Portlock and Dixon*. London: John Stockdale and George Goulding, 1789. http://www.americanjourneys.org/aj-089/.

1790. Meares, John. *Voyages made in the years 1788 and 1789 from China for the northwest coast of America, to which are affixed an introductory narrative of a voyage performed in 1976 from Bengal in the ship "Nootka": Observations on the probable existence of a northwest passage and some account of the trade between the northwest coast of America and China and the latter country and Great Britain*. London: Topographic Press, 1790. Universal Digital Library, http://www.archive.org/details/voyagesmadeinthe002783mbp.

1792. Puget, Peter. *The Vancouver Expedition: Peter Puget's Journal of the Exploration of the Puget Sound, May 7-June 11 1792*, edited by Bern Anderson. *Pacific Northwest Quarterly* 30 (1939): 177–217.

1792. The Quimper expedition of 1790; the Eliza expedition of 1791; the Galiano-Valdes expedition of 1792. Wagner, Henry. *Spanish Explorations in the Strait of Juan de Fuca*. Santa Ana CA: Fine Arts Press, 1933; repr., New York: AMS Press, 1971.

1801. Vancouver, George. *A voyage of discovery of the North Pacific and round the world . . . performed in 1790–95 with the "Discovery" and the "Chatham" under Captain George Vancouver*. Vol. 4, 293–370. London: John Stockdale, 1801. http://www.americanjourneys.org/aj-134/.

1890. Boas, Franz. "Second General Report on the Indians of British Columbia. I. The Lku'ngen" (Songhees). *British Association for the Advancement of Science*, 60:563–82. The Jesup North Pacific Expedition, directed by anthropologist Franz Boas, was conducted from 1897 to 1902 to explore Native cultures on both sides of the Bering Strait and to collect photographs, Native art, and artifacts for museum display.

1913. Edward Curtis. *The North American Indian, being a series of volumes picturing and describing the Indians of the United States, the Dominion of Canada, and Alaska*. Edited by Frederick Webb Hodge. Vol. 9, *Salishan Tribes of the Coast*. New York: Johnson Reprint Co., 1970, 25–30. Vol. 9 contains a short section on the Samish, Lummi, and Semiahmoo. The focus of the selection is the history of how the S'kalakin (or Skolahun) were vanquished by and incorporated into the Lummi tribe.

Mid-Twentieth-Century Works on the Coast and Straits Salish

Starting in the 1930s, several ethnographic studies were published concerning the Coast Salish and Straits Salish. The second book listed, by Bernard Stern, is about the Lummi. Joseph Hillaire was Stern's main consultant for the book.

1930. Haberlin, Hermann, and Erna Gunther. *The Indians of Puget Sound*. University of Washington Publications in Anthropology.

1934. Stern, Bernard. *The Lummi Indians of Northwest Washington*. New York: Columbia University Press; repr., New York: AMS Press, 1969.

1938. Barnett, H. G. "The Coast Salish Indians of Canada." *American Anthropologist* 40:118–41.

1954. Suttles, Wayne. "Post-contact Culture Change among the Lummi Indians." *British Columbia Quarterly*, June–April 1954, 29–102.

1955. Beck, Ethel Fyles. *Lummi Indian How Stories*. Caldwell ID: Caxton Printers.

Mid-Twentieth-Century Audio Recordings

1954. Rhodes, Willard, ed. *Music of the American Indian: Northwest (Puget Sound).* Washington DC: Archive of Folk Culture, Library of Congress. AFS L34. In the mid-twentieth century, Willard Rhodes of Columbia University recorded approximately one thousand Indian songs under the sponsorship of the Bureau of Indian Affairs, and the recordings were made available through the Library of Congress, accompanied by notes. The volume *Music of the American Indian: Northwest (Puget Sound)* is introduced by Prof. Rhodes and Prof. Erna Gunther of the University of Washington. The songs representing the Puget Sound area are from Swimomish, Lummi, Skokomish, Makah, and Quinault. The Lummi songs in the Puget Sound collection are sung by Joe Hillaire.

1950–61. Metcalf, Leon. *The Metcalf Coast Salish Audio Collection*. Burke Museum of History of Culture, University of Washington. Also held by the Archives of Ethnomusicology, Department of Music, University of Washington. Set of recordings (seventy-five reels) of Native Northwest oral tradition and song. The Lummi material in the Metcalf Collection was contributed by Agnes Cagey and Joseph Hillaire. For details about the Metcalf and Rhodes recordings, see the following: Willie Smyth and Esmé Ryan, eds., *Spirit of the First People, Native American Music Traditions of Washington State* (with audio CD recorded at Jack Straw Productions, Seattle, including a song by Pauline Hillaire). Seattle: University of Washington Press, 1999. Appendix 1: Laurel Sercombe, "Ten Early Ethnographers in the Northwest: Recordings from Washington State" (148–68); appendix 2: Judith A. Gray, "Creating and Disseminating Ethnographic Recordings: Washington State Materials in Washington, D.C." (169–80). See also appendix 3, concerning the collections by anthropologist Melville Jacobs (1902–71) of Pacific Northwest linguistic oral tradition and music material (especially of western Oregon and eastern Washington): William R. Seaburg, "Melville Jacobs and Early Ethnographic Recordings in the Northwest" (181–85).

Late Twentieth-Century Works

1972. Gunther, Erna. *Indian Life on the Northwest Coast of North America, as Seen by the Early Explorers and Fur Traders during the Last Decades of the Eighteenth Century*. Chicago: University of Chicago Press.

1972. Martin Sampson (Skagit/Swinomish). *Indians of Skagit County*. Skagit County Historical Series No. 2. 5th printing, 1998. La Conner WA: Skagit County Historical Society.

1974. Suttles, Wayne. *Coast Salish and Western Washington Indians: The Economic Life of the Coast Salish of Haro and Rosario Straits.* New York: Garland Publishing. The first comprehensive study of Straits Salish cultures.

1981. Ruby, Robert H., and John A. Brown. *Indians of the Pacific Northwest: A History*. Norman: University of Oklahoma Press.
1987. Suttles, Wayne. *Coast Salish Essays*. Vancouver: Talonbooks.

Early Twenty-First-Century Works

A number of studies published around the turn of the twenty-first century address issues of Native Northwest history and culture, particularly in relation to contact with Anglo-Europeans. The following is not a comprehensive list, but these are noteworthy works.

1999. Bierwert, Crisca. *Brushed by Cedar, Living by the River: Coast Salish Figures of Power*. Tucson: University of Arizona Press.
1999. Boyd, Robert Thomas. *The Coming of the Spirit of Pestilence: Introduced Infectious Diseases and Population Decline among Northwest Coast Indians, 1774–1874*. Seattle: University of Washington Press.
1999. Miller, Jay. *Lushootseed Culture and the Shamanic Odyssey: An Anchored Radiance*. Lincoln: University of Nebraska Press.
2000. Boxberger, Daniel. *The Ethnohistory of Lummi Indian Salmon Fishing*. Seattle: University of Washington Press.
2000. Harmon, Alexandra. *Indians in the Making: Ethnic Relations and Indian Identities around Puget Sound*. Berkeley: University of California Press.
2000. Seaburg, William, and Pamela Amoss. *Badger and Coyote Were There: Melville Jacobs on Northwest Indian Myths and Tales*. Corvallis: Oregon State University Press.
2000. Stein, Julie K. *Exploring Coast Salish Prehistory: The Archaeology of San Juan Island*. Burke Museum Monographs 8. Seattle: University of Washington Press.
2003. Coupland, Gary Graham, Richard Ghia Matson, and Quentin Mackie. *Emerging from the Mist: Studies in Northwest Coast Culture History*. Vancouver: University of British Columbia Press.
2007. Miller, Bruce Granville. *Be of Good Mind: Essays on the Coast Salish*. Vancouver: University of British Columbia Press.
2008. Thrush, Coll. *Native Seattle: Histories from the Crossing-Over Place*. Seattle: University of Washington Press.

Monographs Published by the Lummi Tribe

The Lummi Tribe (Bellingham, Washington) has published a number of reports by Ann Nugent on issues of concern to the tribe.

1977. *Regulation of the Lummi Indians by Government Officials between 1900–1920*. Lummi Communications.
1979. *The History of Lummi Fishing Rights*. Lummi Communications.

1980. *History of Lummi Legal Action against the United States*. Lummi Communications.
1981. *Schooling of the Lummi Indians between 1885–1956*. Lummi Historical Publications.
1982. *Lummi Elders Speak*. Lummi Historical Publications.

Works Edited by taqʷšəblu Vi Hilbert

One of the great treasures of Native Northwest traditions is the collection of works by Dr. taqʷšəblu Vi Hilbert (Upper Skagit), published primarily by Lushootseed Press (Seattle).

1980. *Ways of the Lushootseed People: Ceremonies & Traditions of Northern Puget Sound's First People*, edited by Vi Hilbert and Crisca Bierwert, in consultation with Thom Hess. 3rd ed., 2001.
1985. *Haboo: Native American Stories from Puget Sound*, edited by Vi Hilbert, based on recordings by Leon Metcalf. Seattle: University of Washington Press.
1991. "To a Different Canoe: The Lasting Legacy of Lushootseed Heritage." In *A Time of Gathering: Native Heritage in Washington State*, edited by Robin Wright. Seattle: Burke Museum and University of Washington Press, 254–58.
1993. *Writings about Vi Hilbert by Her Friends*, edited by Janet Yoder.
1995. *gwəqwulcə Aunt Susie Sampson Peter: The Wisdom of a Skagit Elder* (Skagit/Kikiallus), transcribed by Vi Hilbert, translated by Vi Hilbert and Jay Miller, based on recordings by Leon Metcalf.
1995. *pətius Isadore Tom* (Skagit/Lummi), edited by Vi Hilbert.
1995. *siastənu "Gram" Ruth Sehome Shelton (Klallam/Samish): The Wisdom of a Tulalip Elder*, edited by Vi Hilbert, based on recordings by Leon Metcalf.
1998. *The Clothes That Look at the People: An Ancient Epic Story*, told by xʷhisteməni Johnny Moses (Nuu-chah-nulth and Tulalip), edited by Vi Hilbert, transcribed by Bill Hendry Coté.

Works on Lummi History and Culture

There have been no major works on the Lummi since Stern's book, *The Lummi Indians*, published in 1934 and Suttles' article, "Post-contact Culture Change" in 1954. A comprehensive book on Lummi and Coast Salish history and culture from a Native viewpoint is Pauline Hillaire's forthcoming book and companion media, *Rights Remembered: A Salish Grandmother Speaks on American Indian History and the Future* (Lincoln: University of Nebraska Press), including Lummi songs, stories, and oral history.

Bibliography

Archibald, Jo-ann, Q'um Q'um Xiiem (Stó:lō). *Indigenous Storywork: Educating the Heart, Mind, Body and Spirit*. Vancouver: University of British Columbia Press, 2008.

Averill, Lloyd J., and Daphne K. Morris. *Northwest Coast Native and Native-Style Art*. Seattle: University of Washington Press, 1995.

Berglands, Knut. "The Moon's Sister." In *Coming to Light: Contemporary Translations of the Native Literatures of North America*, edited by Brian Swann. New York: Random House, 1994. 75–80.

Bishop, Robert O., Sr. *Land in the Sky Totem, from Tales Told Me by Joe Hillaire*. Seattle: Shorey Book Store, 1968.

Boyd, Robert. *The Coming of the Spirit of Pestilence: Introduced Infectious Diseases and Population Decline among Northwest Coast Indians, 1774–1874*. Vancouver: University of British Columbia Press; Seattle: University of Washington Press, 1999.

Bringhurst, Robert. "Introduction to John Sky's 'One They Gave Away.'" In *Coming to Light: Contemporary Translations of the Native Literatures of North America*, edited by Brian Swann. New York: Random House, 1994. 225–49.

———. *Masterworks of the Classical Haida Mythtellers*. Vol. 1, *A Story as Sharp as a Knife: The Classical Haida Mythtellers and Their World*. Lincoln: University of Nebraska Press, 1999; Vancouver: Douglas and McIntyre, 2011. Vol. 2, *Ghandl of the Quyahl Llaanas: Nine Visits to the Mythworld*. Lincoln: University of Nebraska Press, 2000. Vol. 3, *Skaay of the Qquuna Qiighawaay*. Lincoln: University of Nebraska Press, 2002.

Brotherton, Barbara, ed. *S'abadeb, the Gifts: Pacific Coast Salish Art and Artists*. Seattle: University of Washington Press, 2008.

Campbell, Joseph. *The Flight of the Wild Gander: Explorations in the Mythological Dimension*. New York: Viking, 1951.

———. *The Hero with a Thousand Faces*. Bollingen Series 27. Princeton NJ: Princeton University Press, 1949.

———. *The Mythic Image*. Princeton NJ: Princeton University Press, 1974.

Cassirer, Ernst. *Mythical Thought*, vol. 2 of *The Philosophy of Symbolic Forms*, translated by Ralph Manheim. New Haven CT: Yale University Press, 1955.

Cranmer, Barb ('Namgis), dir. *Mungo Martin: A Slender Thread* (documentary, 19 mins.). Alert Bay BC: U'mista Cultural Society, 1991. http://www.umista.org/.

Cranmer-Webster, G. "Conservation and Cultural Centres: U'Mista Cultural Centre, Alert Bay, Canada." In *The Care and Preservation of Ethnographic Materials*, edited by R. Barclay, M. Gilberg, J. C. McCawley, and T. Stone. 1986 Symposium of the Canadian Conservation Institute, Ottawa, 77–79.

Cruikshank, Julie, in collaboration with Angela Sidney, Kitty Smith, and Annie Ned. *Life Lived Like a Story: The Lives of Three Yukon Native Elders*. Lincoln: University of Nebraska Press, 1991.

Doniger, Wendy. *The Implied Spider: Politics and Theology in Myth*. New York: Columbia University Press, 1998.

Duncan, Kate. *One Thousand One Curious Things: Ye Olde Curiosity Shop and Native American Art*. Seattle: University of Washington Press, 2000.

Duwamish et al. *Tribes of Indians v. the United States*, Court of Claims of the United States, #F-275, at Olympia, Washington, 1927.

Eliade, Mircea. *Myth and Reality*, translated by Willard Trask. New York: Harper and Row, 1963.

Feist, W. C., and E. A. Mraz. *Wood Finishing: Water Repellents and Water-Repellent Preservatives*. United States Department of Agriculture (USDA) Forest Service, Research Note FPL-0124. Madison WI: Forest Products Laboratory, 1978. http://www.fpl.fs.fed.us/documnts/fplrn/fplrn124.pdf.

Florian, M.-L., R. Beauchamp, and B. Kennedy. "Haida Totem Pole Conservation Program. Ninstints Village, Anthony Island, British Columbia." In *Conservation of Wooden Monuments*. Proceedings of the International Council on Monuments and Sites (ICOMOS) Wood Committee IV, International Symposium, Ottawa, June 1982. ICOMOS Canada and the Heritage Canada Foundation, 1983, 53–82.

Garfield, Viola. *Seattle's Totem Poles*. Bellevue WA: Thistle Press, 1996.

Goodall, R. A., J. Hall, R. Viel, F. R. Agurcia, H. G. M. Edwards, and P. M. Fredericks. "Raman Microscopic Investigation of Paint Samples from the Rosalita Building, Copan, Honduras." *Journal of Raman Spectroscopy* 37 (2003): 1072–77.

Halpin, Marjorie M. *Totem Poles: An Illustrated Guide*. Vancouver: University of British Columbia Press, 1981, 2002.

Harmon, Alexandra. *Indians in the Making: Ethnic Relations and Indian Identities around Puget Sound*. Berkeley: University of California Press, 1998.

Hilbert, Vi (Upper Skagit). "To a Different Canoe: The Lasting Legacy of Lushootseed Heritage." In *A Time of Gathering: Native Heritage in Washington State*, edited by Robin Wright. Seattle: Burke Museum and University of Washington Press, 1991, 254–58.

Hillaire, Pauline (Lummi). *Rights Remembered: A Salish Grandmother Speaks on American Indian History and the Future*. Lincoln: University of Nebraska Press, forthcoming.

———, recorded on *Sharing the Circle: Native Song Traditions of Washington State*, edited by Rebecca Chamberlain. Curriculum guide and CD-ROM. Olympia:

Evergreen (State College) Center for Educational Improvement and the Washington State Superintendent of Public Instruction, Indian Education Office, 2002.

Holm, Bill. *Northwest Coast Indian Art: An Analysis of Form*. Seattle: University of Washington Press, 1965.

Jung, Carl G. *The Archetypes and the Collective Unconscious*, translated by R. F. C. Hull. *Collected Works of C. G. Jung*, Vol. 9, Pt. 1, Bollingen Series 20. Princeton NJ: Princeton University Press, 1959.

———. *Memories, Dreams, and Reflections*. Recorded and edited by Aniela Jaffé, translated by Richard and Clara Winston. New York: Random House, 1961.

———. *Symbols of Transformation*, translated by R. F. C. Hull. *Collected Works of C. G. Jung*, Vol. 5, Bollingen Series 20. Princeton NJ: Princeton University Press, 1956.

Jung, C. G., and C. Kerényi. *Essays on a Science of Mythology*, translated by R. F. C. Hull. Bollingen Series 22. New York: Pantheon.

Lightning, Walter (Samson Cree). "Compassionate Mind: Implications of a Text Written by Elder Louis Sunchild." *Canadian Journal of Native Education* 19, no. 2 (1992): 215–53.

Lister, Kenneth R. *Paul Kane, the Artist: Wilderness to Studio*. Toronto: Royal Ontario Museum Press, 2011.

Mayer, Ralph. *A Dictionary of Art Terms and Techniques*. New York: Harper and Row, 1981.

The Metcalf Coast Salish Audio Collection, 1950–61, Burke Museum of History of Culture, University of Washington. Also held by the Archives of Ethnomusicology, Department of Music, University of Washington.

Miller, Jay. *Lushootseed Culture and the Shamanic Odyssey: An Anchored Radiance*. Lincoln: University of Nebraska Press, 1999.

Moses, Johnny, xʷhistemәni (Nuu-chah-nulth and Tulalip). *The Clothes That Look at the People: An Ancient Epic Story*, edited by Vi Hilbert. Seattle: Lushootseed Press, 1994.

O'Flaherty, Wendy Doniger. *Other Peoples' Myths: The Cave of Echoes*. New York: Collier Macmillan, 1988.

Peterson, Shaun (Puyallup). "Coast Salish Design: An Anticipated Southern Analysis." In *In the Spirit of the Ancestors: Reflections on Contemporary Northwest Coast Native Art*, edited by Robin K. Wright and Kathryn Bunn-Marcuse. Seattle: Bill Holm Center for the Study of Northwest Coast Art and University of Washington Press, 2013.

Report of the Commissioner of Indian Affairs, No. 86 (1854). Isaac I. Stevens, Governor and Superintendent of Indian Affairs, Territory of Washington, to George W. Manypenny. Senate. 49th Congress, 2nd sess. Session Vol. 1. S. Exec. Doc. 1, Pt. 1 (Serial Set Vol. 746). Washington DC: U.S. Government Printing Office.

Rhyne, C. S. "Changing Approaches to the Conservation of Northwest Coast Totem Poles." In *Tradition and Innovation: Advances in Conservation*. London: International Institute for Conservation of Historic and Artistic Works, 2000, 155–60. http://academic.reed.edu/art/faculty/rhyne/papers/approaches.html.

———. "Recent Approaches to the Conservation of Northwest Coast Totem Poles." *Zeitschrift für Kunsttechnologie und Konservierung* 17, no. 1 (2003): 179–84. http://academic.reed.edu/art/faculty/rhyne/papers/totem.html.

Shelton, William (Snohomish). *The Swinomish Totem Pole: Tribal Legends,* accounted by William Shelton to Rosalie M. Whitney. Bellingham WA: Union Printing Company, 1938.

Smyth, Willie, and Esmé Ryan, eds. *Spirit of the First People: Native American Music Traditions of Washington State.* Seattle: University of Washington Press, 1999.

Stein, Alan J. "Indian Tribes Gather in Juanita to Re-enact Signing of 1855 Point Elliott Treaty on May 27, 1933." Essay 1632, August 16, 1999. *HistoryLink.org: The Free Online Encyclopedia of Washington State History.*

———. "Juanita Beach Park (Kirkland)." Essay 4009, October 1, 2002. *HistoryLink.org: The Free Online Encyclopedia of Washington State History.*

Stern, Bernard. *The Lummi Indians of Northwest Washington.* New York: Columbia University Press, 1934; repr., New York: AMS Press, 1969.

Suttles, Wayne. *Coast Salish and Western Washington Indians: The Economic Life of the Coast Salish of Haro and Rosario Straits.* New York: Garland Publishing, 1974.

———. "The Plateau Prophet Dance among the Coast Salish." *Southwestern Journal of Anthropology* 13, no. 4 (Winter 1957): 352–96.

———. "Post-contact Culture Change among the Lummi Indians." *British Columbia Quarterly,* June–April 1954, 29–102.

———. "Productivity and Its Constraints." In *Indian Art Traditions of the Northwest Coast,* edited by Roy L. Carlson. Burnaby BC: Archaeology Press, Simon Fraser University, 1983.

Todd, A. "The Island of Impermanence." In *(Im)permanence: Cultures in/out of Time,* edited by Judith Schachter and Stephen Brockman. University Park: Pennsylvania State University Press, 2008, 41–50.

———. "Painted Memory; Painted Totems." In *Painted Wood: History and Conservation,* edited by Valerie Dorge and Carey Howlett. Pt. 5, *Ethical Considerations,* 400–411. Los Angeles: Getty Conservation Institute, 1998. http://www.getty.edu/conservation/publications_resources/pdf_publications/paintedwood.html.

———. "Totem Pole Conservation: An Ongoing Treatment Program." *Preserving Aboriginal Heritage: Technical and Traditional Approaches.* Proceedings of the 2007 Symposium, Canadian Conservation Institute, Ottawa, Ontario, 2008, 120–26. http://www.cci-icc.gc.ca/bookstore/viewCategory-e.cfm?id=19

University of Washington, Language Learning Center (online), Lummi Straits Salish, Joe Hillaire: http://depts.washington.edu/llc/olr/lushootseed/LUS_007/index.php.

Wainwright, I. N. M., K. Helwig, D. S. Rolandi, C. A. Aschero, C. Gradin, M. M. Podesta, M. Onetto, and C. Bellelli. "Identification of Pigments from Rock Painting Sites in Argentina." In *L'art avant l'histoire: La conservation de l'art préhistorique.*

Journées d'études de la Section française de l'Institut internationale de conservation. Paris, 2002, 15–24.

Wainwright, I. N. M., E. A. Moffat, and P. J. Sirois. "Occurrences of Green Earth Pigment on Northwest Coast First Nations Painted Objects." *Archeometry* 51, no. 3 (2009): 440–56.

Whatcom Museum staff. *A Report: Master Carvers of the Lummi and Their Apprentices*. Photographs by Mary Randlett. Bellingham WA: Whatcom Museum of History and Art, 1971.

Contributors

MELONIE ANCHETA is a professional Northwest Coast Native artist. She is also an independent researcher, writer, and educator on Northwest Coast Native art, paint, and paint technology. For her groundbreaking work, Melonie is acknowledged by the Smithsonian and a number of other institutions as an authority on Northwest Coast pigments. Melonie is writing articles about specific pigments and is working on a book that will place Northwest Coast paint and paint technology on the palette of world history.

BARBARA BROTHERTON (PhD, University of Washington) is an art historian specializing in the arts and culture of the indigenous peoples of the Northwest Coast of North America. She is curator of Native American Art at the Seattle Art Museum and board member of Lushootseed Research, an organization dedicated to the preservation and dissemination of Coast Salish language. Brotherton was the curator of the traveling exhibition *S'abadeb: Pacific Coast Salish Art and Artists* and editor of the companion book.

REBECCA CHAMBERLAIN (MA, Literature, University of Washington) is a Northwest writer, storyteller, scholar, and educator. Her work with elders includes studies of comparative literature and Puget Salish language and storytelling traditions. Since 1996 she has been teaching interdisciplinary programs — focused on writing, literature, poetry, and oral traditions — at the Evergreen State College.

CHIXAPKAID (MICHAEL PAVEL) (PhD, Higher Education, Arizona State University) is a Skokomish tribal member and a traditional bearer of Salish culture within the Pacific Northwest. CHiXapkaid is currently a professor of Native American Studies in education at the University of Oregon and an active traditional artist.

GREGORY P. FIELDS (PhD, Philosophy, University of Hawaii) is a comparative philosopher and interdisciplinary scholar whose main focus is indigenous Pacific Northwest thought and culture. Fields is professor of philosophy at Southern Illinois University Edwardsville and a research associate of the American Indian Studies Research Institute, Indiana University.

VI TAQʷŠƏBLU Hilbert (Upper Skagit, 1918–2008) was one of the last members of her generation who was a native speaker of the Lushootseed language, also known as Puget Salish. She worked and collaborated for more than four decades on the transcription and translation of archival recordings, the development of a dictionary and language curricula, teaching, storytelling, public speaking, and publishing. Vi Hilbert's work was the main force behind the twentieth-century renaissance of Lushootseed cultural and language programs. Hilbert founded Lushootseed Research, now under the direction of her granddaughter, Jill La Pointe.

SCÄLLA PAULINE HILLAIRE (Lummi, b. 1929) is an historian, genealogist, teacher, and conservator of Straits Coast Salish knowledge and culture. She is a graduate of Haskell Indian College and the Evergreen State College. She is a recipient of the Washington Governor's Heritage Award (1996) and the National Heritage Fellowship (2013).

BILL HOLM has been a student of Northwest Coast Native arts and culture for more than sixty years. He is a retired curator of the Burke Museum of Natural History and Culture and emeritus professor of art history and anthropology at the University of Washington.

SCOTT KADACH' ĀAK'U JENSEN has been a carver and instructor of Northwest Coast Native-style art since 1972. His work is represented by the Stonington Gallery in Seattle, Washington, and is included in public and private collections worldwide. In 2010 Fred Sał kaa Fulmer adopted Scott into the Tlingit Chookaneidee Eagle Brown Bear Clan.

FELIX SOLOMON is a Lummi carver committed to bringing back true Straits Salish work and shovelnose canoes. His carving is reminiscent of the type of work done in the late nineteenth and early twentieth centuries by other Straits Salish carvers. Solomon was chosen by the Smithsonian as one of three Natives from across the United States to participate in an educational curriculum documentary about the state of their regional environments. He was also honored by the Smithsonian as the featured artist for Living Earth Day 2012.

ANDREW TODD is a conservator based in Vancouver, British Columbia. He is a specialist in the conservation of fine art objects, sculpture, and outdoor monuments. He has been in practice for twenty-five years and has completed treatments for monumental works in Alaska, California, Washington State, Alberta, and British Columbia. Recent projects include conservation assessments for the Crown Estate in Windsor, United Kingdon, treatment of a totem pole for the Canadian Embassy in Athens, Greece, and on-going projects for the Vancouver International Airport, the Museum of Vancouver, and the Burnaby Village Museum. He has been published by the Getty Conservation Institute and the Canadian Conservation Institute. Before establishing his private conservation practice, he spent seven years with Canada's two major conservation facilities: the Conservation Division of Parks Canada and the Canadian Conservation Institute in Ottawa.

Index

IN THE STUDIES IN THE ANTHROPOLOGY OF NORTH AMERICAN INDIANS SERIES

The Four Hills of Life: Northern Arapaho Knowledge and Life Movement
By Jeffrey D. Anderson

One Hundred Years of Old Man Sage: An Arapaho Life
By Jeffrey D. Anderson

The Semantics of Time: Aspectual Categorization in Koyukon Athabaskan
By Melissa Axelrod

How Mockingbirds Are
By Donald M. Bahr

Lushootseed Texts: An Introduction to Puget Salish Narrative Aesthetics
Edited by Crisca Bierwert

People of The Dalles: The Indians of Wascopam Mission
By Robert Boyd

A Choctaw Reference Grammar
By George Aaron Broadwell

The Lakota Ritual of the Sweat Lodge: History and Contemporary Practice
By Raymond A. Bucko

From the Sands to the Mountain: Change and Persistence in a Southern Paiute Community
By Pamela A. Bunte and Robert J. Franklin

A Grammar of Comanche
By Jean Ormsbee Charney

Dakota Way of Life
By Ella Cara Deloria

Studies in the Anthropology of North American Indians
By Raymond J. DeMallie and Douglas R. Parks

Reserve Memories: The Power of the Past in a Chilcotin Community
By David W. Dinwoodie

Haida Syntax (2 vols.)
By John Enrico

Northern Haida Songs
By John Enrico and Wendy Bross Stuart

Life among the Indians: First Fieldwork among the Sioux and Omahas
By Alice C. Fletcher

Edited and with an introduction by Joanna C. Scherer and Raymond J. DeMallie

Powhatan's World and Colonial Virginia: A Conflict of Cultures
By Frederic W. Gleach

Native Languages and Language Families of North America
(folded study map and wall display map)
Compiled by Ives Goddard

Native Languages of the Southeastern United States
Edited by Heather K. Hardy and Janine Scancarelli

The Heiltsuks: Dialogues of Culture and History on the Northwest Coast
By Michael E. Harkin

Prophecy and Power among the Dogrib Indians
By June Helm

A Totem Pole History: The Work of Lummi Carver Joe Hillaire
By Pauline Hillaire
Edited by Gregory P. Fields

Corbett Mack: The Life of a Northern Paiute
As told by Michael Hittman

The Canadian Sioux
By James H. Howard

Yuchi Ceremonial Life: Performance, Meaning, and Tradition in a Contemporary American Indian Community
By Jason Baird Jackson

Comanche Ethnography: Field Notes of E. Adamson Hoebel, Waldo R. Wedel, Gustav G. Carlson, and Robert H. Lowie
Compiled and edited by Thomas W. Kavanagh

The Comanches: A History, 1706–1875
By Thomas W. Kavanagh

Koasati Dictionary
By Geoffrey D. Kimball with the assistance of Bel Abbey, Martha John, and Ruth Poncho

Koasati Grammar
By Geoffrey D. Kimball with the assistance of Bel Abbey, Nora Abbey, Martha John, Ed John, and Ruth Poncho

Koasati Traditional Narratives
By Geoffrey D. Kimball

The Salish Language Family: Reconstructing Syntax
By Paul D. Kroeber

Tales from Maliseet Country: The Maliseet Texts of Karl V. Teeter
Translated and edited by Philip S. LeSourd

The Medicine Men: Oglala Sioux Ceremony and Healing
By Thomas H. Lewis

A Grammar of Creek (Muskogee)
Jack B. Martin

A Dictionary of Creek / Muskogee
By Jack B. Martin and Margaret McKane Mauldin

Wolverine Myths and Visions: Dene Traditions from Northern Alberta
Edited by Patrick Moore and Angela Wheelock

Ceremonies of the Pawnee
By James R. Murie
Edited by Douglas R. Parks

Households and Families of the Longhouse Iroquois at Six Nations Reserve
By Merlin G. Myers
Foreword by Fred Eggan
Afterword by M. Sam Cronk

Archaeology and Ethnohistory of the Omaha Indians: The Big Village Site
By John M. O'Shea and John Ludwickson

Traditional Narratives of the Arikara Indians (4 vols.)
By Douglas R. Parks

A Dictionary of Skiri Pawnee
By Douglas R. Parks and Lula Nora Pratt

Osage Grammar
By Carolyn Quintero

They Treated Us Just Like Indians: The Worlds of Bennett County, South Dakota
By Paula L. Wagoner

A Grammar of Kiowa
By Laurel J. Watkins with the assistance of Parker McKenzie

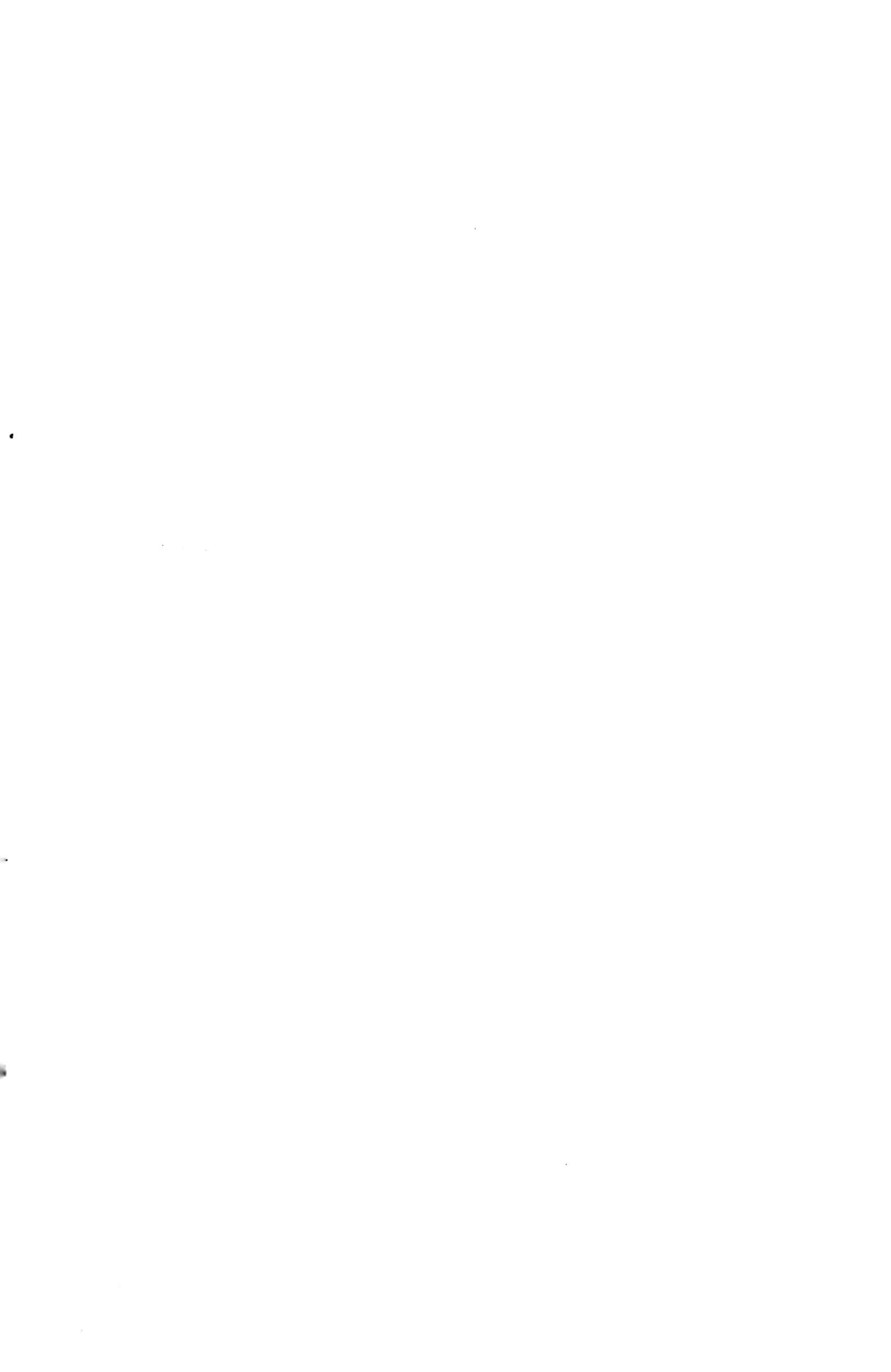